Wellspring of Liberty

Wellspring of Liberty

*How Virginia's Religious Dissenters
Helped Win the American Revolution
and Secured Religious Liberty*

JOHN A. RAGOSTA

OXFORD
UNIVERSITY PRESS
2010

OXFORD
UNIVERSITY PRESS

Oxford University Press, Inc., publishes works that further
Oxford University's objective of excellence
in research, scholarship, and education.

Oxford   New York
Auckland   Cape Town   Dar es Salaam   Hong Kong   Karachi
Kuala Lumpur   Madrid   Melbourne   Mexico City   Nairobi
New Delhi   Shanghai   Taipei   Toronto

With offices in
Argentina   Austria   Brazil   Chile   Czech Republic   France   Greece
Guatemala   Hungary   Italy   Japan   Poland   Portugal   Singapore
South Korea   Switzerland   Thailand   Turkey   Ukraine   Vietnam

Published by Oxford University Press, Inc.
198 Madison Avenue, New York, New York 10016

www.oup.com

Oxford is a registered trademark of Oxford University Press.

Library of Congress Cataloging-in-Publication Data
Ragosta, John A.
Wellspring of liberty : how Virginia's religious dissenters helped win
the American Revolution and secured religious liberty / John A. Ragosta.
    p. cm.
Includes bibliographical references and index.
ISBN 978-0-19-538806-0
  1. Virginia—History—Revolution, 1775–1783.
  2. Virginia—Politics and government—1775–1783.
  3. Church and state—Virginia—History—18th century.
  4. Dissenters, Religious—Virginia—History—18th century.
  5. Freedom of religion—Virginia—History—18th century.
  I. Title.
F230.R17 2010
975.5'02—dc22   2009031552

9 8 7 6 5 4 3 2 1

Printed in the United States of America
on acid-free paper

To my mother and father, Millie and Vince Ragosta,
for teaching their children the joy of learning

Acknowledgments

Any historian can regale those who would listen with stories about the travails of research in various archives: finding shelves empty that should include an important volume, discovering that a text relied on by another author does not quite provide the information or argument suggested, spending hours in front of a creaking microfilm machine (alas, still necessary today) to find that critical pages are illegible no matter the magnification or focus. Handwritten eighteenth-century documents provide an additional opportunity for concentration and headaches. Often, on the all-too-infrequent occasions when I would find the opportunity to visit Peter Onuf's office to discuss this work, in the course of our conversation I would mention the slowness or frustration of research or writing. Inevitably, Peter would end our conversation by asking— already knowing the answer—"Are you still having fun?" All things considered, I have had a great deal of fun in researching and writing this piece and am honored to have had the opportunity to pursue graduate degrees in history, first at George Washington University and then at the University of Virginia. To all who had a part in that endeavor, from professors to librarians, administrators, colleagues, and students, I am deeply grateful. I must mention in particular the initial guidance and constant encouragement of David Silverman, Ken Bowling, and Bob Cottrol of George Washington University.

In terms of this specific project, I am, of course, deeply indebted to the invaluable assistance of Peter Onuf, who has a remarkable ability to formulate ideas and grasp the broad implications and possibilities of incomplete research. In addition, I hope I can do justice to the very insightful suggestions of my dissertation committee: Peter Onuf, Joseph Kett, Chuck McCurdy, and Heather Warren.

I would be remiss not to mention particularly the exceptionally kind assistance of a number of librarians, including those at Alderman Library (especially the government document librarians Anne Benham, Elizabeth Margutti, and Barbie Selby) and the Small Special Collections Library at the University of Virginia, the Robert H. Smith International Center for Jefferson Studies, the British National Archives in London (where I did a good bit of research while celebrating a wonderful twenty-fifth wedding anniversary), the Library of Virginia (especially Brent Tarter's suggestions and assistance), the Union Theological Seminary, the Baptist Historical Society at the University of Richmond, the Rockefeller Library in Williamsburg, and, no less, the Culpeper County Library (where Ann Robson and the rest of the staff always cheerfully assisted in placing odd Interlibrary Loan requests). In addition, I was the recipient of much kind guidance on the use of mapping software by Chris Gist of the Scholars' Lab in Alderman Library. More recently, the editors at Oxford University Press, especially Susan Ferber, have offered very useful advice to a new author of history.

Of course, I am deeply cognizant of the fact that an education is much more than research and writing. Whatever the reception of this work, I could not imagine having pursued this effort without the spectacular opportunity to discuss history, in all of its academic and modern meanings, with such fine colleagues. I will always be indebted to my brilliant and engaging friends from our HIUS 701–702 class and to those who made Peter Onuf's Early American Seminar an exercise worthy of a long night's ride, especially Peter, Andrew O'Shaughnessy, Patrick Griffin, and George Van Cleve.

No one would expect that I could end these acknowledgments without publicly thanking my family. There are innumerable things for which to thank them—for Liz's cups of tea and plates of cookies, for changing our lives and moving to Rixeyville, for holidays and normal days and walks to the river. As any husband and parent can confirm, my life is so intertwined with that of Liz, Greg, and Sarah that I can no longer imagine it without their presence. If they do not enjoy this book—early American history not being a top priority for any of them—I hope that they have enjoyed and appreciated the time in Arlington and Rixeyville when I slowly stopped being a practicing lawyer so that I might pursue a compelling desire to study and teach history to inquiring students. The self-absorbed practice of working on a dissertation would have been unbearable without their constant presence, assistance, and love.

Contents

Wellspring of Liberty

Introduction

The Church of England was the established church of colonial Virginia, and prior to the American Revolution, no British colony was more protective of its established church, nor more abusive of its religious dissenters, than Virginia. Local Anglican vestries collected taxes to support Anglican clergy and to maintain a parish church and glebe land. Regular attendance at Anglican services was mandatory; while the law was often honored in the breach, dissenters from the religious establishment—mostly Presbyterians and Baptists—frequently found themselves fined for their absence. Anglican clergy had the exclusive right to consecrate marriages. The same lay leaders who controlled the colonial church in Virginia were in firm control of the House of Burgesses, and, with the coming of the Revolution, the same establishment leaders controlled the new state government. To any eighteenth-century Virginian, the legal and social dominance of the Church of England was unmistakable.

All of this changed with the American Revolution, but that change was far from obvious or inevitable as the war approached.

In the years between the Great Awakening and the American Revolution, the presence of evangelical dissenters in Virginia swelled. Scotch-Irish Presbyterians from Pennsylvania had been migrating to the Shenandoah Valley in large numbers since the 1730s. After Presbyterian Samuel Davies received a formal license to preach in Virginia in 1747, conversions multiplied, and significant numbers of Presbyterian dissenters began to flow from the Blue Ridge into the Piedmont. In the 1760s, the growth of evangelical Baptists—primarily across the Piedmont, but beginning to enter the Tidewater—eclipsed the growth of Presbyterianism in Virginia, albeit not yet overtaking it in terms of the total number of adherents. By 1775, dissenters accounted for as much as one-third or more of the Virginia population.

The Great Awakening and the growth of dissenting churches challenged the Virginia establishment in more than simply membership. By insisting that all persons were equal in God's eyes and had to experience a relationship with God directly and that the most common person could relate that experience to his fellow man, the dissenters challenged notions of social hierarchy that were at the core of Virginia's social order. Yet the significance of these developments to Virginia society can be easily overstated. While newly formed evangelical churches provided examples of small republican polities that challenged social norms, prior to the Revolution, the government was far from republicanized, and the established church was hardly subject to an easy collapse in the face of an "evangelical revolt." After the limited liberalization of religious toleration that accompanied the Great Awakening, including the licensing of some dissenting ministers, in the ten years prior to the war, dissenters were unable to obtain additional legal reforms, even to be allowed to marry within their own church. In fact, as the Revolution approached, the established church in Virginia was vibrant and growing, dominant in the Tidewater and expanding elsewhere. Although control of the church was largely in the hands of local lay leaders, those same leaders had firm control of the government. The Anglican gentry establishment maintained political and social dominance, although it increasingly chafed at dissenter challenges.[1]

The Baptist interlopers were particularly "enthusiastic," and their outdoor preaching was often viewed as particularly disruptive by both Anglican ministers and lay gentry leaders, especially as evangelical Baptists and Presbyterians made a concerted effort to appeal to Virginia's enslaved community. Further antagonizing establishment leaders, some Baptists were unwilling to seek a license to preach from the General Court in Williamsburg, effectively denying the establishment's authority to control their progress. When questioned by authorities, the ministers would declare that their license to preach was from a higher authority—certainly an insult to a self-respecting member of Virginia's gentry hierarchy. Some dissenters refused to take the oath required to receive a license. For those who were willing, obtaining a license was not always a simple matter. As one Baptist minister described the challenge, "thro' the whole process of this business, from the beginning to the end, obstructions and difficulties lay in the way...and after all this, it was left uncertain and precarious." Even when a license was received, it did not eliminate the political dominance of the established church, establishment taxes, discrimination in favor of Anglican marriage, or the unofficial harassment from Anglican supporters abetted by local officials.[2]

While Presbyterians continued to experience civil discrimination and some degree of persecution, Baptist enthusiasm seemed to invite a violent opposition, especially on the frontier of Baptist expansion into previously strong Anglican counties. The boiling point was reached in 1768 when four Baptist ministers preaching in Spotsylvania County were arrested for preaching without a license. Refusing to commit to not preaching in the county for a year, the Baptists sang hymns to amazed bystanders as they were marched off to prison, and the prisoners proceeded to preach from their jail cell to large crowds, setting a precedent for years of Anglican and dissenter conflict.

With Spotsylvania providing an example for Anglican leaders, albeit a poor one, Baptist preachers faced a flurry of arrests, which they turned to their advantage as a tool to proselytize. By the end of 1774, more than fifty Baptist ministers—over half of those in Virginia—and a handful of others had been jailed for preaching. The arrests continued up to the outbreak of the war, with 1774 seeing the second highest rate of incarceration in the seven-year period. Every dissenter in Virginia must have known or known of several ministers who had been jailed.

More troubling, those attending dissenter meetings were subject to violent assault in the years leading up to the Revolution. Men on horseback would often ride through crowds gathered to witness a baptism. Preachers were horsewhipped and dunked in rivers and ponds in a rude parody of their baptism ritual. Even when Baptist ministers attempted to preach from their jail cells, supporters of the establishment would beat drums or otherwise discourage listeners, sometimes by violently dispersing the crowds. One minister began to preach from his cell only to have his face urinated on; another, his arms outstretched in prayer through the window of his jail cell, cut with a knife. Black attendees at meetings—whether free or slave—were subject to particularly savage beatings.

Early sectarian histories related this persecution, but since then there has been a tendency to underestimate its severity. Yet to appreciate the revolutionary dialogue that unfolded between dissenters and establishment leaders, the perception of the Virginia dissenters at the time must be considered. For them, the persecution was severe and immediate. Persecution did not need to be constant nor ubiquitous to be deeply felt. Even Presbyterians, who were generally spared incarceration and beatings, although there were exceptions, were disturbed by the treatment of the Baptists and the seemingly tenuous nature of religious toleration in colonial Virginia.[3]

As Virginia made the transition from colony to state, the leaders of the new polity were the same establishment leaders who had encouraged or participated in the persecution. Edmund Pendleton (the chairman of Virginia's

Committee of Safety and first speaker of the House of Delegates) and Archibald Cary (first speaker of the Virginia Senate) were committed Anglican leaders, both of whom sat on county benches that incarcerated Baptist preachers before the war. Robert Carter Nicholas, Richard Henry Lee, Edmund Randolph, Benjamin Harrison, and other leaders in the Virginia revolutionary conventions and General Assembly remained staunch supporters of the Church of England and its legal and social privileges.

As a result, when Virginia's political leaders united to oppose Britain, there was a serious question as to whether dissenting members of society would fully support military opposition to the British Crown led by their persecutors. After all, British officials had tended to be particularly solicitous of dissenter interests, and dissenters regularly turned to the Crown for protection from the local Anglican gentry—the same gentry that was to lead the Revolution. While Virginia dissenters were as concerned as their establishment neighbors with taxation without representation and British tyranny, they were also deeply aware of the persecution that the colonial leaders had perpetrated and of their own status largely outside of the Virginia political community. The possibility of an independent state governed by their persecutors without the possibility of British intervention to protect dissent was as much a matter of concern as an opportunity for Virginia's dissenters. In other Southern colonies, such concerns contributed to significant loyalism among dissenters. As the war began, and Virginia's political establishment found that it had to engage the dissenters to mobilize effectively, the tension between dissenters and the establishment, and the contingency of the dissenters' support, became ever more evident.

Before the war—while Baptists and other evangelicals were being incarcerated—dissenters had begun to petition the House of Burgesses over their disabilities. Initially, they did not seek religious freedom but accepted the continued existence of the established church and sought only greater toleration. Their political status—or lack thereof—permitted nothing else. Yet even these limited requests were not met. The House endorsed the notion of expanded toleration in 1772, but the proposal eventually tabled in 1774 was far from adequate—seriously limiting preaching out-of-doors and preaching to slaves, important matters for many evangelicals—and even the moderate reforms that were proposed were effectively blocked by supporters of the religious establishment. A young James Madison, while deeply committed to improving religious freedom in Virginia, was "very doubtful" that any changes could be made given the strength of the Church of England in the House of Burgesses.[4]

Things began to change in 1775 when Virginia's leaders were forced to recognize that they were going to be engaged in a military struggle against Great Britain, the eighteenth century's leading military power. Still, flush with the victories of Lexington, Concord, and Bunker Hill, and with the "rage militaire" dominant throughout the colonies, efforts by Virginia's establishment to engage the dissenters in 1775 were noticeable but carefully circumscribed. Virginia's dissenting preachers were welcomed to preach to their coreligionists among the Continental troops and militia and were exempted from militia musters for the first time, as Anglican ministers had been for many years.

In 1776, however, relations among the establishment and dissenters underwent a fundamental realignment in the face of a war crisis. Military recruiting was lagging badly as the difficulty of forming an effective army and warring with Great Britain became evident. News from Canada was disastrous, with 5,000 men lost in an unsuccessful campaign to the north. While the colonies celebrated General Thomas Gage's abandonment of Boston in the spring, by mid-summer, General George Washington was facing repeated setbacks around New York. Those responsible for mobilizing men and supplies for the patriots, led by members of Virginia's political and religious establishment, were overwhelmed.

In the midst of this crisis, the petitions from the dissenters to the Virginia convention and the new state's House of Delegates changed. Rejecting notions of only improved toleration, they now began to make clear that their full support for the war effort would depend on the establishment's willingness to grant them religious freedom. The establishment's response is also telling: important concessions were made, but full freedom was not forthcoming. For the rest of the war, there was an extended negotiation between establishment leaders and religious dissenters and a series of partial concessions intended to maintain dissenters' support for the war while at the same time maintaining, to the extent possible, some preeminence for the Anglican Church. In the process, the dissenters for the first time found themselves important participants in the political dialogue.

It was under these circumstances the Virginia Convention adopted a constitution and, critically, a Declaration of Rights in June 1776. With the adept maneuvering of freshman legislator James Madison, the Declaration of Rights was modified at the last minute to provide expressly for the "free exercise of religion," rather than simply a broad toleration as suggested in George Mason's original draft. This promise was promptly put to the test.

In little over a week after adoption of that declaration, the convention received a petition from Prince William County Baptists warning that

> We being convinced that the strictest unanimity among ourselves is
> very necessary in this most critical conjunction of public affairs. And
> that every remaining cause of animosity and division may if possible

be removed, have thought it our duty as peacable Christians, to petition for several religious privileges...we have not been indulged with.

Dismissing forever requests only for improved toleration, the Baptists in mid-1776 requested an end to establishment taxes and restrictions on dissenters' worship and marriages, expressly linking their support for the war to these freedoms: "*These things granted*, we will gladly unite with our Brethren of other denominations, and to the utmost of our ability, promote the common cause of Freedom."[5] A flurry of additional petitions from both Baptist and Presbyterian strongholds—including the "10,000 name" petition organized by the Baptists and an official call for freedom from the Hanover Presbytery—dispelled any question about what the dissenters were seeking and offering.

Virginia's establishment leaders were forced to cooperate. After years of failed efforts at reform, in December 1776, while wartime preparation desperately demanded the legislature's full attention, dissenters were exempted from the establishment tax and other religious penalties, and the tax was suspended. This was not a willing concession on the altar of republican principle. Thomas Jefferson later reported that these debates were "the severest conflicts in which I have ever been engaged."[6] The records from the House of Delegates support the notion that reluctant leaders were being forced to come to grips with a new Virginia, one in which the political community would no longer be synonymous with the gentry leaders of the established church and in which dissenters, of western counties and of middling and lower classes, would be agents in the political process. Virginians did not simply prosecute the war as a united republican front in opposition to Britain; the united front was formed by way of negotiation and compromise. While contemporaneous Anglican reporters attempted to minimize the conflict involved—and their soothing rhetoric has too often influenced later histories—it is evident that they were simply putting a conciliatory face on a difficult and unwelcome compromise. Sectarian historians have contributed to this misperception with Anglican historians seeking to minimize the prewar discrimination and evangelical historians seeking to claim a position for their forefathers as disinterested patriots, rather than contingent supporters of mobilization.[7]

Compelling evidence of the nature of the negotiation is provided by the Anglican response to the suspension of the church tax. In 1777, Anglican petitions protested the decision to suspend the establishment tax and exempt dissenters. They urged the House to delay consideration of religious reform until after the war, when they knew that dissenters' leverage would evaporate, arguing that given the controversial nature of establishment and religious regulation, it "should be debated at a time when you have nothing of more importance to engage attention." Knowingly, they identified exactly what the dissenters were doing: "withhold[ing] their concurrence in the common cause until their particular requests are granted,... by such conduct all may be lost." Rather than threatening to withhold support, Anglican petitions recognized reluctantly that if the issue could not be postponed, establishment would have to be sacrificed to unanimity in the war effort.[8] Contrary to their intended purpose, the Anglican protests acknowledged what Virginia's political leaders had already surmised: they would have to make enough concessions to dissenters to maintain their support for mobilization and in so doing could retain the support, even if chagrined, of Anglicans.

The result, though, was not the collapse of the Anglican establishment's political power or prompt adoption of religious freedom. Rather, the dialogue between the political leaders and dissenters was to continue throughout the war with grudging and piecemeal reform paralleling military necessity. In 1777, dissenters were given the right to form their own military companies officered by their own coreligionists; exemption from militia musters for dissenting ministers was also clarified. In 1779, the establishment tax was wholly repealed, rather than continuing the annual suspensions which had been enacted since 1776. In 1780, the General Assembly adopted some vestry reform, and the marriage law was finally modified to legitimate dissenter weddings—subject to a series of limitations.

While Virginia's patriot leaders were negotiating for the support of the dissenters, British leaders, who had historically protected dissenters, did not respond in kind. Certainly, the British understood that religious conflict could encourage loyalism. Not only had royal officials consistently been the protectors of dissenters' rights in colonial disputes, but during the war British officials occasionally played to religious fears, for example, warning American dissenters of the danger to religious liberty from a Congress that would ally itself with a Catholic France. In North Carolina, the royal governor rallied religious dissenters to the king's banner. Yet Virginia Governor John Murray, earl of Dunmore, and British officials generally proved unable or unwilling to mobilize Southern dissenters. One might easily attribute this lacuna to British lack of understanding of America, but the truth is more complex. British officials received regular intelligence from loyalists who, focusing particularly on New England and the middle colonies, saw religious dissent as being at the core of the revolt and Anglicans as being at the center of loyalism. Britain was planning for success, and, given the loyalists' understanding of the role of dissent, British officials envisioned a postwar regime in which the Church of England would be strengthened in America, including the dispatch of bishops. With such a long-term plan, it was simply not feasible for

British officials to drive a wedge between Anglican patriot leaders and dissenters in the South by engaging dissenters in a political dialogue.

The question remains whether the dissenters delivered the support for mobilization sought and promised. The evidence suggests that they did. A number of Baptist ministers who had been incarcerated for preaching prior to the war, and who could have claimed exemptions from service based on war-time reforms, served in a military capacity. This could not be mere happen-stance. In addition, there is substantial evidence that both Baptist and Presbyterian ministers responded to government requests that ministers preach mobilization, requests that were often targeted directly at dissenters, a sign of how much Virginia had changed. Although data on mobilization are very hard to obtain, a county-by-county statistical review suggests that counties with a large dissenter population were at least as likely as Anglican counties to support mobilization for the war in both men and supplies—interesting in itself, given the disabilities and persecution that they faced before the war. Moreover, given their dialogue with establishment leaders, dissenters in Virginia did not evidence the loyalism that played a significant role among dis-senters in other Southern states, dissenters who had far less cause to oppose their local Anglican leaders based on the prewar years than did the dissenters of Virginia.

After the Battle of Yorktown, when dissenter cooperation in mobilization was no longer necessary, the ongoing dialogue between dissenters and the establishment came to an end. For three years, dissenters continued to petition the Virginia House for additional reforms in the area of religious freedom to finish the process of liberalization begun during the war, but with the need for mobilization gone, these pleas were essentially ignored. By 1784, Anglican petitions began to appear that sought to resuscitate the power of the established church, renamed the Protestant Episcopal Church that June. With former establishment leaders still populating the halls of the General Assembly, these Episcopal petitions met with initial success. Establishment leaders rallied to incorporate the Protestant Episcopal Church. More important, the notion of a general assessment to ensure tax dollars to all Christian churches, especially critical to the struggling Episcopal clergy, was initially approved by the House in November 1784 after being championed by Patrick Henry.

Through a series of adept maneuvers, James Madison was able to delay final consideration of the assessment proposal until the General Assembly's October 1785 term. In the interim, the error of the establishment leaders became evident. The politicization of the dissenters and resulting republican-ization of the Commonwealth during the war were irreversible, and the dissenters' voice could no longer be ignored. As a result, a deluge of dissenter protests, together with Madison's famous *Memorial and Remonstrance against Religious Assessments*, utterly undermined the general assessment proposal. By January 1786, the establishment was in full retreat, and dissenters were successful in a campaign to carry Jefferson's Bill for Establishing Religious Freedom into law. As if to provide a capstone for the change in Virginia politics, later that year, the incorporation of the Episcopal Church—and with it any notion that government and church were intimately related—was withdrawn.

Virginia had changed during the Revolution, and the magnitude of that change was now remarkably clear. During the war and its immediate aftermath, Virginia's dissenters wrested religious freedom from the political establishment in a prolonged and difficult negotiation in which they threatened that the price for their wartime mobilization was religious freedom. Equally important, the process itself—forcing the establishment to engage intimately with a far broader population—brought dissenters into the polity, democratizing Virginia's politics.

The Virginia gentry were firmly in control before the war and did not then need to reform in response to evangelical discontent. The rise of dissent did not result in prewar republicanization and did not inevitably lead to disestablishment. Rather, negotiation of disestablishment in return for wartime mobilization politicized the dissenters and proved a key element in the republicanization of the state. The necessity of gaining support and cooperation from the evangelicals required patriot leaders to include freedom of religion within the definition of what they were fighting for; as a consequence of the negotiations, the Virginia polity was reshaped to include the dissenters who had previously been effectively excluded.

This dialogue and negotiation deeply impacted American notions of religious freedom. By the time the U.S. Constitution was crafted in 1787, Virginia had become the most progressive of the new states in protecting religious liberty. The change was so dramatic that in 1789 Virginia, the former bastion of established Anglicanism in colonial America, proved a model for the First Amendment's protection of the free exercise of religion and prohibition on religious establishments. In seeking to understand that process, both jurists and historians have repeatedly turned to the writings of Jefferson and Madison. Although both men were intimately engaged in the fight for religious freedom in Virginia, overemphasis of their work tends to deny an appropriate voice to the dissenters. After all, it was the dissenters who bargained for, and fought for, religious freedom.

That religious freedom was not inevitable. When the war ended, eleven of thirteen new states maintained some form of a Christian oath for participation in the polity and/or an established church. The negotiation with the dissenters in Virginia was not only essential to the adoption of religious freedom there but the developments in that state played a seminal role in the development of religious freedom in the young republic and, thus, in large parts of the world. As a result, the Virginia dissenters' view of what they were bargaining for demands our attention.

Based on both theology and their experience, Virginia's eighteenth-century dissenters had a remarkably robust notion of religious liberty. Their theology required that any commitment to religion be absolutely devoid of government suasion. They emphatically rejected the notion of a "Christian nation" on both religious and political grounds. Similarly, they were insistent that a strict separation of church and state be maintained, not because they sought to create an independent political sphere based on secular liberalism but because they understood the danger that any entanglement posed to both the church and religious belief. Their participation in the political process during the war taught them to value the right to participate while ensuring noninterference in their religious activities. Their petitions repeatedly noted that any government aid to religion was an anathema, as it would inevitably make their ministers servants of and subject to the government. They maintained a strong sense of the right of free exercise, but how could it be otherwise for a people who faced repeated incarceration for "breaching the peace" by preaching in public?

This story rightfully begins with the strength of the colonial Anglican Church and the discrimination and persecution that Virginia's establishment visited on dissenters. The negotiations for freedom are then considered, particularly several hundred religious petitions filed with the House of Burgesses and later the House of Delegates during the crucial period from before the war until the adoption of Jefferson's Statute for Establishing Religious Freedom in 1786.[9] British action and inaction are surveyed next, permitting some conclusions about the lack of a British effort to solicit support from Virginia dissenters during the war. Based on available evidence, an analysis of whether and how the dissenters responded to the call for mobilization, particularly a comparison between actions in Virginia and other Southern states with Anglican establishments, is provided. The crucial period after the war is then reviewed, both to demonstrate the growing reluctance of establishment leaders to make concessions after wartime necessity was removed and the triumphant effort of the newly politicized dissenters to obtain adoption of Jefferson's statute. Finally, the dissenters' understanding of the religious freedom for which they fought is discussed.

For 200 years, sectarian histories have related how Virginia's dissenters, Baptists and Presbyterians, were fighting for freedom during the American

Revolution. And so they were. But the fight was not simply a fight against Britain, it was equally a fight with the Virginia establishment; they fought both for freedom of religion and freedom from British rule. The two were intimately linked, not simply in a theoretical or principled sense but in a very practical sense—they would not have mobilized for the latter without the provision of the former. The immediate (albeit far-reaching) result of the negotiations between the dissenters and establishment was that Virginia witnessed the development of religious freedom and an understanding of that freedom which still speaks loudly today.

Equally important, in the process of that negotiation, Virginia was changed. The establishment gentry were forced to incorporate a broader population—dissenting, western, middling and lower class—into the Virginia polity. Virginia did not begin the war united, and it was far from inevitable that it would fight that way. Before the war, the dissenters were unable to obtain even minor concessions from the establishment; their voices were simply silenced. During the war, with the necessity of recruiting and otherwise mobilizing at the forefront of the minds of political leaders, the dissenters carefully and effectively parlayed threats and offers into a series of religious and political concessions. Disestablishment did not result from the republicanization of Virginia; rather, negotiating disestablishment politicized the dissenters—a process which resulted in republicanization.[10]

Our sense of religious freedom was largely developed in Virginia precisely because this negotiation occurred. At the same time, Virginia was changed: the polity was expanded, and dissenters joined the civil community.

I

Virginians Dissent

A mob collected at one of their [Baptist] meetings and seized the preachers, Barrow and Mintz, and carried them to a water not far distant. There they dipped them several times, holding them under the water until they were nearly drowned, asking them if they believed. At length Mr. Barrow replied "I believe you mean to drown me."

—Semple, *History of the Baptists* (1894)

On any summer Sunday in 1768, as congregants gathered before services at the Little Fork Anglican Church in Culpeper County, Virginia, to discuss recent events, the incarceration in neighboring Spotsylvania County of four Baptist preachers—several of whom had previously been warned out of Culpeper—was almost certainly a topic of conversation. If common practice was followed, local gentry, many of whom were vestrymen, discussed business, politics, farming, and other matters in the church yard until the service was ready to begin—or a bit after—and entered the church in an informal procession that highlighted their social prominence. Certainly local political leaders were there, including county justices, militia leaders, and representatives to the House of Burgesses. By law, all county residents would have been present over the course of a month; there were many dissenters among the "common" people in the community, but because there was no licensed dissenting meeting house in Culpeper in 1768, failure to attend the Anglican Church was subject to a fine. The law was honored in the breach, but Anglican leaders knew that it could be used at whim, particularly to sanction any dissenter who challenged either the church's or their leadership.

Perhaps local leaders saw in Spotsylvania's actions in early June an opportunity to demonstrate their own authority and discourage religious enthusiasm among residents; within a few years, more than a dozen dissenters graced Culpeper's jail—a location that ironically was to host a Baptist church in the early nineteenth century. If so, they were sadly disappointed. As was occurring throughout Virginia, especially in the northern Piedmont, dissent was growing rapidly, and persecution seemed only to feed its rise. Within a few years, several Baptist churches dotted the county, and by the time James Madison was elected to the new U.S. House of Representatives in 1789, Culpeper County provided the margin of victory, and Culpeper Baptists held the electoral balance of power. Of course, this could not be known as residents prepared for services in 1768.

Theologians or sectarian historians might see this mixed scene of political, social, and religious activity in 1768 as evidence of an ailing, secularized church—reason enough for the growth of an enthusiastic, experiential dissenting religion. There is a certain historic and religious chauvinism to that perception. This mixing evidenced the mutually reinforcing nature of colonial Virginia's church, political, and social hierarchy. Eighteenth-century dissenters and Anglicans alike would view the scene outside the Culpeper Anglican church as evidence of the continuing political and social dominance of the latter and continued limitations on the former.

An Established Church and Religious Dissent in Virginia before the Revolution

Designation of the Church of England as the established church of colonial Virginia was far from a mere formality; a host of legal regulations and informal social conventions accompanied it. The scheme closely linked church and state so that local vestries of Anglican laymen had both religious and civil functions—most prominently setting and collecting taxes to support the church and for poor relief. The vestry assessment—taxation without representation for religious dissenters—was usually the highest tax paid by eighteenth-century Virginians. Anglican clergy had the exclusive right to baptize and consecrate marriages, leaving children of those married by dissenting ministers subject to claims of bastardy, with resulting legal incapacities; for example, the bastard children of female servants could be bound out for the benefit of the parish. Dissenters were allowed to preach at funerals, but were sometimes denied the right to do so in a church yard. Anglican vestries were responsible for periodic processing of land boundaries in their parishes and for finding homes for orphans bound out by the county courts, with important consequences for local land disputes and societal relations. Vestries had an obligation to present to grand juries citizens they believed guilty of fornication, adultery, whoredom, blasphemy, swearing, or drunkenness, authority that could be exercised with a studied discretion. As late as May 1776, vestries were given additional authority to assist in appointing collectors and places of payment for government levies denominated in tobacco. Anglican ministers, unlike dissenting ministers, were exempted from militia duty and the tax on tithables. Failure to attend Anglican services regularly or a licensed dissenting meeting house—of which there were few in Virginia at the time—was subject to a stiff fine. Members of the governor's council and general court had to be Anglican. From 1690 to 1740, 60 percent of Virginia burgesses were vestrymen, and the pattern generally continued through the Revolution. Elijah Morton lost his position as justice of the peace in Orange County for being "a promoter of schisms and particularly of the sect called Anabaptists." In theory, all schoolmasters had to be licensed by the Bishop of London and conform to the Church of England. Anglicans generally had access to better educational opportunities than dissenters; not only were local schools usually run by Anglican ministers, but the College of William and Mary, the only institution of higher learning in the colony, was controlled by an Anglican administration and faculty. In the prewar years, religion was a defining characteristic for a Virginian, and both the legal and political dominance of Anglicanism was unmistakable, particularly to a dissenter.[1]

On rare occasions, especially in the Shenandoah Valley, a dissenter would be elected as a vestryman. This apparent evidence of liberality, though, is two-faced. By law, vestries could remove any dissenters who were elected. A protest was filed in 1767 against two Augusta County vestrymen who refused to swear to conform to the Church of England; in 1769, two Augusta vestrymen who would not subscribe were replaced. Although a minority on a vestry could not simply reshape its membership by accusing the majority of dissent, if a majority was accused of not conforming to the Church of England, such cases were referred to the General Assembly. In the once instance identified where this occurred, the vestry was dissolved because "a majority of the vestry...are dissenters," with a new vestry to be elected "conformable to...the church of England." In the end, although a few dissenters sat on Virginia vestries, they were never permitted to challenge Anglican dominance.[2]

Edmund Randolph, an establishment scion, later argued that Virginia's dissenters benefited from "a spirit of mildness [that] was an antidote to the licensed severity of the law." This is revisionist—at best, legal discrimination seen through the eyes of a member of the established hierarchy. For Virginia's eighteenth-century dissenters, legal infirmities and discrimination faced on account of religion did not seem mild. Yet to understand the political dynamic in Virginia before and during the Revolution, to appreciate the complexity of encouraging mobilization among the strong and growing dissenting population, discrimination against dissenters must be perceived from the dissenters' perspective. Care must be taken especially in evaluating apparent leniency in enforcing establishment regulations. William Fristoe, a contemporary Baptist preacher, observed: "Little notice was taken of the omission [in regular Anglican church attendance], if members of the established church; but so soon as the new-lights [evangelical Baptists and Presbyterians] were absent they were presented by the grand jury, and fined according to law." One of the earliest Presbyterians in the Piedmont of Virginia reportedly was fined twenty times for having prayer meetings in his house. Similarly, while the law requiring that schoolteachers be licensed by the Bishop of London was often ignored, Anglican ministers could seek to enforce it when dissenters impinged on their territories, at a minimum harassing dissenting ministers who sought to supplement their income with teaching.[3]

Although the 1689 English Act of Toleration provided considerable relief to dissenters in England, arguments periodically erupted as to whether the act applied in the colony at all. Most famously, Virginia's illustrious Presbyterian minister Samuel Davies disputed the matter with Virginia Attorney General Peyton Randolph. Davies, to silence opposition, sought and received an opinion of the British Attorney General Sir Dudley Rider in 1752 confirming applicability of the Act of Toleration to the colonies. This opinion remained controversial in Virginia, and local colonial officials generally tried to narrow the act's interpretation and apply its requirements strictly, deliberately attempting to restrict the spread of dissent. The act required dissenting ministers to swear an oath to the king, accept the Articles of the Anglican faith (except those dealing with church governance), and be licensed. As interpreted by local gentry in Virginia, both ministers and places of worship had to be licensed with the General Court in Williamsburg, which met only twice a year, requiring a considerable trip for Piedmont and Shenandoah Valley ministers in the period before well-maintained roads. Separate licensing of meeting houses ruled out itinerancy, which was popular among evangelicals. Before an application could be presented, petitioners requesting a license required certification by county magistrates and had to locate an Anglican minister willing to inquire about their adherence to the articles and certify his findings.[4]

Those who preached before seeking a license could be denied licenses, and licensing by county courts was specifically disallowed. When several Baptist preachers arrested in Chesterfield County for preaching without a license offered to take the oaths required by the Act of Toleration before the county court, the court declared that doing so there would not suffice to satisfy the act. Other impediments were created as circumstances required. Fristoe complained that "I knew the general court to refuse a license for a Baptist meeting house, in the county of Richmond, because there was a Presbyterian meeting house already in the county." As he summarized the difficulties,

> thro' the whole process of this business, from the beginning to the end, obstructions and difficulties lay in the way—first to get signers to a petition, second to get a certificate from two acting magistrates in the county from which the petition was sent, thirdly to find the court in such a temper and capable of exercising such generosity as to grant a license, and after all this, it was left uncertain and precarious, and depended on the will and temper of the clergy whether we should succeed or not.

Obtaining a license continued to be a challenge for dissenters up through the war.[5]

Moreover, some dissenting ministers, particularly the more evangelical "Separate" Baptists, opposed the swearing of the requisite oath on principle or believed that seeking a license was to place civil authority over their ministry, which was subject only to the direction of God. Thus, they refused to conform to the requirements of the Act of Toleration, subjecting themselves to "legal" exclusion from preaching. Even when a dissenting minister complied with the act, it did nothing to alleviate the political dominance of members of the established church or end establishment taxes or the legal preferment enjoyed by Anglicans.

This is not to say that dissent was entirely suppressed. In spite of the favored position of the Anglican Church, as early as 1642, Puritans in Nansemond County invited ministers from Boston to come preach, which they did to substantial crowds. This brief flaring of dissent was probably the cause of the 1643 Virginia law requiring that all ministers conform to the Church of England and that nonconformists depart. Nonetheless, by the turn of the eighteenth century, there were a handful of Presbyterians and Baptists worshipping quietly in Virginia, and a growing number of Quakers, but the breadth of dissent was very limited. The few dissenters who entered Virginia in the seventeenth or early eighteenth centuries and were not quickly chased out did little to upset the establishment.[6]

This began to change when, in 1737, Lieutenant and acting Governor William Gooch recommended that the Orange County court license William Williams, a Presbyterian minister itinerating in the Shenandoah Valley—a practice disallowed later. The next year, Gooch accepted a specific request forwarded by the Synod of Philadelphia to permit a Presbyterian population in the valley, perceived in Williamsburg as a buffer against hostile Indians. From that point on, Presbyterian worship became fixed in the colony. This official breach in establishment policy was timely. Although a number of Presbyterians had settled in the valley before Gooch formally accepted their presence, fed by the official sanction and the First Great Awakening, dissent grew rapidly in the middle period of the eighteenth century.[7]

All sources confirm that Virginia's dissenting population experienced strong growth in the decades before the Revolution, but precise figures are impossible to come by, both because of a lack of a detailed census and because defining dissent is complicated by the practice of occasional conformity. Thus, many people who regularly attended dissenting services also attended Anglican services for particular ceremonies; for example, a very large majority of the white inhabitants were baptized in the Anglican Church, and many who might otherwise favor dissenters regularly attended Anglican communion. Moreover, attendees at dissenting meeting houses usually exceeded the denominations' official membership several times over. In any case, the trend was undeniable. While he was an Anglican minister at St. Mary's parish in Caroline County in 1770, Jonathan Boucher said of the dissenters' growing number, "I might almost as well pretend to count the gnats that buzz around us in a summer's evening."[8]

Estimates of dissenters' share of the populace vary dramatically. In 1781–82, when promoting adoption of his Bill for Establishing Religious Freedom, Thomas Jefferson famously claimed that two-thirds of Virginia's population dissented at the beginning of the Revolution. Yet in 1776, when an end to establishment taxes was brought before the General Assembly, he estimated 55,000 dissenters; this would have amounted to 15–25 percent of the white population. Elsewhere, Jefferson said a "majority" were dissenters by the Revolution, but as an early biographer noted, "Mr. [James] Madison thinks that the proportion of Dissenters was considerably less." A 1766 report to the Bishop of London titled "A Brief View of the State of the Church in the British Colonies" estimated that Virginia dissenters were 22 percent of the white population, a robust estimate given the strong growth of dissent from 1766 to 1776. Based on contemporary sources, Jefferson's earlier estimate (15–25 percent) and Madison's observation ("considerably less" than 50 percent) were probably closer to correct in 1776 than the more famous "two-thirds" claim.[9]

Although modern historians disagree on estimates of Virginia's dissenter population in the late eighteenth century, there is no doubt that by the time of the American Revolution dissenters represented a significant share of the population and were growing rapidly. Based on the available estimates, and accounting for regular attendees as well as formal members, dissenters were likely between one-fifth and one-third (if not a bit more) of the white population, with a higher share in the Piedmont, and a substantial majority in the valley and west, but a relatively low share in the Tidewater region. Numbers aside, certainly dissenters' share of the population was highly significant as Virginia sought to mobilize effectively against Britain.[10]

Of course, whatever the growth of dissent, the Church of England maintained dominance both in total numbers and, more to the point, in political power. The Anglican Tidewater continued to be a bastion of legislative power aided by the historic underrepresentation of new, western counties—the east had about one-third of the population and one-half of the delegates—and the deference paid to gentry throughout the colony. The difficulty of travel to Williamsburg and, later, Richmond for western members of the legislature also contributed to Tidewater control of political power. Still, the dramatic growth in dissenters' numbers meant that there were few places wholly impervious to the interlopers; Anglicans maintained political hegemony, but not exclusivity. Moreover, whereas Tidewater gentry maintained a studied underrepresentation of western interests in the legislature, they were far less interested in maintaining an underrepresentation of western recruits to fight a long and difficult war.[11]

A short review of the leading dissenting denominations confirms these general observations. Presbyterians made up the largest group of Virginia dissenters as the Revolution approached. The Scotch-Irish immigrants filling the Shenandoah Valley from Pennsylvania and spreading down the Blue Ridge into the Piedmont, as well as Scottish immigrants to the Piedmont, were primarily Presbyterian (see figure 1.1). These colonial Presbyterians were strict Calvinists (predestinarians) who generally accepted the Westminster Confession of Faith (1646). The fact that the Presbyterian Church was the state church of Scotland (part of Great Britain after the Act of Union in 1707) placed Presbyterians in a somewhat awkward position vis-à-vis Virginia's established church. Not surprisingly, they did not support the Anglican Church, but throughout the period, even to 1786 when the debate over religious freedom was brought to a climax in Virginia, some Presbyterians maintained an ambivalence on the question of state support of religion. In Virginia, though, such ambivalence was never widespread, and the support for broad religious liberty by the majority of Presbyterians as the war proceeded played a key role in the developments under discussion.

While a schism was created in the colonial Presbyterian Church by the Great Awakening, with traditionalists expelling the "new light" enthusiastic evangelicals from the Philadelphia Presbytery in 1741, by 1758 the schism had

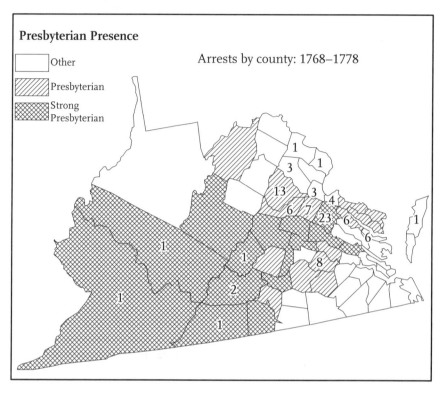

FIGURE I.I. Presbyterian presence by counties, 1776, and dissenter arrests. Presbyterians were particularly populous in the Shenandoah Valley and central Piedmont.

been healed with the evangelicals' dramatic increase in membership playing a critical role in Presbyterians' shift toward a more experiential religion. New Light Presbyterian ministers, notably Samuel Davies in Virginia, often joined in an evangelical appeal to blacks and did not focus on the gentry the way vestry-controlled Anglican ministers did, further alienating themselves from establishment leaders. With Presbyterians continuing to demand a learned clergy, their success in the South was heavily dependent on "missionaries" from William Tennent's "Log College" at Neshaminy, Pennsylvania, and, soon thereafter, the College of New Jersey (later renamed Princeton).[12]

Generally willing to abide by the Act of Toleration, Presbyterians initially caused relatively few problems for authorities, and their status as members of a state church in Great Britain paved the way to relatively cordial relations with many colonial governors, not least with Scottish Governors Robert Dinwiddie and Lord Dunmore. Presbyterian preachers were licensed in Virginia by the General Court beginning in 1747 when Samuel Davies went to Williamsburg, met with Governor Gooch, and received a license to preach at four Piedmont meeting houses. Certainly throughout the French and Indian War, the relationship between Virginia Presbyterians, who were often in the forefront of the frontier fighting, and the colonial government was cordial, if not warm, with Davies playing a noted role in encouraging frontier enlistments. In some areas of the valley, Presbyterians occasionally served on vestries and, as long as the power structure was not threatened, Anglican authorities could ignore the transgression.[13]

Still, even Presbyterians were constantly reminded of the infirmities under which they operated, particularly in the areas of taxes, marriage, and significant political and educational privileges for Anglicans. Nor were Presbyterians immune from active persecution, especially when availing themselves of the evangelical instruments of itinerancy and "enthusiasm." In fact, the whole notion of itinerancy was seen by the Anglican establishment as an assault on stable, local gentry leadership. When Davies first arrived in Hanover County, he was greeted by an order from the governor's council posted where the Hanover Presbyterians met:

> This Board having under their Consideration the Number of
> Itinerant Preachers lately crept into this Colony and the mischievous
> Consequences of suffering those Corruptors of our Faith and true
> Religion to propagate their shocking Doctrines it is Ordered That a
> Proclamation forthwith issue requiring all Magistrates and Officers
> to discourage and prohibit [sic] as far as legally they can all Itinerant
> Preachers whether New Light men Moravians or Methodists from
> Teaching Preaching or holding any Meeting in this Colony and that
> all People be injoined [sic] to be aiding and assisting to that Purpose.

This followed on the prosecution for slander of John Roan, a Presbyterian preacher sent to the Piedmont in 1744–45 by the "new light" New York Synod, who could not resist openly criticizing the Anglican establishment—but who had the sense to flee the colony before he could be seized.[14]

Nor did their willingness to conform to the Act of Toleration suffice to resolve the licensing difficulties experienced by Presbyterians. Thus, when the New York Synod sent John Rodgers to assist Davies, the colonial government denied Rodgers a license ostensibly because he preached before traveling to Williamsburg to make his official application. Reportedly the senior member of the council, acting in the British governor's absence, declared, "we have Mr. Rodgers out, and we are determined to keep him out." Other ministers found their vocation constrained by the limitation of their licenses to specified meeting houses and the ability of authorities in Williamsburg to withhold a license if a minister sought to cover so many meeting houses that authorities could characterize his efforts as itinerancy. When licensed meeting houses were not available, lay members of the church risked prosecution for failure to attend Sunday services at the established Anglican church or for permitting unlicensed ministers to preach at their homes. For example, Joshua Morris of James City was indicted for permitting Roan to preach at his house after Roan was denied a license for his alleged libel.[15]

Still, despite the difficulties, the Presbyterian Church grew, particularly in the valley and middle Piedmont area. It is estimated that by the time of the Revolution, there were over ninety Presbyterian meeting houses in Virginia and approximately seventy Presbyterian ministers.[16]

Baptists, the second largest group of dissenters in Virginia as the Revolution approached, were especially strong in the Piedmont and the most rapidly growing of the dissenting sects. The denomination was broken into "Regular" Baptists (Calvinists), a small number of "General" Baptists (Arminian—believing that saving grace is offered to all who accept it), and evangelical "Separate" Baptists (generally Calvinist). Initially, Separates developed from tension in New England's Congregational Church after the Great Awakening when more evangelical members insisted on a strict requirement that a new member relate a specific conversion experience of being "born again" to join a congregation—rejecting the hard-fought "halfway" covenant championed by the Reverend Solomon Stoddard in 1662—and sought a separation from what seemed to them to be an increasingly worldly Congregational Church. Their strict notions of church discipline continued to set them apart in Virginia as they opposed many social conventions and forms of entertainment that were particularly popular in the Old Dominion, including dancing, horse racing, card playing, gambling, and fiddling.[17]

Since their seventeenth-century growth in England, Baptists, unlike Presbyterians, had always been a marginal group set apart from other churchgoers and seemingly always at odds with government. In the eighteenth century, Baptists seemed to relish their position as nonconformists. They certainly did not have a successful history as a state church like Scottish Presbyterians.[18]

Having moved south and grown rapidly, Separates, in particular, were vociferous in their opposition to aspects of the Virginia establishment. As Separates did not pay their preachers—believing to do so would simply encourage false preachers—they were especially opposed to the church tax to pay Anglican ministers. Furthermore, many Separates refused to abide by the licensing requirements of the Toleration Act, believing them to interfere with Jesus' sole lordship over the church. Consistent with their theology that only a completely free will offering could be acceptable to God, Baptists adamantly opposed all forms of coercion in the area of religion, not only state churches but even infant baptism, risking violation of the law mandating baptism, not to mention receiving the opprobrium of neighbors who thought failure to baptize a child—risking eternal damnation should the child die in infancy—was a particularly pernicious form of child cruelty. These factors, combined with the Separates' enthusiasm in worship and proselytizing, especially among blacks and women, often resulted in them being a primary object of persecution.[19]

As early as 1714, a group of General Baptists was meeting in southeast Virginia. Significant growth of the Baptist denomination waited forty years, however. As the second half of the century began, Regulars maintained strength in the northern Shenandoah and Piedmont. Separates, who seemed to thrive on persecution, became particularly strong "southside," that is, south of the James River, but their preaching and meeting houses were penetrating further north and east as the Revolution approached, contesting space in previously uniformly Anglican counties (see figure 1.2). Tension as these communities clashed resulted in a higher rate of presentments for nonattendance at Anglican

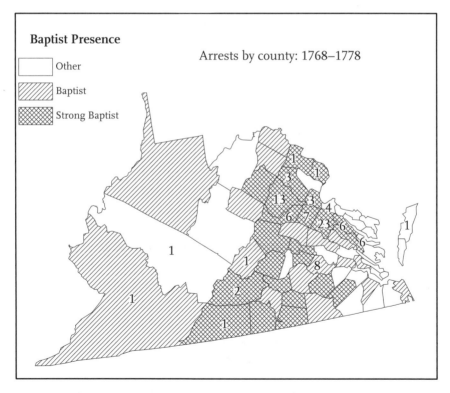

FIGURE 1.2. Virginia Baptist presence by counties, 1776. In the 1760s, the Baptist population exploded in the Piedmont and spread into the Northern Neck, eliciting opposition particularly where it encountered entrenched Anglican interests.

services and other persecution in the Tidewater, where Baptist incursions challenged dominant Anglican cultures.[20]

The lack of formal training for their ministers encouraged the view that eighteenth-century Virginia Baptists were uneducated and of a "lesser sort." One source noted that there was not a single "college-bred man" among the Baptist ministers in prerevolutionary Virginia, further challenging Anglican notions of proper hierarchy. Or, as one Baptist minister explained, "The cant word was, they [Baptists] are an ignorant illiterate set—and of the poor and contemptible class of the people." Yet while certainly the wealthy and powerful of Virginia's gentry tended to be Anglican, as another Baptist noted, most churchgoers from every denomination were "as poor, and as unlearned as we." The Baptists, like the Presbyterians, enticed a few gentry members into their fellowship and were not opposed to using the influence of those gentry members to increase their flock. Still, the independent and relatively democratic structure of their church governance contrasted starkly with the hierarchical structures of the Anglican Church and Presbyterian discipline. Moreover, evangelical Baptist services encouraged close intermixing of congregants, challenging social conventions that insisted a respectable distance be maintained not only between men and women and blacks and whites but also between those of different classes.[21]

Some of the contemporary poor perception of Baptists was due to the fact that they actively recruited blacks (both free and slave) to be converted and preached to and baptized women without their husbands' consent. Inclusion of blacks proved to be an important factor in growth of the Baptists, and it tended to dictate the holding of irregular meetings, sometimes at night, potentially challenging slaveholders' control and contributing to conflict with establishment leaders. Presbyterians also actively recruited among blacks, as did a few Anglicans, but the Baptists presented a particular challenge to the gentry-dominated society by their emphasis on black conversion and willingness to give black members a significant role in their church polity. Although the total number of black Baptists at the time of the Revolution was a small figure, the reputation of promoting slave unrest contributed significantly to the Baptists' conflict with the gentry. For example, one runaway notice published in the *Virginia Gazette* claimed that the runaway "pretends to be very religious, and is a *Baptist teacher.*" This type of publicity was very harmful to Virginia Baptists.[22]

By the time of the Revolution, it is estimated that there were almost 90 Baptist meeting houses in Virginia and approximately 100 ministers.[23]

There was also a small but growing group of German Reformed and Lutheran worshippers in Virginia as the Revolution approached, particularly among German immigrants who moved south from Pennsylvania into the

Shenandoah Valley. As a rule, these sects worked to avoid problems with the established church, sometimes sharing pulpits with Anglicans. General John Peter Muhlenberg, the famous "fighting parson" who led his valley congregation to war, for example, preached to both Lutherans and Anglicans. Virginia contained nine Lutheran and eight German Reformed churches in 1776.[24]

John Wesley and his followers were actively growing colonial Methodism in the mid-1770s, although before and during the Revolution the Methodists pointedly saw themselves as Anglican rather than as dissenters. (The Methodist Church in the United States did not formally separate from the Church of England until 1784.) Methodist preachers were also particularly successful "southside," especially in the Tidewater area, and were also actively recruiting black members. There is some suggestion that as the Revolution approached Methodists became the leading evangelicals in Virginia and attracted a "vast following," but initially Methodist recruiting in the state lagged well behind that of the Baptists and Presbyterians. True, their numbers were growing rapidly but from a very small base in the early 1770s; the first great Methodist revival in Virginia did not occur until 1776.[25]

Quakers and Mennonites comprised a small share of the Virginia population at the time of the Revolution and tended not to agitate for reform, both as a matter of principle and to avoid calling additional attention to their refusal to fight with the militia on the grounds of conscience. During the American Revolution, their initial exemption from military service created tension with other citizens who successfully sought compensating financial support for the government from those unwilling to fight and ultimately required Quakers and Mennonites to provide a replacement if they wished not to serve.[26]

In the wake of the Great Awakening, dissenters in Virginia, especially evangelicals, were rapidly increasing in number and by the time of the Revolution probably constituted one-fifth to one-third or more of the population: a crucial constituency for mobilization against militarily dominant Britain. Several facts concerning the geography of dissent are worth remembering. Disputes tended to flare where dissenters were making the most progress in what had previously been areas dominated by the established church—in the Piedmont and northern neck. The greater concentration of dissenters in the frontier and other relatively less developed regions ensured that dissenters were often familiar with warfare and the use of firearms from Indian skirmishes, as well as hunting, and often owned the rifles that proved to be a boon in some revolutionary battles. As a result, their support for mobilization took on even greater importance with the Virginia legislature occasionally calling specifically on the assistance of backcountry riflemen.[27] Despite the growth of dissent, the disproportionate representation of Tidewater Virginia in the House of Burgesses and later General Assembly, not to mention historic primacy of the establishment, ensured firm control of the assembly and civil polity was maintained by Anglicans. In spite of dissenter growth, Virginia was among the strictest of the Southern colonies in enforcing conformity to the established church. As the 1760s closed, the Anglican Church and its establishment gentry were seeking to tighten controls.

Persecution of Dissenters

As dissenters became a bigger presence and effectively began to challenge Anglican dominance in some areas, their problems with the establishment expanded well beyond the significant legal infirmities and discrimination expressly embedded in the law. Flexible administration of various laws that were neutral on their face could be used by Anglican leaders against dissenters. For example, when Archibald Dick (Anglican rector of St. Margaret's parish), Samuel Hargrave (a Quaker), and Thomas Pittman (who let Baptist Lewis Craig preach at his house) all failed to list chaises for taxation in Caroline County in 1773, Dick was excused by the county magistrates, but the others were each fined 500 pounds of tobacco. Henry Goodloe's family had him declared insane apparently in part based on him permitting the Baptist John Waller to preach in his home. As dissent grew, "absences from the parish church were more strictly observed," and dissenters increasingly fined.[28]

Perhaps even more disturbing to dissenter–establishment relations than legal disabilities, dissenters, particularly Baptists, faced very serious physical assault and incarceration from the latter part of the 1760s until the war. As this physical persecution gained strength and vehemence in the years preceding the Revolution, Presbyterians and other dissenters must have watched with increasing alarm. While scholars have urged caution with dissenters' reports of persecution and have often minimized the persecution or failed to appreciate its scope and impact, the persecution is largely confirmed in court records and other accounts that are so pervasive and consistent as to provide ample support for their general thrust. In any case, there is little question that these reports are highly informative of the dissenters' perception, and the dissenters saw the persecution as a grave threat over the course of many years.[29]

For at least ten years prior to the Revolution, Baptist and, to a lesser extent, other dissenting preachers risked physical attack while preaching. John Waller wrote in August 1771:

whilst Brother William Webber was addressing the congregation,...there came running towards him, in a most furious rage,
Captain James Montague, a Magistrate of the county, followed by the
Parson of the parish, and several others, who seemed greatly exasperated.... Brother Wafford was severely scourged, and Brother Henry
Street received one lash from one of the persecutors, who was
prevented from proceeding to further violence by his companions.

Morgan Edwards, an early Baptist historian who traveled in Virginia in 1772 to
gather information, reported the same incident, saying that the minister of the
parish ran a horsewhip through Waller's mouth as he attempted to preach,
silencing him. "After that the clerk, Buckner, pulled him down and dragged
him to the sherif [sic] who stood at a distance; the sheriff immediately received
him and whipped him in so violent manner (without the ceremony of a trial)
that poor Waller was presently in a gore of blood, and will carry the scars to his
grave." Reportedly, after the beating, Waller (who had been known in his
younger, preconversion days as "Swearing Jack") remounted the stage to preach
and in the process created additional interest in his story, continuing a pattern
of dissenters using persecution as part of their "witness" and to evangelical
purposes. Edwards also reported that David Thomas, a Regular Baptist minister, was pulled down while preaching and threatened with fists and, in another
case, with a gun. Others suffered similar fates. Samuel Harris was driven out
of Culpeper County with clubs and whips and in Orange "was pulled down as
he was preaching, and dragged about by the hair of his head, and sometimes by
the leg....On another time, he was knocked down by a rude fellow, while he
was preaching." Stones and apples were thrown at preachers, and in several
instances they faced men with firearms. John Leland and Daniel Fristoe apparently faced armed assault, and William Fristoe was pursued by an armed
sheriff. William discussed the assaults at some length:

Another time, at the same place, a gun has been brought by a person,
in a great rage, and presented within the meeting house doors,
supposed to shoot the preacher, but was prevented by his own
brother, who suddenly caught the gun from him and prevented the
execution of the wretched design. At another time,...while at
devotion, a mob having collected, they immediately rushed upon
them in the meeting house, and began to inflict blows on the
worshippers, and produce bruises and bloodshed, so that the floor
shone with the sprinkled blood the days following; upon which the
few Baptists in the place concluded they would aim at a redress of
their grievances, by bringing the lawless mob to justice,...A warrant

was applied for, and obtained, for the principal leaders of the
mischief…the result was, in [sic] was deemed a riot, and all were
discharged.

Failure of establishment support for action against violent abuse must have
added to dissenter angst and fear. One Baptist minister, escaping from men
who were attempting to bring him before a magistrate for preaching without a
license, was hunted with dogs.[30]

In other cases, Baptist preachers were dunked—almost drowned—in
mockery of their belief in immersion baptism.

On the first preaching of the Baptists in these parts they met with
violent opposition. A mob collected at one of their meetings and
seized the preachers, Barrow and Mintz, and carried them to a water
not far distant. There they dipped them several times, holding them
under the water until they were nearly drowned, asking them *if they
believed.* At length Mr. Barrow replied "*I believe* you mean to drown
me." After sporting with them thus, they let them go.

Nor was this violent sport an isolated incident. "At another time a lawless mob,
headed by two magistrates, seized Mr. Moore and another preacher who was
with him, and carried them off to duck them." James Ireland, later jailed for
preaching, reported that "sailors were brought on shore from their vessels,
through the influence of the people, in order to take me out into the stream,
hoist me up to the yards arm and so to give me a ducking."[31]

Establishment supporters also disrupted dissenters' meetings with obscene
songs or by playing cards and drinking on the preacher's stage. Nor was physical
assault limited to ministers. A hornets' nest was thrown into one prayer meeting, a (presumably poisonous) snake into another—incidents that could have
caused serious injury and certainly would have caused significant chaos and
fear. Men on horseback would sometimes disrupt meetings by riding roughly
through the crowds of congregants or, as Semple wrote, "They often insulted
the preachers in time of service, and would ride into the water and make sport
when they administered baptism; they frequently fabricated and spread the
most groundless reports, which were injurious to the characters of the Baptists."
Mounted attacks could seriously injure and certainly intimidated even the
stoutest of dissenters. The Baptist preacher Dutton Lane's mother was beaten
by his father for going to Baptist services. One Baptist minister was sued for
baptizing a man's son without his permission, and, though the case was ultimately dismissed, the minister had to pay costs. Meeting houses were directly
attacked. Edwards reports that a mob broke into a Baptist meeting house in

Fauquier County "doing the most slovenly things, breaking their pulpit and communion table in pieces." Threats of abuse were not uncommon. Though many (probably a large majority) of dissenter prayer meetings were uninterrupted, the efforts to break up meetings and physically abuse preachers and congregants were far from rare, and contemporaneous accounts make clear that such abuse was seen by dissenting preachers as an omnipresent risk. Edwards refers to "the *usual* opposition of mobs and the imprisonment of their preachers." These assaults must have had a serious impact not only on those physically injured but also on those who witnessed or heard of the attacks—a group that must have included virtually all Virginia dissenters.[32]

Even greater physical abuse was targeted at the black members of evangelical congregations. James Ireland, a well-known Baptist preacher, recalled that at one meeting with a large number of slaves "the patrolers [sic] were let loose upon them.... I was equally struck with astonishment and surprise, to see the poor negroes flying in every direction, the patrolers seizing and whipping them, whilst others were carrying them off prisoners, in order, perhaps, to subject them to a more severe punishment." Ireland also reported that when crowds gathered outside his prison cell to hear his preaching, some members were threatened "whilst the poor negroes have been stripped and subjected to stripes."

Evangelizing to the 40–45 percent of Virginia's population that was enslaved was a central element of religion for Baptists and some evangelical Presbyterians and an important element in the rapid growth of dissent. At the same time, evangelicals' appeal to blacks was another factor in hardening the resolve of the gentry to oppose dissenters' inroads, often violently. Animosity was fueled by the perception of the gentry that dissenters' preaching to slaves without owners' consent and at irregular hours challenged owners' authority and, according to some owners, encouraged runaways, creating deep animosity between evangelicals and many Anglican leaders. A newspaper article, reportedly written by Attorney General John Randolph, specifically attacked the Baptists for "Slaves [drawn] from Obedience to their Masters," and runaways were sometimes attributed to evangelical influence. One slave owner asked his overseer to keep slaves away from evangelical preachers who "put most of my...Negroes crazy with their new Light and their new Jerusalem."[33]

Nor was the persecution limited to Separate Baptists, although they certainly received the brunt of the abuse. Regular Baptists and, to a lesser extent, Presbyterians faced discrimination and physical assault. As historian Jewel Spangler notes, eight of the eighteen original ministerial members of the Ketocton Regular Baptist Association were jailed or attacked. Presbyterians are also apparent in the list of those persecuted, although disaffection toward

Presbyterian ministers appeared to subside somewhat when Baptists took their place as the focus of abuse.[34]

Although this "informal" chastisement of dissenters cannot always be laid at the feet of officials or Anglican ministers, it often appeared to have official sanction—providing a sound basis for dissenter alienation from establishment leaders. When magistrates participated in disrupting meetings, attendees who would not disperse on official orders faced fines; others were fined for refusing to testify against dissenting ministers. In any case, the disruption and intimidation clearly originated with supporters of the established church, and dissenters could not help but conflate these problems with the legal infirmities imposed by the political establishment.[35]

Beyond the physical abuse and intimidation, from 1768 through 1778, more than fifty dissenters were jailed for preaching without a license, for a generic "disturbing the peace," or for related offenses—many on numerous occasions and for extended periods (see figure 1.3). In one case a preacher was jailed for having married a couple in violation of the requirements that an Anglican minister preside. More ominously, several ministers were seized and charged with sedition or mutiny, with one warrant claiming that they "Teach and Preach Contrary to the Laws and usages of the Kingdom of Great Britain, raising Sedition and Stirring up Strife amongst his Majestie's Liege People," and another justice of the peace insisting that the dissenters were "raising factions in the minds of his majesty's Subjects." Others were jailed for permitting unlicensed preaching at their homes. Samuel Mackie and his son, also named Samuel, were jailed for allegedly hurting a drunk who sought to break up the Presbyterian worship service at their home. Some ministers were seized by officials but released with a warning to leave the county. Adding to the dissenters' burdens, dissenting congregants were presented to courts for attending "illegal preaching." To put these arrests in context, based on available reports that likely understate the number of instances in which dissenting ministers were dragged before courts, half or more of the Baptist ministers in Virginia at the time of the Revolution had suffered a jail term for preaching—ensuring that all dissenters would be deeply conscious of the problem.[36]

Incarcerations began in early June 1768 in Spotsylvania County, when four Baptist preachers were jailed, and continued regularly for six years. Although some historians have suggested that open persecution was waning as the war approached, 1774 saw the second highest rate of incarceration in the period, with one arrest as late as 1778 in Accomack County. Fristoe concludes that "times grew such there appeared no probability of escaping prison without a license could be obtained, and to obtain them was difficult—for by this time the members of the general court had taken prejudice, being all of the established church, they resolved

FIGURE 1.3. Essex Courthouse—Beale Memorial Baptist Church: The Essex Courthouse, built in 1728 (excluding the belfry), was the scene in 1774 of the trial and imprisonment of four Baptist preachers for "preaching and expounding the Scriptures contrary to law. " The building later became the Beale Memorial Baptist Church.

to discountenance the Baptists, and decreed to license but one place in a county." One Piedmont farmer commenting on the arrests noted that "at last they let them alone but not until the british war Commensed [sic]" in April 1775.[37]

On being brought before magistrates at a court session, which often occurred after several weeks of incarceration, dissenting ministers were generally offered freedom for a commitment (with a sizable bond) that they would not preach in the relevant county for a period of at least a year. Some took the oath—either abiding by it or ignoring it as an ill-gotten agreement. Samuel Harriss, a well-known Baptist preacher, having sworn an oath not to preach in Culpeper County for a year and a day, broke his bond within weeks; declaring that his agreement not to preach had been made with the "devil," he assured his listeners that the devil was a "perfidious wretch" with whom bargains need not be kept. Breach of such an oath could lead to incarceration, though, as Joseph Spencer found in Orange County. Others refused the offer of a bond on principle and remained jailed for extended periods. Many of the preachers languished in jail for months and faced several jail terms (see appendix A).[38]

Eighteenth-century penal conditions were never good, but the conditions faced by dissenters were often exacerbated. Magistrates, always Anglicans, on occasion ordered jailers to limit the dissenters' food or deny them use of the jail yard. When Waller and several colleagues were imprisoned for preaching in Middlesex, he reported that the jailer was given "a charge not to allow us to walk in the air until Court day." The ministers reported that "the prison swarmed with fleas," and they were fed on bread and water for several days until their friends found out about their need. Elijah Craig was held in an inner cell to prevent preaching through a window. James Ireland reported that his jailer would not admit visitors without the payment of a fee but did honor him with the presence of drunks from the jailer's tavern. In other instances, jailed dissenters were plagued by the burning of pepper pods and brimstone outside of their cells, particularly when they would begin to preach. "In addition to confinement, those of the vulgar sort took occasion to collect disagreeable and ill-favored trash, nauseous combustables, and burn them in the prison window which filled the close dungeon with smoke that made it difficult for him to breathe or support life." David Tinsley was incarcerated for four months in Chesterfield "in the depth of winter....The suffocating effects of burning tobacco and red pepper were applied to the door and window of his cell." Ireland claimed that his jailer attempted poisoning; in another instance, explosives were detonated under his cell. Jeremiah Moore's incarceration in Alexandria was accompanied with a threat from the magistrate: "You will lie in jail until you rot."[39]

When imprisoned preachers tried to preach from their cells—being deeply devoted and recognizing that their suffering could provide an important foil for preaching, as did establishment officials, belatedly—their efforts often met additional persecution. Men with knives waited outside the cell window of John Weatherford and cut his hands and arms when his enthusiasm for preaching caused him to extend them to his listeners in supplication through the window; the assaults left him scarred for life. Another minister had his face urinated on when he approached his prison's window to preach. Other efforts to interfere with jailhouse preaching included singing obscene songs, beating drums, or ringing bells during a minister's efforts. In discussing his time in the Culpeper jail, Ireland related that men on horseback would ride through the crowds gathered outside of the prison to hear preaching and would threaten attendees; blacks would be whipped. Archibald Cary, a powerful burgess and Chesterfield County magistrate, had a wall erected around the county jail yard and broken glass placed atop the wall in an effort to stop preaching from jail. (This effort was defeated by the listeners fastening a cloth to a stick, which they would wave above the wall when a group had gathered to hear preaching.) Others were physically abused, often violently, for preaching from jail.[40]

It was also evident that the persecution originated with local gentry, not royal officials, who had always been more solicitous of dissenters. The increased level of official persecution began when Lieutenant Governor Francis Fauquier died in 1768 and a local member of the Anglican gentry, John Blair, became acting governor. Arrests increased again several years later on the death of Baron Botetourt when another local member of the gentry was placed temporarily in the executive seat. The extent to which arrests had roots in tension with local gentry is clear when one considers the geographic distribution of arrests—occurring where dissenters, Baptists in particular, were penetrating areas previously dominated by Anglicans (figures 1.1 and 1.2).

> It is to be observed, also, that these persecutions took place chiefly in the older counties, that is, in the counties lying along the great rivers of tidewater Virginia and in the northeastern part of the colony. This is just the country and the society that bred the men who led the Revolution, and we remember that among the staunchest patriots were some who at first were strong for the mother country and for the Mother Church.[41]

Early sectarian histories describe abuse of dissenting preachers and laymen in vivid terms, sometimes tending toward martyrology. There can be little question, though, of the general impression the persecution must have formed on dissenters. With half of the Baptist ministers in Virginia before the American

Revolution suffering some jail time, no dissenter in the colony could have been unaware of the extent and seriousness of the problem; not only was it widely reported in the press, but local networks of communication among dissenters must have spread the stories—probably enhancing them to some degree— quickly and broadly. Such exaggeration might tend to increase animosity between the establishment and dissenters and increase dissenters' fears. Moreover, there were likely scores of incidents that have not come down through history that were fodder for local gossip and anxiety. Cooperation among some Baptists and Presbyterians, such as the occasional sharing of meeting houses, contributed to the broad dissemination of stories of official abuse. Though the precise extent of the persecution may never be known, any effort to minimize its seriousness misses the implications it had for dissenters' perception of local gentry as the Revolution approached.[42]

The growth of persecution in the years of colonial crisis is critical in understanding the relationship of the establishment and dissenters during the Revolution. As one nineteenth-century historian explained, "the Baptists pursued the Church Establishment with a vindictive hatred that is repellent, . . . They saw their fellows and neighbors arrested and thrust like common malefactors into the county jails for the alleged crime of preaching the Gospel of peace."[43] What was remarkable was the extent to which these dissenters, having faced serious legal discrimination, physical abuse, and incarceration, and in spite of their bitterness and "vindictive" animus, were later willing to mobilize to support the war led by the same Anglican persons who had visited persecution on them.

Strength of the Anglican Establishment

To appreciate the problem faced by Virginia dissenters as the American Revolution began, one must also appreciate the continued strength of the Anglican establishment. Anglicans were the largest religious denomination in Virginia and were hardly vulnerable to an easy evangelical revolt. As a philosophical matter, for 1300 years governmental leaders believed that virtue was central to a functioning government—especially a republican government, religion to virtue, and an established church to the success of religion; this doctrine, shared broadly in the eighteenth-century colonies, was not easily challenged. With such a foundation, Anglicanism remained vibrant throughout the period, especially in Virginia, where the patriarchy maintained dominance socially and in church affairs. Many of the problems that did plague the Anglican Church during the Revolution were also experienced by other denominations.

Recent research provides an excellent antidote to prior suggestions of a deep malaise in the prerevolutionary Church of England. In the years preceding the Revolution, Anglicanism evidenced key indicators of strength: it was growing; correcting a problem from earlier in the century, nearly all Virginia parishes had a rector, and as many as three-quarters or more of those ministers were Virginia born, born in other American colonies, or had lived in Virginia prior to receiving ordination.[44]

Local Anglican rectors retained significant prestige throughout the period, whatever damage had been done to their reputations by the Parson's Cause when some of their members challenged popular restraints on their tax-supported salaries—a case that shot young country lawyer Patrick Henry to fame for arguing against the clergy and "losing" the case when the Reverend Maury received one penny in damages. Eighteenth-century Anglican ministers had significant social standing and intermarried with many of the "best" Virginia families. A number of Anglican parsons held positions on county benches. The powerful William Byrd told a correspondent that "clergymen of good character are no where better respected." The necessity of a costly education and the willingness of increasing numbers of candidates for Anglican ministry to make the voyage to England for ordination—an expensive and time-consuming trip that meant risking a 20 percent likelihood of death—demonstrate the continued appeal of the position.[45]

More to the point, any seeming weakness in the ecclesiastic structure of the Anglican Church in America (particularly the lack of an American bishop) or in the status of Anglican ministers in Virginia should not be confused with weakness in the continuing dominance of lay Anglican leaders. The establishment at issue here was sociopolitical—relating to community standards and governmental control—rather than theological. In fact, the dominance of the laity in the Virginia Anglican church, the same laity that controlled political institutions, tended to strengthen the ties between church and state in the colony. It is not insignificant that in Virginia men continued to dominate church membership, unlike the growing dominance of women—who lacked political influence—in New England churches.[46]

Anglicans dominated the mechanisms of government at all levels with a large share of officials down to the level of local justices being current or former vestrymen. Bishop Meade found that no more than three members of Virginia's 1776 convention, which agreed to independence and framed Virginia's first constitution, were *not* vestrymen. Key political leaders during this period were among those most dedicated to Anglican hegemony and most adamantly opposed to liberalization of toleration for dissenters. Nor should the control that these church leaders exercised over government be underestimated. Before the Revolution a small number of leading burgesses exercised very broad power over the mechanisms of government, particularly through control of the speaker's office, key committees, and the governor's council. A study by historian Charles Sydnor suggests that seven men constituted Virginia's power elite from 1761 to 1774—Peyton Randolph, Robert Carter Nicholas, Richard Bland, Benjamin Harrison, Edmund Pendleton, Richard Henry Lee, and Archibald Cary; the majority of them were devoted churchmen. Pendleton and Cary, both of whom sat on benches that incarcerated dissenting preachers, became the first speakers of the Virginia House of Delegates and the Virginia Senate, respectively. Pendleton personally protested efforts to begin a Presbyterian congregation in Caroline County. In speaking of efforts to end the religious establishment, Jefferson states that "our greatest opponents were Mr. Pendleton and Robert Carter Nicholas; honest men, but zealous churchmen." Cary ordered the jailing of several Baptist preachers and the construction of the jail yard wall to discourage preaching. Lee and Harrison were strong defenders of the established church. Not only did Anglican leaders continue to control the mechanisms of government, they worked diligently to limit religious reforms throughout the war and beyond.[47]

Nor were political leaders isolated from the broader Anglican laity in supporting the established church at the expense of dissenters. In 1762, Devereux Jarratt, who later became a famous evangelical preacher in the southside, decided to seek ordination in the established church rather than the Presbyterian Church, noting that "the general prejudice of the people at the time against dissenters and in favor of the church, gave me a full persuasion that I could do more good in the church than anywhere else." One Piedmont planter noted that Separate Baptists "weare [sic] held in contempt by most of the people." Ireland, on being incarcerated for preaching, recognized that persecution instigated by Anglican ministers "received the hearty concurrence of their parishioners."[48]

Although there were broad eighteenth- and nineteenth-century reports of the clergy's supposed shortcomings, more recent studies dispel the myth that a substantial share of Virginia's Anglican clergy were miscreants, thereby explaining a fall from power. In fact, the often lurid criticism of late-eighteenth-century Anglican ministers cannot be taken at face value; much of the criticism was sectarian. Even Bishop Meade's often repeated criticisms of the Anglican clergy, which have formed the foundation of much of the history of Anglican declension, might be put down to tension among the evangelical and traditional wings of the Episcopal Church. Moreover, the increasing share of the clergy who came from Virginia or other colonies suggested that any problems with the quality of the clergy were rapidly diminishing. One study shows that whereas three-quarters of Virginia's clergy in 1776 were recruited in Virginia, three-quarters of those charged with misbehavior had been recruited abroad. The trend clearly favored an effective local clergy. Reports of low attendance are also exaggerated. A small number of "communicants" may evidence the lack of the prerequisite confirmation among congregants (which required a trip to London for a bishop's blessing) or the seriousness with which eighteenth-century Anglicans took Paul's admonition that to take communion unworthily is to bring damnation on oneself; George Washington, for example, was a steady congregant, but never a communicant. Nor can the established church be dismissed as rapidly losing influence as the Revolution approached to the pro-British Toryism of its members. Methodists and New England Anglicans certainly suffered from the accusation, but Toryism among the Anglican ministry in Virginia was less than has often been reported and was very limited among the substantial majority of the parsons who had been born in the colonies or lived there before ordination. As one Baptist historian conceded, Anglican Toryism among foreign-born ministers did contribute to more general post hoc claims of dissoluteness.[49]

In any case, whatever the problems with the clergy, the continuing strength of the Anglican laity can be seen in its effective opposition to efforts to improve toleration in the years leading up to the war. As the persecution of the dissenters increased, particularly after 1768, there were more vocal calls for greater toleration, particularly a growing petitioning campaign by the dissenters against their legal infirmities. Yet while the House of Burgesses endorsed generally the notion of improved toleration, several facts became clear. No one at the time was seriously anticipating an end to legal discrimination or the establishment; improved toleration of a still dissenting church was all that was being discussed. More important, the Anglican political establishment made it clear that no reforms would pass unless they were consistent with its wishes. Thus, draft legislation in 1772 included restrictions on night meetings (particularly relevant for recruiting slaves) and itinerancy. Out of concern that the outspoken dissenters would pass some of their insubordinate spirit on to the slaves, legislation was to "guard against the Corruption of our Slaves" by carefully regulating dissenting preachers. Robert Carter Nicholas, treasurer of the Commonwealth, chairman of the Committee for Religion, and a strong supporter of the Anglican Church, intended this legislation to prescribe the activities of the dissenters within safe spheres of activity. Yet even this limited reform could not pass the House of Burgesses. With an increase in Baptist revivals and increased criticisms of the established church by dissenters, relationships between dissenters and establishment leaders deteriorated in key respects. In early 1774, James Madison was "very doubtful" of the success of

Baptist and Presbyterian petitions for additional religious toleration because of the strength of the Church of England in the legislature and because Anglicans were seeking even greater restrictions.[50]

Although some historians have suggested that the Great Awakening democratized political institutions and dramatically weakened the established church, this was not the case in Virginia as the American Revolution began. Religious affiliation was still a defining characteristic, legally and socially, and Anglicans maintained a firm control on positions of power. Dissenter influence might have been growing, but it continued to be seriously restrained.[51]

Britain's Historic Role as Supporter of Dissenters

Growing antagonism between Virginia's dissenters and the Anglican elite over religious discrimination and persecution must be juxtaposed with the fact that British officials had historically been protectors of dissenter interests. Dating to the Glorious Revolution of 1689, the association of the British Crown with protection of dissenters' religious rights in colonial America was strong. A brief review of the treatment of dissenters in eighteenth-century Virginia confirms the protective role of royal officials. In 1738, British Governor William Gooch welcomed Presbyterian settlement of the backcountry, promising religious toleration to the prospective immigrants from Pennsylvania. In 1747, with Presbyterianism growing in the Piedmont, and in the face of local Anglican opposition, Gooch supported Samuel Davies as the first dissenting minister licensed by the General Court in Virginia. Within a year, the governor's council—Virginia gentry—led the effort to stem Presbyterian incursions in the Piedmont by blocking the licensing of Davies's assistant, John Rodgers, in spite of the efforts of the royal governor. Davies's response was to obtain an opinion of the British attorney general supporting the application and breadth of the Act of Toleration. The local elite continued their efforts to undermine that interpretation in spite of the intervention of royal officials. In 1768, a scathing letter attacking imprisoned Baptist preachers and questioning applicability of the Act of Toleration was printed in the *Virginia Gazette*; this letter is generally thought to be the work of the Virginia Attorney General John Randolph. Dissenters, well aware of the tension between efforts of the local elite and English law, intentionally appealed to English precedents permitting local licensing of meeting houses and itinerant preaching in their efforts to ease licensure problems in the 1750s and 1760s.[52]

Beyond legal rights under the Act of Toleration, persecution of Virginia's dissenters flared precisely when the governor's palace in Williamsburg was vacant of a British official. For example, in 1750, when county courts began to issue licenses to dissenting ministers, perhaps based in part on the precedent of William Williams's licensure by Orange in 1737, Virginia's native elite put a stop to it, insisting that only the General Court, which met only twice a year in Williamsburg, requiring a long and expensive journey for many dissenting ministers, could issue licenses. These restrictions came about when Thomas Lee, local president of the council, was acting as governor. Once again, British officials attempted to intervene to protect dissenters from the local Anglican elite. The British Lords of Trade, responding to an inquiry from Lee, admonished that "a free Exercise of Religion is so valuable a branch of true liberty, and so essential to the enriching and improving of a Trading Nation, it should ever be held sacred in His Majesty's Colonies." The affiliation of royal officials with protection of dissenter interests continued up to the war; arrests of dissenters flared in 1768, after the death of Governor Fauquier. With dissenter persecution reaching new heights, Presbyterian clergy addressed the new governor, Lord Botetourt, on his arrival in 1769, insisting that no subjects were more committed to the king and offering to give proof of their allegiance. Botetourt responded: "It is the King's express command, that liberty of conscience be allowed to all his subjects, so they be contented with a quiet and peaceable enjoyment of the same." Both Botetourt and his predecessor expressly promised protection under the Act of Toleration. Unfortunately for dissenters, arrests again increased after the death of Lord Botetourt in 1770.[53]

Anxiety that Britain intended to implant an Episcopal bishop in America contributed substantially to the colonial crisis in New England and the middle states, but in Virginia opposition to a colonial bishop did not greatly alienate dissenters from royal authority and was more rooted in the Anglican laity's desire not to lose any of its existing control over the church than in opposition by dissenters. An extended discussion of an episcopate in the *Virginia Gazette* among Anglican laymen and clergy makes clear that the issue was primarily about church control, but both sides sought to use dissenters as a foil—one warning dissenters of the dangers of an episcopate, the other insisting that dissenters would be protected, while at the same time arguing that opposition to an episcopate was generated by dissenters.[54]

With persecution and discrimination associated with local Anglican leaders who maintained control of the patriot movement, and protection affiliated with royal officials, Virginia dissenter support for the rebellion against Britain was highly contingent. As the Revolution approached, Virginia did not present a homogenous citizenry easily united in opposition to British rule. While the number of dissenters in Virginia grew to a substantial share of the population, those dissenters still faced critical legal discrimination and increasingly serious, sometimes vicious persecution. Incarceration of dissenters for preaching was rampant from 1768 through 1774. With the Anglican establishment healthy and in firm control of the mechanisms of government, this seemed unlikely to change. Yet while establishment leaders continued to control the polity, they were not in a position to force dissenters into mobilization once hostilities with Britain began, nor was there an effective opportunity for dissenters to force the establishment to recognize religious liberty prior to the war.

How, then, did Virginia successfully mobilize for the American Revolution in the face of this serious rift? The negotiations between dissenters and establishment leaders that followed open hostilities with Britain proved to be the essential element in obtaining and maintaining dissenter support for the war effort and, beyond that important but parochial concern, in both the development of religious freedom in Virginia and the republicanization of the Virginia polity. Without wartime necessity, there is little reason to believe that religious liberalization would have occurred at the time; indeed, the experience of the other colonies suggests otherwise.

Pleading for Reform and Demanding Freedom

These things granted, we will gladly unite with our Brethren of other denominations, and to the utmost of our ability, promote the common cause of
Freedom.

—Prince William County Baptists, June 20, 1776

As Virginia's colonial leaders contemplated armed opposition to British rule,
they were well aware of the difficulties they faced in launching a military
challenge to the eighteenth-century superpower. They would need the broadest
possible support if they were to mobilize successfully, including that of
Virginia's rapidly growing population of dissenters. In fact, as military necessity
increased, the state's political leaders were particularly interested in gaining
the service of the riflemen from the frontier regions dominated by dissenters.
Given the gentry's continuing effort to minimize and control dissent and
prewar persecution of dissenters led by Anglican establishment leaders, a vexing problem was posed for Virginia's leaders.

At the same time, given their peculiar position outside of establishment
society, Virginia dissenters had to choose whether to support the war effort at
all. Certainly they shared other colonists' concerns with British corruption,
arbitrary government, taxation, and lack of representation. In fact, western
counties—in which the dissenters were concentrated—were seriously underrepresented in the colonial assembly and particularly sensitive to questions of
representation. Still, to the extent that their establishment compatriots were
fighting to protect their liberties, Virginia's dissenters were painfully aware of
their civil disabilities and the legal discrimination against them, not to mention

the serious persecution at the hands of the local establishment and its supporters. Nor could they easily forget that they had relied on British officials to
protect religious toleration in the face of a belligerent local establishment. In
other Southern colonies, where they had far less cause to distrust their local
leaders, dissenters sometimes proved reluctant to join the patriot movement.

Given these realities, the ambiguous position of dissenters in Virginia led
to a complex and extended negotiation in which establishment leaders sought
dissenter support for mobilization while the dissenters insisted that the
problem of religious freedom be addressed by the gentry leadership immediately, not after the crisis as members of the establishment urged. This is not to
say that key political leaders—certainly Thomas Jefferson and James Madison—
did not welcome the opportunity to establish liberty of conscience. Yet even
these remarkable leaders would not have been successful on the basis of erudi-
tion alone. Madison seemed to recognize at the time that intellectual arguments for liberty of conscience would likely require political support to be
successful. Writing a friend on January 24, 1774, Madison bemoaned the
presence in Virginia of a "diabolical Hell conceived principle of persecution...to their eternal Infamy the Clergy can furnish their Quota of Imps for
such business. This vexes me the most of any thing whatever. There are at this
[time] in the adjacent County not less than 5 or 6 well meaning men in close
Goal for publishing their religious Sentiments which in the main are very
orthodox." In this context, presaging the difficult political negotiations to come,
he observed that "Political Contests are necessary sometimes as well as military...to instruct in the Art of defending Liberty and property."[1]

Historians have increasingly noted growing divisions in Virginia at the
time of the Revolution based on class and race and the concomitant problems
posed for effective mobilization, but although class conflict certainly contributed to the complexity of mobilization, religious dissent in the Piedmont and
frontier posed a more vexing problem. Disputes that have been identified as
class conflicts in revolutionary Virginia were largely over issues of recruiting
and enlistment, a not uncommon historic phenomenon. These were largely
resolved by addressing aspects of recruiting and enlistment especially by
accommodation at the local level. They rarely involve crosscutting social and
political issues requiring statewide reform in unrelated areas like those posed
by religious dissenters.[2]

Strong evidence of the gentry's continued control of the polity and the lack
of consensus among religious groups as the war began is found in the fact that
prior to the outbreak of hostilities, prospects for religious peace in Virginia
were dim. Even the limited legislative efforts to expand toleration from 1769 to
1774 failed in the face of opposition from Anglican leaders. Virginia's political

leadership did not change significantly with the war, and the new state's assembly continued to be dominated by the same Anglican establishment that had supported discrimination against and persecution of dissenters. The same pattern was evident in local governing regimes. Nor had support for the established church among the people been undermined before the war.[3]

One must dispel the notion that the Great Awakening (circa 1730s to 1750s) had democratized political institutions in Virginia prior to the American Revolution. The Great Awakening was a powerful force for growth in evangelical religion, and certainly the tenets and structure of the evangelical denominations emphasized the claims of individual conscience and helped plant democratic principles among the populace. Still, the idea that fundamental changes in the political structure republicanized Virginia before the war and presaged relatively easy adoption of religious liberty is inconsistent with the continued discrimination against and persecution of dissenters and their inability to have even moderate reforms adopted prior to the war. On the other hand, by the mid-1780s, the political activism and power of dissenters were undeniable. The process of establishment leaders engaging them in some of the era's most important political debates during the war politicized the dissenters, creating a fundamental social and political redefinition of Virginia.[4]

Thus, when historian Rhys Isaac asks "whether the patriot movement in Virginia may be understood as in part a defensive response from the traditional order to the transformations in popular orientation toward authority manifested in the spread of evangelism," he may have it exactly backward. The wartime negotiations demonstrate that as those in authority moved decisively toward challenging British control and forming new governmental institutions, the necessity of gaining the support and cooperation of the evangelical masses required patriot leaders to include liberal personal freedoms, particularly religious liberty, within the definition of what they were fighting for. Rather than republicanization inevitably leading to the patriot movement and disestablishment, the process of negotiating disestablishment, necessitated by the movement, politicized the dissenters, which proved to be a key element in the republicanization of Virginia.[5]

The negotiation between dissenters and the political establishment is most evident in several hundred petitions dissenters filed with the Virginia legislature and the Anglican response from 1768 to 1786 (see figure 2.1.). Whereas petitioning was a common means of communication with government in the eighteenth century, prior to these negotiations for religious freedom in Virginia, petitions generally tended to address local or personal problems. For example, earlier religious petitions might request changes in parish boundaries or relate to the composition of vestries or a minister's position. During

FIGURE 2.1. Virginia's House of Burgesses: From the colonial period through 1780, when the capitol was moved to Richmond, petitions were received in the House of Burgesses and General Assembly in Williamsburg (reconstructed by Colonial Williamsburg). Special thanks to the Colonial Williamsburg Foundation.

the war, petitioning occurred on a previously unheard-of scale, involving extraordinary numbers of participants—in one case 10,000 signatures on one petition—and relating religious issues to the grand struggle that consumed the Commonwealth's attention. Petitioning was no longer only a matter of seeking a redress of a specific local grievance; by integrating a far broader spectrum of people into the political dialogue on a far broader range of issues, it was an exercise in forming a new commonwealth.

Discussion of these negotiations in correspondence appears to be limited, in part, by concern not to offend anyone's "honor" by expressly suggesting ulterior motives for supporting the Revolution and in part because many dissenting ministers, especially Baptists, were relatively unlettered. Anglican petitions often (correctly) accused dissenters of seeking quid pro quo support for the war, but those same petitions make it clear why the matter had to be handled delicately by dissenters. Thus, the Hanover Presbytery insisted shortly after the war that "we have hitherto restrained our complaints . . . that we might not be thought to take any advantage from times of confusion, or critical situations of Government in an unsettled state of Convulsion and war, to obtain what is our clear and uncontestable right." This may sound eminently reasonable, but it was blatantly false. The Presbytery's perceived need to renounce use of leverage speaks to the difficulty of identifying clearly negotiations that did occur.[6]

These negotiations can be best understood by considering several successive periods. From 1768 to 1775, dissenter concerns over arrests and persecution led to pleas for improved toleration, pleas that rose considerably in volume and tone as the war broke out. In 1776, with the easing of the initial rage militaire and the necessity of a difficult mobilization foremost in the minds of the new government, dissenters changed the substance of their requests, now insisting on religious freedom in return for their support, and the establishment had to make major concessions. With the issue unresolved by the 1776 reforms, negotiations continued regularly on various aspects of religious freedom from 1777 through 1780. Then, through 1786, the nature and content of the negotiations changed again when the end of serious fighting eliminated the driving need for dissenter cooperation in mobilization and establishment leaders sought to recoup lost ground. In considering each period, it is important to keep in mind the corresponding progress of the war and various crises of recruiting and mobilization, including some instances of active resistance by the citizenry to recruiting, all of which affected the tenor of the dialogue between dissenters and the establishment.[7]

1768–75: Unsuccessful Pleas for Greater Tolerance

As persecution of dissenters flared in 1768 and subsequent years, the legislature was slow to respond. Nor were dissenters able to force an effective response; their lack of status in the Virginia polity did not lend itself to a political resolution of their problems. In 1770, groups of Baptists began to file petitions with the House of Burgesses seeking moderate reform. Initially, they asked only that they be allowed to preach outside of meeting houses designated in licenses and that their ministers receive the same exemption from mustering for militia duty as ministers of the Church of England. As incarcerations increased, Baptists filed a series of similar petitions seeking improved treatment under the "spirit" of the Act of Toleration.[8]

It appeared that progress was being made when, in 1772, a committee of the House of Burgesses was asked to propose a law to extend toleration without impairing the legal privileges enjoyed by Anglicans, but when drafts were circulated, the law did not go far enough in accommodating dissenters' concerns. It was evident that the proposal was motivated in large part by establishment efforts to prevent evangelical preaching from encouraging slave autonomy. The proposal continued to require licensing of dissenting ministers for a fee and restricted meeting places and times, and it would have required dissenters to preach in meeting houses with the doors open (to discourage any inappropriate discussions) and limited preaching to slaves or to outdoor assemblies, a hallmark of dissenting evangelicals. While dissenters—especially Baptists—objected to the narrowness of the proposed reforms, they pointedly denied any interest in complete religious freedom or an end to the establishment, seeking only the "same kind Indulgence, in religious Matters, as Quakers, Presbyterians, and other Protestant Dissenters, enjoy." In 1774, David Thomas, a leading Baptist preacher who had been brutally attacked on several occasions, could still assert: "We lay no schemes to advance ourselves, nor make any attempts to alter the constitution of the kingdom to which as men we belong....We freely pay all taxes, levies, &c....And in one word, we comply with all the laws of our country without exception." The same deferential tone was evident in a petition from Peaks of Otter Presbyterians as late as May 1774 claiming only continued tolerance, as long as Presbyterians abided by the law. Yet while dissenters denied any claim for full religious freedom, establishment forces opposed even the limited reforms requested. In spite of repeated efforts in the House of Burgesses to bring in a bill, no changes to the legal establishment were made.[9]

Given the political dominance of the establishment, change was not expected any time soon. In early 1774, James Madison wrote his friend and confidant William Bradford that such

> incredible and extravagant stories were told in the House of the
> monstrous effects of the Enthusiasm prevalent among the Sectaries
> and so greedily swallowed by their Enemies that I believe they lost
> footing by it and the bad name they still have with those who pretend
> too much contempt to examine into their principles and Conduct and
> are too much devoted to the ecclesiastic establishment to hear of the
> Toleration of Dissentients, I am apprehensive, will be again made a
> pretext for rejecting their requests.

Although Baptist entreaties had been joined by other Protestant dissenters, Madison was "very doubtful" of their success because of the strength of the Church of England in the legislature and because some Anglicans were seeking even greater restrictions on dissent.[10]

Within months, though, as colonial leaders' attention turned to seeking an effective and unified response to British adoption of the Intolerable Acts, a distinctly different voice began to creep into the dissenters' claims and petitions. As early as September 1774, as Virginia's delegation wrestled with its colonial colleagues in the First Continental Congress in Philadelphia, Virginia dissenters began to emphasize the relationship between Christian doctrine and opposition to "violent usurpations of a corrupted Ministry." Baptists in Lunenburg County, noting with approval the meeting of the Continental Congress, asked "every Christian Patriot" to join the struggle against Britain. Shortly thereafter, in a petition written in November 1774 (but received by the House of Burgesses after word of open conflict in Lexington and Concord reached Williamsburg), the Hanover Presbytery, on behalf of "all the Presbyterians in Virginia in particular; and all Protestant Dissenters in general," took the opportunity to point out problems with the limited 1772 proposal for improved toleration. Still, in 1774 the Presbyterians sought only increased toleration, noting a willingness to take an "oath of allegiance" and register their places of public worship. Seeking to demonstrate resolve to seemingly indifferent (if not hostile) Anglican burgesses who were increasingly focused on the conflict with Britain, the Presbyterians added that "the subject is of such solemn importance to us, that comparatively speaking, our lives and our liberties are but of little value. And the population of the Country, and the honour of the legislature, as well as the interest of American liberty, are certainly most deeply concerned in the matter." A similar petition from Baptist and other dissenters seeking improved toleration was received on June 13, 1775. The House ordered both petitions to lie on the table.[11]

After fighting began in New England, petitions increasingly linked religious liberty and the patriots' cause. On August 16, 1775, the Baptist General Association sent a petition to the Virginia Convention, which had assumed effective governance of the colony. The status of the Baptists was of particular concern to colonial leaders: not only had they suffered the brunt of persecution at the hands of the establishment, but Baptists had sometimes been known as pacifists and, after 1774, rumors were being spread from New England that the Baptists maintained a "Coolness," if not hostility, to the patriot movement. The Reverend Ezra Stiles of Yale, based in part on conversations with Robert Treat Paine, a Massachusetts delegate to the Continental Congress, recorded in November 1774 that the Baptists "will leave the general Defence of American Liberty to the Congregationists to the Northward and the Episcopalians to the Southward," and "avail themselves of this opportunity to complain to England of Persecution."[12] Thus, it was of crucial importance to the patriots that the Virginia Baptist convention of 1775 declared that the war was "just" and "it was lawful to go to War, and also for us to make a Military resistance against Great Britain." Yet in doing so, the Baptists tellingly noted that they were "distinguished . . . from the Body of our Countrymen by appellatives and sentiments of a religious nature." Still, the Baptists assured Virginia's leaders that they saw themselves as "members of the same community in respect of matters of a civil nature." Lest anyone misunderstand the importance of their support, the Baptists reminded the Assembly that they represent a "brave and spirited people," of whom "some have inlisted, and many more likely so to do." Notably, while the 1775 Baptist Association meeting reportedly condemned the establishment tax and called for broader religious freedom, these issues were not expressly mentioned in the petition to the Virginia Convention at this time. Even the newspaper accounts mentioning other issues were ambivalent; the *Virginia Gazette* noted some Baptists believed religious scruples forbid paying the establishment tax, but the Baptist General Association left its members "peaceably to pay, if they were free [as a matter of conscience] so to do, or to suffer the spoiling of goods, for conscience sake, without resistance, yet they unanimously look upon it to be a grievance, which they should rejoice to see redressed." The actual petition filed with the Virginia Convention omitted this discussion altogether and concluded only with a request that Baptist ministers be permitted to preach to the soldiery, a request quickly brought to the assembly's floor by Patrick Henry and equally quickly granted. At the same time, responding to a long-standing complaint, dissenting ministers finally joined Anglican ministers in gaining exemption from militia musters. Years later, James Madison reportedly recalled that the Baptists "when hope was sinking...declared that the tenets of their religion did not forbid their fighting for their country, and that the pastors of their flocks would animate the young of their persuasion to enlist for our battles."[13]

The role of the extremely popular Patrick Henry in the dispute over religious freedom continued to be important (see figure 2.2). Henry was an Anglican, but by disposition he was inclined to support dissenters' claims for more freedom, not only based on a principled love of liberty but because his mother had introduced him to evangelical preachers early in life. In fact, his power as a speaker is often compared to that of the Reverend Samuel Davies, reportedly one of the most compelling eighteenth-century preachers; his mother had often taken young Patrick to hear Davies, and an evangelical tone was evident in many of Henry's most famous speeches. Moreover, Henry's maternal grandfather, Isaac Winston Sr., had been indicted and fined for permitting Presbyterians to preach on his land, an affront that must have rankled the passionate lawyer. It was not happenstance that Henry had gained political fame with a fiery speech against Anglican clergy in the Parson's Cause. In another case (likely an apocryphal story), the young Henry reportedly rode on horseback to witness a court proceeding against imprisoned Baptist ministers and, unable to restrain himself, rose after the prosecutor had presented the indictment and taking it from the table roared, "Did I hear an expression, as of a crime, that these men,...are charged with,—with—what?,—preaching the

FIGURE 2.2.   Patrick Henry: Having gained fame in leading lay opposition to the prerogatives of the Anglican clergy, Patrick Henry played a leading role supporting dissenters in early Virginia battles for religious freedom (although this would change in 1785). Special thanks to the Virginia Historical Society.

Gospel of the Son of God? Great God! Great God! Preaching the gospel of the Son of God—Great God!" That indictment was dismissed. Although most sources view this story as a later fabrication, it was certainly consistent with Henry's reputation and would have been warmly received in eighteenth-century Virginia. Henry is known to have defended some imprisoned Baptist preachers, reportedly paying bail anonymously when one minister could not afford it, and certainly he came naturally to the reforms requested in 1775.[14]

Still, whatever the minor reforms, by the end of 1775, the Anglican leadership was maintaining a tight control on the reins of government. Although the tone and content of dissenters' requests were waxing with the conflict with Britain, they were still carefully circumscribed. That changed when 1776 presented a crisis of legitimacy for the government and a mobilization crisis, crises that were addressed by showing enough flexibility on religious issues to maintain a united front against the British opposition.

The End of Rage Militaire and Beginning of Dissenter Demands

After the dispatch of somewhat more pointed petitions at the end of 1774 and 1775, dissenters' calls on the Virginia House for redress lay relatively dormant until spring 1776. Real reform seemed to have little purchase as patriots enjoyed the successes of battles at Lexington, Concord, and Bunker Hill, and British General Thomas Gage was trapped in Boston. Yet while American patriots celebrated Gage's retreat from beleaguered Boston in April, as the summer of 1776 approached, they were waiting anxiously for renewed and escalated fighting. British reinforcements, including German mercenaries, were known to be making their way to America. In June, the Continental Congress realized that state enlistments were falling far short of the troops needed, and it was forced to adopt a bounty. Then came news of the debacle in Canada with the loss of 5,000 American soldiers; soon, General George Washington's defeats in and around New York brought even greater gloom. Recognizing that a prolonged crisis loomed ahead, the Second Continental Congress in May advised the colonies to draft new constitutions for their governance, and the Virginia Convention sent a resolution to the Continental Congress urging it to declare independence. Interestingly, in the midst of these growing concerns and the immediate and desperate need for men and materials to support the war effort, Archibald Cary—Anglican scion of a leading Virginia family, soon to be speaker of the new Virginia Senate, and nemesis of Virginia dissenters—was directing recruiting and procurement in central Virginia. The stage was set for the dissenters to force their way into an active role in the polity.[15]

As patriot confidence turned to deep concern in 1776, Virginia's dissenters began to suggest that more might be needed to obtain their full support for the war. An April letter to the *Virginia Gazette*, signed only from "A Dissenter," noted pointedly that if they were to be successful, Virginians had to stand united when either their political or their religious rights were assaulted. "To this end, the dissenters (equally attached to America's liberty) ought to petition their rulers for the removal of that yoke, that in these fearce [sic] times has become more grievous, in paying the established clergy, and being still obliged to have the solemnization of matrimony performed by them." The writer's suggestion that dissenters mobilize politically to demand their rights took on a note of warning to Virginia's troubled leaders, ending with "a word to the wise is enough."[16]

In this environment, Virginia was among the first of the new states to respond to Congress's call for new organic laws when it adopted its June 1776 constitution. Of crucial importance, Article 16 of the Virginia Declaration of Rights was among the first written government declarations of religious freedom, a right to worship as one chooses, as distinguished from mere toleration of dissent authorized in the Act of Toleration or earlier colonial charters. George Mason's original draft of the declaration called only for "the fullest tolerance in the exercise of religion." Perhaps remembering that dissenting ministers had been jailed under a system of "toleration," James Madison, in his first term in office, objected that tolerance was far from freedom and gained the support of the wildly popular Patrick Henry in introducing an amendment providing that "all men are equally entitled to the full and free exercise of [Religion] accordg to the dictates of Conscience; and therefore that no man or class of men ought, on account of religion to be invested with peculiar emoluments or privileges" (see figure 2.3). Yet when Henry was asked whether the amendment would impair the religious establishment, he disclaimed any such intent, undermining the proposal that he had just offered. A frustrated Madison was forced to draft a second amendment (introduced with the help of Edmund Pendleton), which recognized that "all men are equally entitled to enjoy the free exercise of religion." Pendleton, an establishment ally, apparently supported Madison's amendment to avoid more radical proposals. The final language of the declaration reflected Madison's efforts, noting that "all men are equally entitled to the free exercise of religion," but retained an ambiguity that would have been avoided by the Henry amendment.[17]

Adoption of this important and remarkable declaration did not resolve the question of dissent. Article 16 was immediately interpreted by some as providing only toleration, whereas others insisted that full religious freedom, including disestablishment, was contemplated. Friends of the establishment noted that even after Article 16's adoption, the convention's actions demonstrated that Anglicanism continued to be the established religion. In early July, for example, the Virginia Convention directed the Episcopal Church to end the prayers for the king and pray instead for the local magistrates. Years later, Pendleton, the president of the convention and the person who actually

FIGURE 2.3. James Madison: In his first term as a delegate, the young James Madison played a critical role in adoption of Article 16 of Virginia's Declaration of Rights guaranteeing "religious freedom." Madison's later career would prove even more important to development of religious liberty. Library of Congress, Prints and Photographs Division, Washington, D.C.

introduced the critical language, explained that Article 16 did not contemplate disestablishment; it "rather seems to forbid coercion in matters of Faith and modes of worship, than to remove the establishment; and that laws for the latter purpose were necessary to be passed by the Assembly, was the Opinion of all at the time."[18]

Whatever the legal merits of the conflicting claims, clearly, Article 16 did not eliminate the practical infirmities faced by Virginia's dissenters. Discriminatory laws and penalties were still on the books. Dissenters demanded more than dramatic words. In this context, with a cooling of the rage militaire of 1775 and the military situation having turned more desperate, previously mild dissenter requests for improved toleration took on a new, more assertive tone.

Eight days after adopting the Declaration of Rights, while the Virginia Convention struggled with forming a new constitution for an independent state, it received a petition from the Prince William Baptists with a dramatically reformulated request. This petition, written in May while the colony considered independence and the need for a new constitution, began by noting:

> This colony with others is now contending for . . . liberties of mankind
> against the enslaving schemes of a powerful enemy. . . . We being
> convinced that the strictest unanimity among ourselves is very
> necessary in this most critical conjunction of public affairs. And that
> every remaining cause of animosity and division may if possible be
> removed, have thought it our duty as peaceable Christians, to petition
> for several religious privileges . . . we have not been indulged with.

A more portentous opening—a powerful enemy, need for "unanimity," the "peaceable" nature of the Baptists, and the denial of their religious privileges—could not have been provided to Virginia's leaders as they faced growing problems with mobilization. Dismissing forever requests for greater toleration in a society with an established church, Baptists now insisted on an end to establishment taxes and restrictions on dissenters' worship and marriages, expressly linking their support for the war to these freedoms: "*These things granted*, we will gladly unite with our Brethren of other denominations, and to the utmost of our ability, promote the common cause of Freedom."[19]

Herein lay a threat and an opportunity, one that must have struck Archibald Cary and other establishment leaders hard as they struggled to provide men and materials for the war and eliminate the threat of a seaborne Governor Dunmore, who was still operating off the Virginia coast. Certainly Virginia's leaders were aware that North Carolina's royal governor had rallied over 1,000 Scotch Highlanders and Regulators, largely dissenters, to the king's banner in early 1776 before they were defeated at Moore's Creek Bridge. In this context, Virginia's political leaders had to recognize that the Baptist petition was not simply a request from fellow patriots united in the cause for improved treatment. Instead, they found themselves engaged in a difficult negotiation with dissenters whose firm support was essential if Virginia was to play its part in a successful revolution. The ensuing dialogue marked a change from the period when Anglican Tidewater gentry leaders could simply govern as they saw fit, without directly engaging those from other regions, classes, and religions. Now dissenters were becoming active participants in the political process.[20]

Two months later, Baptists meeting in convention in Louisa took the matter up in a letter to the state's first governor, Patrick Henry, reminding him that "you have always distinguished yourself by your zeal and activity" for Virginia and a "constant attachment to the glorious cause of liberty and the rights of conscience." Governor Henry responded promptly, promising to "guard the rights of all my fellow citizens, from every encroachment" and hopefully (perhaps anxiously, if not accurately) noting "that those religious distinctions which formerly produced some heats are now forgotten...that the only contest among us, at this most critical and important period, is, who shall be foremost to preserve our religious and civil liberties." Virginians must now "perish or triumph together."[21]

Although Henry's admonition that Virginians must be united or fail was accurate, he deceived himself if he believed that previous religious "heats" would be forgotten. With the Declaration of Rights in hand but establishment taxes still being assessed, and with the war effort proceeding poorly, dissenters continued dramatically to increase their call for religious freedom, subtly—and sometimes not so subtly—linking that freedom to support for the war. In the next key missive, received by the General Assembly on October 11, residents of heavily Presbyterian Prince Edward County noted that they "heartily approve" of the new constitution and Declaration of Rights because Article 16 would "relieve us from a long Night of ecclesiastic Bondage." The petitioners then warned the political leaders that they expected that "without Delay, you would pull down" the establishment. Virginia's leaders had to be sensitive to the implications of such a plea; the Presbyterians clearly linked the issue to the war by noting that such action would "blot out every vestige of British Tyranny and Bondage." The need for support from western riflemen and reports that some western counties, the same areas that had seen some opposition to Virginia recruiting officers, were threatening to abandon Virginia and establish their own independence, heightened political leaders' interest in appeasing the Presbyterians.[22]

Less than a week later, the House received the "10,000 name" petition from "the Dissenters from the Ecclesiastic establishment" which had been organized by the Baptists, but included many non-Baptist signatories. To put this figure in perspective, Virginia's total population at the time is estimated at 400,000 to 600,000, of which approximately 40–45 percent was enslaved; thus, although the signatories were not exclusively white males, over 10 percent of the adult white male population apparently signed. The 10,000 name petition specifically noted that establishment levies constituted taxation without representation. This call to end the establishment and guarantee religious equality so that internal "animosities may cease"—particularly given the express admonition that unanimity was needed in the war effort—was difficult to overlook.[23]

Two days later, a remonstrance from freeholders and, critically, militia of Augusta County, another Presbyterian stronghold, noted that Virginians' "unanimity has made them formidable to their enemies," but warned that "their unanimity will be ever preserved by giving equal liberty to them all; nor do the[y] crave this as the pittance of courtesy but...as their patrimony which cannot be withheld from them without the most flagitious fraud, pride and injustice, which if practiced may shake this continent and demolish provinces." If the militia's participation in this process failed to focus establishment leaders adequately on the implications for mobilization, the Augusta petition made clear that failure to act would risk a violent reaction, noting that the petitioners "firmly believe attempts to repeal an unjust law can be vindicated beyond a simple remonstrance addressed to the legislators."[24]

Any doubt that Presbyterians had wholeheartedly joined the call for religious freedom as a condition for wholehearted support of the war was dispelled by an October 24 petition from the Hanover Presbytery. This missive, based on the Declaration of Rights and natural rights philosophy, prominently noted the dispute with Britain. Virginia's legislative leaders, including establishment stalwarts who populated the Committee for Religion, could not miss the change in tone and content from prior Presbytery petitions. The petition noted that dissenters have

> ever been desirous to conduct themselves as peaceable members of
> the civil Government; for which reason, they have hitherto submitted
> to several ecclesiastic burthens [sic] and restrictions that are
> inconsistent with equal liberty. But now when the many & grievous
> oppressions of our mother Country have laid the Continent under
> the necessity of casting off the yoke of tyranny,... we flatter ourselves
> that we shall be freed from all the encumbrances which a spirit of
> Domination, prejudice, or bigotry hath interwoven with most other
> political systems.

The Presbyterians' specific request was prefaced with a recognition that "in a land where all of every denomination are united in the most strenuous efforts to be free; we hope and expect that our Representatives will chearfully concur in removing every species of religious, as well as civil bondage." The Presbyterians concluded that "this being done," it will inure to the "great honour and interest of the State."[25]

Additional petitions peppered the assembly in late 1776, calling for an end to the establishment tax and pledging, for example, that, "this granted," dissenters "shall ever wish well to the commonwealth, and shall always do every thing in their Power to defend it." The war with Britain, and "consideration, that by the joint & strenuous endeavors of every one our Liberty" could be defended, provided the context. Yet petitioners would "determine to bleed...before they submit, to any form of Government, that may be subversive of these religious Privileges that are a Natural Right." The logic was inescapable: support for the new government—including mobilization—was absolutely essential, and it would turn on the new government's treatment of "religious Privileges." To ensure that the importance of their requests would not be missed, the Augusta County committee warned of the "Vast Number of Dissenters from the Established Church in this Colony" and that establishment tends to embitter "the Hearts of every Virtuous American now Strugling [sic] in Defence of the Common Rights of Mankind."[26]

Responses from the established church tended to confirm the fact that dissenters were negotiating an understanding about the relationship between their support for the war and religious freedom. A petition from Anglican clergy and one from Methodists (who until 1784 were "in communion with the Church of England") sought continuance of the establishment. A group of Anglican ministers personally pressed their opposition to disestablishment on members of the assembly in Williamsburg in late 1776. An Anglican essayist argued in the *Virginia Gazette* that the majority of people would be "aggrieved" by disestablishment and might "be sickened" of support for the Revolution, complaining bitterly that dissenter warnings about the risk to the unanimity of support for the war effort were disingenuous. The establishment author was angry that a previous apparent Virginia consensus on British misrule now seemed inadequate to generate the needed support. "Why then should unanimity forsake us, as long as we continue in the same situation? If it does, it must be because some people require more than others for having ventured less, and only having done, to say the most, as much."[27]

With several petitions, newspaper letters, Anglican ministers buttonholing delegates, and a previously firm control on the leadership, Anglicans thought their response was adequate to at least obtain a delay, particularly given the press of other war-related matters. The problem the establishment faced was not a lack of Anglican response; rather, the dissenters were in a position to demand reforms, and the patriot, Anglican leadership decided it could not risk further delay. The Anglicans were finding that it is far more difficult to oppose someone else's liberty than to fight for one's own.

The Anglican letter in the *Gazette* elicited a biting response reportedly penned by Caleb Wallace, moderator of the Hanover Presbytery and son-in-law of one of the Augusta members of the General Assembly; Wallace had been sent to Williamsburg by the Presbytery to lobby for reforms. While he would later give up the ministry and become a member of Kentucky's first supreme court, during the war he was actively involved in the dispute over religious freedom. He was in a particularly efficacious position given that he shared ties with James Madison from time spent together at the College of New Jersey and, after his second marriage in 1779, a family connection with Patrick Henry. As a frequent clerk for the Presbytery, his name would appear repeatedly on key Presbyterian petitions.

In November 1776, Wallace's letter to the *Gazette* warned that "at a time when the salvation of our country confessedly depends on the aid and exertions of every party, does not policy loudly forbid any irritating refusal to the reasonable demands of thousands of valuable citizens?" In fact, the presence of dissenting ministers in Williamsburg lobbying the legislature—and presumably making more pointed demands orally—certainly contributed to establishment leaders taking their concerns and threats seriously. For example, at the end of 1776, Wallace joined the delegates in Williamsburg for six to eight weeks in an effort to encourage disestablishment. In the end, Virginia's leaders concluded that their fellow Anglicans were unlikely to refuse to fight because of concessions to dissenters. The alternative danger, however, loomed large.[28]

These petitions and newspaper exchange arrived amid an ongoing military conflict, which, by the end of 1776, many patriots were viewing with apprehension. After the first flush of patriotic fervor and success faded, state leaders were forced to come to grips with waning military ardor, mounting battlefield losses, and the difficulty of maintaining a volunteer army. One contemporary Baptist minister explained, "The state legislature became sensible that a division among the people would be fatal to this country." With crucial fiscal and military issues pressing, the Virginia Assembly was forced to turn to the question of religious freedom despite Anglican lobbying, calls for delay, and the press of other business. Radical reforms would be needed.[29]

The 1776 petitions were initially referred to the Committee for Religion, a committee which the conservative Edmund Pendleton, speaker of the House, had appointed in an attempt to support the status quo.

> To the chairmanship of the committee he [Pendleton] appointed Carter Braxton. He had also named to membership the most conservative man in the House, Robert Carter Nicholas. Pendleton had told Jefferson earlier that he counted upon these two to "assist in watching and breaking the spirit of party, that bane of all public councils."[30]

The sparse pages of the *Journal of the House of Delegates* demonstrate the efforts of Pendleton and other establishment supporters to resist reform. As the first session of Virginia's General Assembly got under way in October, the dispute clearly escalated. Petitions kept arriving and more members were added to the Committee for Religion—undermining Pendleton's effort to pack the committee—until, on November 6, the House of Delegates passed a surprising resolution to permit any member to sit on the committee. Disputes must have still plagued the committee's efforts under conservative leadership, however, and on November 9, the committee was discharged from any consideration of the petitions, with the demands for religious liberty and Anglican responses referred to the Committee of the Whole House. On November 19, the House adopted a resolution calling for an exemption of the dissenters from establishment taxes, continued regulation of religion, and retention of property by the then established church. A smaller committee (including Robert Carter Nicholas, Thomas Jefferson, George Mason, Patrick Henry, and James Madison) was appointed to draft a bill, but apparently its progress was also impeded. Evidencing the intense debate over these matters, when Jefferson temporarily left the House for personal reasons, the proposed bill was amended to soften the blow on the established church, calling only for a suspension of taxes and specifically reserving the question of a general tax assessment to benefit all religious sects. The limited bill apparently did not repeal prior acts penalizing nonattendance or requiring particular "modes of worship." This was only remedied by Jefferson's hurried return to the House.[31]

After years of failed attempts to improve toleration and limit the establishment, on December 9, 1776, with a war government struggling to mobilize the populace, dissenters were exempted from establishment taxes. At the same time, establishment taxes were suspended, a practice continued annually until 1779. The General Assembly also repealed penalties for nonattendance at Anglican services. Licensing of ministers and houses of worship was left legally ambiguous, although the removal of penalties effectively seemed to undermine it. Still, that reformers were forced to accept suspension (rather than elimination) of establishment taxes and that the question of a general assessment to benefit all religion was expressly reserved, as well as vestry control of poor relief and the Anglican monopoly on marriage, are further evidence of the continuing authority and power of the establishment. Jefferson bemoaned the fact that although 1776 brought partial success, "our opponents carried in the general resolutions of the comm[itt]ee of Nov. 19, a declaration that religious assemblies ought to be regulated, and that provision ought to be made for continuing the succession of the clergy, and superintending their conduct."[32]

As if to counter any suggestion by Anglican apologists or later historians that these reforms were quickly or easily granted to dissenters, Jefferson later referred to these debates as "the severest conflicts in which I have been engaged." The records from the House of Delegates bear out this conclusion and support the notion that a reluctant gentry was being forced to come to grips with a new Virginia, one in which the political establishment would no longer be synonymous with the established church and in which dissenters of western counties and of middling and lower classes would be agents in the political process.[33]

An alternative view was urged from the start by those with particular interests. For example, Edmund Randolph, an Anglican advocate, argued that the establishment tax was easily repealed as Anglicans "dreaded nothing so much as a schism among the people, and thought the American principle too pure to be adulterated by religious dissension. They therefore did in truth cast the Establishment at the feet of its enemies." Randolph added that the 1776 reforms were made with only limited Anglican opposition; "the advocates for the church were apparently unconscious of its [the December law's] imbecility [i.e., impact on the religious establishment]. It was enervated by mental inactivity." Randolph conceded that "if the church and the dissenters could have been brought to such an issue that the Establishment was in danger, the band of union might not have been totally free from fracture." Yet the petitions and newspaper accounts and the committee machinations evident in the *Journal* demonstrate that the established church and dissenters *were* brought to such an issue, and that the establishment, after serious opposition and having limited the reforms' impact as much as possible, facing wartime necessity, had to recede. Pendleton joined Randolph's effort at early revisionism, and their views were subsequently embraced by sectarian historians of the nineteenth century who sought to minimize any notion of conflict in the revolutionary process as they claimed a central role for their denominational predecessors as principled patriots rather than interested and contingent bargainers. In fact, Randolph and Pendleton put a conciliatory face on the matter. Jefferson's testimony confirms what is clear from the record: the negotiation over religious freedom was perhaps the most complex and difficult ever faced by the Virginia House because it evidenced the creation of a new Virginia. Although the results were later evident—the key role of Baptists and Presbyterians in Virginia's war effort and their intimate participation in the polity after the war—the process itself, the give-and-take of difficult negotiations, was central to these developments.[34]

Over the years, as interest revised reporting (if not memory), Virginia's previously dissenting sects increasingly and correctly claimed an important role in the struggle for liberty without noting that they had bargained for religious freedom with strong indications that their support had a price. It was critical, after all, that after the war the former dissenters were able to claim the mantle not only of "real republicans" in the political process but also disinterested patriots in the glorious cause. Yet if there was any doubt about the nature and intensity of the negotiations from the petitions and other sources, what followed—both the Anglican response and the continued negotiation—confirmed that the dissenters had forced their way into the polity by insisting on religious freedom in return for their support for the war effort and that the establishment leaders had been forced to engage the dissenters in an extended negotiation that created and legitimated their position in the polity.[35]

Continued Negotiation and the Anglican Response

The suspension of establishment taxes did not end the establishment, nor did it resolve the problem of religious liberty. Dissenters still faced restrictions on marriage and were subject to poor taxes and regulation from Anglican vestries, among other infirmities. The question of a general assessment was left unresolved. The Church of England was technically still the established church, subject to regulation by government, and Anglican leaders had been successful in ensuring that establishment taxes were suspended rather than repealed.

The 1777 response to reform by Anglican petitioners is particularly telling. Whatever the logic of the negotiations, and whatever the change in content and tone of dissenters' petitions from 1774 to 1776, one might question the extent to which the dramatic change in religious liberty was made not on the basis of revolutionary principle but in a bargain for dissenter support for mobilization. After all, certainly some legislators supported elimination of the religious tax and reform of the establishment before the war, and many dissenters would have mobilized in any case. One can easily avoid conclusions about the extent of suasion applied to the legislature, especially by underestimating the strength of the establishment and the political clout of those who opposed liberalization, not to mention failing to focus on the conditional language used by the dissenters throughout 1776. Yet the established church itself provided strong evidence that the concessions on religious liberty were part of a difficult negotiation for support of the war effort.

Shortly after establishment taxes were suspended, exasperated Anglican petitions—which, consistent with the social status of their authors, tend to be printed rather than handwritten—objected angrily that dissenters were insisting on religious freedom before offering full support for mobilization, urging that in the present "critical situation" nothing should divert the legislature from indispensable war measures. Recognizing that it was necessary to "make men unanimous in the defence of liberty," "inhabitants" (read Anglicans) of Mecklenburg County sought continued support for the established church.

Importantly, they concluded that they "would by no means wish to see Churchmen adopt the principles of Dissenters, withhold their concurrence in the common cause until their particular requests are granted, for by such conduct all may be lost." The Anglicans knew exactly what the dissenters were doing and hoped that making the deal explicit would force dissenters and legislators to shy away from it in the name of unanimity in the struggle and Southern honor. Anglicans from across the Commonwealth joined in this protest, filing similar or identical petitions through 1777 and into 1778. The Anglican petitioners understood that the dissenters anticipated a quid pro quo deal for support, support that went to the heart of military preparedness. At the same time, Anglicans published an intellectual appeal for continuing an establishment—*The Necessity of an Established Church in Any State; or, an Humble Address to the Legislators of the Commonwealth of Virginia*. Like their petitions, it seemed to fall on deaf ears of legislators fixated on mobilization.[36]

Having objected to what they viewed as inappropriate pressure from the dissenters, Anglican supplicants could only hope to delay consideration of religious freedom past a crisis that increased dissenters' leverage, urging legislators that given the controversial nature of religious regulation, it "should be debated at a time when you have nothing of more importance to engage your attention." With the press of war-related business, this seemed a reasonable request. Rather than threatening to withhold support, though, Anglicans recognized reluctantly that "if only withholding from a competent number of ministers of the gospel fixed salaries is the most likely means to make men unanimous in the defence of liberty, as has been urged, we should be very sorry indeed if there could be one found of that reverend order who would repine at the success of the measure." Taking any other position would have made the Anglicans guilty of exactly what it was they were criticizing dissenters for—and probably would not have been credible.[37]

Anglican calls for delay may have acted as a call for all deliberate speed to those who saw in the dispute an opportunity to promote religious freedom. Shortly thereafter, Jefferson warned in his *Notes on Virginia* that the time to establish liberties firmly was during the conflict, as had Madison in 1774. "It can never be too often repeated, that the time for fixing every essential right on a legal basis is while our rulers are honest, and ourselves united. From the conclusion of this war we shall be going down hill. It will not then be necessary to resort every moment to the people for support." Jefferson went on to warn that "the shackles, therefore, which shall not be knocked off at the conclusion of this war, will remain on us long, will be made heavier and heavier, till our rights shall revive or expire in a convulsion." His prediction that the end of the war would mark the zenith for religious and other liberties was proven inaccurate in large part because of the redefinition of Virginia's political structure that resulted from the war and the gentry's necessity of negotiating with dissenters and incorporating them into the political framework. Of course, this could not be known at the time. The same underlying point made by Jefferson was made by Baptist minister William Fristoe: "The consideration of these things, stimulated and excited the Baptists in Virginia to use every effort, and adopt every measure embracing that particular crisis as the fittest time to succeed, which if past by might never offer again, and they and their posterity remain in perpetual fetters under an ecclesiastic tyranny."[38] In fact, the Anglican petitions appear to have had the opposite of their intended effect. They made Virginia political leaders' options clearer: they could give dissenters whatever religious freedoms seemed necessary to maximize their support for the war while maintaining the support (albeit somewhat begrudging) of the Anglican establishment.

This pattern continued for the remaining years of the war, but the political efforts of Anglican leaders prevented a collapse of the religious establishment or full granting of religious liberty. Rather, the dissenters and Virginia's political leadership continued to spar as one group sought greater liberty and the other support for mobilization while attempting to minimize the impact on the established church. Throughout this period, there was an exchange of requests and demands and, slowly, concessions by the political leadership as necessary to maintain continued support.

Legislative concessions to dissenters came in multiple forms. As recruiting became more difficult, the General Assembly began to eliminate or narrow exemptions from the general requirement that all free men muster with the militia, from which continental drafts were also made. In 1775, 1776, and 1777, the House eliminated exemptions for overseers, Quakers and Mennonites (requiring them to hire a substitute if they wished to avoid service), copper workers, some millers, and students and faculty at the College of William and Mary. Yet with a crisis in recruiting growing, dissenting ministers were exempted in 1775, and the requirements for qualifying as an exempted minister were clarified in 1777 such that dissenting ministers could more readily claim an exemption as long as they would take an oath of loyalty. While other exemptions came under extreme scrutiny, the exemption for dissenting ministers was kept in place and expanded.[39]

In 1777, concerned by the express reservation of a possible general tax assessment to support religion in the 1776 legislation, the Hanover Presbytery filed a petition objecting to any such assessment, viewing it as undoing the good that had been accomplished with adoption of the Declaration of Rights and the suspension of establishment taxes. The Presbytery noted that the suspension of establishment taxes tended to inspire its members with confidence in government. Baptists joined the objection to a general assessment. In spite of the broad protests from Anglicans, the question of a general assessment was left on the table and establishment taxes were again suspended. More immediately, with an eye to the recruiting problems faced throughout Virginia, dissenting sects were given the right to raise their own continental companies, led by their own coreligionists, to help fill Virginia's quota.[40]

By contrast, beginning in 1777 and continuing through 1778, the General Assembly received a string of Anglican petitions objecting to the "alarming" progress of dissenters. These petitions objected to the abandonment of the established church by the General Assembly, noting the breach of faith with ministers who had pursued ordination with an expectation of continued public provision of ecclesiastical salaries, and to the preaching of the dissenters, particularly the use of outdoor and night meetings, a lightly veiled reference to preaching to slaves. The petitions sought increased restrictions on dissent, including licensing of ministers, and some action to provide government funding for churches. Given the progress of the war and objections of dissenters, these petitions were ignored or simply tabled.[41]

The year 1778 was relatively quiet for religious issues in the General Assembly—and not coincidentally an optimistic year for mobilization with General Horatio Gates's victory over General John Burgoyne at Saratoga in October 1777, France's entry into the war in February 1778, Washington coming forth from Valley Forge with a more professional and effective army in the spring, and British General Henry Clinton's retreat across New Jersey—but it did not pass without some renewal of dissenter complaints. Presbyterian petitioners sought a relaxation of requirements concerning the use of oaths, with various oath requirements applying to voters and civil and militia officers being objected to by evangelicals. By May 1779, the assembly permitted solemn declarations in the place of oaths for those of religious scruples regardless of denomination. Though a relatively minor reform, it was another response to dissenter demands and a further step in the process of bringing dissenters fully within the polity.[42]

A new-found official support for dissenters and their public legitimization was evidenced in other ways as well. After being dunked in 1778 in Isle of Wight County, Baptist ministers David Barrow and Edward Mintz sued four men involved in the attack. The perpetrators were bonded for good behavior and required to pay costs for not appearing at a hearing. As one modern observer noted dryly, "The men who instigated this attack on the two ministers probably did not expect the sentence of the court."[43]

In 1779, with the war seemingly stalemated and recruiting lagging badly,[44] the simmering negotiations concerning religious liberty again came to a boil. In May, facing repeated calls for dissolution of various vestries and a general dissenter opposition to the Anglican vestries' continued civil capacity, the General Assembly took up a bill on vestry reform and for appointment of over-seers of the poor to replace the vestries' civil functions. Although it was repeat-edly brought forward, defenders of the status quo were able to delay this bill through 1779, but it resurfaced in 1780. In addition, the Baptist association once again objected to marriage laws that required an Anglican minister to per-form the ceremony or at least be paid a fee if a dissenter was to perform the service. With Anglican ministers' salaries suspended and many ministers suffering serious financial hardship, the General Assembly was not yet pre-pared to eliminate this important source of income.[45]

More fundamentally, a heated battle began over proposals for a broad legislative statement of religious freedom and counterproposals for adoption of the long-delayed general assessment. In May, as part of a general reform of colonial laws to comport with the independent status of Virginia, the General Assembly took up Jefferson's Bill for Establishing Religious Freedom, which was initially drafted in 1777. By fall 1779, a series of petitions from dissenters urged its passage. A petition from largely Presbyterian Augusta County said the bill was "agreeable to our Declaration of Rights" and an appropriate means "for Laying a Permanent foundation to maintain that Liberty which we are so Earnestly, if so [missing text] contending for." Baptists meeting in Amelia County wrote: "That the said bill, in our opinion, puts religious freedom upon its proper basis; prescribes the just limits of the power of the State, with regard to religion; and properly guards against partiality towards any religious denom-ination; we, therefore,...wish it to pass into law." Another petition from Augusta stated that Jefferson's bill was based on "just, catholic & political prin-ciples" and urged that it be adopted. A November 1 petition from "Church of England men, Presbyterians, Baptists & Methodists" in Amherst County whole-heartedly supported the Bill.[46]

Overall, however, in 1779 there were more petitions in opposition to Jefferson's bill from supporters of the established church, many seeking adop-tion of a "general assessment for the support of Religious Worship." On the same day that the House received the Augusta petition supporting the bill, it received one from Lancaster County urging that the bill should be tempered by a requirement of licensing of preachers so as to avoid "Licencious [sic] Freedom." Other petitions objecting to the bill prominently called for opposition to evan-gelical appeals to enslaved blacks. A November 10 petition from Amherst County supported a general assessment and restrictions on any "Catholic, Jew,

Turk or Infidel" in any civil capacity; it noted that it had been read and approved by the militia at muster, indicating that the Anglican petitioners were learning from the dissenters' example.[47]

In the midst of this heated debate, on October 25, a general assessment bill to benefit all Christian denominations was introduced. After being read a second time, however, the bill was repeatedly delayed from consideration by the whole House and eventually failed as the assemblymen realized that given deteriorating wartime conditions, it was no time to antagonize dissenters.[48] On the defeat of the general assessment, an effort to eliminate the establishment tax, rather than continuing its suspension, was finally introduced into the House. With the war far from won, the assembly again acted to mollify dissenters and, after suspending the establishment tax each year from 1776 through 1778, finally repealed it in December 1779. Once again, some sense of the intensity of the debates in the House can be gathered from the clipped references in the official journal.[49]

The extent of change in the political community is further evidenced by comparing the 1776 Committee for Religion, which Pendleton had configured to impede reform, to the committee that drafted the final repeal of the establishment tax. In addition to George Mason, the 1779 committee included French Strother of Culpeper, who had reportedly once freed a Baptist minister from jail by substituting a slave, and Beverley Randolph, who, despite family connections with warm establishment supporters, was no friend to the church establishment. Yet their work still met resistance. The House struck from the repeal bill approved by the committee Mason's preamble, which read:

> To remove from the good People of this Commonwealth the Fear of being compelled to contribute to the Support or Maintenance of the former established Church, And that the Members of the said Church may no longer relye upon the Expectation of any Re-establishment thereof, & be thereby prevented from adopting proper Measures, among themselves, for the Support and Maintenance of their own Religion and Ministers.

Establishment leaders were not willing to accept that their cause was wholly lost.[50]

Necessity, not acceptance, dictated the formal end of establishment taxes. Of course, with Anglicans still holding out hope for a return to some form of establishment and financial support for clergy, passage of Jefferson's famous Bill for Establishing Religious Freedom would have to await further developments. Given that urgent war legislation took priority in the Virginia House, the time devoted to religious matters in 1779 speaks to the supreme importance that the General Assembly was forced to place on the reforms demanded by the dissenters.

Although it was certainly a crucial victory, final repeal of the establishment tax did not end the negotiation of religious liberty between the dissenters and the wartime government. In May 1780, at a time when the Virginia legislature was grappling with a Southern war and the dramatically increased necessity of recruiting resulting from the loss of the Virginia Continental Line at Charleston, a concern soon heightened by the evaporation of the militia at Camden, a Baptist petition from Amelia again objected to restrictions on marriage and vestry laws concerning the poor. The next month the Baptist association meeting in Spotsylvania County "heartily approve[d]" of the repeal of the establishment tax, but remonstrated for the right of dissenting ministers to solemnize marriages. These Baptists did not forget to remind the assembly that their search for "equal Religious, as well as civil Liberty" was supported by the fact that they "demean our selves as good Citizens and peaceable Subjects of the Commonwealth." The issue was made more pointedly in the petition from the Sandy Creek Baptists who, in words that Jefferson certainly would have approved, specifically attacked the plea of those who argue that "it is not now a proper Time to proceed to such Affairs, let us first think of defending ourselves." Invoking the Declaration of Rights, the dissenters suggested that there is no more appropriate time to resolve the matter of religious freedom "than when contending with those who endeavor to tyrannize over us." In November 1780, Baptists also asked that the assembly correct problems arising from continued control of poor laws, and taxation to support those laws, by vestries conformable to the Church of England.[51]

Lest the General Assembly forget that continued agitation for religious liberty and material support of the Commonwealth were intertwined, petitions from Cumberland County in 1780 began by reminding the assembly that it is "a fundamental principle of Government that protection and Allegiance are reciprocal." Showing heightened confidence in their role in the political process, these petitioners went on to attack some Anglican ministers, urging that the assembly adopt a test oath, which a "true Whig" would never refuse, and that "non-juring preachers" be silenced and their taxes doubled because it appears just that "those who are exempted from Rendering Personal service as Soldiers should yield a Larger proportion of their Wealth." A Prince Edward County petition of the same date offered the same recommendation, and the matter was taken up by a series of identical petitions from Buckingham County from December 7, 1780. In less than two weeks, though, Anglicans from Cumberland County responded that the earlier petitions were targeted at Anglican ministers, and they blamed "turbulent & disorderly" New Light Presbyterians. Still, the

Anglicans felt it crucial to add that although many Anglican ministers would not take the oath out of conscience—given their oath for the king at ordination—they had given the American cause sufficient evidence of loyalty.[52]

With the movement of the seat of war to the Southern theater and a series of American defeats, concerns for recruiting and, more generally, support of the revolutionary government were reaching a peak. In this environment, the General Assembly again, grudgingly, had to make just enough changes to ensure continued dissenter support. In June, vestries were replaced by over-seers of the poor in seven, primarily Presbyterian, western counties. In December 1780, Virginia finally permitted dissenting ministers to perform the marriage ceremony. Unlike Anglican ministers, though, they had to obtain a license, which was restricted to one county, and the number of dissenting min-isters that could perform marriages in any given county was limited. As early Baptist historian Robert Semple noted, "To resist British oppressions effectu-ally, it was necessary to soothe the minds of the people by every species of policy. The dissenters were too powerful to be slighted, and they were too watchful to be cheated in an ineffectual sacrifice." Still, the piecemeal and incomplete nature of this reform again demonstrated the effective rear guard action of establishment supporters.[53]

Contrary to claims that religious freedom and disestablishment came about quickly and easily, petitions and related documents through 1781 evidence an extended and, at the end of the Revolution, incomplete back-and-forth between political leaders and dissenters. Before the war, the political and ecclesiastic establishments were essentially the same; as the war approached, the strength of the Church of England was growing. In spite of their rapidly growing num-bers, and in spite of the assistance of some visionary political leaders, the dis-senters were unable to obtain significant reforms or improved toleration prior to the war. A conjunction of political necessity in the midst of war and the dis-senters' persistent demands and warnings were central to the establishment of religious freedom in Virginia.

From the vantage point of 200 years later, one tends to see the results of conflict—including the development of religious freedom—but may miss the deep contingency and discord that produced the results, much less the process of change itself. The exigencies of war mobilization forced the political estab-lishment not only to engage dissenting sects and expand their direct represen-tation to some extent by incorporating new western counties as the war continued—a factor that proved crucial in the ultimate adoption of Jefferson's Bill for Establishing Religious Freedom—but also partake in a complex and extended negotiation for religious freedom with citizens who previously had not been major participants in the political process. This result was forced on the establishment because of their need to unify Virginia in the face of a war with Britain, as well as by the threats from dissenters that they might withhold full support for the war effort. Only the threat to military mobilization could have moved the establishment to cede its hegemony as it struggled with managing a faltering government.

The change, though not easy or quick, was monumental. During the war, dissenters participated in the political process in a manner in which they had heretofore been effectively excluded. This process of petitioning and negotiating changed their status. The political establishment was forced to expand its concept of the Virginia polity, and the state was changed in an irreversible manner. While nineteenth-century sectarian historians were quick to embrace the results—often claiming primacy for their coreligionists as "true" Virginias and Americans because of their patriotic contribution to the war effort—those historians gave less attention to the process, perhaps in an effort to minimize any contingency.

Contrary to the suggestion that the prerevolutionary development of the evangelical polity was the source for revolutionary fervor and laid a foundation for the development of early American democracy, in Virginia, it was in the cauldron of the Revolution itself that evangelicals were able to join the polity, thereby democratizing it, and, with their establishment conegotiators, create an environment that produced the postwar development of a vibrant democratic debate on multiple issues. Rather than evangelical religion itself being a cause of the Revolution, the Whigs' need for broader support proved to be the well-spring of liberty by requiring political leaders to enlist the evangelicals in the war, not only playing an important role in winning the military conflict but also leading to a uniquely American development of the modern state, first and most impressively in the development of religious freedom and separation of church and state. Democratization in this context then mediated development of every aspect of the young republic. Perhaps this was part of what Benjamin Rush meant when he wrote, "I hope with the history of this folly, some historians will convey to future generations, that many of the most active and useful characters in accomplishing this revolution, were strangers to the formalities of a Latin and Greek education."[54]

The success of the complex and difficult negotiations between dissenters and their erstwhile protagonists begs a question: could Britain, the former protector of dissenter interests, have appealed to Virginia's dissenters successfully on the issue of religious toleration? Given the history (not to mention British efforts elsewhere in the rebellious colonies), this would have seemed like an appropriate forum to seek loyal support. Britain's failure to do so was intimately tied up with the question of the proper political role of religious dissent in the British colonies.

British Plans for Success

The great Source of this religious Contention and Disorder lies in the defective Constitution of our colonial Policy. Every Church has its Pretensions to take the lead.... The War is...at the Bottom very much a religious War, and every one looks to the Establishment of his own Party upon the Close of it. And indeed, upon the Issue, some one Party ought to predominate,... It is perhaps impossible to keep the ecclesiastical Polity out of the Settlement without endangering the Permanency of the cure.

—Ambrose Serle to Lord Dartmouth,
November 8, 1776

The initial success of royal Governor Josiah Martin in North Carolina in rallying dissenters to the king's banner raises intriguing possibilities for Virginia. After all, had there been a different result at the Battle of Moore's Creek Bridge in early 1776, Martin might have been able to mobilize and maintain significant support for royal authority in North Carolina with dramatic consequences for the war. Given the prewar antagonism between Virginia's dissenters and the Tidewater gentry controlling the state's patriot movement, a long historic pattern of royal officials protecting dissenter interests in the state, and the dramatic growth of dissent there before the war, one might also have expected a forceful effort from Governor Dunmore or authorities in Britain to encourage similar support among Virginia's dissenters. If successful, such an effort could easily have disrupted the internal Virginia polity—a crucial source of men and supplies for the Continental Army.

In fact, British officials were not unaware of the possibility of using their historic role as protectors of dissenting interests to appeal to American dissenters. In an effort to conciliate dissenters in New York in 1775, immediately after hostilities broke out, British officials finally, after repeated refusals encouraged by local Anglican leaders, agreed to the legal incorporation of Presbyterian and Dutch Reformed churches. When Benjamin Franklin led a delegation seeking to garner support for the American cause from French Canadians, Guy Carleton, the British commander in Canada, successfully reminded the Canadians of British support for dissenter rights, particularly in the Quebec Act in 1774, and American hostility toward Catholicism. Later, after the capture of John Burgoyne's army at Saratoga and the official entry of France into the war as an American ally, Britain's Carlisle Commission appealed to American Protestant dissenters against a Continental Congress which had entered an alliance with Catholic France. On October 3, 1778, after the commission's efforts to negotiate peace by making concessions just short of recognizing American independence were rebuffed by the Continental Congress, Sir Henry Clinton, commander of British forces in America and a member of the Carlisle Commission, published a manifesto appealing directly to the American populace. The commission warned those Americans concerned with religious toleration that the Continental Congress had negotiated with a "foreign power," France, which had been "averse to toleration and inveterately opposed to the interests and freedom of the places of worship... and that Great Britain from whom they are for the present separated, must both from principles of her constitution and of protestantism be at all times the best guardian of religious liberty, and most disposed to preserve and extend it." Given England's raw history of religious disputes and intolerance of Catholics, and the colonists' severe reaction to Britain's decision to grant Canadian Catholics the right to practice their religion in the Quebec Act, this warning of an alliance between the new Congress and a "popish" king could have had a serious impact on dissenters had they believed that Britain would more readily protect their religious liberty and had British officials been in a position to engage the issue seriously. The point was not wholly lost on its intended audience. Robert Honyman, a doctor in Virginia, noted in his diary that the Carlisle Commission had warned Congress that it should unite with people who shared their language and religion, rather than entering into an "insincere... foreign alliance." Nor were patriot leaders unconcerned with such efforts to sow religious discord; after the war, Presbyterian officials, referring in particular to the alliance with Catholic France, reported with relief, "when we consider the unwearied attempts of our enemies to raise dissension by every topic that could be supposed inflammatory and popular, the harmony that has prevailed not only between the allied powers, but the troops of different nations and languages acting together, ought to be ascribed to the gracious influence of Divine Providence."[1]

Given the historic association of Britain with protection of dissenter interests and the continued control of the Virginia polity by dissenters' protagonists, the appeal to dissenters in the Carlisle Commission, not to mention Governor Martin's relatively successful appeal to dissenters in North Carolina, raises several questions. Would such an appeal from Lord Dunmore, early in the war, have met with similar or even greater success than that experienced by Martin in North Carolina? Could Britain have made a more targeted and serious appeal to Southern (especially Virginian) dissenters to encourage loyalism or, at least, discourage support of the patriot movement? The simple answer is Dunmore did not, and Britain could not.

Dunmore's Search for Loyalists

John Murray, fourth earl of Dunmore, had never been a popular governor in Virginia. Even his short war against Shawnee Indians to obtain land sessions in present-day Kentucky—always a way to curry popularity in the American frontier—a conflict that he was pleased to have known as "Dunmore's War," did not give his reputation a lasting lift. Once war between Britain and the colonists broke out, he spent more than a year diligently trying to rally loyalists to the king's banner.[2]

Dunmore, however, never had even the initial success that Martin enjoyed when he rallied loyalists to Moore's Creek. There are a number of reasons for this, most notably Dunmore's decision to appeal to slaves (of rebels) to fight for the king (in return for which they would obtain their freedom) incensed most white Virginians. Dunmore also lacked Martin's experience in working with the concerns of western dissenters. Thus, he sought to encourage Indian attacks on the frontier, again alienating most Virginians and especially western Presbyterians, while remaining silent concerning the Presbyterians' earlier avowal to Lord Botetourt of their unmatched loyalty to the king and willingness to prove it during the period of British–colonial political tensions. Dunmore did offer frontiersmen a clear title to their land should they join his forces, certainly an enticement, but they might also have seen some irony in the fact that the Royal Proclamation line of 1763 had contributed significantly to their land problems. More to the point, while royal officials were undoubtedly associated with protection of dissenters' interests, Dunmore did not address the question of protection of dissenters' religious liberty from a local Virginia establishment that had consistently discriminated against and persecuted them. In any case, once Dunmore alienated the frontier by his effort to encourage Indian raids and slave rebellion, any cooperation was highly unlikely.[3]

In fact, Dunmore seemed largely oblivious to the tension between the local establishment and dissenters in Virginia and the possibility of dissenter support of the Crown. Thus, he wrote Lord Dartmouth in December 1774:

> With regard to the encouraging of those, as your Lordship likewise exhorts me, who appeared, in principle averse to those proceedings [of the Continental Congress], I hope your Lordship will do me the Justice to believe, I have left no means in my power unessayed to draw all the assistance possible from them to His Majesty's Government; but I presume your Lordship will not think it very extraordinary, that any persuasions should have been unavailing, against the terrours, which on the other hand, are held out by the Committees, independent Companies etc. so universally supported, who have set themselves up, superior to all other Authority, under the Auspices of their Congress.

He went on specifically to note that the nonimportation/exportation agreements adopted by the Continental Congress imposed a particular burden on the lower sort, but he failed to recognize or seek to exploit the possibility of encouraging loyalism among the lower class, which had a somewhat disproportionate number of dissenters. Perhaps Lord Dunmore's aristocratic roots and aspirations blinded him to all but Virginia's Anglican gentry. Certainly, the difference in Governor Martin's correspondence of the same period is striking.[4]

In fact, by 1776, while still trying unsuccessfully to rally effective support in Virginia, Dunmore was so benighted as to think that the assembly's offense of ordering Anglican clergy to excise the prayers for the king from their services would enrage the populace—seemingly ignorant of the leadership role of Anglican laity in controlling the new state and the extent to which changes in their dominance were demanded by dissenters whose assistance was needed for wartime mobilization. Thus, Dunmore told Lord Germain in June 1776,

> yet I am well convinced it [Virginia's declaration of its independent status] is quite repugnant to the wish of most. Their having ordered the Prayers for the preservation of His Majesty and those of His Trinity etc. to be erased and substituted others for their Congress, Conventions etc. in their place, I am well convinced (though this Colony is by no means remarkably over religious) that this change will have a wonderfull effect on the minds of the lower Class of

People, who I am satisfied even now only wait for an Army able to protect them, which Army I doubt not were they landed, they would immediately join. Even many of those I am satisfied that now appear in arms against us, would willingly change Sides.

In spite of his brave declarations, Dunmore was never able to maintain more than desultory support among white Virginians.[5]

With as much as one-third or more of the Virginia population dissenting and the new state legislature being forced to make concessions to their interests, and in spite of Martin's initial success in North Carolina, Dunmore could not see past the Church of England and its gentry leadership. This was an opportunity missed. Of course, one cannot assume that a British appeal to dissenters in Virginia, in the face of the patriots' forceful efforts to obtain dissenter support and other reasons for dissenters' patriot sympathies, would have been successful. Dunmore, though, seemed more focused on making war against colonials than seeking to co-opt their support.

More generally, Britain, too, focused almost entirely on Anglican loyalists. Its understanding of the war and its plans for a new colonial regime after Britain's inevitable military success would permit nothing else.

Britain's Plan for Postwar Religion

Whatever Dunmore's failings, British officials also did not make a consistent appeal to dissenters, particularly those in the South who had faced persecution from local officials. Of course, one might conclude that the British leadership simply failed to understand the war at all—why the Americans were in revolt, why early British efforts to negotiate failed, and why repeated American military defeats did not end the resistance. Perhaps colonial religious controversies were of the same ilk. Yet looking beyond Virginia, it becomes evident that other factors impaired any serious effort by Britain to capitalize on dissenter loyalty to the Crown and disenchantment with Virginia's establishment leaders.

In Britain, any linkage between royal officials and protection of dissent in America was substantially impaired by the extent to which English dissenters aligned with "real whigs" and "commonwealthmen" against government interests in the political disputes of the 1760s and 1770s. For example, Joseph Priestley's 1774 (anonymous) *Address to Protestant Dissenters* expressly called on English dissenters to help unseat the government of Lord North. Colonial dissenting interests, particularly in New England, were known to be in close communication with the English dissenters who plagued Tory officials. For

British policy makers, this English experience tended to obscure the Crown's role as protector of dissenters in America and the possible support of the dissenters.[6]

When British officials did focus on religion in America, all that they could see were the apparent problems generated by dissenters, that is, non-Anglicans, in New England and the middle states. From very early on in the colonial conflict, Tories in America accused dissenters in New England of creating and inflaming the dispute, and British officials were led to believe that dissenters in New England and the middle states, particularly Presbyterians—seen by many British officials as inheritors of a Scottish legacy for rebellion—were at the heart of the colonists' disloyalty. Based on the role of dissenters in political conflicts in England, royal officials were well disposed to accept such an understanding. As a result, when British officials, confident of their ultimate success against an American rabble, planned for the postwar regime, a substantially stronger religious establishment was contemplated, not stronger protection of dissent.[7]

Even had they wished to engage dissenters, once patriots had effectively seized local governmental institutions, British officials simply lacked an effective forum for doing so. Although the British army could seek to encourage militarization of loyalists (and did so with some success, particularly in New York, Georgia, and South Carolina), the military was not in a position to engage dissenters in the political process as were Virginia's new leaders. The result was that Britain was simply unable to appeal effectively to Southern dissenters. Britain lacked both an ideological and a political ground for negotiation.

Both before and during the war, British officials were fed a regular diet of "intelligence" that implicated the "black regiment" of dissenting ministers— first New England Congregationalists and then middle colony Presbyterians—in fomenting the revolt. Dissenters' efforts in America were seen as a challenge to both the Episcopal Church and the monarchy. This view was expressed by important colonial officials, such as Massachusetts Governor Thomas Hutchinson, Massachusetts Chief Justice Peter Oliver, and Joseph Galloway, speaker of the Pennsylvania colonial House of Representatives and a member of the first Continental Congress, as well as Anglican leaders, such as Charles Inglis of New York, later the first Anglican bishop in Canada. Oliver clearly found the initial causes of the conflict in the dissenters of New England; in his history of the origins of the war, finished in 1781 while in exile in England, he explained that "had the force of [religious] Enthusiasm been well understood, & what Power the dissenting Clergy had over the Minds of the People in *America*, it would have been a great Error in Politicks not to have suppressed the Growth of such a Weed, as hath poisoned both *Old* & *New England*." These views were certainly made known to his British acquaintances before 1781. Hutchinson reflected similar concerns when he opposed creating official fast days as requested by patriots in 1774 because to do so "was only to give an opportunity for sedition to flow from the pulpit." Galloway explained that dissenting preachers' "spirits and enthusiasm were equally intolerant of the rules of the established church and government." In 1779, he testified to British authorities that as the conflict reached a crisis in 1774, opponents of the Crown were "Congregationalists, Presbyterians and smugglers." Inglis related a very similar view to ecclesiastical leaders in London, but he also reported to the secretary of the Society for the Propagation of the Gospel in Foreign Parts in late 1776 that it was "past all Doubt, that an Abolition of the Church of England was one of the principal Springs of the Dissenting Leaders' Conduct; & hence the Unanimity of Dissenters in this Business, their universal Defection from Government."[8]

These views, even if true—and at best, they were gross oversimplifications—held for the Northern but not for the Southern colonies where Anglicanism was established and dissenters were struggling for their rights. Yet the British ministry was apparently unable to make such a distinction. The prevalence of Anglicanism in the South simply encouraged the ministry to believe, despite growing evidence, in the latent dominance of loyalism in that region and to look for loyalism among Anglicans throughout the colonies. Both the problem with dissenters and the latent loyalism of Anglicans were viewed as endemic. Galloway wrote the influential Charles Jenkinson, a confidant of both King George and Lord North, that

> a particular sect of religious People whose Principles naturally lead them to an admiration and love for Democracy, almost universally embrace the sedition against Government, . . . but few of the Church of England and other Sectaries, except men of Bankrupt and desperate Fortunes, . . . did not oppose or refuse to be connected with a design . . . of throwing off their subordination to the British State.

In a joint letter in 1780, optimistic Anglican clergy in New York wrote that "dissenters in general, and particularly Presbyterians and Congregationalists were the active Promoters of the Rebellion"; by contrast, the clergy explained, Anglicans "from their Infancy imbibe Principles of loyalty, and Attachment to the Present State"; dissenters "from their infancy, imbibe Republican, levelling Principles, which are unfriendly to the Constitution." Loyal Americans, overwhelmingly Anglicans, convinced the ministry that dissent was not a religious problem but a political one, and not an opportunity but a problem in need of a solution. Having earlier expressed an opinion "that much of this Controversy has been fomented by Presbyterian Preachers, with a View to the Extirpation of the Church of England from the Colonies," and that a final settlement would require "the full Establishment of the Church," certainly including a local bishop, Ambrose Serle, formerly Lord Dartmouth's private secretary and at the time serving with Admiral Richard Howe in New York, reported in his journal in 1777 that he had "visited Mr. Inglis in the morning & talked over with him, the Subject of the full Establishm[en]t. of the Church of England, on which we agreed, and are to have a meeting with the Revd. Mr. Seabury & the Attorney Genl. [Kempe] to consider further of it." Serle later convinced Galloway of the same point and undoubtedly made his views known to Admiral Howe.[9]

Anglican leaders in Britain fed this view and encouraged the notion that problems in America arose from failure to support the colonial establishment more aggressively. By 1777, Archbishop of York William Markham was blaming the dispute in America on "fanatics and sectaries" and the government's failure to support adequately the colonial Anglican establishment. This view was attacked by British Whigs, such as the duke of Grafton and the earl of Shelburne, both supporters of America, but opposition from those sources was hardly likely to change the views of ministerial officials during the course of the war. Even John Wesley, with his close ties to the ministry, contributed to the view that the Revolution was led by a cabal supported by Congregationalists and Presbyterians.[10]

Key British officials concurred, and the view was one of long standing. As tensions with the colonies increased in the 1760s, Secretary of War William Barrington assured General Thomas Gage of his agreement that the Massachusetts mobs were "stimulated by their fanatic clergy who have taken up a strange ungrounded fear of episcopacy. This I preach to all our ministers." Gage reported in the relative calm of 1770 that mobs were, for the time, quiet and that "some attribute this change to Whitefields's sermons, who has been some time amongst them, preaching up subordination to government, and obedience to the laws." This fit well with government theory and policy. North Carolina Governor Martin had written the earl of Dartmouth from New York, November 4, 1774, "the same spirit of division [between Episcopalians and Presbyterians] has entered into or been transferred to meet other concernments." Officials in Britain, certainly influenced by the drumbeat from America, took a similar line. William Knox, Under-Secretary of State, wrote to Lord Dartmouth circa 1774–78 in an effort to explain the colonial unrest: "a Dependent Church seems as necessary as dependent Governments to preserve the connection between Great Britain and her Colonies." Or, as Horace Walpole quipped after open hostilities began, "Cousin America has run off with a Presbyterian parson." In reflecting on the war, Guy Carleton, governor of Quebec from 1768 to 1778 and commander of all British forces in America from 1782 to 1783, "even asserted that had there been bishops in America before the war, the leaders of the Revolution would not have secured such a favourable response to their propaganda."[11]

These views were inadvertently fed by American supporters in Britain. Edmund Burke, for example, in his Speech on Moving Resolutions for Conciliation with America in March 1775, argued that:

> The [American] people are Protestants; and of that kind which is the
> most adverse to all implicit submission of mind and opinion. This is
> a persuasion not only favourable to liberty, but built upon it. I do not
> think, Sir, that the reason of this averseness in the dissenting
> churches, from all that looks like absolute government, is so much to
> be sought in their religious tenets, as in their history.... The Church
> of England too was formed from her cradle under the nursing care of
> regular government. But the dissenting interests have sprung up in
> direct opposition to all the ordinary powers of the world; and could
> justify that opposition only on a strong claim to natural liberty.... But
> the religion most prevalent in our northern colonies is a refinement
> on the principle of resistance; it is the dissidence of dissent, and the
> Protestantism of the Protestant religion ... agreeing in nothing but in
> the communion of the spirit of liberty.

Of course, although it was not Burke's intent, this description tended only to harden the views of those loyal to the British Crown and ministry that too much freedom had been provided to American dissenters and the established church wrongly allowed to languish. With an implicit knowledge that to be effective, civil and religious institutions required a close bond, British officials could not fathom another means to understand the religious elements that repeatedly reared their heads in the disputes surrounding the American Revolution. The conclusion of Serle that the Americans were "Oliverian," for "inculcat[ing] War, Bloodshed & Massacres," referring to a symbol of religious strife that still deeply moved British policy makers, is indicative of the inability of British officials to see American dissent in anything but an adversarial manner as the war proceeded.[12]

Thus, to the extent that British policy makers focused on religion in America during the war, they generally saw dissent as a problem that caused or contributed heavily toward the war and would have to be remedied when the war was won. Leniency toward dissent—failing to impose vigorously the state church, including an episcopate—lay at the root of the problem of dissenter opposition. As a result, rather than seeking to co-opt dissenters, British authorities employed Anglican propagandists. Anglican Tory ministers Reverend

Jonathan Odell and Samuel Seabury were hired by General Howe to write propaganda for Britain for local distribution at £50 a year. As tensions rose, the Reverend John Vardill of New York's King's College, in London serving as a government pamphleteer, wrote Dartmouth urging "upon the government the necessity of supporting loyal Anglicans now that the Dissenters could be seen for the rebels they truly were."[13]

These reports and positions significantly influenced the vision of British officials as they planned for the inevitable success of their war effort. Thus, a postwar settlement was understood to include a strengthened Anglican Church in America with local bishops, not improved religious freedom. In 1776, Serle, then serving with a triumphant Admiral North in New York, urged his former patron, Dartmouth, to consider in a postwar settlement that "the War is...at the Bottom very much a religious War, and every one looks to the Establishment of his own Party upon the Close of it." After the war, Britain must remedy "the defective Constitution of our colonial Policy. [In which] Every Church has its Pretensions to take the Lead." "It is perhaps impossible," Serle concluded, "to keep the ecclesiastical Polity out of the Settlement, without endangering the Permanency of the cure. There will never be a fairer Opportunity, nor a juster Right, to fix the Constitution of America in all respects agreeable to the Interests and Constitution of Great Britain, than upon the Conclusion of this War." In his private journal, Serle added, "Republican Presbyterianism can never heartily coalesce with Monarchy & Episcopacy." Similarly, New York Anglican minister Charles Inglis gave specific advice to his superiors at the Society for the Propagation of the Gospel in Foreign Parts on what was necessary in a post-war settlement.

> Then will be the Time to make that Provision for the American
> Church which is necessary, & place it on at least an equal Foot with
> other Denominations, by granting it an Episcopate, & thereby
> allowing it a full Toleration. If this Opportunity is let slip, I think
> there is a Moral Certainty that such another will never again offer, &
> I must conclude in that Case that Government is equally infatuated
> with the Americans at present.

Stability was impossible in a state permeated by dissent; the solution, of course, was to strengthen Anglicanism and restrict dissent. Remarkably, even as the war raged, a committee of three British bishops was appointed in 1777 to reconsider the need for an American episcopate, but wartime apparently was recognized as an inauspicious environment for such action. Still, the effort was not rejected; British officials contemplated addressing these problems once peace under British rule was reestablished (as they expected). Knox, an unofficial advisor on postwar colonial policy, prepared a plan for an episcopal establishment that would tend to "combating and repressing the prevailing disposition of the Colonies to republicanism, and exciting in them esteem for monarchy." The possibility that British success would be accompanied by a firmer establishment was not lost on American patriots. Early American historian David Ramsay explained that for Presbyterians, "from independence they had much to hope, but from Great Britain if finally successful, they had reason to fear the establishment of a church hierarchy."[14]

Given the reliance of the British ministry on the views of its loyalist supporters, British policy makers could neither see nor exercise the opportunity that may have existed to rally dissenters to the royal banner. At least in Virginia, the result was a fundamental reversal of roles: during the war, the former Tidewater establishment, which had been responsible for the discrimination and much of the persecution visited on Virginia's dissenters, became patrons of dissenter interests in the legislature and, as a result of extended and complex negotiations, politicized dissent. On the other hand, royal officials, historically the protectors of dissent and in spite of prewar assurances of unbridled loyalty from Virginia Presbyterians, increasingly saw the future of British North America as being dependent on a strengthening of the Church of England and, with efforts to enlist Western Indians and slaves, antagonized many dissenters who might have otherwise supported royal authority.

A second serious problem also tended to undermine any possibility of fruitful cooperation between British officials and dissenters. Once the war began and patriots had usurped control of local government institutions, there was simply no political space in which British officials could readily negotiate with dissenters to create an opportunity to bring them into the British polity and invest them in the British success. Once the mechanisms of government were controlled by patriot forces, British officials could not engage in realistic (and certainly not immediate) discussions for concessions or politicization of potential civilian allies. Thus, while military positions could be and were offered to loyalists when the British army was in a particular area, the absence of British civil institutions seriously impaired interaction with the vast majority of the populace. Of course, the use of loyalists in military operations was dependent on direct support of the British army and suffered when the army was not present or left after having "pacified" an area. Thus, while Governor Martin expected in 1775 and early 1776 that North Carolina dissenters would rally to the king's banner, Britain's failure to provide support when they did so significantly impaired future efforts to enlist loyalists, as Lord Charles Cornwallis woefully discovered as he crossed North Carolina in 1781. Whatever the problems with militarizing loyalists, as British Commander-in-Chief Jeffrey

Amherst recognized, loyalists had to be put in control of a functioning government, as well as military positions, if locals were to develop a real stake in the political success of Britain, but little was accomplished in this regard.[15]

Georgia was the one place where British military success was followed by a serious effort to renew British civil authority during the war, thereby "Americanizing" not just the military aspects but the political and religious aspects of the war as well. For a period of time in 1780 and early 1781, this effort resulted in some success. Elsewhere, efforts were limited, in part because General Clinton, commander of British forces in America during the closing years of the war, was an opponent of wartime efforts to establish civil government.[16] The absence of political ground on which to engage dissenters in Virginia and elsewhere would have made any effort to cooperate with dissenters very difficult, even had the ministry been inclined to encourage it.

John Wesley and Loyalism in Virginia

In spite of Dunmore's failure and Britain's inability to engage dissenters effectively, Virginia's patriots were concerned that such an appeal would be made, and some were convinced that Britain was using religion as a tool to disrupt Virginia's mobilization. Certainly such fears would heighten patriot interests in conciliating dissent. The most intriguing bit of evidence in this regard is an anxious letter from a patriot recruiter to Virginia officials concerning British efforts to co-opt the growing Methodist population in the southside Tidewater and the Eastern Shore near the end of the war.

> A certain sett [sic] of Preachers called Methodists are preaching the doctrine of passive obedience, and point out the horrors of war in so alarming a manner that it has caused many to declare that they wou'd suffer death rather than kill even an enemy—this is a new doctrine and inculcated by some sensible preachers from England, which I am told is paid by the Ministry through Wesley for this purpose—it must be discountenanced, or all torys [sic] will plead religion as excuse, and get license to preach.

One patriot Anglican minister in Virginia, to the consternation of a Methodist preacher who was present at the time, publicly declared that Methodists were "sent here by the English ministry to preach up passive obedience and non-resistance." The anxiety of Virginia's leaders was undoubtedly fed by the growing pacifism of Virginia's Methodists, not to mention reports of open loyalism among Methodists on Maryland's Eastern Shore. Earlier, Devereux

Jarratt, a leading Anglican preacher in the southside of Virginia with a strong Methodist leaning, reported that when Thomas Rankin, one of Wesley's lieutenants touring America, spoke at a revival, the congregants were deeply moved, and "the unhappy dispute between England and her colonies, which just before had engrossed all our conversation, seemed now in most companies to be forgot." These were hardly words of encouragement to a local Anglican elite seeking to mobilize the populace. In this context, the rapid growth in Methodism in the early years of the war takes on an entirely new, menacing, and political (rather than purely religious) significance.[17] Moreover, the fact that Methodists were still part of the Church of England (until 1784) created the opportunity for the British ministry to engage them more effectively without compromising its view of a postwar ecclesiastical settlement. Add to this the observation that the especially close relationship of the Wesley brothers— Charles an even stronger Tory than John—to Lord Mansfield and Lord Dartmouth gave "something of a more authoritative cast to what is said by him [John] on this occasion," and an intriguing opportunity for counterrevolutionary efforts presents itself.[18]

In spite of the intriguing possibilities, there is no real evidence that the British were seeking to manipulate dissent in America by appealing to American Methodists or paying Wesley to do so. Nor is this a matter of historical oversight: Wesley's vocal and effective Toryism in England has received extensive scrutiny. As the conflict between the American colonies and the metropole increased, Wesley initially evidenced some sympathy for the colonists' position; most famously, in June 1775, he wrote letters to Lord Dartmouth and Lord North indicating that "he did not think the measures which had been taken with regard to America could be defended 'on the foot of law, equity or prudence.'" Wesley went on to warn of strong disaffection in the British hinterlands to the loss of trade brought on by the American dispute. By October, however, with the extent of the American military rebellion and the challenge to British authority becoming evident after reports of Bunker Hill reached England, and with the king having issued a proclamation labeling the Americans rebels in August, Wesley's position had shifted to being clearly and emphatically Tory with the publication of *A Calm Address to the American Colonies*, an abbreviated version of Dr. Samuel Johnson's pamphlet *Taxation No Tyranny*.[19]

What was criticized by protagonists as Wesley's newfound Toryism was not really new at all. In the 1760s, partially in response to criticism that had been leveled at British Methodists, Wesley had been a strong Tory, supporting King George and his ministry against growing and vocal domestic opposition. With Methodists in England subject to official censure and unofficial violent attack, Wesley was committed to maintaining his position, believing that the loyalty of the Methodists to the Crown would be rewarded with acceptance or at least neutrality by officials in ecclesiastical disputes between Methodists and other Anglicans. As American protests led to war against the Crown and the Crown made clear its views that the so-called patriots were traitors, Wesley's apparent support for the Americans evaporated.[20]

As the American war dragged on, Wesley became increasingly vocal and increasingly Tory. In 1776, he published *A Seasonable Address to the More Serious Part of the Inhabitants of Great Britain, Respecting the Unhappy Contest between Us and Our American Brethren with an Occasional Word Interspersed to Those of a Different Complexion.* The next year, he wrote *A Calm Address to the Inhabitants of England,* which specifically appealed to British Methodists for loyalty to the Crown. In 1778, Wesley twice engaged printers to publish first *A Serious Address to the People of England, with Regard to the State of the Nation,* and then *A Compassionate Address to the Inhabitants of Ireland.* In all, he issued eight pamphlets or open letters opposing the American patriot movement.[21]

Importantly, Wesley's actions were not focused on American Methodists at all. Each of these works was aimed at encouraging support of the government by Methodists in Britain. In fact, although his first *Calm Address* was nominally addressed to the colonies, he had a British audience in mind for that publication as well. A contemporary reviewer in the *London Magazine* wrote, "This *calm address* was printed to *inflame* the breast of the English against their American brethren." Copies of *A Calm Address* were sent to New York for distribution, but a friend of Methodist interests wisely had the copies destroyed—although certainly Wesley's loyalism became well known in America. In contrast, his direct appeals to Americans only encouraged neutrality. In March 1775 in a letter to Thomas Rankin, Wesley told American Methodist preachers, "say no word against one or the other side," and avoid politics—interesting advice in light of his own actions in England. Charles Wesley also told Rankin to take neither side. As if to emphasize the point, Wesley recalled all the British Methodist preachers in America, and all but Francis Asbury complied.[22]

Throughout the period, Wesley made it clear that his real concern was with vocal domestic unrest in Britain and the possibility of revolution in England. After the 1775 publication of *A Calm Address,* Wesley wrote in his journal: "Need any one ask from what motive this was wrote? Let him look round: England is in a flame!—a flame of malice and rage against the King, and almost all that are in authority under him. I labour to put out this flame." He traveled to Bristol in February 1777 to discourage domestic unrest. Later he endorsed a proposal for the enlistment of British Methodists in local militia to repel a possible invasion after France entered the war, a far cry from the pacifism of Virginia Methodists.[23]

Wesley angrily responded to claims that he was paid by the ministry, not-ing that at his station in life—he was seventy-three years old in 1776—and hav-ing refused numerous opportunities for personal advancement, he was not interested in ministry support. He declared in a letter to *Lloyd's Evening Post* that he wrote *A Calm Address* "Not to get money." "Not to get preferment for myself or my brother's children." "Not to please any man living, high or low." Rather, he sought to quiet British unrest and to end the war. Certainly, as the British ministry struggled with domestic opposition and flagging recruiting, it welcomed and encouraged support from one of Britain's most popular minis-ters. Although Methodists were still a very small share of the English population, Wesley preached twenty to thirty times a week across England and had extraor-dinary influence. Trading on that popularity, the ministry ordered distribution of his *Calm Address* at parish churches. There is also an indication that the ministry offered him remuneration and advancement, but apparently the Methodist minister rejected such offers other than a contribution of £50 for a chosen charity. Other offers of ministry support were simply turned away.[24]

Despite the rational concern of Virginia recruiters, the British ministry did not utilize Wesley or others to encourage loyalism among Virginia dissenters. Even in the case of Methodists, in which encouragement at that time would not necessarily have been inconsistent with a postwar episcopate, Britain sought to pacify and neutralize the revolt. In fact, for the first several years of the war, the disdain of British officials for American fighting ability tended generally to dis-courage British efforts to enlist military support among the Americans, much less American dissenters. British officials were certainly uninterested in engaging in a dialogue or creating any new political mechanisms that might have brought local dissenters more fully into the polity, potentially republican-izing the system. Any thought of modifying colonial political structure was focused on strengthening the control from Britain and of British institutions, such as the Anglican Church. Thus, the issues of Wesley's reaction to the war and the ministry's reaction to Wesley are emblematic of British treatment of religious dissent during the war. The ministry's concern was focused clearly on assuaging domestic (rather than American) dissenters and did not presage substantial changes in the American political structure. At the same time, the fact that fears of ministry support of American Methodists existed and were expressed by patriot officials suggests that those officials would give even greater attention to their relations with dissenters.

Governor Dunmore sought to awaken loyalism in Virginia for well over a year, but apparently he never appealed directly to dissenters. Episodic actions by British officials during the war suggest that they were aware of the potential importance of dissenters to effective mobilization in America, and one might have expected them to convert that awareness into action, capitalizing on the historic association of royal officials with protection of dissenters. Yet the British failed to do so. When the topic was considered, British strategists did not see the issue of religious toleration as presenting a significant opportunity; in fact, they concluded that they had been far too tolerant during the colonial period and planned a much strengthened Anglican Church as part of the postwar regime, effectively precluding action during the war to use improved toleration or religious freedom to encourage support. Nonetheless, patriots were troubled by the threat of British-encouraged loyalism among religious groups, especially the Methodists. As a result, rather than being an impediment to successful mobilization, the differences between Virginia's establishment leaders and dissenters became an opportunity to encourage mobilization and broaden participation in the revolutionary polity while the war reversed the position of the local elite and the British government in terms of the promise to dissenters.

That Virginia's establishment leaders sought to encourage mobilization among dissenters is clear. What is less clear is whether dissenters did, in fact, mobilize to meet the promise and hope of the negotiations. Addressing this issue requires some comparative analysis of the mobilization of the dissenters and establishment supporters in Virginia. Equally, consideration of the role of dissenters in other Southern colonies that did not benefit from such intense negotiations might inform the answer.

Did the Dissenters Fight?

Governor Henry of Virginia has published a proclamation...recommend[ing] to the clergy of all denominations to stir up the people & incite them to enter in to the service, which they generally comply with most heartily, especially those famously called dissenters & most of all the Presbyterians who have always been furious in the cause.

—Robert Honyman, *Diary, 1776–1782*
(March 4, 1777)

Religious denominations in the early nineteenth century wrapped themselves in a patriotic mythology concerning the Revolution, recounting their unequaled role in winning the war to encourage their own growth. Sectarian sources trumpeted a virtually universal patriotism of Baptists and Presbyterians. In 1784, the Hanover Presbytery reported, "we shun not a comparison with any of our brethren for our efforts in the cause of our Country." Robert Howell declared in *The Early Baptist of Virginia* that during the war "not a Baptist could be found in Virginia, minister or layman, who did not espouse, and at every sacrifice and to the last extremity defend, the cause of liberty." Robert Howison agreed that "no class of the people of America were more devoted advocates of the principles of the Revolution, none were more willing to give their money and goods to their country, none more prompt to march to the field of battle, and none more heroic in actual conflict than the Baptists of Virginia."[1] Claims for the unmatched role of sectaries outside of Virginia were equally broad and even less well founded. The Presbyterian Synod of New York and Philadelphia sent a pastoral letter in May 1784 claiming "the general and almost universal attachment of the Presbyterian body to the cause of liberty," a claim certainly not justified by activity in the South. Ernest Thompson states that Scotch-Irish Presbyterians supported the Revolution "almost to a man," albeit later conceding a bit more realistically that "Presbyterians, other than the Scots, for the most part gave . . . their full support." One early Baptist historian concluded that "we have no record of so much as one thorough Baptist story [sic]."[2] Although these claims made great press, they did not always provide a fair characterization nor, certainly, adequate documentation. Unfortunately, such early sectarian histories, while usually emphatic about the triumphal role of their coreligionists, have been often accepted or rejected without careful scrutiny.

These heroic accounts leave us with the question as to whether Virginia's dissenters mobilized effectively as promised in the negotiations with establishment leaders. After all, with the discrimination and persecution that the Anglican political establishment had visited on dissenters prior to the war, it was far from evident that dissenters would fully support mobilization against Britain called for by those same establishment leaders. William Cathcart, another nineteenth-century Baptist historian, explained:

> It was a serious thing for our Baptist fathers to throw away this refuge [the British Crown], this last hope in many a gloomy day, and trust their religious rights to men who were executing laws full of tyranny up to the commencement of the Revolution. And it was a little difficult to join the same military company with the tax-gatherer who had robbed you by due process of law, the constable who had lodged you or your widowed sister or mother in prison because conscience forbade the payment of a tax to support religion, or the jailer who had put you in the stocks or scourged you for preaching Jesus, or with the justice who had condemned you.

Given the number of dissenters who had been jailed or beaten for preaching, Cathcart's admonition should not be dismissed as mere hyperbole. In fact, prewar antagonism between local establishment leaders and dissenters in other colonies and Britain's historic role as a defender of dissent often contributed to loyalism among dissenters in other states who had far less cause to distrust their establishment leaders than did those in Virginia, particularly the scores of dissenting leaders who had personally suffered persecution. These challenges were not merely left unanswered at the altar of republican principle. As historian Richard Beeman notes, "shared belief in the ideological abstractions of republicanism, . . . is certainly not sufficient explanation for the unity of allegiance within the Virginia backcountry, for Baptists and Anglicans seem to have shared the principles of republicanism in the Carolina backcountry as well, yet unity obviously did not automatically follow." Considered from that perspective, if Virginia's dissenters did mobilize effectively, that fact provides additional evidence to understand and analyze the course of negotiations with establishment leaders.[3]

Unfortunately, eighteenth-century military records do not list the religious affiliation of recruits, and, even if they did, the lack of accurate aggregate data on denominational support by colony or county would make evaluation of such information difficult. As a result, alternative means must be considered to evaluate dissenters' support for mobilization.

Clergy Mobilization

Evaluating the relative mobilization of various denominations can begin by considering mobilization of their clergy. The social prominence of eighteenth-century clergy suggests that their activity might provide a reasonable means to assess mobilization of their congregations. Several factors complicate such a review, however. Evaluating dissenting ministers' actions is made more difficult by the relative lack of journals, letters, and sermons. Published collections of revolutionary sermons have very limited entries from Virginia, much less from the state's dissenting population. Baptist ministers in Virginia were largely unschooled, making analysis of their support for the American Revolution particularly difficult. Furthermore, at least some dissenting ministers claimed to eschew a political position for religious reasons. Still, available information shows a pattern of dissenting ministers supporting the war; whereas Anglican ministers tended to be better represented in high-ranking political and military positions during the Revolution, the prevalence of dissenting ministers in the military, especially given exemptions from muster for dissenting ministers after 1775, is telling.[4]

Initially, an evaluation might be made by identifying the share of the clergy of each denomination that were loyalists. Although this is a relatively easy comparative analysis, it is also largely unhelpful. As the sectarian histories urge, there are no recorded instances of loyalists among the Virginia Baptist and Presbyterian clergy. There were several pacifist Baptist ministers in the state, including the Reverend Martin Kaufman in the Shenandoah Valley who had a Mennonite background and John Koontz in Culpeper, but Baptists generally disassociated from the pacifists, and in any case, pacifism cannot be equated with Toryism.[5] At the same time, a substantial number of Anglican clergy were British loyalists. After a detailed study, historian Otto Lohrenz concludes that thirty-one of Virginia's Anglican ministers showed, at some time, disapproval of revolution (with twenty-two neutrals and fifty-two patriots); his estimate of loyalists includes, perhaps too conservatively, eleven clergy who were "irresolute... both Tories and Whigs at different stages during the Revolution." These irresolute ministers, many of whom supported the patriot movement initially but tired of the war and the demand for independence, might have been classified patriots or neutrals. A similar analysis by Nancy Rhoden, while a bit less conservative with the irresolute clergy, is of the same general order (twenty-eight loyalist Anglican clergy, fifty-eight who supported the patriots, and forty-four neutral). William Parks and R. S. Thomas suggest a much lower rate of loyalism among Anglican ministers, but their analyses are probably somewhat too sympathetic to Anglican interests. George MacLaren Brydon, in his detailed history of Virginia's early Anglican Church, notes that seventy Anglican ministers declared loyalty to America while nineteen "disappeared" from public records after the establishment salary was eliminated; these may have been loyalists unwilling to take an oath or may simply have had to make a living; some were elderly and retired or died.[6] For these purposes, a precise figure is not necessary; a reasonable estimate is that between 50 percent and 75 percent of Virginia's Anglican ministers supported the patriot movement; loyalists accounted for 15–30 percent, with the remainder neutral. It is noteworthy that loyalism among the native-born Anglican clergy was quite low. In any case, while the extent of Anglican loyalism has often been overstated and is difficult to determine with precision, all the sources agree that there were a number of loyalist Anglican ministers; there is no doubt that loyalism among Baptist and Presbyterian ministers in Virginia, even if not nonexistent, did not begin to approach that of Anglican ministers.[7]

Still, looking alone to the share of loyalism among the clergy is likely to be a poor surrogate for mobilization of denominational laity given that Anglican ministers had taken loyalty oaths to the king as part of the ordination ceremony, and a significant share of them were born in Britain. In this regard, the Anglican clergy were simply not representative of the laity. Nonetheless, other evidence of active involvement in political affairs, preaching, and mobilization in support of the Revolution, while showing the dominant place of Anglicans in the prewar social hierarchy, also demonstrates at least as effective mobilization by Baptists and Presbyterians, more so in critical respects.

When the First Continental Congress called on each colony to enforce a trade embargo against Britain by appointing county committees, a very substantial share of Virginia's Anglican ministers were elected to serve on the resulting Committees of Safety, which assumed political leadership of the opposition to Britain in the early days of the Revolution, a far higher share than in the case of Presbyterians and Baptists. Here, too, other studies have documented this phenomenon. Lohrenz provides a detailed review of Committees of Safety, finding that twenty-five Anglican ministers were elected to county committees; three declined (apparently as latent Tories); of the twenty-two who served, eighteen played particularly active roles. Of the approximately 125 Anglican ministers at the beginning of the war, this suggests that over 17 percent served on county committees. Anglican ministers were serving on the committees in twenty of sixty Virginia counties. This is a remarkably high participation rate for clergy in the political committees that controlled Virginia as it broke from Britain.[8]

While some dissenting ministers served on various county committees, the dissenters could not begin to match the contribution of the Anglican clergy either in absolute terms or the percentage of their ministers who served. Presbyterian ministers served on the county committees in Bedford (David Rice), Fincastle (Charles Cummings, chairman), Louisa (John Todd), Prince Edward (Richard Sankey and Samuel S. Smith), and Washington Counties (Charles Cummings, chairman, after the formation of Washington County in 1777). Reuben Ford, in Goochland County, was apparently the only Baptist minister to serve in this capacity. Had the Presbyterian and Baptist ministers participated on committees at a level comparable to that of the Anglicans, there would have been seventeen Baptist committee members and thirteen Presbyterian.[9]

This evidence also does not support a negative inference concerning mobilization by Virginia dissenters. Given the social and political position of dissenters and Anglicans before the war and eighteenth-century social hierarchy, it should be no surprise that proportionally more Anglican ministers served on the committees in the early days of the conflict. Moreover, the committees, whose primary functions were replaced by the time of the 1776 Virginia Constitution, were active during a period when dissenters' claims for religious freedom—and concomitant promises to support the state leadership—were only beginning to gain a favorable hearing from the establishment. If anything, this evidence suggests that in the early period of the war Anglicans continued to dominate the political system, that many of Virginia's leaders continued to hold dissenters at arm's length, and that republicanization of the polity had to await the revolutionary conflict.

A similar pattern is evident in the appointment of chaplains and surgeons, with Anglican ministers dominating these prestigious positions in Virginia. Such appointments certainly evidenced support of the patriot cause, but the relative absence of dissenting ministers is again more indicative of the strength of prewar social hierarchy (and lack of formal education, in the case of Baptists) than lack of support for mobilization by dissenters. As William Taylor Thom explained in his nineteenth-century study: "Of course, these positions [chaplaincies] would go to the clergy of the Establishment, ten shillings a day and all. The Baptists could hardly hope to get any of the appointments."[10]

Lohrenz identifies eighteen Virginia Anglican ministers as chaplains (fifteen military, three legislative). There were a number of Presbyterian chaplains—including Amos Thompson, Philip Vickers Fithian, Charles Cummings, Andrew Hunter, Joseph Rhea, Robert McMordie, Daniel McCalla, and John Todd—but still proportionately far less than the Anglicans. Several Baptist ministers visited military camps specifically to preach to Baptist recruits, but none appear to have been formally appointed as chaplains. Here again, as one early historian noted of chaplains: "A vast number were appointed more for their outside general influence, than because they were earnest, self-denying ministers of God." Similarly, with respect to surgeons, at least two of Virginia's Anglican ministers filled the role; there is no indication of dissenting ministers serving in this capacity.[11]

A far more interesting picture appears, however, when enlistment by Virginia clergy is considered. There are certainly well-known instances of Virginia clergy taking up arms and, on occasion, leading their congregations to war. Most famously, Peter Muhlenberg, an Anglican minister from the Shenandoah Valley, was appointed colonel of the Virginia Eighth (German) Regiment and rose to the rank of major general. As his last clerical function, on January 21, 1776, Muhlenberg is said to have preached a sermon based on Ecclesiastes 3:1–8 ("There is a time for everything, and a season for every activity under heaven: . . . a time for war and a time for peace") and concluded by removing his clerical robes to reveal his uniform and ordering a drummer to beat for an enlistment to begin on the spot. While some question this oft-repeated story, its long lineage and absence of early contradictory statements suggest that it has at least some basis in truth. Undoubtedly, the former Anglican rector became an important military leader. Before the war, Muhlenberg preached to valley Lutherans as well as Anglicans, and both the Anglicans and Lutherans claim him as one of their own. Yet he was ordained by the Bishop of London so that he might become rector of the parish church in Dunmore (later Shenandoah) County and was apparently never formally ordained in the Lutheran Church. He is appropriately considered Anglican for these purposes.[12]

Several other Anglican ministers also provided military service. Charles Thurston of Frederick County was a colonel. James Madison, a future bishop of Virginia and a cousin of the future president of the same name, organized students at William and Mary into a militia and saw active service as a captain during several raids. Samuel McCroskey, Isaac Avery, and Benjamin Sebastian served. Adam Smith of Botetourt Parish was a private soldier in a campaign against the Cherokees. In addition, Robert Andrews gave up his position as an Anglican rector and enlisted to support his family, becoming initially a chaplain and then a major general of militia during the Yorktown campaign.[13] Neither Baptist nor Presbyterian ministers could match the rank of Anglican ministers serving in the military, again evidencing the social rank of Church of England ministers before the war and Anglican control of the polity. The total extent of dissenting ministers' military service, however, provides a very different picture.

Baptist ministers, in particular, appear regularly on the rolls. Especially interesting is the number of Baptist ministers willing to serve even though they had personally suffered persecution at the hands of the establishment. Dissenting ministers' service even when not (perhaps especially when not) commissioned as officers, likely played an important part in encouraging mobilization among dissenting congregations. The impact of clergy enlistment on their congregations was likely also enhanced by the 1775 expansion of exemptions from militia muster to include dissenting ministers licensed by their own societies. In fact, while Anglican ministers who enlisted tended to dissolve their clerical ties, with Muhlenberg being the most famous example, Baptists and Presbyterian ministers who took up a weapon to fight alongside their congregants seemed to maintain their ministry and establish a new level of authority and prestige in the community.

Given the dominance of Presbyterians in the Shenandoah Valley, a substantial share of the recorded service of Presbyterian ministers was in the various campaigns against the Indians or involved short-term militia service when the valley appeared threatened. Charles Cummings, sometimes referred to as the "fighting parson of Fincastle County," engaged in fighting Indians during the war and served as a chaplain on the 1776 expedition against the Cherokees. William Graham, rector of Liberty Hall (the predecessor of Washington and Lee University) and an important participant in the battle over religious liberty (especially in 1784–85), served as captain for his congregation (Timber Ridge and Hall's Meeting House). John Blair Smith, also an active participant in the debates over a general tax assessment for religion in 1784–85, was captain of students at Hampden-Sydney Academy. John Todd, who signed several petitions on religious freedom as moderator of the Hanover Presbytery, including the critically important petition in October 1776 that demanded an end to the establishment tax, is listed as a colonel in the Louisa militia, and Benjamin Erwin is listed as an ensign in Rockingham. It is not clear, however, whether any of these latter four participated in active duty. Several other Presbyterian clergy apparently also had at least some military service during the war, including Samuel Doak, John McMillan, and James Mitchel. A number of Presbyterian ministers, including William Graham, Archibald Scott, James Waddell, and John Brown, served informally in 1781 when British Colonel Banastre Tarleton threatened the valley after surprising Thomas Jefferson and the Virginia General Assembly in Charlottesville.[14]

Compared to either the Anglicans or Presbyterians, a large number of Baptist ministers provided active military service. Most notably, at least nine Baptist ministers who had suffered significant persecution for their prewar preaching served during the Revolution. William McClanahan, a Baptist minister who had suffered incarceration, formed a company of the Culpeper Minutemen. The Reverend David Barrow, who had been seized and dunked in response to his preaching, served in the army. Joseph Anthony, who had also suffered imprisonment, served as an officer. Jeremiah Moore, who had been jailed and attacked by a mob led by a magistrate, served as a corporal. John Burrus (imprisoned in Caroline County), John Shackleford (imprisoned in Essex and King & Queen Counties), John Young (imprisoned in Caroline County), John Weatherford (imprisoned in Chesterfield County), William Webber (imprisoned in Chesterfield and Middlesex Counties), and John Corbley (imprisoned in Orange and Culpeper Counties) served. Ambrose Dudley, a Separate Baptist preacher, became a captain in the Virginia Line. Baptist ministers Lewis Conner, John Courtney, Robert Murrell, William Cave, and William E. Waller also saw active service, several for extended periods.[15]

In addition, a Joseph Spencer of Orange County became a captain in the Continental Line, and a Joseph Spencer was jailed in Orange County before the war for preaching as an unlicensed Baptist, although he heatedly denied being an Anabaptist. Lewis Little concludes that the jailed preacher and captain were one and the same. Although this is probably correct, there is some question in this regard. While Captain Joseph Spencer fought at Brandywine (September 11, 1777) and supposedly endured the rigors of Valley Forge (1777–78), a Joseph Spencer signed a petition in Orange County asking for a division of the county docketed by the General Assembly on November 17, 1777. (A Joseph Spencer from Orange County reappears as a friend of James Madison in the battle over adoption of the constitution.) Although Spencer was likely another persecuted Baptist minister serving in the military, some caution here is necessary.[16]

In any case, the participation of Baptist and Presbyterian ministers in the military, including at least nine Baptists who had personally suffered persecution at the hands of the establishment, and a number of others who certainly suffered the indignities of being dissenting ministers in prerevolutionary Virginia, suggests that dissenting ministers, as they had promised, responded strongly to calls for mobilization, with their example inevitably serving as a forceful exhortation to their congregants.

In fact, looking beyond personal service, Virginia's political establishment probably saw the most useful role for dissenting clergy in encouraging their congregants to support the war. Community leaders' support of enlistment and provision of material support were central to Virginia's ability to mobilize, and dissenting ministers' roles in the community were increasing with the size of their congregations. There is some indication that precisely this support is what establishment leaders were seeking as they negotiated liberalized restrictions on religious liberty. Edmund Randolph, for example, noted that dissenting ministers' style of preaching and experience in public exhortation particularly suited them to recruiting. "The Presbyterian clergy were indefatigable. Not depending upon the dead letter of written sermons they understood the mechanism of haranguing and had often been whetted in disputes on religious liberty so nearly allied to civil." Nicholas Cresswell, an English traveler in Alexandria, recorded in 1776 that "the Presbyterian Clergy are particularly active in supporting the measures of Congress from the Rostrum, gaining proselytes, persecuting the unbelievers, preaching up the righteousness of their cause and persuading the unthinking populace of the infallibility of success." Baptist ministers played a similar role. In 1775, when the Baptists petitioned the House of Delegates for improved toleration and specifically declared that the war was "just" and their members free to enlist, "they tendered the services of their pastors in promoting the enlistment of the youth of their religious persuasion." Reportedly James Madison often later recalled that the Baptists "when hope was sinking...declared that the tenets of their religion did not forbid their fighting for their country, and that the pastors of their flocks would animate the young of their persuasion to enlist for battles."[17]

The vicissitudes of recruiting and the dynamics of negotiations seemed to drive specific government requests for the support of dissenting clergy. In February 1777, shortly after dissenters were exempted from establishment taxes, and with the war and recruitment going very badly, Governor Patrick Henry issued a proclamation seeking to improve recruiting for the Continental Army. In that proclamation, he specifically called on all officers of the state and asked "the clergy of every denomination, to exert in their several stations that influence which they possess over the people." Contemporaries believed this call was directed particularly to and taken up by dissenting ministers. Dr. Robert Honyman recorded in his diary that

> Governor Henry of Virginia has published a proclamation abolishing
> the scheme of raising volunteer companies it is thought to be a
> hindrance to the recruiting men for the regular regiments; among
> other things in the proclamation he recommends to the clergy of all

denominations to stir up the people & incite them to enter in to the service, which they generally comply with most heartily, especially those famously called dissenters & most of all the Presbyterians who have always been furious in the cause.

The call for "clergy of every denomination" to come to the aid of the state was itself a recognition of the growing role of dissenters in the new commonwealth.[18]

In January 1778, with George Washington's army still suffering at Valley Forge and before France agreed to enter the war, "Mr. Jeremiah Walker of the Baptist Society" was approached by Governor Henry, with the concurrence of the governor's council, to use his influence with the Baptists to increase enlistments. Henry's decision to turn publicly to Walker is significant. Not only had Walker been heavily persecuted (jailed in Chesterfield, fought in James City, sued in Lunenburg), he also played a key role in drafting and presenting the Baptist petitions seeking improved religious liberty. Walker had participated in the petitioning process since at least 1772 and continued to do so throughout the war; along with the Reverend John Williams, he had signed the letter on behalf of Baptists congratulating Henry on his election as the first governor of the state of Virginia and urging him to support religious liberty. Walker was later involved in the May 1780 petition against the marriage and vestry laws. Not unimportantly, Walker was also reportedly one of the most effective preachers in the state, called by one contemporary the "greatest preacher I ever heard." In 1778, presumably well aware of Henry's and Walker's discussions and seeing an improved opportunity to press the negotiations, Walker and Elijah Craig, who had also been repeatedly jailed for preaching, were appointed by the Baptist General Association to lay grievances before the assembly, especially opposition to a proposed general assessment.[19]

Evidence also suggests that as the dialogue with the state political leadership continued, dissenting ministers took extra pains to encourage support for mobilization. For example, Presbyterian Caleb Wallace considered joining the service as a military chaplain but concluded (perhaps conveniently) that he was more useful staying at home encouraging support. When Presbyterian John Blair Smith, described as one of the best recruiters in the state, hurried to join Prince Edward militia marching to meet Nathaniel Greene at Guilford Court House in early 1781, he arrived at an evening encampment late and with badly blistered feet; he was advised by military officers that he would serve his country best by returning to his pulpit and exhorting in favor of mobilization.[20]

The active role of a number of dissenting ministers in enlisting recruits has been recorded; these included Presbyterians John Blair Smith, William Graham, and Caleb Wallace and Baptists Jeremiah Walker, William McClanahan, and

Elijah Craig. David Rice, a Presbyterian minister and member of the Bedford County Committee of Safety, preached sermons that "opposition to the claims of the British Parliament are very just and important...resistance is justified by the laws of God and the dictates of common sense." Presbyterians John Brown, Archibald Scott, and James Waddell also urged support for the war. Presbyterian Charles Cummings "contributed much to kindle the patriotic fire which blazed forth so brilliantly among the people of Holston in the Revolutionary War." Baptist minister Daniel Marshall "was unremitting in his patriotic appeals in behalf of the struggle for independence, notwithstanding he was several times warned and threatened by the British soldiery."[21]

These ministers' role as opinion leaders could be highly significant for mobilization. William Sprague, who collated biographical information on early ministers in the nineteenth century, provides one example involving a Presbyterian minister who was actively involved in the pursuit of religious freedom:

> On a certain occasion, when, by invitation of the Executive authority
> of the State, it was resolved to raise a volunteer company of riflemen,
> to go into active service, there appeared much backwardness in the
> men to come forward,—he [William Graham] stepped out, and has
> his own name enrolled, which produced such an effect that the
> company was immediately filled, of which he was unanimously
> chosen Captain; and all necessary preparations were made for
> marching to the seat of war, when General Washington signified to
> the Governors of the States, that he did not wish any more volunteer
> companies to join the army.

While their military service was laudable, the exhortation of dissenting ministers in favor of mobilization probably provided their most significant contribution to the cause of the Revolution in Virginia.[22]

Anglican ministers also preached in favor of the patriot cause, and certainly, many of them would be known by their congregations as patriots. Perhaps the most celebrated of the surviving Anglican patriotic sermons is that of the Reverend David Griffith, later the first bishop-elect of Virginia, on December 31, 1775, for which the Virginia Convention resolved to express its thanks and appreciation. In that sermon, Griffith defined the bounds of obedience to civil authority and, in a passage that came closest to encouraging express support for the rebellion, explained,

> but it is high time that the mists of errour should be removed from
> the eyes of every American, from every friend to truth and justice;
> that while selfish and unworthy motives actuate some, others may

not be prevented, by bigotry, from uniting in the most important
cause that ever engaged their concern.

I would not be thought to stand here "*a mover of sedition*" or an
advocate of licentiousness. It would ill become this sacred place, and
the character of a minister of the gospel of Christ, to inspirit rebellion
and foment disorder and confusion: But it becomes us, highly, to
remove every impediment from the progress of truth and justice to
espouse the cause of humanity and the common rights of mankind.

Other Anglican ministers were also known to preach in support of the revolutionary government, including John Bracken, Charles Clay, Thomas Dade,
Alexander Balmaine, Thomas Smith II, and John Campbell. Yet Muhlenberg's
example notwithstanding, there are few recorded instances of Anglican clergy
actually urging military enlistment from the pulpit and fewer still of Anglican
ministers joining their congregants as enlisted men. Of course, there may be
many reasons for this lacuna. Certainly, few of the sermons of this era survive.
Furthermore, Anglican worship in the latter part of the eighteenth century
tended not to lend itself to such passionate appeals. Anglican minister William
White, while supporting the patriots, explained that he "never beat the ecclesiastical drum. . . . Being invited to preach before a battalion, I declined and mentioned to the colonel . . . my objections to making of the ministry instrumental
to the war."[23] Still, the consistency and importance of preaching mobilization
by dissenting ministers is not matched in the record of Anglican ministers.

Although the extent of preaching and exhortation cannot easily be quanti-
fied, it is evident that such support was part of what establishment leaders
expected of dissenters in return for greater religious freedom, that political
leaders called on dissenters to make good on such commitments, and that generally, dissenting ministers did take an active part in encouraging enlistment
and mobilization in support of the war effort.

A clear pattern of Anglican ministers' participation in political and high-ranking military roles, especially early in the war, certainly evidences Anglican
support for the war but also shows that social hierarchy continued to dominate
in the early war years and that the republicanization of Virginia had not yet
occurred. There is an equally clear pattern of dissenting ministers participating
in enlistment and recruiting (even among those who had been directly persecuted) and of the new government's direct call for their support. It seems highly
unlikely that these men took up arms in defense of a new regime that they
believed, independence won, would return to religious persecution. William
Fristoe, a Baptist minister who had suffered attacks for preaching, explained:

It would leave us to the sore reflection, what have we been struggling for? For what have we spent so much treasure?...Why hear the heart-affecting shrieks of the wounded, and the awful scene of garments enrolled in blood, together with the entire loss of many of our relations, friends, acquaintances and fellow citizens—and after all this, to be exposed to religious oppression, and the deprivation of the rights of conscience, in the discharge of the duties of religion, in which we are accountable to God alone and not to man?

Caleb Wallace made the same point on behalf of the Presbyterians: "If this [establishment] is continued, what great advantage from being independent from Great Britain?"[24]

Given the persecution and marginalization that plagued dissenting ministers before the war, their level of military participation appears to be the direct result of extensive negotiations with their former persecutors. At the same time, the loyalism (and neutrality) that did exist among a significant share of Virginia's Anglican clergy, and the hesitancy of some to participate directly in supporting the war effort, suggests an abandonment of their traditional roles as community leaders—positions that were increasingly filled by dissenting ministers. Thus, the negotiations not only pulled dissenters into the military but also increasingly politicized them in this manner as well, contributing to the republicanization of Virginia.[25]

Data on Mobilization

Although eighteenth-century records do not permit a full analysis of enlistment by denomination, available data do permit consideration of the mobilization of dissenters in counties with some or strong Baptist and Presbyterian presence. Given a substantial interest in sectarian sources in aggrandizing the role that their fellow sectaries, particularly ministers, played in the war, these data provide an important tool to check and confirm conclusions drawn from anecdotal information. This analysis suggests that as the war and improvements in religious liberty progressed, Baptist and Presbyterian areas of Virginia generally mobilized more effectively than did Anglican areas.[26]

Data from 1776—collated by Thomas Jefferson—show a relatively limited variation in the enlistments by counties based on the presence of dissenting churches (see table 4.1). While the lowest response rate at the time was from counties designated as "Other" (Anglican for these purposes), 6.1 percent of their militia was raised for service; this compares to an average of only 6.8 percent; no group of

TABLE 4.1. County Response to Mobilization in 1776

Counties	1777 Militia	Raised 1776	Percentage
Baptist (15)	12700	894	7.0
Strong Baptist (22)	19444	1346	6.9
Presbyterian (15)	10522	738	7.0
Strong Presbyterian (15)	16896	1100	6.5
Other (Anglican) (15)	7884	480	6.1
Total	48779	3330	6.8

Note: Counties adjusted to reflect 1777 configuration; Williamsburg included. Corrects several figures absent in TJ Papers based on Library of Congress copy.

Source: Papers of Thomas Jefferson, 2:130–32.

counties had a higher response rate than 7 percent. This suggests that even early in the war the counties with a high dissenting population were mobilizing at least proportionately to their abilities. It is worth noting that the mobilization rate for "Other" counties is reduced substantially by the very low response rate from Eastern Shore counties where British Governor Dunmore continued to raid.

A more dramatic picture emerges by 1780–81 when the strongest response to specific requisitions for men and supplies came from counties designated as "Strong Baptist" and "Presbyterian," 48.5 percent and 49.8 percent, respectively, compared to an average response rate of 43.2 percent. (As one might expect, the data also show a generally higher response to the requisition of supplies than to the requisitioning of troops.) Mobilization in the "Other" counties (35.1 percent), those most strongly controlled by Anglicans, was the lowest, albeit only marginally lower than counties designated "Baptist." Still, the percentage spread in the county responses is much higher than those from early in the war, and the change suggests growing support from counties with significant dissenting interests. Significantly, the figure for Anglican counties is most seriously affected by an extremely high "no return" rate, 80 percent, suggesting that their level of support might be overestimated (see table 4.2).

This analysis tends to corroborate anecdotal evidence concerning the practice of the clergy, showing that especially as the war (and negotiations and religious liberalization) progressed, dissenting counties generally responded to official requests for support more effectively than counties dominated by Anglicans. Given the serious persecution and discrimination that preceded the war and the dominance of Anglican counties in the General Assembly, the willingness of dissenting counties to mobilize at least as effectively as Anglican counties supports the notion that Virginia dissenters and political leaders engaged

TABLE 4.2. Overall Response to Requisitions, 1780–1781

Counties	1780 men	1781 men	Supplies	Average
% Response				
Baptist (20)	21.2	38.2	59.5	35.2
Strong Baptist (25)	45.7	29.3	57.8	48.5
Presbyterian (15)	45.6	21.8	53.7	49.8
Strong Presbyterian (20)	27.9	29.3	49.1	35.6
Other (Anglican) (15)	39.8	28.1	25.4	35.1
Total	38.4	28.3	56.7	43.2
No Response %				
Baptist	45.0	85.0	73.7	67.9
Strong Baptist	32.0	72.0	36.0	46.7
Presbyterian	6.7	86.7	33.3	42.2
Strong Presbyterian	40.0	70.0	70.0	60.0
Other (Anglican)	66.7	86.7	86.7	80.0

Note: Average in first part of table is average of all county entries, so category weight not equal.

Source: See Appendix B.

in a complex negotiation for mobilization in support of the war effort in return for religious freedom and that the dissenters made reasonable efforts to implement their commitments to mobilize.

Dissenter Experience in Other Southern Colonies

While dissenters in other southern colonies had not suffered nearly as much religious discrimination or persecution at the hands of their local establishments, they were in fact much less likely than their Virginia coreligionists to support the patriot movement with vigor, or, more precisely, they were far more likely to evidence loyalism or neutrality. This raises important questions about the role of the Virginia negotiations in encouraging mobilization.

In North Carolina, as the Revolution approached, relations among the establishment and dissenters were deeply influenced by the Regulator movement of 1766–71 in which western North Carolinians protested against authority exercised by an eastern, gentry elite, particularly gentry control and abuse of the land recording system. While some North Carolina dissenting clergy urged their members to avoid armed support for the Regulators, and Governor William Tryon sought to pacify Scotch-Irish Presbyterian opposition through appeals of Presbyterian ministers who supported the Crown, inevitably, the western-based Regulators were heavily dissenter, both Baptist and Presbyterian, and the force that defeated them at the Battle of Alamance in 1771, largely from eastern North Carolina, was dominated by that colony's Anglican establishment.[27]

After the Alamance defeat, Regulators were required to swear an oath of loyalty to the Crown while their economic, political, and legal concerns generally continued to be ignored by the eastern elite and appointed county leaders. As in Virginia, the same eastern, Anglican elite who controlled the colony provided the leadership for the Revolution in North Carolina.[28] By comparison, former Regulators were well aware that North Carolina's last royal governor, Josiah Martin, had made serious efforts to address their concerns. Moreover, to encourage loyalty among dissenters as the Revolution approached, Martin specifically appealed to immigrants from the Scottish Highlands by promising land, remission of taxes, and forgiveness of arrears on quitrents. In issuing a proclamation demanding loyalty, he appealed to support among evangelicals by chastising the rebel leaders who "extravagantly profane even the most sacred name of the *Almighty* to promote their flagitious purpose of exciting rebellion." As a result, Martin confidently reported to his superiors in London in early 1775 that "people in the Western Counties of this Province, which are by far the most populous, will generally unite in support of Government…with the aid of a considerable Body of Highlanders [largely Presbyterian] in the midland counties." Several months later, he made clear that he expected support not only from the Presbyterian Highlanders but also from the interior of the colony generally, where Baptists were concentrated, telling Dartmouth that he "should be able to draw together…out of the interior Counties of this Province, where the People are in General well affected, and much attached to me, at least two thirds of the fighting men in the whole Country."[29]

Thus, as the American Revolution began, perhaps it was no surprise that when loyalists from North Carolina rallied to the king's banner at the Battle of Moore's Creek Bridge on February 27, 1776, the group was dominated by several hundred former Regulators (likely dissenters) and 700 Scottish Highlander Presbyterians. Many more Regulators initially heeded Governor Martin's call to arms, but reportedly went home before the battle when they found out that the British regulars and Martin, whom they had expected to join them in person, had been delayed and would not be meeting them at Moore's Creek.[30] The drubbing taken by the royalists at Moore's Creek Bridge at the hands of a smaller group of patriots quieted western North Carolina for a number of years, but it certainly did not bring the dissenters to support the patriot movement. In February 1779, when British Colonel Archibald Campbell issued a proclamation rallying American Tories to the defense of Augusta, Georgia, 700 loyalists from North Carolina, many Scottish Highlander Presbyterians, heeded the call before being badly beaten at Kettle Creek, Georgia. A year later, a similar rallying of North Carolina loyalists in the backcountry—again, certainly many dissenters among them—was led by John Moore, who had been second in command at Kettle Creek; the gathering at Ramsour's Mill in June 1780 met with a similar result, however, when 400 patriots expecting the imminent arrival of reinforcements attacked and dispersed 1,000 loyalists. Loyalists dominated by dissenters rose at least three times in North Carolina during the war.[31]

The prominence of Presbyterian Highlanders in many reports should not suggest that loyalism among North Carolina dissenters was limited to Presbyterians or laymen. After Moore's Creek, at least one Presbyterian minister, a Reverend John McLeod, fled North Carolina to join loyalist forces in New York and sought to encourage other North Carolinians to join him. Certainly there was also a substantial Baptist contingent among the North Carolina loyalists. James Childs, a North Carolina Baptist minister, urged his congregation not to support the patriots. Childs reportedly warned "Shew him [Childs] a great man with a half moon in his hatt and Liberty Rote on it and his hatt full of feather [and] he would Shew you a devil...he did not value the Congress nor Commityer no more than a passell of Rackoon Dogs for he got his [commission?] from the king and the field offessers got their Commission from Hell or the Devil." North Carolina Baptist minister William Cook also signed a Tory paper, "The Protest," but was hauled before a county committee and, to avoid more severe treatment, sought instruction, ultimately issuing an apology. James Perry, another North Carolina Baptist minister, was brought before the Anson Committee of Safety, apparently as part of a group that sent allegedly seditious letter to the legislature in 1777. Several of the Baptist ministers, after chastisement, repented, but the difference in dissenters' support for mobilization in Virginia and North Carolina is still notable.[32]

Recognizing the role of dissent among Carolina loyalists, in 1776, Joseph Hewes, a North Carolina delegate to the Continental Congress, asked a committee of Presbyterian ministers in Philadelphia to appeal to their brethren in North Carolina, and at about the same time the Continental Congress ordered "that two Ministers of the Gospel be applied to, to go immediately amongst the Regulators and Highlanders in the Colony of North Carolina, for the purpose of informing them of the nature of the present dispute between Great Britain and the Colonies." Hewes explained to a North Carolina correspondent, "we have prevailed on the Presbyterian Ministers here [Philadelphia] to write to the Ministers and congregations of their Sect in North Carolina,...these people are staunch in our cause and have promised to set their Brethren in North Carolina right." In an earlier letter, 200 copies of which were distributed in North Carolina, Philadelphia Presbyterian ministers warned their North Carolina coreligionists that "if you will offer yourselves to voluntary slavery, and desert the loyal sons of liberty of all denominations in the most honourable and important contest, we can have no fellowship with you." Contributing to this effort to pacify North Carolina Presbyterians, the Reverend Jonathan Witherspoon in 1778 wrote an "Address to the Natives of Scotland Residing in America." In spite of these efforts, these appeals had limited success; North Carolina's dissenting Regulators were simply too well aware that their old Anglican protagonists were leading the Revolution and that British colonial leaders had often sought to protect their interests.[33]

None of this is to suggest that a very large share of dissenters in North Carolina were necessarily loyalists, but the difference between the virtually unanimous patriotism among the Virginia dissenting ministers and the apparently unmatched patriotism of their congregations, in spite of the role of their prewar persecutors in leading the patriot movement, is striking.

Interestingly, the 1776 North Carolina Constitution did support religious liberty and some separation of church and state and did so in a manner ostensibly more fulsome than early efforts in Virginia. Discrimination in the provision of marriages by dissenting ministers was also eliminated in North Carolina in 1776. Yet unlike Virginia, there was no extended and intimate dialogue in North Carolina in which dissenters and establishment leaders negotiated support for the patriot movement in return for support for religious liberty. When North Carolina patriot leaders sought to discourage loyalism among the former Regulators, they sent a delegation made up of a county justice who had participated in the criminal conviction of Regulators, an Anglican militia officer who had fought against the Regulators at Alamance, and a Presbyterian minister who had denounced their efforts. The lack of dialogue in North Carolina among the establishment leaders of the Revolution and different religious groups appears to have had a significant impact on the relative patriot and loyalist support. After all, Virginia dissenters were not innately more cooperative with eastern Anglican leaders than dissenters in North Carolina; rather, the negotiations themselves contributed to the relative unanimity in Virginia.[34]

Failure to develop effective political institutions in western North Carolina became a major impediment when eastern leaders sought dissenter support for the Revolution. In fact, there is some suggestion that in changing suffrage requirements in 1775 so that one needed to be a freeholder to vote for a member of a county committee, North Carolina establishment leaders were specifically seeking to disenfranchise many poor, recently emigrated Presbyterian Highlanders. The fact that the new North Carolina state assembly was far smaller than its colonial assembly, dramatically increasing the apparent distance between local concerns and the legislature, could not have helped, especially in western counties, which had been historically underrepresented. For example, from 1770 to 1780, as the underrepresented backcountry sought an increased role in the polity, the number of adult white males per assemblyman shrunk slightly in Virginia from about 432 to 423, whereas the figure rose dramatically in North Carolina, from 274 to 618. Not only was the overall rate of representation kept relatively constant in Virginia, but with the creation of new western, largely dissenting counties, representation in the Virginia backcountry improved substantially. Thus, Thomas Jefferson's data from 1776 show an average of 526 militiamen per Anglican county and over 1,100 militiamen per county with a strong Presbyterian influence, with very large discrepancies between the number in Anglican counties and other dissenting counties (refer to table 4.1). By the end of the war, however, the number of militiamen in counties with a strong Presbyterian influence had dropped to 721, with comparable drops in other dissenting counties, while the average number from Anglican counties had remained relatively constant. Unlike the situation in North Carolina, Virginia governmental institutions permitted an effective dialogue among western dissenters and the eastern establishment so that dissenters could join the polity and reasonably be urged that their interests lay with the patriots. A critical tangible means of demonstrating those interests was the negotiation with the Virginia establishment of religious freedom.[35]

In South Carolina as well, many Piedmont loyalists were Presbyterian or Baptist and had a well-seated suspicion of eastern Anglicans based on a history of eastern control of political and economic institutions. The result was significant Toryism and a high rate of neutrality among the South Carolina backcountry dissenters. Still, South Carolina dissenters could not point to persecution beginning to approach that suffered by dissenters in Virginia. Here, too, the lack of dialogue between establishment and dissenter groups in South Carolina contributed to this situation.[36]

As in Virginia and the Carolinas, the dissenters in Maryland, growing in number, were required to pay taxes to support Anglican ministers and faced a number of formal and informal means of discrimination, although certainly Virginia dissenters had been treated much more harshly before the war. Methodism, in particular, was active on the Maryland Eastern Shore immediately before and during the war. While John Wesley continued to support a communion with the Church of England, Eastern Shore Methodists were sensitive to the disadvantages and opposition they faced from the established church and its local leaders—not to mention their tax obligations to support Anglican clergy—and were relatively unenthusiastic about the patriot movement. For example, Francis Asbury—who was active in Maryland before the war until the test oath drove him out in 1778 and who led American Methodists after the war—was particular resentful of the treatment of Methodists by Anglicans. Nor was the opposition restricted to Methodist congregants. William Paca told Governor Johnson on September 6, 1777, "I am sorry to inform you of an insurrection of Tories...headed by some scoundrel Methodist Preachers." As compared to dissenters preaching support for the patriot movement and mobilization in Virginia, at least one Methodist minister in Maryland openly preached for the king, stirring up significant opposition to the patriots. Other Methodist ministers in Maryland were equally suspect.[37]

One might note that Methodists were also the most Tory of Virginia sects, but there were significant differences. Loyalism on Maryland's Eastern Shore was not limited to Methodists. Furthermore, sources note more active Toryism among Maryland's Methodists, including armed opposition to state authorities and direct provision of aid to the British, whereas pacifism was more often the complaint against Virginia Methodists. Finally, the Toryism of Maryland Methodists was actively promoted by their preachers.

As in the case of the Carolinas, and in contrast to the situation in Virginia, Maryland patriot leaders failed to engage dissenters effectively during the war. Maryland Methodist ministers were not exempted from militia service, subjecting at least eight to incarceration for failure to serve. In fact, facing Methodist opposition from the Eastern Shore, Maryland's leaders adopted a law requiring a loyalty oath from preachers, which implied a willingness to bear arms and without the normal exemption permitting a solemn affirmation by those of religious scruples, an oath that Anglican leaders knew Methodist preachers would not give on principle. Failure to take the oath subjected one to large tax penalties and a prohibition on preaching. As a result of violations of this law, Maryland officials jailed more than twenty Methodist ministers during the war, a marked contrast with Virginia, where regular incarceration of dissenting ministers effectively ended with the war and exemption of dissenting ministers from military service was finally provided. Similarly, treatment of other pacifists, including Quakers and Mennonites, was far harsher in Maryland than in Virginia, with at least one Dunker hanged in Maryland.[38]

Myriad factors contributed to the different realities in Virginia, the Carolinas, and Maryland, but it is clear that loyalism among dissenters was far more common in these other new states than it was in Virginia. In fact, as a general matter, other Southern states saw a much higher rate of loyalist emigration to

Britain during and immediately after the war than did Virginia. The extended dialogue between establishment and dissenters in Virginia and the willingness to expand dissenter representation were certainly important parts of that milieu. The absence of similar changes in the polity in the other Southern states explains in part the greater difficulty faced by their establishment leaders in incorporating dissenters effectively into the war mobilization.[39]

As the American Revolution raged around and in Virginia, dissenters faced a particular choice of whether to rally to the support of a new government led by their former persecutors. They did so, at least in part as a result of the negotiations for religious liberty. Action by dissenting ministers, particularly their pronounced efforts to preach mobilization and the military service of previously persecuted Baptist ministers, strongly suggests that these patterns did not simply emerge spontaneously. Rather, they were the result of an extended and considered negotiation with establishment leaders. Appeals from the Virginia government for ministerial support suggest the same. By the end of the war, as religious liberty had been substantially ensconced in the structure of the new state government, Richmond increasingly found itself relying on effective mobilization in counties with a strong dissenting presence. The pattern of substantial loyalism among dissenters in other Southern colonies seems altogether absent in Virginia, in spite of the exceedingly raw prewar dissenter–establishment relations in the latter. As Virginia's dissenters participated in the political discussions—primarily through their petitions, but also by the particular participation of key dissenting ministers in discussions in Williamsburg and Richmond and growing legislative representation of western counties—they became part of the polity. This participation was an important factor in supporting effective dissenter mobilization in Virginia and, over time, played an important part in changing the state from a relatively closed, hierarchical society controlled by Tidewater, Anglican elite to a far more republican system.

Yet in spite of these negotiations and the substantial gains made during the course of the Revolution, and in spite of the dissenters' effective mobilization in support of the war effort, religious freedom was incomplete at the war's end, and dissenters continued to petition for reform. With hostilities over, however, dissenters seemed to realize that they might face renewed resistance from Anglican leaders who retained their control of the legislature. As a result, conclusion of the war seemed to make complete religious freedom recede further. Whether and how dissenters could complete the work that was begun would occupy their political efforts after the war.

After the War

Resolved,...the people of this Commonwealth, according to their respective abilities, ought to pay a moderate tax or contribution annually for the support of the Christian religion, or of some Christian church, denomination, or communion of Christians, or of some form of Christian worship.

—Adopted (47–32), *Journal of the House of Delegates*
(November 11, 1784)

After Lord Cornwallis's surrender at Yorktown on October 19, 1781, the Revolutionary War continued for almost two years until the Treaty of Paris was signed. Yet while the war nominally continued, there seemed to be little question among Virginians in the waning days of 1781 that there was cause for celebration. As Virginia Governor Thomas Nelson wrote in October, "this Blow [Yorktown], I think, must be a decisive one, it being out of the Power of G.B. to replace such a Number of good Troops." In spite of continued desultory appeals for support from the Continental Congress, the great pressure for mobilization was eliminated.[1]

The shift in the winds of war and dissipation of the need for mobilization caused a new shift in the political fortunes of Virginia's dissenters. Unfortunately, full religious freedom had not yet been obtained. Even with the 1780 amendments, which authorized marriages by dissenting ministers, dissenters still faced discrimination in the area of marriage. Their ministers had to be licensed by a county court to perform marriages; they could only perform marriages in their own county, and only four dissenting ministers of each denomination could be licensed within a county. Their Anglican counterparts faced none of these restrictions.[2] Anglican vestries continued to be responsible for poor relief, both control of poor taxes and administration of relief (except in seven western counties where reform had been implemented during the war). Dissenters feared that relief subject to such Anglican control could be influenced by "Party Motives."[3] Some dissenters complained that glebes, churches, and other property that had been purchased through general taxes should not continue to be held exclusively by Anglican parishes, as the act that exempted dissenters from establishment taxes had provided.[4] Most fundamentally, there was persisting ambiguity in the protection of religious liberty in Virginia, particularly as it affected church–state relations. The Anglican Church was still nominally the established church, with its mode of worship specified in legislative enactments. Furthermore, since 1776, Virginia had on several occasions considered whether to adopt a general assessment—a government tax to benefit all (or at least all Christian) ministers—and a test or oath act requiring that one swear to certain doctrines before holding office was still a possibility (some form of which had been adopted in most of the new states).

The possibility of a general tax assessment to support religion was of particular concern to dissenters. This matter had been expressly reserved in the 1776 act ending the establishment tax on dissenters. With ministers' incomes having suffered severely, a bill was introduced in 1779 to provide a general assessment for all Christian denominations; that bill also laid down rules of acceptable doctrine, including belief in God, a future state of rewards and punishment, and the divine inspiration of the Old and New Testaments. With strong dissenter opposition and the war moving south—figuratively and literally—the 1779 bill was tabled, but the effort was not abandoned. With the end of the war, Virginia dissenters were very conscious of the fact that their liberties were incomplete and were far from guaranteed.

After Yorktown, Tidewater Anglican leaders—still in control of the General Assembly—saw little reason to accede to further dissenter demands for redress of inequities and improved freedom. With the pressure for mobilization removed, the assembly's response to the regular requests from dissenters for further reform turned from attentive to languid. While many historians have seen adoption of Thomas Jefferson's Statute for Establishing Religious Freedom in 1786 as the natural continuation of the process of liberalization of religious freedom after 1775, such a rarefied perception fails to appreciate the extent to which the postwar legislative machinations provide further evidence of the continued strength of the Anglican establishment, of the nature of the wartime negotiations, and of the fundamental change in Virginia's political process wrought by that dialogue between the dissenters and establishment (see figure 5.1).

FIGURE 5.1. Thomas Jefferson: Remembered for his drafting of the Virginia Statute for Establishing Religious Freedom, Jefferson also played an important part in the end to establishment taxes and religious penalties in 1776. Library of Congress, Prints and Photographs Division, Detroit Publishing Company Collection, Washington, D.C.

Petitioning without Response

Beginning in 1781, once dissenter support for mobilization was no longer needed, continued dissenter petitioning met a wall of silence. This contrasted sharply with circumstances during the war when, in spite of the pressing demands of the war—indeed, because of them—and in spite of repeated Anglican calls for delay, religious issues and dissenters' demands were regularly at the center of the Virginia legislature's agenda. Not so once the war ended.

As early as November 22, 1781, just over a month after Yorktown, petitioners from Prince Edward County, a Presbyterian stronghold, sought dissolution of Anglican vestries and an end to their administration of the poor tax. Less than a month later, that petition was deferred to the next session, when it was rejected. A more detailed Baptist petition of June 3, 1782 also asked for an end to Anglican vestries' governmental functions and added a request to end discrimination in the context of marriages. The first request was, again, rejected; the second deferred to the next session, when no action was taken.[5]

In 1783, the pace of dissenter petitioning accelerated a bit when petitions from Amelia, Essex, and Powhatan County Baptists sought reforms of both marriage and vestry laws. The tone of these petitions was a bit sharper— particularly urging their claims based on dissenters having taken an equal place with members of the establishment in the crisis of war. Frustrated Essex County Baptists noted that action on their grievances was called for "as we have joined with our Brethren in the same Cause of Liberty" and that nothing should remain to "disappoint our Expectation." Amelia County Baptists argued somewhat indignantly that "we cannot conceive that our conduct has been such in the late important Struggle as to forfeit the Confidence of our Countrymen, or that the Church-of-England-Men have rendered such peculiarly meritorious Services to the State, as to make it necessary to continue the invidious Distinctions which still subsist," and Powhatan Baptists urged that they had "freely embarked with our fellow-citizens, in the common struggle for liberty & while we were opposing our enemies in the field . . . part of our petition was granted, but our liberties in full, together with those of other dissenters, are not yet" guaranteed. The Powhatan Baptists not only asked for resolution of their grievances but noted prophetically that they hoped "that no law may pass, to connect the church & state in the future." All were to no avail. Despite the increased pace of petitioning, the questions of vestries and marriages were again taken up by the House in the second session of 1783, but Anglican opponents of reform were once again able to prevent any action from being taken.[6]

On May 26, 1784, the General Assembly received two additional petitions urging further liberalization. The first was from Baptists meeting in King & Queen County. The second—an extended discussion of developments in Virginia concerning religious liberty—came from the Hanover Presbytery. The Presbyterians began by reminding the assembly of their hope that the problem of religious liberty would have been resolved during the war. "An entire and everlasting freedom from every species of ecclesiastical domination, a full & permanent security of the unalienable right of Conscience & private judgment; and an equal share of the protection & favour of Government to all Denominations of Christians, were particular objects of our expectation, and irrefragable claim." Noting that people continued to confuse "the distinction between matters purely religious, and the objects of human Legislation," the Presbytery joined Baptist complaints over vestry laws and restrictions on marriages by dissenting ministers. The Presbytery also observed that the Anglican Church still benefited from quasi-official status and complained that it "is actually incorporated & known in law" and permitted to take and own property as a body, "while other Christian communities are obliged to trust to the precarious fidelity of Trustees chosen for the purpose." A May 8, 1784, letter in the *Virginia Gazette and Weekly Advertiser* more accurately stated that the Anglican Church was "virtually" incorporated, but the effective imbalance in treatment of the institutions was clear. The Presbyterians asked that all churches be treated equally, implying that Presbyterian churches wished to incorporate on a nondiscriminatory basis. In speaking of the war, the growing irritation of the Presbytery was evident:

> We are willing to allow a full share of Credit to our fellow
> citizens, . . . for their spirited exertions in our arduous struggle for
> Liberty, we would not wish to charge any of them, either ministers or
> people, with open disaffection to the common cause of America, or
> with crafty dissimulation or indecision, till the issue of the war was
> certain, so as to oppose their obtaining equal privileges in Religion;
> but we will resolutely engage against any monopoly of the honours
> and rewards of Government by any sect of Christians more than the
> rest, for we shun not a comparison with any of our brethren for our
> efforts in the cause of our Country, . . . and therefore esteem it
> unreasonable that any of them should reap superior advantages for,
> at most, but equal merit.

This convoluted formulation was intended to do exactly the opposite of what it purported: avoid comment on denominations' support for the war. Equally disingenuous was the suggestion that Presbyterians had "hitherto restrained our complaints from reaching our Representatives that we might not be thought to take any advantage from times of confusion, or critical situations of Government in an unsettled state of Convulsion and wars, to obtain what is our clear and uncontestable rights." In any case, this effort, too, fell largely on now deaf establishment ears.[7]

This lengthy and dissimilating Presbytery petition was drafted by a young John Blair Smith, twenty-seven years old at the time and the second rector of Prince Edward Academy, a Presbyterian school shortly to be renamed Hampden-Sydney College (see figure 5.2). Although only ordained in 1779, Smith was an important member of the Presbytery as rector of one of its two

FIGURE 5.2. John Blair Smith: After the war, the Presbyterian president of Hampden-Sydney College initially supported a general assessment to benefit Christian teachers until members of the Presbyterian laity and other Presbyterian ministers rallied against the idea. From Morrison, Alfred J., "College of Hampden-Sydney Dictionary of Biography 1776–1825" (Hampden-Sydney, 1921), plate opposite page 47. Special thanks to Hampden-Sydney College.

schools; not insignificantly, both Patrick Henry and James Madison sat on the board of the Academy. With Reverend William Graham, rector of the second Presbyterian school, Liberty Academy in the Shenandoah Valley (later Washington and Lee University), Smith played a leading role in the events that followed concerning religious liberty and the proposed general assessment. Ironically, it was John Smith's brother, the Reverend Samuel Stanhope Smith, who encouraged the Presbytery to bring Graham to Virginia; Graham proved to be a foil to John Blair Smith's abortive support for a general assessment and was a leader in the campaign for adoption of Jefferson's statute (see figure 5.3).

FIGURE 5.3. William Graham: The president of Presbyterian Liberty Academy (later Washington & Lee University) helped to lead the Presbyterian assault against any form of government support for religion. Special thanks to Washington and Lee University.

At this time, though, with Smith's missive for the Presbytery emblematic, dissenters' pleas for greater freedom and an end to discrimination based on their wartime service were waxing with little apparent effect, a marked departure from the experience during the war. Without the necessity of dissenter support for mobilization, the legislature largely ignored dissenters' continuing requests for further liberalization.[8]

Establishment Resurgent

As time went on, Anglicans saw an opportunity not simply to ignore dissenter requests but to use their continued legislative dominance to revive their flagging church. Beginning at the end of 1783, the Virginia General

Assembly heard a renewed Anglican voice asking for greater state participation in religious matters. First and foremost, Anglicans (Episcopalians after a spring 1784 convention) sought to revive the notion of a general tax assessment to support Christian ministers. As a large share of the population continued to be nominally Episcopalian, such a scheme would effectively guarantee the salaries of Episcopal clergy, stabilize a financial situation that had plagued the clergy since the suspension of the establishment tax in 1776, and encourage renewed calls to the ministry, which had been suspended during the war and in the years immediately thereafter because of the unavailability of ordinations in Britain for American applicants—in short, help renew a clergy in serious disarray. The Episcopalians also sought the right to incorporate formally to hold property as a corporate body. Thus, churches and glebes, which had been expressly left to the Anglican Church when establishment taxes were eliminated, could be better managed and used to support Episcopal ministers. Recognizing that a return to the former exclusive establishment was not practical, the Episcopal community did not see either measure as discriminatory, suggesting that an assessment would benefit all (or at least all Christian) denominations and claiming that any church body might choose to be incorporated.[9]

The Anglicans were not only consciously seeking to recapture ground but recognized that dissenters had lost their primary leverage when the need for wartime mobilization ended. The Reverend David Griffith, who played a leading role in Anglican reorganization and incorporation of the Episcopal Church, and who was the first Virginia nominee for ordination as an Episcopal bishop, noted that while Anglicans should try not to antagonize dissenters unnecessarily, the dissenters' position was undercut by the removal of the common danger. Griffin concluded that during the war it would have been unwise to "interrupt that union which was so necessary for our mutual security and preservation," but the time was now ripe for action.[10]

A general assessment was broached again publicly in a letter in the September 13, 1783, Richmond *Virginia Gazette or American Advertiser* urging that "nations are happy only in proportion as they are *virtuous*" and insisting on the necessity of government support of Christian denominations to support that virtue. Noting the disheartening decline of public virtue during the war and emphasizing the common view that virtue was necessary for sound republican government, and religion for virtue, the author concluded that government had an obligation to support religion. This was a powerful argument in eighteenth-century Virginia as the central role of virtue and religion to sound government was widely conceded, even by those most in favor of full religious liberty. Apparently anticipating opposition to the assessment proposal, nonetheless, the writer expressed confidence to the legislature that "no presbytery can awe your deliberations."

This newspaper volley was supported by an establishment petitioning campaign, with seven petitions between November 1783 and November 11, 1784, urging a general assessment to support Christian ministers, several of which also called for permitting churches to be incorporated. A request from Lunenburg County was received on November 8, 1783, asking that "the reformed Christian religion [be] supported and maintained by a General and equal Contribution of the Whole State upon the most equitable footing that is possible." The Lunenburg petitioners, claiming that they represented "all Sects and Denominations" within the state, endorsed a "free and universal Toleration," but thought that a general assessment would be consistent with that toleration if each taxpayer chose the denomination to which funds would be directed. For these petitioners, religious freedom required only equal treatment of sects, or of Protestant Christian sects, but did not portend a separation of church and state. Before the month was out, Amherst Anglicans joined in seeking legislative action to support "All the sincere & pious Christians of every Denomination." Echoing the words from the *Virginia Gazette* (possibly having been written by the same hand), these petitioners assured the General Assembly, hopefully, that "no big-oted Presbytery can awe your Deliberations," and their call for action was accom-panied by continued support in the newspapers. The Lunenburg petition elicited an initial favorable response from the Committee for Religion, but it was tabled by the House on November 15, 1783. The Amherst petition was referred to the House, but no action was taken on it in that session.[11]

As the legislative session began in May 1784, additional petitions arrived in Richmond calling for a general assessment to benefit Christian ministers; sur-prisingly, little was heard in opposition from dissenters. In an effort to clothe themselves with the public interest, the pro–general assessment petitioners again took up the need for "public virtue" that had been undermined by the demands of the war. From a recognition that religion was essential to public morals, the leap to the necessity of public support for religion seemed small. Thus, Warwick County petitioners reminded the legislature "that it is essen-tially necessary for the good Government of all free States, that some legislative attention should be paid to religious Duties." Powhatan petitioners agreed that "Encouragement & Support of Piety, true Religion, and Learning,...is one of the great Bulwarks of Liberty." Not only did these petitions seek to confirm a governmental role in supporting religion, the authors also sought to reassert their role as societal leaders in this important area.[12]

Having done little for the Episcopal Church other than running inter-ference since 1775, the reaction of the legislature to these new requests was favorable. On May 27, 1784, the Committee for Religion again endorsed the notion of a general assessment. The commanding Patrick Henry urged adoption, noting that other states had such a tax. While James Madison and several others opposed this action, Anglican power in the General Assembly was still deeply seated, and the prospects of the provision were good, certainly far better than the Anglican Church had enjoyed since 1776.[13]

What developed at this point appears to be a coordinated plan by which supporters of the Episcopal Church would seek an assessment and incorporation and, finally, agree to reform marriage and vestry laws to ensure passage of the laws they desired. Having approved an assessment at the end of May and noting expressly petitions from the Episcopal and Presbyterian churches, the Committee for Religion agreed in early June that "incorporation ought to be extended to all other religious societies within this Commonwealth, which may apply for the same." At the same time, referencing memorials from Baptist and Presbyterian churches, the committee finally endorsed vestry and marriage reforms. The resolution from the Committee for Religion was presented to the House by Wilson Miles Cary, a relative of churchman Archibald Cary, who had played a key role in seeking to silence dissent before the war and, with him, a delegate to the 1784 convention that organized the Episcopal Church in Virginia. A law equalizing marriage requirements promptly passed the House in June, only to die with the end of the session in the more conservative Senate. With time in the spring session short, all of these matters were carried over to the fall. In a dramatic change from the war years, in the summer of 1784, it was Episcopalians who were stirring the political pot for action and seemed to be doing so successfully. James Madison, having just returned to the Virginia legislature after four years in the Continental Congress, said of the early 1784 developments:

> Several Petitions came forward in behalf of a Genl. Assessm[en]t which was reported by the Come. of Religion to be reasonable.... The Episcopal Clergy introduced a notable project for re-establishing their independence of the laity. The foundation of it was that the whole body should be legally incorporated, invested with the present property of the Church, made capable of acquiring indefinitely— empowered to make canons & by laws not contrary to the laws of the land, and incumbents when once chosen by Vestries to be immovable otherwise than by sentence of the Convocation. Extraordinary as such a project was, it was preserved from a dishonorable death by the talents of Mr. Henry. It lies over for another Session.

Madison could only await the reconvening of the legislature to seek to derail the reinvigorated establishment effort.[14]

Shortly after the General Assembly reconvened on October 30, 1784, religious liberty and church/state relations again took the "principal attention" of the Virginia polity. This was a marked change in the situation since the end of the war. As an indication of the direction of the leadership, Speaker John Tyler, a Patrick Henry partisan, appointed a conservative Committee for Religion, including many older men who were strong supporters of the Episcopal Church. On November 11, the Committee of the Whole House on the State of the Commonwealth voted forty-seven to thirty-two that there should be "a moderate tax or contribution annually for the support of the Christian religion, or of some Christian church, denomination, or communion of Christians, or of some form of Christian worship." Importantly, as Madison and his colleagues endeavored to slow the apparent establishment juggernaut and subject its renewed effort to public scrutiny, the vote on this resolution—and many of the related votes that followed—was recorded, which was not normal procedure in the House. Henry and his supporters voted in the affirmative, Madison in the negative. The matter was then referred to a committee chaired by Henry for drafting an assessment bill.[15]

Supporters of the Episcopal Church effectively received another boost that same day when a Baptist petition arrived from the first joint convention of the Virginia Regular and Separate Baptists, convened at the Dover meeting house as the Baptist General Committee. The new committee, formed from four Baptist associations, was charged "to consider all the political grievances of the whole Baptist society in Virginia, and all references from the District Associations, respecting matters which concern the Baptist society at large." Formation of the General Committee provides considerable evidence of the politicization of dissenters, as it was formed for the express purpose of representing all Virginia Baptists before the General Assembly, a far cry from previous Baptist associations, membership in which was largely doctrinal. That the constitution of the General Committee specified that remonstrances to the General Assembly must come from the committee is also evidence of the Baptists' growing political sophistication. In this petition, the new Baptist political body sought resolution of the vestry and marriage issues but did not mention the general assessment. Oddly, the minutes of the Dover meeting indicate that the Baptists specifically rejected a general assessment, but this was not recorded in their petition to the assembly. In fact, the Baptist request in their petition "that all Distinctions in your Laws may be done away, and that no order, or Denomination of Christians in this Commonwealth, have any Separate Privileges allowed them more than their Brethren of other Religious Societies" may have been read by some as an implicit approval of both a general assessment and a nondiscriminatory incorporation act. Certainly the Baptists' plea for marriage and vestry reform, which Episcopalians apparently intended to bargain for a general assessment, fit the assembly's program.[16]

Key political leaders, seeking again to assert their historic leadership of both church and state, supported the general assessment. Patrick Henry used his considerable skills and unmatched influence to urge its adoption as a means to rescue civic virtue. Other supporters came from the gentry establishment, including the very popular revolutionary Richard Henry Lee, who explained to Madison that "Refiners may weave as fine a web of reason as they please, but the experience of all times shows Religion to be the guardian of morals—and he must be a very inattentive observer in our Country, who does not see that avarice is accomplishing the destruction of religion, for want of a legal obligation to contribute something to its support." Establishment stalwart Edmund Pendleton supported the assessment, as did John Marshall, Benjamin Harrison (governor in 1783–84 and speaker of the House in 1785), Spencer Roane, and Philip Barbour. Even George Washington appeared to support the assessment; in declining George Mason's request that he sign Madison's *Memorial and Remonstrance* against an assessment, Washington wrote Mason,

> Altho' no mans Sentiments are more opposed to *any kind* of restraint
> upon religeous principles than mine are; yet I must confess, that I am
> not amongst the number of those who are so much alarmed at the
> thoughts of making People pay towards the support of that which they
> profess, if of the denominations of Christians; or declare themselves
> Jews, Mahomitans or otherwise, & thereby obtain proper relief.[17]

Future governor John Page, a staunch supporter of the Episcopal Church, must have reflected the views of many members of the assembly when he urged on his friend Thomas Jefferson—who, unfortunately for opponents of an assessment, was acting as ambassador to France at the time—the necessity of a general assessment to save the Episcopal Church and prevent the victory of "Enthusiastic Bigottry," a reference to evangelicals.

> Fontaine [an Episcopal minister] has been almost starved; Andrews
> [ditto] has quitted his Gown, he says, to avoid starving. Nothing but a
> general Assessment can prevent the State from being divided
> between immorality, and Enthusiastic Bigottry. We have endeavored
> 8 years in vain to support the rational Sects by voluntary
> Contributions. I think I begin to see a Mischief arising out of the
> Dependence of the Teachers of the Christian Religion on their
> individual Followers, which may not only be destructive to Morality
> but to Government itself.[18]

With the assessment proposal evidently headed for easy enactment, the Presbytery of Hanover, which had repeatedly opposed a general assessment during the war, offered what appeared to be lukewarm support in another extended petition, again written by the energetic John Blair Smith. This petition significantly boosted the assessment's prospects. Presbyterian minister John Holt Rice, who was in a position to know, wrote in 1826, "The general belief was that the measure [the assessment] would be carried in spite of all opposition. Under this impression, the Presbytery resolved to attempt by remonstrances to the Legislature, so to modify the plan, as to make it as harmless as possible." Certainly, the Presbytery's apparent endorsement was full of caveats, noting that "should it be thought necessary at present for the Assembly to exert this right of supporting Religion in General by an Assessment on all the people; we would wish it to be done on the most liberal plan," and that the legislature should adopt no articles of faith, as had been proposed in 1779, nor regulate modes of worship. Still, the Presbytery's position, as penned by Smith, had clearly shifted, expressly stating that the legislature had authority to enact a general assessment, compared to wartime insistence that such proposals confused civil and religious authority. The net effect of the Presbytery petition was enormous and allowed supporters of an assessment to claim overwhelming public support. Madison's anger boiled over:

> The Episcopal people are generally for it [a general assessment], tho' I think the zeal of some of them has cooled. The laity of the other Sects are equally unanimous on the other side. So are all the Clergy except the Presbyterian who seem as ready to set up an establishment which is to take them in as they were to pull down that which shut them out. I do not know a more shameful contrast than might be formed between their Memorials on the latter & former occasion.

Madison's reaction evidenced the difficulty faced in stopping the assessment given the approval of the establishment leaders in the House and the perception advanced in Richmond of its broad public support. In fact, through mid-November, no opposing petitions had been received in response to the seven petitions supporting an assessment.[19]

Less than a week after receipt of the Baptist and Presbyterian petitions, in an apparent attempt to conciliate opponents and further co-opt dissenters, the General Assembly passed a resolution calling for a bill to end discrimination in the areas of marriage and vestries—in spite of years of delay by Anglican supporters, a resolution now adopted without recorded opposition. As in the spring, a resolution was also adopted supporting incorporation of "all societies of the Christian religion, which may apply for the same." This latter resolution was also the subject of a recorded vote (sixty-two in favor, twenty-three opposed) with (not surprisingly) Henry supporting and Madison opposing. Adding to the legislative maneuvering, the committee to draft the bill on incorporation was headed by Carter Henry Harrison, a supporter of the established church, and included Henry. The committee to bring in bills on marriage and vestries included Madison.[20]

Within weeks, a new marriage law had been enacted removing most remaining restrictions on dissenters, and the Protestant Episcopal Church had been incorporated with the prospect of other churches being incorporated in the future. Edmund Pendleton stressed the nondiscriminatory nature of the enactments when he reported to Richard Henry Lee, then serving in Congress:

> The [Incorporation] act was preceded by a resolution that they would
> pass laws for incorporating any society of Christians, who should
> desire it. I am not able to discover in this law, any thing which can
> justly alarm any other society, no more than in another bill, ... for a
> general assessment to support religious teachers, with a right of
> appropriation in the prayer [sic]; yet in both some very sagacious
> gentlemen, can spy designs to revive the former establishment,
> which I believe, do not exist in the minds of any member of that
> church, the clergy and a few monarchy men excepted.

The Act for Incorporating the Protestant Episcopal Church passed in a (recorded) vote of forty-seven to thirty-eight.[21]

Several things are notable about these reforms. The marriage law was not enacted without controversy and was only accepted after difficult negotiations with a more conservative Virginia Senate, dominated by Episcopalians, which demanded continued prohibition on marriages by itinerants. With Methodist evangelicals particularly dependent on itinerants at this time, it is possible that Senate leaders were targeting them, and it may not be happenstance that as the Senate met Methodists were meeting in Baltimore officially to break relations with the Episcopal Church.[22] Furthermore, whereas the November 17 resolutions for reform provided that vestries were to be replaced with overseers of the poor, failure to address this issue in 1784 must have excited dissenters' suspicions about apparently resurgent Episcopal power. More significantly, whatever its intent, the decision to incorporate the Episcopal Church directly, rather than adopting a general incorporation law that any religious (or civic) institution could use, as suggested by the November resolution, and the decision to specify aspects of Episcopal Church governance in the incorporation act deeply angered Presbyterians and helped sink any hope for their cooperative support, even if guarded, for an assessment. Establishment supporters were surprised by the vehemence of continued opposition, particularly as the provision in the incorporation bill that had ostensibly been most objectionable—incorporation of the clergy separate from the laity—had been removed. Evidencing the growing tension generated by the terms of the incorporation bill, Madison, reversing his prior position, voted in favor of the incorporation act, later explaining that his support served the more important goal of defeating the assessment bill as he desperately sought to play both sides, placating supporters of the Episcopal Church and driving a wedge between Presbyterians—now vociferously opposed to this incorporation act—and Episcopalians. As Madison explained to Jefferson "a negative of the [incorporation] bill too would have doubled the eagerness and the pretexts for a much greater evil, a general assessment, which there is good ground to believe was parried by this partial gratification of its warmest votaries."[23]

Unfortunately for Episcopal stalwarts, in the period between adoption of the resolution in favor of an assessment and the bill's actual consideration, Henry was elevated to governor, removing from the House the assessment's most powerful floor leader. Henry's election to governor is often characterized as a plan by Madison to remove Henry from the assessment debate. Writing James Monroe shortly afterward, Madison reported: "Mr. Henry the father of the Scheme is gone up to his Seat for his family & will no more sit in the H. of Delegates, a circumstance very inauspicious to his offspring [the assessment]." Yet one might question Madison's brilliant engineering of a reverse palace coup. Benjamin Harrison, having completed three terms as governor, could not run again; Henry was a logical choice for governor and appeared more than willing to accept. Bishop Meade's nineteenth-century history argued that it "appears likely that the Madison party worked successfully to help get Henry out of the House," but also notes that Henry must have been sure of the assessment's success and that he had other reasons to accept the position, including that Richmond was a "more interesting place for his aristocratic wife and gave access to more potential husbands for his marriageable daughters," both of whom were married within eighteen months of his election. Virginia's early archivist, H. J. Eckenrode, suggested that Henry was a silent coconspirator in his removal from the legislative debate over assessment because of its unpopularity with the "people," but this speculation may be a bit too melodramatic and may emanate from wishful thinking of those who hoped that Henry would not risk his popularity by championing an assessment bill, a wish that obviously proved futile. Some indication of Henry's interest is provided by the fact that even after he was elected governor but before his term began, he accepted the chairmanship of the committee to draft the assessment bill. In any case, in a very tight and crucial battle to delay adoption of the assessment, Henry's absence from the floor of the House proved critical.[24]

Although the general assessment had a substantial majority of support on November 11, over these ensuing weeks of legislative positioning, Madison skillfully moved to placate supporters and mobilize opposition. Helpfully, petitions in opposition to an assessment also began to arrive, although through 1784, more petitions supported the assessment.[25] Throughout the debate, Madison and his allies continued to insist on recorded votes, which may have contributed to some supporters of the general assessment being defeated at the polls before the critical 1785 term. Sometime in late December, Madison made one of his rare floor speeches, echoing dissenters' arguments that religion was not within the jurisdiction of the House and that any assessment would trap the legislature into questions of orthodoxy. Finally, on December 24, 1784, by a margin of forty-five to thirty-eight, Madison was able to gain a delay in the final consideration of the assessment so that the proposed bill might be publicized and the citizenry asked for its views. With Madison working to narrow support for an assessment, this vote to delay was carried by the western, largely dissenter delegates, with delegates from counties formed after 1776 voting eleven to one in favor of the delay, and five of the six delegates who actually switched their votes from supporting a general assessment to seeking postponement coming from heavily dissenter counties. Equally important, immediately after agreeing to the delay, the House adopted a resolution providing for printing the proposed bill, along with the vote to delay its consideration, for distribution throughout the Commonwealth so that the opinion of the people might be heard.[26]

This request for the views of the people played an important part in the ultimate defeat of the assessment. The *Virginia Journal and Alexandria Advertiser*, for example, printed the bill and the vote for delay on March 17, 1785, shortly before new elections. This was followed by a letter opposing the assessment bill and urging Virginians to elect representatives "most favorable to the religious, as well as to the civil rights of their constituents" and to send petitions opposing the assessment. A week later, another letter opposing a general assessment urged instead support for Jefferson's Bill for Establishing Religious Freedom. The *Virginia Journal* later published Madison's *Memorial and Remonstrance* against an assessment. This newspaper campaign, however, met opposition from the *Virginia Gazette or American Advertiser*, which published additional letters supporting an assessment.[27]

All told, 1784 evidenced a dramatic reversal in treatment of religious issues by Virginia's leadership. Whereas the war years were marked by intense negotiations and dialogue among the establishment and dissenters with regular liberalizations on multiple fronts to satisfy dissenter demands, and the immediate postwar years were marked by establishment leaders quietly ignoring continued dissenter claims, 1784 saw an effort by the establishment to regain some of what had been lost. Initially, it appeared to be very successful: the Protestant Episcopal Church had been incorporated and a general assessment seemed to be on the verge of adoption.

Anglican leaders, however, appeared ignorant of how much had changed in the Old Dominion. Madison's careful maneuvering to permit the assessment to be referred to the people was, in fact, its death knell and, as the former dissenters flexed their political muscle, the result was not only defeat of the assessment and repeal of Episcopal incorporation but the adoption of Jefferson's Statute for Establishing Religious Freedom, putting an end to Virginia's establishment.

Dissenters Flex a Newfound Political Muscle

With the delay engineered by Madison, passage of the general assessment no longer appeared a fait accompli. The Presbyterians had an opportunity to revisit the issue, and other sects, notably the Baptists, had an opportunity to rally in opposition. What ensued was a massive petitioning of the General Assembly against an assessment. Once again, though, the tone of the petitions changed. Now, rather than the supplicants who hoped for improved toleration in 1775 and religious freedom in 1776, or the disgruntled dissenters who sought final reforms from 1781 to 1784, the dissenting churches rose in coordinated campaigns to demand a political resolution in the name of political equals who had played a key role in the Revolution. Throughout 1785, it became clear that the dissenters were wholly politicized—not only demanding reform in a petitioning campaign but doing so in a public and coordinated manner with dozens of local petitions taking up the cry from organized sectarian leaders. The effort of Virginia's Tidewater gentry to recapture some stature for the formerly established church was simply swept away.

The politicization of the dissenters was first evidenced in their own internal struggles, including the organization of the Baptist General Committee in the fall of 1784 expressly for political purposes. A similar process of internal debate became evident in Presbyterian actions. By May 1785, when the Hanover Presbytery again met, the clergy, who traditionally commanded broad deference in the Presbyterian Church, were confronted by a petition from Augusta County laity demanding to know what the clergy had intended by the November 1784 petition supporting a general assessment, even if with caveats. Recognizing not only that the general assessment was not inevitable but that their own laity was deeply troubled by their prior stance, the Presbyterian clergy quickly corrected their position. On a motion "whether they approve of any kind of an Assessment by the General Assembly for the support of Religion," they decided that the "Presbytery are unanimously against such a Measure." Additional meetings of Presbyterians were called throughout the summer and fall in an effort to mobilize opposition. A Presbyterian convention at Bethel on August 10, advertised in the newspaper to encourage broad participation, emphatically rejected any assessment and urged local meetings to do the same. The petition from the Bethel convention, copied by many local Presbyterian communities, began by reminding the House that the Presbyterians during the war had "willingly defended it [the state] with the foremost, & at the risk of every thing dear to us," but this petition was clear and emphatic about Presbyterian opposition to a general assessment and took up the old dissenter insistence that the legislature was powerless to intervene in this manner.

> We oppose the Bill ~ Because it is a Departure from the proper line of
> Legislation ~ . . . It establishes a precedent for further Encroachment,
> by making the Legislature a judge of religious Truth ~. If the
> Assembly have a right to determine the preference between
> Christianity & the other Systems of Religion that prevail in the world,
> they may also, at a convenient time, give a preference to some
> favoured sect among Christians.[28]

The Presbyterian reversal was a rebuke to John Blair Smith, who reportedly did support the notion of an assessment to support Christian ministers and was certainly willing to accept an assessment to block what he viewed as the greater evil—direct legislative incorporation of the Episcopal Church. Smith wrote Madison in June 1784 complaining angrily that, based on his review of the House of Delegates' Journal, the Episcopalians were seeking incorporation of the clergy separate from the laity, which was "unjustifiable, & very insulting to the members of their communion." Beyond the issue of clergy/laity relations, using language paralleled in the Presbytery's November 1784 petition, Smith indicated that what disturbed him most was the suggestion in the Episcopal petition favoring incorporation that the legislature would "*enable,* them to regulate all the spiritual concerns of the Church &c." Smith was adamant that no action be taken that favored the Episcopal Church or suggested legislative control of the church polity.[29]

Smith's fixation on incorporation, and acquiescence (even if limited) on an assessment, may have been used strategically by Madison and his allies to rally opposition to the assessment. Thus, on November 17, 1784, after the House had approved a resolution "for the incorporation of all societies of the Christian religion, which may apply for the same," Harrison's committee was ordered to bring in a bill "to incorporate the Clergy of the Protestant Episcopal Church." The reasons for this critical shift in language—adopting exactly the "clergy" language that incensed Smith and applying it only to the Episcopalians—are not altogether clear. The previous petition from Presbyterians seeking a non-discriminatory incorporation bill had been upstaged by the November 12 Presbyterian petition, which specifically opposed incorporation of the clergy of the Episcopal Church. On the other hand, Madison may have seen in the language used on incorporation an opportunity to undermine what he saw as a dangerous alliance between the Presbyterians and Episcopalians on the question of a general assessment. Such an effort to sow dissension among the Presbyterians and Episcopalians may have been facilitated by the arrival in Richmond the next day (November 18) of Presbyterian representatives, John Todd and the agitated John Blair Smith. No doubt Madison took up with these gentlemen the question of the Presbyterian's apparent shift to acquiescing in the general assessment. In any case, by December 11 when the incorporation bill was introduced, it was again simply referred to as "A Bill for incorporating the Protestant Episcopal Church."[30]

While Madison's specific efforts to unhinge any Presbyterian–Episcopal alliance are not recorded, shortly after the Presbyterian about-face in early 1785, Madison reported to Jefferson that

> The Presbyterian clergy have at length espoused the idea of the
> opposition [to the general assessment], being moved either by *a fear
> of the laity or a jealousy of the episcopalians*. The mutual hatred of these
> sects has been much inflamed by the late act incorporating the latter.
> *I am far from* being *sorry for it as a coalition between them* could *alone
> endanger our religious rights* and a tendency to *such an event had been
> suspected.*

While the origin of the chameleon-like changes in language on incorporation are not clearly identified, and the Presbyterians continued to oppose incorporation in 1785, the breach in apparent Episcopal/Presbyterian unity in December 1784 contributed to the Presbytery's shift in focus to what the laity (and Madison) saw as the greater danger—a general assessment. The clear rejection of an assessment by the Presbyterians in 1785 proved critical.[31]

The Baptists—who had been oddly publicly silent on the assessment in 1784—also organized in opposition in 1785. In May, the Kehukee Baptist Association, led by John Leland and David Barrow, called on its members to petition against the assessment. The issue was rejoined at meetings in Powhatan on August 13 and in Orange County on September 7. Baptist and Presbyterian opposition was joined by Quakers, Methodists, and some Episcopalians. The result was a flood of petitions in opposition from across the state. Madison wrote Jefferson:

> The steps taken throughout the Country to defeat the Genl.
> Assessment, had produced all the effect that could have been wished.
> The table was loaded with petitions & remonstrances from all parts
> against the interposition of the Legislature in matters of Religion.
> A General convention of the Presbyterian church prayed expressly
> that the bill in the Revisal [Jefferson's Statute for Establishing
> Religious Freedom] might be passed into a law, as the best safeguard
> short of a constitutional one, for their religious rights.

No one, not even the most devoted establishment gentry, could miss the change in political fortunes.[32]

On the reconvening of the Assembly, it was clear that the general assessment was at best in deep political trouble under the relentless assault of dissenters. Some indication of the changing tide is evident in the decision of the new speaker, Benjamin Harrison, an establishment supporter, to appoint Zachariah Johnston, a prominent Shenandoah Valley Presbyterian, as the chairman of the Committee for Religion. Johnson's inclination is evident in what is reported of a speech that he gave on the assessment:

> I am a Presbyterian, a rigid Presbyterian as we are called; my parents
> before me were of the same profession; I was educated in that line.
> Since I became a man, I have examined for myself, and I have seen
> no cause to dissent [from Presbyterianism]. But, sir, the very day that
> the Presbyterians shall be established by law, and become a body
> politic, the same day Zachariah Johnston will be a dissenter. Dissent
> from that *religion* I cannot in honesty, but from that establishment
> I will.

Reflecting a bitter opposition to any intermixing of church and state, Johnson made clear that taking funds under even a nondiscriminatory general assessment would make the Presbyterian Church "a body politic." Under these circumstances, the assessment proposal never received a third reading. William Henry Foote reported that the bill was taken up by the Committee of the Whole, but votes could not be obtained to return the bill to the floor of the House; "when the question was called the bill was lost in the committee by a majority of three votes." Foote also reports that John Blair Smith, perhaps a bit humbler after the difficulties of 1784 and, no doubt, Madison's opprobrium, was given the opportunity to appear before the committee in November 1785 and argued effectively against the assessment.[33]

Several aspects of the 1785 debate are worthy of special consideration. First, not surprisingly, Presbyterian flirtation with the general assessment in 1784 led to a warm sectarian battle about which denomination had the greatest influence on the proposal's defeat—and thus a claim to be the "true" proponents of American religious freedom. Certainly the Baptist position had been more consistent, and they were responsible for the most popular of the petitions opposing the assessment, but the political clout of the Presbyterians—and the importance of getting the Presbytery to reverse its apparent approval of an assessment in 1784—should not be underestimated. William Wirt Henry concludes that the Presbyterians were so much more populous than Baptists at the time that opposition to the general assessment became known as "a Presbyterian movement," although this may reflect a continuing bias against the more radical Baptists. Madison, unwilling to credit Presbyterian influence after his deep anger at their limited endorsement of an assessment in the previous session, noted that the greatest opposition to the general assessment was from "the middle and back Counties, particularly the latter," where Presbyterians dominated. Similarly, Edmund Randolph wrote Arthur Lee shortly before the 1785 assembly session began: "Religion will form a capital figure in the debates of the next Assembly. The Presbyterians will have a sufficient force to prevent the general assessment, possibly to repeal the act of incorporation. The delegates from those counties in which the majority is of that persuasion are expected with full and pointed instructions on both heads." Of course, the Presbyterians had contributed to the risk of adoption of a general assessment with their November 1784 petition guardedly supporting it. In any case, the adamancy with which each denomination sought to seize the role of political "kingmaker" in defeat of the assessment and adoption of Jefferson's statute is telling; each group, previously largely excluded from the polity, sought to claim the mantle of successful participants in the political process.[34]

Second, there is some suggestion that the proposed assessment bill had a significant impact on the election of 1785. Certainly that seems to have been Madison's and his allies' intent in demanding recorded votes and on having the bill printed with a list of those voting for and against delay in December 1784. Madison recounted that "the printed Bill has excited great discussion and is likely to prove the sense of the Community to be in favor of the liberty now enjoyed. I have heard of several Counties where the late representatives have been laid aside for voting for the Bill, and not a single one where the reverse has happened." Edmund Pendleton, in an April letter, suggested to Richard Henry

Lee that the election might be difficult for those supporting the assessment. Others reported that the 1785 election was particularly sharp for a number of reasons.[35] On the other hand, the impact of the bill on the election is difficult to prove analytically because the election results do not show a clear pattern between those supporting and opposing the December 24 vote to delay the general assessment. In the end, the political demands of dissenters throughout the state, linked with the increasing number of western legislators in the House, was more significant than the election of 1785. With delegates from the new counties of Harrison and Nelson in the 1785 House, the net increase in delegates from western counties since 1776 was 32 of 156 members; this is particularly significant given the lopsided voting of western (dissenting) counties against an assessment. Still, western votes alone would not have defeated the general assessment, particularly given the continued lower attendance rate from distant western counties; for example, in the critical 1784 vote to delay, only 40 percent of delegates from counties formed after 1776 voted, compared to 58 percent from older counties more likely to be dominated by Episcopalian gentry leadership. In any case, the perception of the political impact of the proposal and opposition to it evidences a change in the political fortunes of former dissenters, with opposition to an establishment proposal now appearing as a political asset.

Third, during the summer of disquiet in 1785, Madison was convinced by George Mason and George Nicholas to draft his *Memorial and Remonstrance against Religious Assessments*. This *Memorial*, initially an anonymous publication, has long held an important place among icons of American religious liberty as a classic statement of the reasons for a clear separation of church and state and has been credited by the Supreme Court as evidencing the meaning of religious liberty protected by the First Amendment to the U.S. Constitution; the leading authority refers to it as "one of the truly epoch-making documents in the history of American Church-State separation."[36]

The *Memorial* has fifteen clauses posing arguments in opposition to a general assessment and, more generally, any state involvement in religion. The arguments include a reference to Article 16 of the Virginia Declaration of Rights that only reason and conviction can direct conscience and that religion was not, therefore, within the jurisdiction of the assembly, and that the bill is "adverse to the diffusion of the light of Christianity." In response to the argument that civic virtue was necessary to a republic and religion to civic virtue, Madison did not question the necessity of civil virtue or of religion to promote it; rather, he explained that historically establishments had done more harm than good to the cause of religion. Thus, whereas a republic needed civic virtue, and civic virtue religion, religion most emphatically did not need (indeed, it suffered from) government intervention.[37]

Yet although the *Memorial* may be one of the most eloquent statements on religious freedom in history, the pivotal role that it played in the 1785 campaign against a general assessment and adoption of the Statute for Establishing Religious Freedom is often overstated, implicitly diminishing the political influence as well as the ideology of the Baptists and Presbyterians. In terms of the volume of petitions and signatures, the *Memorial* was dramatically over-shadowed by an eloquent Baptist petition that expressed deep concern over the potential damage that a general assessment—and the resulting entanglement of government and religion—would do to the churches and, in particular, its inconsistency with "the Spirit of the Gospel." One count shows that the House of Delegates received thirteen copies of the *Memorial and Remonstrance* with 1,552 signatures but twenty-nine copies, with 4,899 signatures, of various versions of the "Spirit of the Gospel" protest. Presbyterians tended to rally around a simple petition that endorsed the detailed position taken at the Convention at Bethel; versions of that Presbyterian petition also received far more signatures than the *Memorial*. This is not to diminish the continuing significance of the *Memorial and Remonstrance* as a statement of the necessity of religious freedom and strict separation of church and state, but in Richmond, in the fall of 1785, the petitions under which the table groaned owed more to the political demands of former dissenters.[38]

Fourth, whereas the opposition to the measure ultimately overwhelmed its proponents, the substantial support for the general assessment and the extent to which its defeat in 1785 was the result of a critical and difficult political battle in response to an optimistic and resurgent establishment can easily be under-estimated. Washington wrote to Mason with apparent confidence that the majority of people seemed to support the assessment. George Nicholas noted his belief that "a majority of the counties are in favor of the measure but I believe a great majority of the people against it." Adoption in the county-dominated House of Delegates was a very real possibility.[39]

Even the petitioning is not as one-sided as some suggest. After November 11, 1784, when the measure received a favorable vote in the General Assembly, seventy-nine petitions were received in opposition to a general assessment, and twenty supported it; this count ignores the seven supportive petitions received on the subject from November 1783 until November 1784.[40] Furthermore, the opposition was geographically widespread, especially if one includes the 1783–84 petitions, not to mention the petitions supporting an assessment from the Episcopal clergy and, initially, the Hanover Presbytery. William Foote's report that even after the influx of petitions the proposal to bring the assessment forward for a third reading was defeated by only three votes in the Committee of the Whole is an indication of how highly contested this matter was; it is clear that the former establishment continued to have considerable influence in the legislature.[41]

Finally, it has also been suggested that the economic malaise of the postwar period undermined a general assessment. Certainly economic conditions were adverse to a new tax and the state was still struggling with tax collection generally (never mind Virginians' legendary resistance to any tax); yet this factor can easily be overstated. In the spring of 1784, when these issues again came to the attention of the assembly, agricultural prices were rising, and 1784 was apparently a good crop year, with tobacco exports increasing rapidly, albeit both crops and prices were weak later in 1785. Economic issues and opposition to taxes generally are rarely mentioned in the scores of petitions. "The Humble Petition of a Country Poet" accompanying one Baptist petition urged expressly that the matter was not a question of taxation generally.

> Tax all things; water, air and light,
> If need be; yea, tax the *night*,
> But let our brave heroic minds
> Move freely as celestial winds.

Moreover, although economic conditions might contribute to the defeat of the general assessment, they have a tenuous relation to the adoption of the Statute for Establishing Religious Freedom. Some of the support among historians for the alleged importance of fiscal considerations was a post hoc creation emanating from Hugh Blair Grigsby's early discussion in his *History of the Virginia Federal Convention of 1788*, but Grigsby mischaracterizes a number of aspects of the debate in an effort to suggest that Virginians were not really opposed to a religious assessment. In the end, although economics were not irrelevant, they appear to have played a minor role in the defeat of the assessment.[42]

For those members of the former establishment who in 1784 believed that their political control would permit the resurgence of the Episcopal Church, 1785 demonstrated how seriously the polity in Virginia was changed by the American Revolution and the negotiations for religious liberty. In the face of what appeared to be almost certain passage of a general tax assessment to support religion, effective political opposition from dissenters proved critical.

An End to Establishment

With the proposal for a general assessment rejected, the dissenters, with the assistance of James Madison's legislative skills, turned to a permanent end to the establishment and adoption of Jefferson's Statute for Establishing Religious

Freedom, codifying the religious freedom that the dissenters had long sought. While before the Revolution no colony more carefully protected its established church nor more aggressively discriminated against and persecuted dissenters than Virginia, by early 1786, with the adoption of the statute, no state provided broader protections to religious freedom or did so in terms nearly as eloquent. Nothing could speak more clearly to the fundamental change in the Virginia polity that resulted from the war and, in particular, the forced dialogue between dissenters and establishment leaders.

The push for Jefferson's bill was made compelling not only by the general outpouring of sentiment for religious freedom evidenced in the 1785 petitions against a general assessment but by the fact that a number of those petitions specifically endorsed the Bill for Establishing Religious Freedom. Nonetheless, Madison later reported that the bill passed with "warm opposition." Most notably, when the bill was brought to the floor, an effort was made to replace Jefferson's ringing preamble with Article 16 of the Declaration of Rights, thereby removing some of Jefferson's rationalist justification for religious freedom, perhaps with a hope of leaving some ambiguity as to the statute's scope and intent. The unease among conservatives was not surprising; Jefferson's preamble (as proposed) declared:

> Almighty God hath created the mind free...yet chose not to propagate it [religion] by coercions...but to extend it by its influence on reason alone,...that our civil rights have no dependence on our religious opinions, any more than our opinions in physics or geometry;...that the opinions of men are not the object of civil government, nor under its jurisdiction; that to suffer the civil magistrate to intrude his powers into the field of opinion and to restrain the profession or propagation of principles on supposition of their ill tendency is a dangerous fallacy, which at once destroys all religious liberty,...; that it is time enough for the rightful purposes of civil government for its officers to interfere when principles break out into overt acts against peace and good order; and finally, that truth is great and will prevail if left to herself; that she is the proper and sufficient antagonist to error, and has nothing to fear from the conflict unless by human interposition disarmed of her natural weapons, free argument and debate; errors ceasing to be dangerous when it is permitted freely to contradict them.[43]

With strong momentum in favor of religious liberty, the proposal to excise the preamble was defeated easily in the House, in a vote of thirty-eight to sixty-six. The bill was then passed on a vote of seventy-four to twenty and

sent to the Senate. The more conservative Senate also insisted on an amendment to remove Jefferson's preamble, with this effort led by none other than
the dissenters' old nemesis, Speaker Archibald Cary. Given Senate intransi-
gence, this proposal was ultimately defeated only by Madison's agreement to
accept several specific amendments, including deletion of the suggestion
that God intended to propagate religion based on the "influence on reason
alone" (an anathema to those relying on the "revealed" religion of Scripture,
including some dissenters who were critical to the bill's adoption) and
Jefferson's assertion that "the opinions of men are not the object of civil
government, nor under its jurisdiction"—albeit retaining Jefferson's admonition that only when "principles" led to concrete "acts" was government
action appropriate. Madison later sought to explain the changes to Jefferson,
who was sensitive about edits to his drafting, by noting that although these
amendments "somewhat defaced the composition, it was thought better to
agree to than to run further risks, especially as it was getting late in the
Session and the House growing thin."[44]

Effectively codifying a position that dissenters had advocated since at
least 1776, Jefferson's bill passed into law in Virginia on January 19, 1786,
providing

> That no man shall be compelled to frequent or support any religious
> worship, place, or ministry whatsoever, nor shall be enforced,
> restrained, molested, or burthened [sic] in his body or goods, nor
> shall otherwise suffer on account of his religious opinions or belief;
> but that all men shall be free to profess, and by argument to main-
> tain, their opinions in matters of religion, and that the same shall in
> no wise diminish, enlarge, or affect their civil capacities.[45]

Shortly after adoption of the Statute for Establishing Religious Freedom,
the House finally passed legislation to create overseers of the poor in all
counties, removing the poor tax and orphans from control of Episcopal vestries. In the same session, a committee was appointed to review the act of incorporation, and a bill to amend the act received two readings, but the House
adjourned before final action was taken. While the 1786 Episcopal convention
recommended "to the several parishes to present petitions" opposing repeal of
incorporation, and several dozen petitions were received, with the Statute for
Establishing Religious Freedom in place and clear Presbyterian and Baptist
opposition to an individual act of incorporation and the apparent church/state
entanglement, in the fall session of 1786, the House resolved to let any church
hold property, repeal Episcopal incorporation, and repeal all laws on governance of church worship or polity.[46]

The issue of old church property was bantered about Virginia for thirty more years. The 1786 act repealing incorporation again confirmed ownership of all property held by denominations, meaning that the Episcopal Church could keep the old Anglican churches and glebes. In 1787, Presbyterians renewed their request for pre-1776 glebes to be sold and churches and plate to be made available for public use. The same year, the newly United Baptist Churches of Christ in Virginia, combining the Regular and Separate Baptists, voted in committee by a margin of only one vote to continue to pursue the old glebes and church property. Initially, the House firmly rejected this complaint. Yet by 1799, under a stream of Baptist protests, the Presbytery having decided to let the matter lie, the Virginia legislature repealed prior acts vesting glebes in the Episcopal Church. A method of sale was enacted in 1802 whereby overseers of the poor could sell glebes that were vacant or became vacant. Not surprisingly, that statute was challenged in Virginia courts as a taking of property that had legally and repeatedly been vested in the Episcopal Church. While the Virginia courts upheld the statute, the U.S. Supreme Court ultimately struck it down. Interestingly, the Virginia Supreme Court would have ruled the act unconstitutional had not Edmund Pendleton, an Episcopal stalwart, died the night before issuing his opinion; his successor on the court, St. George Tucker, cast the decisive vote in the statute's favor. Unfortunately for the Episcopal Church, before the U.S. Supreme Court acted, a great deal of property had been disposed of.[47]

The Statute for Establishing Religious Freedom was welcomed heartily by the dissenters and, for that matter, many of the formerly established church. Over time, Jefferson's statute, and the debate surrounding its adoption, played a central role in the development of religious freedom in America.

Even though squabbles continued, with the adoption of the statute, the dissenters had effectively achieved and codified the religious liberty that was so lacking before the Revolution and for which they had negotiated and fought. The achievements in this postrevolutionary period, however, varied markedly from the careful and continuous negotiations that occurred during the war when establishment leaders desperately needed dissenters' support but carefully parried reform whenever possible, and certainly differed from the prewar period of establishment legislative hegemony. Establishment leaders stopped their dialogue and efforts to conciliate with the end of the war; in fact, they sought to reinvigorate the established church through state support. Yet they failed to realize that the negotiations during the war had politicized the dissenters and forever expanded the Virginia polity. Unlike the complex, piecemeal negotiations of the Revolution, the defeat of the general assessment and the adoption of the Statute for Establishing Religious Freedom in 1785–86 was a permanent political settlement of the religious problems that had vexed Virginia for many years. The postwar political disputes between dissenters and establishment leaders were emblematic of a new dynamic in which the politicization of those formerly disenfranchised contributed to a republicanization of Virginia. The entire process of negotiation and reform during the war created a base of legitimacy for dissenters; then, after an initial period of establishment resurgence, the dissenters were able to capitalize on that newfound political legitimacy to achieve what seemed wholly impractical before the war. Contrary to the view that republicanization occurred before the war as a result of the Great Awakening, or that religious liberty was developed in a postwar compromise between dissenters and establishment intellectuals, the crucible of war gave birth to both. Although religious differences were increasingly politically sublimated in the new republic, the former dissenters—western, middling class—were not.[48]

Although no one would question that Virginia had adopted broad protections for religious freedom at the behest of the former dissenters, there continued to be strong debates in the early republic, and into our time, about what religious freedom entailed, with broadly differing views from different groups and different regions. Given the story of their wartime negotiations, careful consideration should be given to the following question: what did Virginia's religious dissenters mean by religious freedom?

6

What Did They Fight, and Bargain, For?

The notion of a christian Commonwealth, should be exploded forever, without there was a Commonwealth of real Christians. Not only so, but if all the souls in a government were saints of God, should they be formed into a society by law, that society could not be a gospel church, but a creature of state.

—John Leland, *Virginia Chronicle* (1790)

By 1786, as Americans began the process that eventually led to the adoption of the federal constitution and Bill of Rights, there would have been nearly unanimous agreement across the young country that religious freedom was protected. Yet the meaning of religious freedom varied from state to state and community to community. For Virginia's former dissenters, the meaning was broad and deep, both based on their political experience as outsiders in a polity with a religious establishment and based on a theological commitment to unbridled worship free from any coercion. Given the historic role of Virginia's dissenters in the development of religious freedom in the state, and the seminal role Virginia soon thereafter played in framing religious freedom for the new nation, careful consideration should be given to the dissenters' understanding of what it was they fought for.

In exploring this issue, it is perhaps unavoidable that one use the structure of the First Amendment concerning the "establishment" of religion (as in "Congress shall make no laws respecting an establishment of religion") and its "free exercise" (as in "or prohibiting the free exercise thereof"). Of course, the language of the First Amendment was not agreed on until 1789, but the concepts involved were of long standing. The operative provision of Jefferson's statute includes the same dichotomy, limitation on government authority followed by a guarantee of freedom of worship, and the same was reflected in numerous dissenter petitions.

The question of "establishment" raises issues relating to whether the new nation was to be a "Christian nation," discrimination among sects or between religion and irreligion, and, more generally, separation of church and state. Essentially it focuses on restrictions on government action. The issue of free exercise raises questions concerning whether authority exists to regulate religion and when, if ever, religious tenets justify an exemption from an otherwise valid law that is facially neutral toward religion. It focuses on control of private action. While establishment and free exercise issues are not mutually exclusive, this dichotomy provides a useful structure for considering dissenters' understanding of the meaning of religious freedom.

Establishment

There is little question that dissenters saw an end to the "establishment" of religion in Virginia as essential both to the development of religious liberty and to their willingness to support the patriot war effort. Certainly, their experience with the Anglican establishment, both its control of the church and its control of government, informed their understanding of religious freedom, as did their theology and ideology of government. Each of these factors, and the clear evidence of their petitions, demonstrates that dissenters fought for a strict disestablishment and clear separation of church and state.

One reason that the breadth of early Virginians' conception of religious liberty is often underestimated is the view that the state's prewar establishment was mild and could not justify a strict limitation on government power or a demand for separation of church and state. This, though, ignores the dissenters' perspective. Although it is true, as John Leland pointed out, that persecution in Virginia never "stained [Virginia soil] with vital blood" (that is, dissenters had not been killed), the discrimination and persecution dissenters faced was widespread and serious. Moreover, on principle, for dissenters and their supporters the issues were the same as those confronted in European religious strife. Not only did Thomas Jefferson warn of a bloody European history of church/state entanglement in urging adoption of his statute, but dissenters relied on the same history. In opposing the general assessment, for example, petitioners from Accomack County warned that it threatened to be the "first link which Draws after it a chain of horrid consequences, and that by Degrees it will terminate in who shall preach, when they shall preach, where they shall preach, and what they shall preach... kindling Smithfield's fires in America." Even minor impairment of religious rights could lead to major interference; as James Madison warned in his *Memorial and Remonstrance*, "it is proper to take alarm at the first experiment on our liberties." Similar language was used by the dissenters. To suggest that an allegedly mild establishment led to mild demands for religious freedom is to ignore not only Virginia dissenters' experience with the establishment but the theological and ideological bases for a strict separation of church and state urged by the dissenters.[1]

Christian Nation

Of course, there is no question that a large majority of eighteenth-century Americans were Christian; nor is there a question that most of them wanted the new nation to stay that way and believed that doing so would be good for the country. Many, certainly the Virginia dissenters, supported religious freedom for non-Christians, but that did not change their hope and belief that Christianity would succeed in a diverse religious marketplace. Moreover, while the demand for disestablishment overwhelmed Virginia's Episcopal hierarchy, the dissenters, establishment supporters, and even Enlightenment thinkers believed that Christian virtue and religion were essential to the progress of a republican nation. This was a generally held belief in eighteenth-century America. George Mason wrote to Patrick Henry in 1783 that "Justice & Virtue are the vital Principles of republican Government." George Washington's Farewell Address in 1796 warned, "Let us with caution indulge the supposition that morality can be maintained without religion." The Northwest Territory Act, adopted by the same Congress that adopted the First Amendment, recognized that "religion, morality, and knowledge, [are] necessary to good government and the happiness of mankind."[2]

The necessity of religion, in particular Christianity, for the health of a republic was widely accepted, but the issue in the Christian nation debate was what role the government should have in supporting or even endorsing that result. What was not accepted, at least in Virginia, was that the state had any necessary or even productive role in encouraging or endorsing religion or Christianity. Madison's *Memorial and Remonstrance* had directly challenged that notion. As Madison was fighting the general assessment in Virginia, the Congress of the Confederation rejected a proposal to support religion in the Northwest Territory by setting aside land for its use; Madison wrote to James Monroe that

> Cong[res]s. Had expunged a clause contained in the first [report on the Land Ordinance] for setting apart a district of land in each

Township, for supporting the Religion of the Majority of inhabitants. How a regulation, so unjust in itself, so foreign to the Authority of Congs. So hurtful to the sale of the public land, and smelling so strongly of an antiquated Bigotry, could have received the countenance of a Commtee is truly matter of astonishment.

What was left in the Northwest Territory Act was the very general observation that religion and morality, like knowledge, are necessary for good government. Similarly, in drafting his Farewell Address, while recognizing the importance of religion, Washington rejected a suggestion by Alexander Hamilton that he ask rhetorically "does it [national morality] not require the aid of a generally received and divinely authoritative Religion?"[3]

A shift in the historic understanding of the mutual roles of church and state has contributed to confusion on this matter. Philip Hamburger, in his bulky *Separation of Church and State*, explains that arguments concerning religious liberty changed from the early eighteenth century, when they focused on the supposition that religion needed government, to the end of the century, and the argument that government needed religion. Hamburger urges that based on this new focus on the necessity of civic virtue, many dissenters accepted the proposition that the United States must be a Christian nation. The relevant syllogism is: republican government needs morality and virtue, morality and virtue need (the Christian) religion, therefore government should support or at least endorse religion. Very few questioned the assumptions; yet what was at issue—what Virginia's dissenters emphatically rejected—was the validity of the conclusion.[4]

The critically important 1785 Presbyterian petition recanting support for a general assessment noted the "happy influence of Christianity" on society, but made it clear that Christianity's influence was "never known...in the history of its progress, so effectual for this purpose, as when left to its native excellence and evidence to recommend it...free from the intrusive hand of the civil magistrate."[5] Dissenters urged that the benefit of religion to society (and government) was enhanced by leaving religion wholly out of the sphere of government. Moreover, they understood that any support or endorsement by government, even any government declaration of a Christian nation, much less limiting any government benefits to a particular religion or sect, would interfere with religion. Dissenters' understanding of these issues was intertwined with three interrelated concerns: any government support or even endorsement interfered with their free will offering to God, support or endorsement would corrupt the church, and both support and endorsement were beyond government's authority.

Theologically, the necessity of a completely free acceptance of God was central to the eighteenth-century evangelicals, especially the Baptists. The implication was that any endorsement of religion by government, even a declaration in favor of Christianity, would tend to encourage religion based on the power and authority of government, rather than God, interfering with that free will offering. Leland explained that "if a creed or faith, established by law was ever so short and ever so true; if I believed the whole of it with all my heart, should I subscribe to it before a magistrate, in order to get indulgence, preferment or even protection, I should be guilty of a species of idolatry, by acknowledging a power, that the head of the church, Jesus Christ, has never appointed." The whole notion of a national religion was to suggest that in some way adherents to that religion were more patriotic or better citizens, thereby influencing religious choices, an anathema to evangelicals.[6]

Government endorsement or support of religion not only interfered with individual choice but threatened to corrupt the church. As one dissenter explained, "the State, I say, has always corrupted the Church." This could occur in at least two ways: any state support of the church would make the ministers providers of "public services" and, thus, subject to some level of (corrupting) legislative control. Any government endorsement or support would also bring into question the sincerity of advocates and, as a result, the legitimacy of proselytizing. Thus, although Jefferson insisted that religion must not interfere with government, dissenters insisted with at least equal adamancy that government not interfere with religion, even by endorsing it.[7]

Dissenters had long objected that any establishment would effectively make religion a public service and ministers public servants. Any formal alliance with government inevitably meant influence, and that meant corruption. Baptist minister William Fristoe noted "when legislatures undertake to pass laws about religion, religion looses [sic] its form, and Christianity is reduced to a system of worldly policy." If that occurs, legislators "must in reality assume the prerogative of judging who are, and who are not worthy to receive the public benefice. And of consequence, our religious principles, as well as preachers must be subject to their [illegible], and stand, or fall according to their determination." If a law either supported or endorsed Christianity, or in any way made benefits contingent on ones affiliation, then legislators or regulators would have to specify what was Christian. This would corrupt religion because religious questions were influenced by governmental decisions. A petition from Powhatan County during the assessment debate explained that a critical problem with the general assessment was that "the Sheriffs, County Courts, and Public Treasury are all to be employed in the management of many laws for the express purpose of Supporting Teachers of the Christian Religion." The

Freeman's Remonstrance argued that such entanglement of church and state has "always corrupted, and often ruined one another; as wine and water mingled, turns to vinegar."[8]

Objections to state interference or endorsement of religion also hinged on the deleterious impact that it would have on the legitimacy and efficacy of evangelizing. Baptists, in particular, shared the concern expressed in Section 12 of the *Memorial and Remonstrance* that church/state cooperation not only threatened their independence but would undermine their ability to proselytize effectively. Madison explained that any preference for Christianity would have the perverse tendency to discourage non-Christians from emigrating here, where they might be converted, and encourage states in "darkness" to discriminate against Christians, again interfering with proselytizing. Petitioners from Botetourt County reasoned that creating a Christian commonwealth through a general assessment would foolishly discourage "two thirds of the human race from coming into our country upon equal terms." Government endorsement might suggest that ministers adopted Christianity in anticipation of some political approval or emolument. Money, per se, was not the issue; any appearance of preference had the same effect. In a 1786 petition relating to incorporation of churches, the Baptists of Buckingham County warned that government leaving churches alone "is the only way to convince the gazing world, that Disciples do not follow Christ for Loaves, and that Preachers do not preach for Benefices."[9]

More generally, dissenters were adamant that making the country a Christian nation was beyond the authority of government, both as a religious and civil matter. From a religious perspective, not only did religion not need aid or endorsement, but such intermixing of civil and religious issues would suggest some civil authority in an area that was exclusively religious—an authority that was inconsistent with Christ's control of the church. The seminal Presbyterian 1776 petition demanding an end to establishment indicated that any state involvement in religion, rather than benefiting religion, was inconsistent with Christian doctrine. "Neither can it be made [to] appear that the Gospel needs any such civil aid. We rather conceive that when our Blessed Saviour declares his *kingdom is not of this world*, he renounces all dependence upon State Power." The same notion was joined by a petition from Amherst urging that the signatories were "Fully Persuaded...That the Religion of Jesus Christ may and ought to be committed to the Protection Guidance & Blessing of its Divine Author." In 1784, the Baptist General Committee told its members that it is "repugnant to the spirit of the gospel for the legislature thus to proceed in matters of religion [general assessment]; that the holy author of our religion needs no such compulsive measures for the promotion of his cause." This formed the basis of the dramatic "Spirit of the Gospel" petition that swept Virginia. Baptists had a long history of opposing civil interference in religion. Seventeenth-century Baptist theologians made this point, stating "that the magistrate is not to meddle with religion or matters of conscience,...because Christ is the King and Lawgiver of the church and conscience."[10]

Even more seriously, Virginia's dissenters rejected the notion of restricting any elements or privileges of the polity to Christians or even declaring this a "Christian nation" because to do so was to exceed the proper authority of civil government, and once the proper line of government authority was crossed, there was little to stop government control of religion and full establishment. The Hanover Presbytery's October 24, 1776, petition seeking an end to establishment stated emphatically that

> there is no argument in favour of establishing the Christian Religion,
> but what may be pleaded with equal propriety for establishing the
> Tenets of Mahomed by those who believe the Alchoran; or if this be
> not true, it is at least impossible for the Magistrate to adjudge the
> right of preference among the various Sects that profess the
> Christian Faith, without creating a Chair of Infallibility which would
> lead us back to the Church of Rome.

Baptists in opposing a general assessment had explained "Farewel to 'the free exercise of religion', if civil rulers go so far out of their sphere as to take the care and management of religious affairs upon them." Even the most general preference for Christianity was simply "quite out of the province of any Legislature upon earth." This concern went beyond the question of providing aid. "If you can do any thing in Religion by human Laws you can do every thing." Presbyterians agreed that breaching the line of separation threatens a new establishment of "any Sect they [the legislature] think proper." This was why incorporation of the Episcopal Church so worried dissenters in 1784, and why Madison was able to use that incorporation to rally opposition to a general assessment. Madison reported to James Monroe that the Presbyterian change of heart on a general assessment may have been due to their becoming "alarmed at the probability of further interferences of the Legislature, if they once begin to dictate in matters of Religion."[11]

These concerns were clearly evidenced in the debates over the general assessment and Jefferson's statute. Many establishment supporters sought support for or limitation of some political rights to Christians. The *Virginia Gazette*, in response to Jefferson's draft Bill for Establishing Religious Freedom, urged that Christianity should be established while "Jews, Mohamedans, Atheists or Deists" should be tolerated but not permitted to hold office. An

Essex County petition urged that "no person not being Protestant nor profess-ing the Christian Religion and living in conformity to the same, be permitted to hold or exercise any Civil Authority." Lunenburg petitioners agreed. In the view of those supporting a general assessment, religious freedom required only nondiscrimination among Christian denominations, and the proposed assessment was "impartial as to preclude the remotest Jealousy of Preference to any Denomination of Christians." At times, language in dissenter petitions also seemed to make nondiscrimination among Christians their object. In 1784, in a petition drafted by John Blair Smith, the Presbyterian clergy sought an equal share "to all Denominations of Christians." Yet the fact that discrimination was the immediate object of a particular complaint does not mean that a nondiscriminatory establishment of "Christianity" or even declara-tion of its primacy would be supported by dissenters, as other petitions and declarations made clear.[12]

Although support for a Christian commonwealth was forcefully presented by those supporting a general assessment, it was equally forcefully rejected by the dissenters, who defeated the general assessment and supported Jefferson's statute. Baptist Elder John Leland, in his 1790 recollection of Virginia's battle for religious freedom, declared "the very idea of toleration is despicable, it sup-poses that some have a preeminence above the rest to grant indulgence; whereas all should be equally free, Jews, Turks, Pagans and Christians." Leland added that "the notion of a christian Commonwealth, should be exploded forever, without there was a Commonwealth of real Christians. Not only so, but if all the souls in a government were saints of God, should they be formed into a society by law, that society could not be a gospel church, but a creature of state."[13]

In fact, the proposed general assessment essentially would have made Virginia a Christian nation, as was provided in South Carolina. Dissenters rec-ognized that the proposed system was nondiscriminatory, benefiting them as much as others. Yet they opposed the nondiscriminatory system on principle as an establishment, a term that Madison's *Memorial and Remonstrance* repeat-edly used to refer to the assessment. The November 1785 petition from Presbyterian clergy (reflecting a number of other petitions) explained that even a general assessment or preference for Christianity generally was unjust and dangerous. "If the Assembly have a right to determine the preference between Christianity & the other Systems of Religion..., they may also,...give a preference to some favoured sect among Christians."[14] A petition from Chesterfield County insisted,

> let Jews, Mehometans, and Christians of every Denomination injoy
> religious liberty, as the declirATION of rights has invited them in
> which says no man or set of men are instituted to exclusive or

separate emoluments or privileges from the community but in
consideration of having rendered singular services to the state.
[T]herefore thrust them not out now by establishing the Christian
religion lest thereby we become our own enemys and weaken this
infant State.... Let the Church of Christ and religion alone.

Fristoe added that an assessment to benefit Christianity was unfair to "avowed
infidels." Dissenters' reasoning was broad enough to cover test and oath
requirements as well as assessments and ministerial support.[15]

A number of modern legal historians and pundits seek to dismiss these
statements by dissenters. Thomas Curry argues that it "would appear...that
Virginians changed and broadened the meaning of establishment from an
exclusive state preference for one church to one that embraced many churches
or Christianity in general. Such was not the case, however. They used the concept...without forming in their minds a clear distinction between an exclusive
and non-exclusive establishment." This is revisionist. As dozens of petitions
(not to mention Madison's *Memorial and Remonstrance*) make clear, the dissenters were emphatically arguing against any establishment of or aid to religion, whether exclusive or nonexclusive. That was, after all, the whole point of
the general assessment.[16]

The issue was not merely financial support of churches; nor was the battle
fought merely in passing or as dicta in a substantive dispute over taxes. When
Jefferson's statute was before the General Assembly, for example, there was an
effort to insert "Jesus Christ" in the preamble, a change that would support the
"Christian nation" moniker without any financial aid. Dissenter petitions that
had deluged the assembly, however, were inconsistent with this; the "Spirit of
the Gospel" petition, the most popular petition, evidenced a concern for those
"who are not professors of the Christian Religion." In the face of dissenter
demands for full religious freedom, their legislative supporters emphatically
rejected the proposed amendment adding "Jesus Christ." Jefferson recounted
the story thus:

Where the preamble declares that coercion is a departure from the
plan of the holy author of our religion, an amendment was proposed,
by inserting the word "Jesus Christ,"...the insertion was rejected by
a great majority, in proof that they meant to comprehend, within the
mantle of it's [*sic*] protection, the Jew and the Gentile, the Christian
and Mahometan, the Hindoo, and infidel of every denomination.

The *Journal of the House* does not expressly record a discussion concerning this
amendment, but this does not mean that the proposal was not made, likely in
the Committee of the Whole. Madison records the episode somewhat differently,

but to the same effect. Of course, the preamble to the statute does not itself provide actionable rights, but such language would cross the line that dissenters sought to establish and could be used to influence future courts, policy makers, and legislators. As Madison explained, inclusion of "Jesus Christ" "would have been, to imply a restriction of the liberty defined in the Bill, to those professing his religion only." Virginia's dissenters, and their legislative supporters, specifically, intentionally, and emphatically rejected such an approach.[17]

Religion versus Irreligion

A more complex question arises over whether dissenters believed that government can support religion generally as opposed to irreligion (or no religion). That is, although state-supported promotion of Christianity or conditioning government benefits on one's particular religion were clearly eschewed by Virginia's dissenters and their legislative supporters, can government promote all religion broadly defined? For example, after the Virginia Convention ratified the federal constitution, much to the consternation of Patrick Henry and his supporters, Henry led the effort to propose amendments to the constitution; the proposals included a provision that would have prohibited any governmental action that "favored or established" any particular "sect." One might conclude that the intent was only to prohibit discrimination among religions but to permit nondiscriminatory aid to all religion, as opposed to irreligion (albeit, based on the assessment debate, one might equally conclude that Henry was implicitly referring to Christian sects). Confusing the question further are statements by dissenters that appear to call only for nondiscrimination among religions. For example, the 10,000 name petition sought reform "so every Religious Denomination being on a Level animosities may cease."[18]

Such language does not demonstrate that dissenters intended to limit their fight against establishment merely to antidiscrimination among confessed religions; rather, it happened to be the immediate object of their attack at that time. At other times, dissenters' language was considerably broader; a number of petitions expressly demanded equal rights for "pagans" and "infidels," obviously inconsistent with government support or endorsement of any religion. In 1790, John Leland, speaking on the question of test oaths and qualification for office, and mimicking Jefferson's argument in Notes on the State of Virginia, explained, "if a man merits the confidence of his neighbors, in Virginia, let him worship one God, twenty Gods or no God—be Jew, Turk, Pagan, or infidel, he is eligible to any office in the State." Presbyterian clergy warned against "ancient distinctions among the Citizens on account of religious opinions." The logic of dissenters' opposition to establishment applies equally to any government benefit or limitation of government privileges for any or all religion: government lacked the authority to address religion, government corrupted religion, and any government influence would undermine the completely free will offering of obedience to God.[19]

There is certainly no indication that had the general assessment proposal included non-Christian denominations it would have been accepted. To the contrary, the May 1785 resolution of the Presbytery to oppose the assessment referred generally to "any kind of an Assessment . . . for the support of Religion." In fact, some proponents of an assessment argued that it should apply to all religions; Richard Henry Lee wrote to Madison that

> The declaration of Rights, . . . rather contends against forcing modes
> of faith and form of worship, than against compelling contribution
> for the support of religion in general. I fully agree with the presbyte-
> rians, that true freedom embraces the Mahomitan and the Gentoo as
> well as the Christian religion. And upon this liberal ground I hope
> our Assembly will conduct themselves.

This view, though, like the assessment for the Christian religion, could not rally adequate support. As Madison reported to Jefferson, an effort to liberalize the proposed general assessment such that all religious teachers would be covered by its provisions came to naught when "the *pathetic zeal of the late Governor Harrison* gained a like majority for reinstating discrimination." Of course, that discriminatory provision was then soundly defeated as inappropriate government interference in religion.[20]

Separation of Church and State

Beyond the possibility of discrimination in favor of Christianity or religion, or even endorsement, dissenters' understanding on the proper role of government and religion makes clear that government should not intervene in religion, even in a nondiscriminatory manner—not simply to maintain the purity of government and protect the interests of minorities but to protect the interests of religion. Given their ideology and theology, they argued generally for a strict separation of church and state.

The most often cited authority on separation of church and state is Jefferson's 1802 letter to the Danbury Baptist Association in which he emphatically stated: "I contemplate with sovereign reverence the act of the whole American people [the First Amendment] which declared that their legislature should 'make no law respecting an establishment of religion, or prohibiting the free exercise thereof,' thus building a wall of separation between Church & State." The breadth of that understanding from a historical perspective, how- ever, has been questioned by some historians who have challenged both the principled nature of the declaration and its acceptance beyond the Enlightenment elite. James Hutson, chief of the Manuscript Division at the Library of Congress, argues that Jefferson's letter was primarily a political document and did not reflect a broad principle. This flies in the face of Jefferson's express statement to his attorney general, Levi Lincoln, that the letter gave him an opportunity "of sowing useful truths and principles." Jefferson recognized that the letter also gave him the opportunity to tweak his federalist opponents in New England, and the views expressed would not be to the liking of the New England Congregationalists (still established in Massachusetts, Connecticut, New Hampshire, and Maine), as Hutson well establishes, and Jefferson edited the letter to omit language that might have been politically explosive. These issues are beside the point; the statement left in was a statement of principle.[21] More important here, Thomas Buckley argues that while Virginia's dissenters were "willing to embrace Jefferson's legislation in terms of the freedom it guaran- teed their own activities and the coup de grace it administered to what had once been an overbearing established church, they did not accept its author's philos- ophy on separation of church and state." The wartime petitioning experience suggests that dissenters understood separation of church and state as an impor- tant principle and one they wholeheartedly endorsed.[22]

On principle, the dissenters' views were clear: religious liberty required that "no law may pass, to connect the church & state in the future." Dissenters believed not only that religion did not need government but that government involvement was affirmatively harmful to religion, and as a matter of natural law and constitutional structure, government had no authority in this area whatsoever. As Leland explained, "THE principle, that civil rulers have nothing to do with religion, in their official capacities, is as much interwoven in the Baptist plan, as *Phydias's* name was in his shield." Dissenters made the point that any union or alliance confused the earthly role of officials and otherworldly authority of God and threatened to corrupt both. A petition from Botetourt County during the assessment debate explained, "Civil Government & Religion are, and ought to be, Independent of Each other. The one has for its object a proper Regulation of the External conduct of men....; [the other] our internal or spiritual welfare & is beyond the reach of human laws." A newspaper letter urging opposition to the general assessment echoed this view; it would "turn his [Christ's] Ambassadors into State men, which is to alter their divine mission, to degrade their sacred character, and debase them to secular interests, and to carnal compliances.... The Church and the State, are two societies, and in their nature and designs, as different as Heaven and earth." While there was opposition in Virginia to the dissenters' argument that the state and religion "cannot even form the most distant connexion," that opposition came from those supporting the general assessment and demonstrates further that severing that connection was exactly what was sought by the dissenters who opposed the assessment.[23]

The breadth of the petitions makes clear that the issue was not just the payment of ministers but what the Supreme Court has come to call "entanglement" of church and state. The point was made in a nineteenth-century Baptist history relating that the resolutions adopted in the eighteenth century had "the ring of giant right rising from the rack of persecution and oppression. It was the war cry of every Baptist voiced by Lewis Lunsford.... 'The unlawful cohabitation between Church and State, which has so often been looked upon as holy wedlock, must now suffer a separation and be put forever asunder.'"[24]

Principled opposition to any connection as ill-advised and beyond government authority was not limited to financial connections. For example, a series of petitions rejected vestries' civil obligations—by then essentially limited to assessing and allocating poor relief—in part for wrongly employing religious officers in a civil function. As Virginia grappled with a plethora of new civil and institutional obligations, the state had to await a more opportune time to disentangle itself completely from its mixed ecclesiastic and civil role, which it did shortly after adoption of Jefferson's statute. Minor, politically expedient exceptions bedeviled those opposed to church/state connections for some time, and continue to do so today. The point here is that dissenter objections to Episcopal vestries' civil functions and to incorporation of the Episcopal Church by the legislature is further evidence of their demand for separation of church and state.[25]

Nor was opposition to church/state interaction a change in the dissenters' position from the understanding of religious freedom central to wartime negotiations and urged from the start of the Revolution. When the notion of a general assessment was first raised in 1776, both Presbyterians and Baptists rejected it as entangling church and state. Subsequent, qualified support that some Presbyterian ministers gave an establishment in 1784—believing it was inevitable—was overwhelmed by opposition in 1785, opposition which the Presbytery then agreed was "unanimous."[26]

Much confusion can be generated by overly broad and shifting definitions. For example, Hamburger's *Separation of Church and State* launches into a lengthy discourse arguing that eighteenth-century evangelicals did not support separation of church and state, but one of Hamburger's central assumptions is that separation of church and state involves both restrictions on government, that is, preventing government action that results in alliances, unions, or entanglement with religion, and restrictions on private action, namely, preventing churches or clerics from being involved in government or politics. Noah Feldman introduces a similar confusion when he characterizes the separation question as "whether faith should inform political debate." To understand the dissenters' position, the two issues must be carefully distinguished. The issue of separation of church and state to dissenters, and as a constitutional matter, relates only to restrictions on government action and, as Leland explained, the action of persons "in their official capacities." As Baptists noted in endorsing Jefferson's bill, the issue was defining "the just limits of the power of the State." Although some dissenters (and Jefferson) urged restrictions on clerical involvement in politics, these arguments were only prudential, based on what a minister's congregation should demand as a matter of contractual obligation, not constitutional limitations. Many eighteenth-century evangelicals had no intention of limiting their own right to comment on political matters; indeed, they believed that private religious activity in the public (nongovernmental) sphere was wholly appropriate and protected by a separation of church and state and free exercise.[27]

Eighteenth-century dissenters in Virginia were emphatic, though, that government should not be engaged with religion and, indeed, had no authority to do so. Hamburger dismisses dissenter arguments about the limits of civil power by urging that they only "focused on the distinction between religious and civil jurisdictions," as if restrictions on civil jurisdiction have nothing to say to separation of church and state. As Virginians repeatedly made clear, the fact that the state had no jurisdiction in matters of religion was fundamental to removing government from involvement with religion. Jefferson's statute explained that "the opinions of men are not the object of civil government, nor under its jurisdiction." Thus, when Botetourt County petitioners, echoing the views of other dissenters, insisted that "Civil Government & Religion are, and ought to be, Independent of Each other," Hamburger simply confuses the matter by concluding that while historians "interpret[] the word 'independent' as suggesting 'separateness,' . . . it seems to have referred to the traditional distinction between the jurisdiction of the two kingdoms [civil and religious]." Although Hamburger's analysis of restrictions on and opposition to some private religious activities developed in the nineteenth century is highly informative, it should not hide the very real demands for separation of church and state as part of religious freedom made by eighteenth-century Virginians.[28]

Public Disputes over Religion

In a smattering of cases, the Supreme Court has suggested that the establishment clause is primarily intended to discourage public disputes concerning religion. For example, in *Locke v. Davey*, a Washington state law that provided college scholarships for any study except the ministry was upheld in part based on the notion that the First Amendment was intended to minimize civil conflict that might result from such scholarships, raising public controversy concerning religion to a constitutional level. This would have been an anathema to eighteenth-century dissenters. Although their goal was not to encourage disputes, they did not see religious freedom removing religion from the public sphere. In fact, they were being introduced to the public sphere through the vehicle of seeking religious freedom. The cases in which the notion of discouraging pubic disagreement has surfaced have been sporadic and not very consistent and certainly are difficult to jive with the dissenters' understanding of religious freedom.[29]

Free Exercise

Comments by eighteenth-century dissenters supporting the need for "free exercise" of religion or "rights of conscience" are ubiquitous, but understanding what that meant to them is more difficult. Dissenters clearly understood that government could not directly regulate worship or a religion's internal affairs. Facing proposals to restrict the time or place of worship or who could participate, Prince William County Baptists, in the first of the Baptist petitions that clearly sought freedom of religion rather than merely improved toleration, asked "that we be alowed [*sic*] to worship God in our own way, without interruption." A petition from Presbyterian Prince Edward County insisted that the assembly "define accurately between civil and ecclesiastic Authority; then leave our Lord Jesus Christ the Honour of being the sole Lawgiver and Governor of his Church." Minutes of the Hanover Presbytery refer to a petition (now missing) asking the assembly "to abstain from interfering in the government of the church."[30]

Here again, for dissenters, government simply lacked authority to regulate religion directly. As explained in the Baptist "Spirit of the Gospel" petition, "any Majestrait or Legislative Body that takes upon themselves the power of Governing Religion by human laws assumes a power that never was committed to them by God or can be by Man." This concern for government interference with the internal regulation of a church was instrumental in contributing to the 1786 repeal of the 1784 Virginia statute incorporating the Protestant Episcopal Church. Although the legislature needed to release the Episcopal Church from previous statutory obligations relating to its form of worship, and many opponents of the 1784 incorporation recognized the necessity of a general, nondiscriminatory incorporation law, the specific requirements in the

1784 law concerning governance of the church—though drafted by Episcopalians and adopted unchanged by the legislature—were viewed as utterly inappropriate for legislative action, and that law was promptly repealed after adoption of Jefferson's statute. As a Baptist petition explained, "if the members of the Protestant Episcopal Church prefer Episcopacy to any other form of Government, they have an undoubted Right as free Citizens of [the] State to enjoy it; But to call in the aid of Legislature to Establish it, threatens the freedom of Religious Liberty in its Consequences."[31]

For theological reasons, dissenters insisted that government be wholly divorced from regulation of worship and religious functions. It was essential that people had complete freedom to worship as they thought best. Leland explained, "every man must give an account of himself to God, and therefore every man ought to be at liberty to serve God in a way that he can best reconcile to his conscience. If government can answer for individuals at the day of judgment, let men be controlled by it in religious matters; otherwise, let men be free." A similar argument was made by the Presbyterian clergy: "It is the duty of every man for himself to take care of his immortal interests in a future state, where we are to account for our conduct as individuals; and it is by no means the business of a Legislature to attend to this." The depth of this belief is evident in the Baptists' extended battle over child baptism. In the face of establishment arguments that refusal to baptize infants was cruel, subjecting unbaptized children who died to eternal damnation, and laws mandating child baptism, Baptists insisted that even this was an act of coercion that could influence the baptized child when grown to adulthood and was wrong because only a completely free choice could be pleasing to God. Regulation of religious actions, being essentially coercive, was inappropriate. For dissenters, the coming judgment necessitated complete freedom of worship.[32]

Beyond direct regulation of worship or a church polity, the question of free exercise becomes more complex. It was clear in Virginia after adoption of Jefferson's statute that free exercise meant that the government could not penalize mere religious opinion; actions alone could be regulated. Thus, Jefferson's statute notes

> to suffer the civil magistrate to intrude his powers into the field of opinion and to restrain the profession or propagation of principles, on supposition of their ill tendency is a dangerous fallacy which at once destroys all religious liberty ... it is time enough for the rightful purpose of civil government for its officers to interfere when principles break out into overt acts against peace and good order.

Dissenters would certainly have agreed.[33]

The more difficult question arises when someone claims a right to an exemption from a law mandating or prohibiting action that is facially neutral to religion. Numerous examples can be contemplated: oath taking, military service, medical procedures, work rules, and so on. Unlike the issue of establishment, where discriminatory action by government against irreligion in favor of religion is inconsistent with freedom of religion, here discrimination is sought, in the form of the government restraining its hand, in favor of those who take action or oppose taking action for religious reasons.

In recent years the Supreme Court has reversed itself and generally eschewed any such exception. One reason for the Court's reversal is that it largely abandoned restricting free exercise protections to religion at all, endorsing protections for strongly held philosophical beliefs, and once that limitation is removed a free exercise exception to facially neutral laws becomes excessively broad. Yet divorcing protection for the free exercise of "religion" from a deity (or deities) is not only inconsistent with the general understanding of the term now and in the eighteenth century but is inconsistent with the historical foundation of the religious freedom. As dissenters insisted and as Madison explained in the *Memorial*:

> This duty [of worship we owe to our Creator] is precedent, both in order of time and in degree of obligation, to the claims of Civil Society. Before any man can be considered as a member of Civil Society, he must be considered as a subject of the Governour of the Universe: And if a member of Civil Society, . . . do it with a saving of his allegiance to the Universal Sovereign. We maintain therefore that in matters of Religion, no man's right is abridged by the institution of Civil Society and that Religion is wholly exempt from its cognizance.

Caleb Wallace, the long-serving clerk of the Hanover Presbytery who was intimately involved in debates over religious freedom, made the same point, noting that "it appearing then that when men form the social compact each reserves to himself the right of choosing and acting for himself in what relates to religion and conscience." Conflating a philosophy or firmly held belief with religion undermines this justification for exempting free exercise from government authority in the first place. Although there may be good reasons to protect a citizen's strongly held belief, such reasons cannot take precedence to laws enacted by representatives under the social compact absent an express reservation and certainly lack the historical and theoretical antecedents of the First Amendment.[34]

The question remains whether Virginia's dissenters would have seen an exemption from otherwise neutral laws as a necessary element of free exercise.[35]

Ellis West and Michael Malbin, focusing on Jefferson and other political leaders, argue that a free exercise exemption from a neutral law is inconsistent with Lockean notions of freedom through law, notions at the core of the founding fathers' fight for liberty. Judge Michael McConnell, recognizing that Locke would not support such an exemption (requiring, instead, a faithful person to accept nondiscriminatory civil penalties), points out that although Jefferson's views on religion and the polity are Lockean, Madison (and, he might add, the dissenters) approached the issue from a different perspective. Thus, for Jefferson (and Locke) "liberty of conscience meant largely freedom from sectarian religion, rather than freedom to practice religion in whatever form one chooses," whereas Madison (and the dissenters) had a "far more sympathetic attitude toward religion" and saw the issue as one of government interference with religion. Of course, this may be unfair to Jefferson, because, as McConnell recognizes elsewhere, his notions of religious liberty were much more robust than Locke's, but in any case, the dissenters' views were based on a different, more expansive rationale than Locke's.[36]

As dissenters believed that the right to free exercise predates the social compact and takes precedence to it, exemption from otherwise valid laws for free exercise, within limits, makes sense. Other elements from Virginia's historic struggle for religious freedom support and help define a free exercise exemption. In 1776, during the debate over Virginia's new constitution, Madison publicly grappled with the scope of free exercise in response to a provision in George Mason's draft Declaration of Rights. Madison's first proposed amendment to the draft focused primarily on replacing Mason's call for broad "toleration" with the notion of religious freedom. That proposal read:

> all men are entitled to the full and free exercise of it [religion] accordg
> to the dictates of Conscience; and therefore that no man or class of
> men ought, on account of religion to be invested with peculiar
> emoluments or privileges; nor subjected to any penalties or disabil-
> ities, *unless under color of religion, any man disturb the peace, the*
> *happiness or safety of society.*

The italicized language in this proposal was from Mason's original draft. When this amendment failed, Madison suggested an alternative including a far broader free exercise provision, presumably more consistent with his own belief: "all men are equally entitled to enjoy the free exercise of religion, according to the dictates of conscience, *unpunished and unrestrained by the magistrate, Unless the preservation of equal liberty and the existence of the State are manifestly endangered.*" Neither limit on free exercise was included in the final version of Article 16. Rhys Isaac concludes that the omission of Mason's "disturb the peace, happiness, or safety of society" was meaningless; "we may be sure that the representatives who consented to omit such a stated exception did so from a sense of its redundancy rather than from any principled disapproval of its intent." The subsequent history is to the contrary. Mason's use of the term "happiness"—regulation was appropriate when religious exercise interfered with the "happiness" of society—inferred a far broader right of legislators to restrict free exercise than Madison's proposal. This type of expansive language on government authority to restrict free exercise was only adopted by Delaware; most other states restricted governmental action in opposition to free exercise to ensuring "peace" and "safety," as did Virginia, ultimately. Presumably these states concluded that allowing government to restrict free exercise based on legislators' perception of the "happiness" of citizens was to give government too broad of an authority. In fact, a similar argument that government should have the authority to regulate religion to maintain "social tranquility" had been used by those opposed to Jefferson's statute.[37]

Jefferson's statute states that any action that is based on the exercise of religion is protected unless a violation of "peace and good order."[38] Similar language was used repeatedly by the dissenters, but their remonstrances even more clearly espoused the view that some affirmative harm was required if the state was to interfere with free exercise. The Baptist minister Leland explained that "the legitimate powers of government, extend only to punish men for working ill to their neighbours, and no ways effect the rights of conscience." Elsewhere, Leland insisted that government had no right to restrict free exercise in "time, place or manner." This notion was a long-standing part of Baptist and dissenter doctrine. Dr. Benjamin Avery, a leading apologist for eighteenth-century English dissenters, in a letter prepared for the English Dissenting Deputies in 1743 objecting to a Connecticut law restraining "enthusiasm" and "itinerancy," wrote "but great and manifest as those Mischiefs are, Wee [sic] cannot be of Opinion that, the Magistrate has anything to do with the matter; but to see that the publick peace is preserved; that there are no Riots or Tumults, and that his Subjects are not allowed to assault, hurt, maim, wound, plunder or kill one another in those Religious Contests." William Sweet reports that a Baptist leader in exile in Amsterdam in 1611 explained that "the magistrate is not by virtue of his office to meddle with religion or matters of conscience, ... but ... to handle only civil transgressions (Rom. VIII), injuries and wrongs of man against man ... for Christ only is the king and lawgiver of the church and conscience (James IV.12)."[39]

While Leland, for example, expressly opposed exempting ministers from taxes or military service, he did so because he opposed providing government benefits or indulgences to clergy simply because of their calling, that is he opposed establishment or any entanglement between church and state. Free exercise did not demand no payment of taxes (although how to treat a religiously based claim for exemption from military service could be a more complicated matter). Leland explained the matter himself: "should a man refuse to pay his tribute for the support of government, or any wise disturb the peace and good order of the civil police, he should be punished according to his crime, let his religion be what it will; but when a man is a peaceable subject of state, he should be protected in worshipping the Deity according to the dictates of his own conscience."[40]

The language—in dissenter statements and in the statute—requiring a threat to "peace and good order" would seem to limit government's ability to penalize acts within the free exercise of religion without some showing of a particular injury arising from the religious exercise beyond the mere fact that the acts are covered by a generally applicable law. Yet some, most notably Supreme Court Justices Antonin Scalia and John Paul Stevens, have argued that the eighteenth-century notion of disturbing the peace was so broad as to include any illegal act. This reading makes restrictions of government action to instances affecting "peace and good order" wholly circular; any violation of the law qualifies. Under such a reading, protection of free exercise only prohibits actions regulating religion per se, and there is no free exercise exemption from a general law, violation of which would be understood to disturb the "king's peace." On its face, this broad reading of the early meaning of "disturbing the peace" and "licentiousness" is certainly open to question. For example, the nineteenth-century *Dictionary of American and English Law* defines "breach of peace" as "offenses against public order," either actual, constructive (going armed into public or challenging someone to fight), or apprehended (issuing threats), and "licentiousness" as "doing as one wills, regardless of the rights of others." That is, disturbing the peace was to harm others or take action posing an imminent threat.[41]

Others have cited a Virginia dissenter for the notion that any illegal action was understood to disturb the peace. "An anonymous Virginian wrote in 1777 of Christian sects that 'quarrel' with one another, 'they ought to be punished, not as professors of religion, but as disorderly members of the Commonwealth.'" Even if one were to accept such a narrow reading of the admonition against "quarrel[ling]," a fuller recitation of that dissenter's views gives a different impression:

> Are not the Magistrates of every State armed with the legal sword?
> Surely then they have sufficient power to suppress any riot, or
> tumult, or insurrection that may happen among the subjects of every

sect or party...But when one [sect] is by law exalted by dominion above the rest, this lays the foundation of envy, and debate, and emulation, and wrath, and discord, and confusion; if not of war, bloodshed, and slaughter, in the end:—Being all indulged alike...what cause can they have to quarrel with one another? And if any of them do so, they ought to be punished, not as professors of religion, but as disorderly members of the Commonwealth.

This is far from a clear endorsement of the restrictive position on free exercise and, in fact, seems to comport with evangelicals' view that government was restricted to enforcing the "second tablet" (the Fifth through Tenth Commandments), that is, harm to others.[42]

The restrictive interpretation is problematic because it calls into question why legislators and dissenters repeatedly included the "disturbing the peace" limitation on a government's right to act, suggesting some affirmative harm to society.[43] In any case, whatever the merits of linguistic and etymological arguments on the breadth of free exercise, the history of dissent in Virginia provides a clearer picture. Dissenters often opposed facially neutral oath requirements as an unjust imposition on their religious objection to swearing. More seriously, numerous preachers were imprisoned before the Revolution for breach of peace. "Magistrates began to issue their warrants, and sheriffs had their orders to take up the *disturbers of the peace*." The early Baptist historian Robert Semple complained, "it seems by no means certain, that the law in force in Virginia authorized the imprisonment of any person for preaching. The law for the preservation of peace, however, was so interpreted, as to answer this purpose; and, accordingly, whenever the preachers were apprehended, it was done by a peace warrant." Of course, the breach in question was simply public preaching without a license; no allegation was made that any affirmative harm or injury was caused.[44]

Dissenters certainly believed that the protections for religious freedom bargained for during the war would prohibit imprisonment simply for preaching publicly. More broadly, dissenters insisted that government regulation not be permitted to interfere with their religious practices. By mid-1777, perhaps with the arrests and earlier harassment of Presbyterian ministers in mind, the Hanover Presbytery warned that one of the dangers of government action relating to religion was that the government could dictate "who shall preach; what they shall preach; to whom, when, and at what places they shall preach." It is simply unfathomable that they intended to leave such questions to the discretion of sheriffs and magistrates in determining that noninjurious religious gatherings were a breach of peace which, in spite of free exercise, were unprotected.[45]

Of course, this does not suggest that free exercise is an unlimited right. Affirmatively harmful actions can be regulated. Furthermore, when free exercise is impinged by an otherwise neutral regulation, the test to determine whether free exercise should trump such a law might be anything from a balancing of interest test to a requirement that the government show a compelling interest to interfere with free exercise (something similar to Madison's "manifest" threat theory).[46] In some cases, determining what the imposition on religion would be of enforcing a generally applicable law and comparing that to the state's interest in discouraging harmful actions would be difficult. To use an eighteenth-century example that was clearly under contemplation, the gathering of large groups of slaves was commonly prohibited. Could a minister absolve himself from liability under such a statute by claiming that it interfered with his free exercise? Probably not; the state made a rational decision from an eighteenth-century perspective that large groups of slaves posed a real danger, and it is far from clear that restricting such preaching would significantly impair free exercise (whereas such preaching would seem not to have met Madison's test for government interference in free exercise). Alternatively, the proposed toleration act of 1772 would have prohibited the baptizing of a slave without his or her master's permission. This would have posed a more complicated problem. Presbyterians in 1775 specifically warned that if someone made a profession of faith, it was their "duty to admit him into our Church." A Baptist preacher made the same point, explaining that "when persons give us a satisfactory account of their conversion, declare their agreement with us in judgment, and withal bear an honest report, and have a good character; we esteem ourselves bound in conscience to receive them; having no authority from CHRIST to reject any such little ones who believe in him."[47] In any case, the dissenters' experience strongly suggests that something more than simply engaging in a breach of peace, defined as any action declared illegal, is required to justify interference with free exercise. Whatever the difficulty, if the voice of Virginia's dissenters is to be properly privileged, some exception from otherwise neutral laws for the free exercise of religion must be recognized.

Some have argued that these positions are inconsistent—that one cannot oppose nondiscriminatory aid to religion and support exceptions to general laws for "religious exercise." Virginia's dissenters did. Of course, not all positions are perfectly consistent, but the apparent inconsistency here evaporates when one considers the issue from dissenters' perspective. The issue to the dissenters was not one of preventing all aid to religion to neutralize religion. Rather, the issue was one of preventing any entanglement from impairing religion by way of government action, although dissenters certainly recognized that this approach would also be better for the civil polity. Thus, it is not inconsistent to insist that government not interfere in religion by aiding or endorsing it affirmatively or by imposing restrictions that interfere with its free exercise.

In fighting for freedom, Virginia's dissenters had a very specific and very broad notion of what it was for which they were fighting. Their understanding of religious freedom was fueled by a deep devotion to religion, their theological understanding of the centrality of individual devotion (especially among the Baptist, but also among Presbyterian evangelicals), and an equally deep devotion to the necessity of keeping government from being entangled with religion. This understanding was consistent with almost 200 years of Baptist learning and the difficult experience of all of Virginia's dissenters with the establishment before and during the war.

Specifically, dissenters were emphatic that the government should not—indeed, could not within its proper sphere—give any special privileges to any sect or to Christianity generally. They rejected proposals to make this a "Christian nation." Of course, they insisted on a disestablishment of religion, but more fundamentally, they insisted on the separation of church and state; that is, they opposed not only government aid to religion but any union or entanglement as well. In large part, they recognized that involvement with the government or aid from the government would corrupt religion, inevitably making it in some way a creature of the state. Any government benefit to religion would inevitably make civil officials judges of religion. More fundamentally, interference in religious matters was simply beyond the legitimate authority of government. This was a line that dissenters believed could not be crossed; to grant government power in the area of religion would permit a government, if it so chose, to adopt a full establishment. Equally, the dissenters insisted that government must guarantee a free exercise of religion that would prevent it from regulating religion directly and require that it allow religious activity that did not harm the "peace" or "safety" of the commonwealth. Although the breadth of that limitation was never clearly defined, it certainly included a right to preach publicly without molestation.

Crucially, the dissenters' understanding was defined by a real concern for religion. Some urged that government and the civil polity and those expressing minority viewpoints must be protected from the potentially deleterious impact of the use of religion in a public venue—certainly important considerations—whereas the dissenters based their understanding of religious freedom on the need to prevent an entanglement to protect religion itself. Viewed in this manner, there is no inconsistency in requiring a strict disestablishment, including a broadly defined separation of church and state, while at the same time insisting that government accommodate private religious activity that does no real harm.

In the course of the past 200 years, the dissenters' understanding of religious freedom, much like the story of their fight for religious freedom, has not always been adequately recognized. Even once those historical developments are recognized, though, the question remains as to whether the views of Virginia's dissenters should be given particular prominence. They were, after all, initially a minority in one state. Before leaving their story, some consideration might be given to how and why it should be remembered.

Epilogue

> This Court has considered the happenings surrounding the Virginia General Assembly's enactment of "An act for establishing religious freedom,"...written by Thomas Jefferson and sponsored by James Madison, as best reflecting the long and intensive struggle for religious freedom in America.
>
> —*McGowan v. Maryland*, 366 U.S. 420, 437 (1961)

Before the American Revolution, no colony more carefully protected its established church or more aggressively persecuted dissenters than Virginia. By 1786, no state provided protections for religious freedom nearly as broad or as eloquent as those in Virginia's Statute for Establishing Religious Freedom. This transformation in Virginia, the largest and most populous state, became a clarion call and a bellwether for similar transformations throughout the young republic. Eleven of the thirteen new states had test acts or establishments at the end of the Revolution, but these were slowly eroded or eliminated over the course of the nineteenth century, with the Virginia experience proving a model for religious freedom and, specifically, for the adoption of the First Amendment to the U.S. Constitution in 1791.[1]

There is a broad agreement among judges, lawyers, and historians about the significance of the Virginia experience. For example, in ruling that the First Amendment religion clauses were binding on the states as part of the liberty guaranteed by the post–Civil War amendments, the Supreme Court stated in *Everson v. Board of Education*, the "movement toward this end [religious liberty] reached its dramatic climax in Virginia in 1785–86." "This Court has previously recognized that the provisions of the *First Amendment*, in the drafting and adoption of which Madison and Jefferson played such leading roles, had the same objective and were intended to provide the same protection against government intrusion on religious liberty as the Virginia statute [for Establishing Religious Freedom]." Later, Chief Justice Earl Warren summarized thus: "This Court has considered the happenings surrounding the Virginia General Assembly's enactment of 'An act for establishing religious freedom,' . . . written by Thomas Jefferson and sponsored by James Madison, as best reflecting the long and intensive struggle for religious freedom in America, and as particularly relevant in the search for First Amendment meaning."[2]

Historians generally agree. Leo Pfeffer explains: "Nor can there be any doubt that together, the 'Memorial and Remonstrance' and the Virginia Statute furnished a historic basis for the adoption" of the First amendment. Anson Stokes states in his exhaustive *Church and State*, Virginia's statute "influenced the American theories of Church-State separation and religious freedom more than any other historical factor." Jon Butler says simply, "the Virginia debate and the Act for Establishing Religious Freedom directly affected the conceptualization and passage of the First Amendment." Martin Marty concludes that "the Virginia event, by common consent, was the most decisive element in an epochal shift in the Western world's approach to relations between civil and religious spheres of life after fourteen centuries."[3]

Perhaps not surprisingly, in seeking to understand that Virginia experience, courts and commentators often turn to the writings of James Madison and Thomas Jefferson. Both the majority and dissent in *Everson v. Board of Education* gave preeminence to Madison's *Memorial and Remonstrance* in adoption of Jefferson's statute, although the dissent's explanation for doing so was more eloquent:

> [The] Remonstrance is at once the most concise and the most
> accurate statement of the views of the *First Amendment's* author
> concerning what is "an establishment of religion." Because it
> behooves us in the dimming distance of time not to lose sight of
> what he and his coworkers had in mind when, by a single sweeping
> stroke of the pen, they forbade the establishment of religion and
> secured its free exercise.

The dissent concluded that Madison's *Memorial* "killed the Assessment Bill." Jefferson's views, especially his 1802 letter to the Danbury Baptist Association referring to a "wall of separation" between church and state, have also been the object of much judicial and historical cogitation.[4]

Yet there is an extent to which this focus on Jefferson and Madison tends to undervalue the role of the dissenters and has contributed to a certain historical forgetfulness. Without taking anything from Madison's or Jefferson's enormous contributions, the statute and *Memorial and Remonstrance* and their authors' arguments were, after all, in some sense secondary. The change in Virginia politics that allowed adoption of religious liberty had far more to do with the dissenters' views than the erudite reasoning of Madison and Jefferson. The history of the rise of religious liberty in Virginia speaks in a much different voice: it speaks in the voice of religious dissenters.

As our collective memory has placed Jefferson and Madison at the center of a secularist reading of the First Amendment, we can forget that Virginia's evangelical dissenters were more essential to the development of religious free-dom and at least as adamant on a strict separation of church and state and robust free exercise. The conflict between dissenters and Virginia's Anglican establishment is also a challenge to the view of many historians that in the formation of a new, pluralistic American nation, religious freedom was inevi-table. That teleologically tainted conclusion tends to undervalue the fight for religious liberty. Finally, republicanization, at least in Virginia, was neither the result of the religious awakening of the mid-eighteenth century nor of liberal principles of revolutionary leaders, although both played a part. In Virginia, a complex, lengthy, and highly contested negotiation sought support for mobili-zation in return for religious freedom and, of necessity, brought dissenters from across the new commonwealth and across social and economic lines into the polity. This proved to be foundational in the development of Jeffersonian republicanism.

This history lost its potency in part because the dissenters' interests turned elsewhere. After 1786, the Baptists continued to object to the fact that Episcopal churches were permitted to hold church buildings and glebes that had been purchased with tax dollars in the years before the Revolution, with Episcopalians countering that religious freedom had been granted to dissenters based in part on an understanding that their church would retain this property. Even for the more radical Baptists, the matter was not without controversy, and the Baptist General Committee decision to pursue the matter after 1786 passed by only one vote, whereas the Presbytery officially dropped the matter. After repeated complaints from a growing Baptist population, the Virginia General Assembly passed a law in 1802 providing that as glebes became vacant, they should be sold and the funds provided to overseers of the poor; this law was held uncon-stitutional in 1815, but by that time, much of the property had been sold. The point here, though, is that despite the apparently heated debate, this continuing battle over church property was a sideshow, even to many evangelicals. After all, the issue was not what should be the relationship between church and state but how to respond to and disentangle a former relationship. In the broader scheme of church health and evangelical success, the property proved to be of limited significance. Certainly the Episcopal Church, for reasons having little to do with the seizure of the glebes, suffered serious problems through the early nineteenth century. Moreover, whatever the property settlement, the energy of the evangelical sects, particularly the Baptists and the Methodists, was very successfully diverted to proselytizing and joining the social and political mainstream in Virginia and throughout the South.[5]

Here historical forgetfulness was not entirely accidental. Often in the nineteenth century, Baptist and Presbyterian historians would allude to their role in establishing religious freedom in Virginia, although in their effort to claim a triumphant part in the success of the Revolution and establish their credentials as patriotic Americans, they often understated the extent of the conflict and negotiation inherent in that process. Certainly they did not wish to revisit the threat not to support wartime mobilization or the loyalism of some coreligionists elsewhere in the South. The trend was evident already in May 1784 when the Hanover Presbytery insisted, in spite of clear evidence to the contrary, that it had "restrained our complaints [during the war]…that we might not be thought to take any advantage from times of confusion, or critical situations of Government." Episcopalians equally sought to recharacterize history, urging that the former establishment was mild and development of religious freedom was a cooperative venture between Anglicans and dissenters. While Baptist and Presbyterian sectarian historians joined in a heated and sometimes fantastical battle over which denomination should take primacy in the success of their efforts, with both Baptists and Presbyterians insisting, for example, that they were the source of Jefferson's statute and Madison's *Memorial and Remonstrance*, downplaying the contested nature of the dispute tended to sublimate the evangelicals' role altogether.[6]

This collective forgetfulness was abetted by the extraordinary success of Jefferson and Madison—Madison as "father of the constitution" and Jefferson as father of a movement. The Virginia experience was constantly in the background as Americans struggled with how to balance religious freedom and societal needs and historic expectations in the early republic, and it was perhaps natural that Jefferson's and Madison's names, and especially the products of their drafting—Jefferson's statute and Letter to the Danbury Baptists and Madison's *Memorial and Remonstrance*—became associated with these developments. These documents were repeatedly published over the course of the nineteenth century, particularly where local church/state disputes erupted. Slowly states eliminated restrictions that limited civil rights to Protestants or Christians or demanded some confession of faith by office holders; slowly antiestablishment doctrines were expanded—reforms that were often accompanied by explicit or implicit reliance on Jefferson or Madison and, in the early nineteenth century, by political support from evangelicals. By 1878, when the Supreme Court declared emphatically in *Reynolds v. United States* that the crucial antecedents of the First Amendment can be found in Jefferson's statute and Madison's *Memorial and Remonstrance*, the story of Virginia dissenters' intense and contingent negotiations was largely lost, although the broader influence of these developments, identified with Jefferson and Madison, continued to expand.

In the twentieth century, developments concerning religious liberty have seemed to accelerate as questions of religious freedom have been largely federalized since the Supreme Court declared that states are also subject to the First Amendment as a result of the post–Civil War amendments to the U.S. Constitution and as increased diversity (not to mention litigiousness) has forced the courts to confront a perplexing array of problems relating to religious liberty. Throughout this period, the Court has continued to interpret the First Amendment's religious freedom clauses with particular deference to Madison and Jefferson.

Although Jefferson and Madison certainly played essential roles, the highly circumscribed focus on them results in a historic perspective of the First Amendment that undervalues the dissenters' role and misdefines the source of America's religious freedom. This restricted focus has contributed to attacks on the Court's fulsome view of the antiestablishment and free exercise clauses. Ironically, Virginia dissenters' religious autonomy and theology demanded a very broad reading of religious freedom that some seek to dismiss today as "secularist" in part by the almost exclusive focus on Jefferson and Madison. Of course, the precise application of that history today, particularly by courts and lawyers in complex legal disputes, is another matter altogether. Yet if nothing else, claims that a strict separation of church and state are solely a modern, secularist addition to the First Amendment or that the founding generation shared a notion that the United States must be understood as a "Christian nation," can be dismissed.

Though the centrality of the Virginia experience among historians and courts generally seems secure, there are several reasons why the experience of the dissenters in particular should be more fully privileged. If Jefferson's statute and Madison's *Memorial* are relevant history, the dissenters' understanding at the heart of development of those iconoclastic documents is at least as relevant. The statute is certainly a historic antecedent of the First Amendment, and the dissenters' petitions and the negotiations they evidence were antecedents of the statute and provide *"reliable* evidence of [the nature of the] consensus within the legislature" when Jefferson's statute and earlier reforms were adopted, even if that consensus was initially necessitated by wartime mobilization. To say that Jefferson's statute was the culmination of a ten-year struggle requires one to consider the struggle, which was emphatically not a dry intellectual debate between Jefferson and establishment leaders on Lockean doctrine. Because of dissenters, these issues took center stage during the Revolution when, as Anglican petitions repeatedly complained, the General Assembly had "more immediate" tasks. Dissenters played the crucial role in the end to establishment taxes and the defeat of the general assessment bill, which paved the way for Jefferson's statute. Madison made a similar point in a related context, urging that to the extent one looked to the history of the ratification of the constitution, one should look beyond the views of the founders to the views of the "nation."[7]

At a fundamental level, the development of religious freedom in Virginia was a negotiation in which the political establishment ceded religious liberty in return for support for mobilization, support the dissenters provided. Thus, there was a "deal" for religious liberty; as a result, dissenters had a legitimate expectation that they would receive something in return for their mobilization. In such circumstances, the intent of the dissenters on what they were trading for takes on even greater significance; it honors the bargain that was made. Although it may be ironic that Virginia's dissenters, who were persecuted before the war by the establishment, came to define what religious establishment and religious freedom meant, this was the result of the political compromises necessitated by war.

Finally, there is broad agreement that no single individual influenced adoption of the First Amendment as much as James Madison. Yet to the extent that Madison's view of the meaning of religious freedom is given central importance and his shepherding adoption of the Statute for Establishing Religious Freedom and the First Amendment is credited, it is particularly relevant that Madison's election to both the Virginia ratification convention and the first federal Congress depended on support of former dissenters and an understanding that he would pursue constitutional protections for religious freedom. Presumably, the dissenters' support was based on an understanding that the religious freedom that Madison agreed to pursue would be the freedom that they sought.

Various sources record Madison's electoral involvement with the Baptists differently, but the essence of the story remains the same. The Virginia Baptist General Committee unanimously agreed in March 1788 that the proposed federal constitution did not adequately protect religious liberty, and numerous Baptists joined Patrick Henry's vocal opposition to the constitution. Madison's father warned him of growing Baptist opposition. Virginia's ratification of the constitution, and effective formation of the federal union, hung in the balance.[8]

Thus, it was an ominous development when Baptist John Leland, "probably the most popular [preacher] of any who ever resided in this State," opposing the constitution as written and supporting Henry's demand for amendments prior to ratification, declared as a candidate for the Virginia convention from Orange County, a Baptist stronghold and Madison's home. Opposition was joined by the popular Orange County Baptist minister Aaron Bledsoe, who had suffered arrest for preaching before the war. Friends urged Madison to come to Orange and speak with Leland, warning him that his other electoral opponent, Thomas Barber, "amoungs his Friends appears, in a General way the Baptus's, the Preachers of that Society are much alarm'd fearing Religious liberty is not Sufficiently secur'd thay pretend to other objections but that I think is the principle objection, could that be Removed by sum one Caperble of the Task I think thay would become friends to it." On the eve of the election, Madison met with Leland concerning rights of conscience, and Leland withdrew from the race, urging support for Madison, reportedly at a public gathering on election day. Senator John S. Barbour explained that

> If Madison had not been in the Virginia Convention, the constitution would not have been ratified, and as the approval of nine States was necessary to give effect to this instrument, and as Virginia was the ninth State, if it had been rejected by her, the constitution would have failed (the remaining States following her example), and it was through Elder Leland's influence that Mr. Madison was elected to the Convention.[9]

The next year, after Madison was denied a position in the U.S. Senate by the Virginia legislature, dominated by Patrick Henry—still angry over his defeat in the ratification convention—Madison's election to the House of Representatives was threatened by a strong antifederalist campaign (running none other than James Monroe). Again, "there was a strong Baptist sentiment, and in most of [the counties in his district] the Baptist element was large enough to hold the balance of power." A decisive win in strongly Baptist Culpeper County proved critical to his election. As the editors of his papers explain, during the campaign, Madison

> denied rumors of his reported opposition to a bill of rights, lest gossip cost him the support of the dissenting religious sects, notably the Baptists, who were politically active not only in Culpeper but throughout the district. Soon after returning home JM wrote Baptist preacher George Eve to reassure him that his devotion to the cause of religious liberty had not abated and that he now favored adding to the

Constitution a declaration of fundamental rights, including "the rights of Conscience in the fullest latitude." Pastor Eve responded by actively promoting JM's candidacy among his flock, as did the Reverend John Leland, the leader of the Virginia Baptists.

Madison was undoubtedly aware of his electoral debts to the former dissenters.[10]

As promised, Madison introduced amendments in the first federal Congress, indicating as he did so not only their necessity for the good of the republic (particularly bringing into union reluctant Rhode Island and North Carolina—both Baptist bastions—which initially refused to endorse the U.S. Constitution because of a lack of express protection of fundamental rights, especially religious liberty) but a sense of obligation to his constituents, a group in which both Baptists and Presbyterians had strong influence. The progression of events—the initial decision of the Baptist General Committee and Orange County Baptists to oppose the constitution, Leland's candidacy and election eve change of heart, Madison's campaign letter to the Baptists, and the electoral role of the Baptists in both Madison's election to the convention and to the House of Representatives—suggests that the view of the dissenters was particularly weighty for Madison not only during the debates in Virginia but in his efforts to obtain the First Amendment.[11]

Philip Hamburger speculates that Madison's views on religious liberty, in particular opposition to any alliance between church and state, moderated between drafting the *Memorial* in 1785 and the First Amendment debates in 1789. Chief Justice William Rehnquist has implied the same. The role of the former dissenters and religious freedom in Madison's electoral success and his actions as president, not to mention his later summary of the battle for religious freedom in his "Detached Memorandum," put the lie to such a suggestion. As further evidence of Madison's interest in supporting the dissenters' views on religious freedom, he found it relevant to report to President George Washington that "one of the principal leaders of the Baptists lately sent me word that the amendments [the proposed Bill of Rights] had entirely satisfied the disaffected of his Sect, and that it would appear in their subsequent conduct." Under such circumstances, in seeking to divine Madison's intent in urging adoption of the First Amendment, it is not unreasonable to give particular consideration to the meaning of religious liberty understood by Virginia's dissenters.[12]

In a second exercise in historical forgetfulness, many have questioned the extent of contingency in the development of religious freedom in America, suggesting that religious freedom was largely inevitable and relatively easily developed, a natural outgrowth of the pluralism of colonial America, itself fed by

British mercantilist interests and European persecution of dissenters. These factors conspired to make America a haven for religious dissenters fleeing strife in Europe and resulted in both government and ecclesiastic institutions with significant inherent weaknesses. Many of the leading historians of American religious history, including Nathan Hatch, Sidney Mead, and Perry Miller, "have argued that most Americans were not following the cloud and pillar of high principle, but that they started walking down the road to religious freedom without knowing it."[13]

Certainly pluralism and dissent made America ripe for religious freedom and, if a new nation was to be formed, some accommodation was inevitable. For some analysts, these factors made development of a separation of church and state and of religious freedom "irreversible" by at least the time of the Great Awakening. Perhaps, although even if some form of religious liberty was inevitable, "what?" and "when?" were wide-open questions. Answering those questions in Virginia, and the influence that the Virginia experience would have on the young nation, depended both on the agency of dissenters (and their Enlightenment supporters) and effective assertion of principle.[14]

The contingency in the dissenters' battle in Virginia should not be gainsaid. While nineteenth-century sectarian historians sought to minimize conflict, the notion that religious freedom was readily embraced by Virginia's gentry simply obfuscates the struggle between Virginia's religious establishment and dissenters, the strength of the establishment in the state before the war, and the persecution and discrimination visited on dissenters. In fact, some of the factors supporting the presumed inevitability of religious freedom were double-edged; for example, the lack of complete ecclesiastic structure in Virginia, including the absence of a domestic bishop, simply served to further aggrandize the role of the gentry laity, which ran both church and state. As Jefferson recognized, the successful attack on that structure was one of the most difficult and important battles of the American Revolution.[15]

Could religious freedom in Virginia have been established during the Revolution without that conflict? No. Could it have been established without the intellectual underpinning provided by Jefferson and Madison and their dissenting supporters? Perhaps, but the foundation would not have been so plumb, nor perhaps spread so far. The Enlightenment rationale, joined with the dissenters' ideology, was essential to address concerns about virtue in a republican society, checks and balances in government, the relationship of government and religion, and the vibrancy of religion in a society that demands a separation of church and state. Had the foundation been off, by even a few degrees, through the course of history the line of development may have deviated substantially so that the plural establishment advocated in Virginia and

initially adopted in Maryland, Georgia, and South Carolina might have tri-
umphed, or the notion of a government-supported establishment with toleration of dissenters (as in Massachusetts) might have become the model. Virginia
dissenters, both their political influence and their driving ideology, and the
negotiations which brought them into the polity were essential, but Jefferson's
and Madison's intellectual justification became central to liberalization elsewhere, liberalization often supported by evangelicals. If the question is who
exercised agency and how in developments of political structures essential to
the winning of religious liberty that continued to evolve into the nineteenth
century and beyond, the political and social conflict and contest between dissenters and establishment leaders must be more fully considered.

There is, then, a third matter. This period, and events surrounding the
Revolution, produced a groundswell of political interest on the part of the
broader populace, with common men (quickly followed by common women)
recognizing, demanding, and fighting for a place in society that was so much
more distant in the colonial days of British Empire. In Virginia, the necessity of
establishment leaders negotiating with dissenters over religious freedom was
critical to those broader developments. The crucial change in the Virginia polity
embodying that transformation occurred not before the Revolution, as a result
of a religious awakening, or after the Revolution, as a consequence of the
formation of a republican government, but as part of the challenge the
Revolution itself. The social and political and religious ramifications were foundational not only for Virginia but for the new nation. What followed was the
Jeffersonian "Revolution of 1800" and Jacksonian democracy as the flow of history consumed the stream of republicanization that was fed in Virginia by a
challenge to the established hierarchy by religious dissenters.

During the American Revolution, Virginia's religious dissenters demanded
religious freedom in return for their full support for mobilization. The resulting negotiations changed Virginia's polity such that after the war, efforts to
reinvigorate the establishment failed, and dissenters ushered into law Jefferson's
heroic Statute for Establishing Religious Freedom. Readers may consider the
consequences of that fight on the development of religious freedom and, more
generally, on the nature of the young republic. Certainly, standing alone, the
struggles and expectations of Virginia's dissenters cannot answer questions in
current constitutional disputes nor define historic developments. Yet it is clear
that the current legal and historic literature and judicial decisions have failed
adequately to listen to the voice of Virginia's dissenters, and they must be
heard.

Appendix A: Persons Persecuted for Religion, Eighteenth-Century Virginia, Post-1763

Physical Persecution and Arrest

Name	County/Description
Afferman, John	Middlesex: beaten for participating in worship. Little, 516.
Alderson, John	Botetourt: reportedly jailed for marrying a couple outside church (or failing to pay parson's fees). Little, 457, 516. Apparently age seventy-five at time. Rennie, App 1:257. Regular Baptist. Simpson, II:61.
Ammon, Thomas	Culpeper: jailed for preaching, 1774. Little, 516; Rennie, 262. Separate Baptist. Simpson, II:61.
Anthony, Joseph	Chesterfield: jailed three months for preaching, 1771. Little, 516; Gewehr, 127. Chesterfield: Jailed 1770–71, offered to take oath but court said doing so in county would not suffice. "Prosecution," 416; Lutz, 98. Separate Baptist. Rennie, 257.
Baker, Elijah	Accomac: pelted with stones/apples; jailed (fifty-six days) in 1778: attempt to Shanghai. Little, 469, 473, 516. Separate Baptist; arrested for vagrancy in 1778. Rennie, 175, 257.
Banks, Adam	Culpeper: jailed, 1774. Little, 516; Rennie, 262. Jailed/arrested for holding prayer meeting. Riley, 66; Curry, 37.
Barrow, David	Nansemond: ducked and nearly drowned by twenty men, dragged and driven out, 1778. Benedict, II:249, note (not lower sort, "well-dressed men"). Regular Baptist. Simpson, I:5.
Bledsoe, Aaron	Baptist arrested for preaching. Carroll.
Burruss, Jacob	Caroline: Baptist, indicted for permitting "unauthorized" services, dismissed, 1768. Campbell, 201–2.

Name	County/Description
Burrus, John	Caroline: jailed for preaching, 1771. Little, 516, 235, 246–47. Caroline: indicted for "illegally preaching" and failure to attend, fined for the latter, 1768. Campbell, 201–2. Separate Baptist. Simpson, III:112.
Carter's Run	Meeting house broken into and perpetrators "doing the most slovenly things," pulpit and communion table broken up. Edwards, 90.
Chambers, Thomas	Orange: jailed, 1768. Little, 516; Rennie, 262.
Chappawomsick	Stafford: Regular Baptists. Violent opposition by gang led by Robert Ashby (about forty): harassed during worship, leading to a "bloody fray"; threw "live snake…into the midst of them while at worship"; hornets nest; brought guns to disperse. Edwards, 29; Benedict, II:31. Cursing and swearing while performing baptisms. Edwards, 30, quoting Fristoe.
Chastain, Rane	Chesterfield: ordered to leave county or go to jail. Little, 516. Separate Baptist. Simpson, I:6.
Chewning (Choning), Bartholomew	Caroline: preaching/teaching contrary to law, sentenced to jail or bond for good behavior, jailed, 1771. Campbell, 212–13, 436. Caroline: jailed. Little, 516, 235; Rennie, 262. Baptist exhorter "soon turned out" of jail. Semple, 102.
Chewning, Betty	Caroline: Baptist, refused summons to testify at Waller trial, fined 350 lbs. tobacco, 1772. Campbell, 222.
Chiles (Childs), James	Spotsylvania: jailed for preaching, 1768. Little 516, 93, 106–7, 203. (Patrick Henry reportedly argued case and obtained release, although Little thinks unlikely.) Separate Baptist. Rennie.
Clay, Eleazer	Chesterfield: man sought to whip, failed. Little, 516. Separate Baptist. Simpson, I:7. Member gentry. Rennie, 257.
Clay, John	Father of Henry Clay; jailed for preaching. Little 516, 218–19 (citing Bailey, *Trials and Victories*); Lutz, 99. Separate Baptist. Simpson, I:8. Jailed 1770, member gentry. Rennie, 258.
Corbley, John	Culpeper: taken from pulpit, dragged and beaten, jailed for preaching; Orange: jailed for preaching. Little, 516, 137–38. Regular Baptist. Simpson I:9. Culpeper: jailed 1769; Orange: jailed 1768. Rennie, 258.
Craig, Elijah	Culpeper: jailed for preaching twice, claimed put on rye bread and water (one month); Orange: jailed for preaching for seventeen to eighteen days, 1768. Little, 131. Edwards claims moved to inner cell to stop preaching. Little, 135, 516. Culpeper and Orange: jailed. Benedict, II:292. Separate Baptist. Simpson, I:11.

Name	County/Description
Craig, Joseph	Spotsylvania: apprehended but escaped, 1768. Little, 516, 127; Rennie, 263. Chased by dogs. *Religious Herald*, April 6, 1871. Persecuted Culpeper and Orange. Simpson, III:117, citing Craig. Craig claims he was taken four times, jailed once in Caroline County. Separate Baptist. Simpson, III:117.
Craig, Lewis	Spotsylvania: indicted and tried but not imprisoned (1766–67?); jailed for preaching (four weeks) (1768); Caroline: arrested and required to bond; jailed for preaching (three months), with Pendleton on bench, 1771. Little, 516, 53 et seq., 235, 249. Caroline: arrested/jailed for preaching contrary to license, sentenced to jail or bond, jailed, 1771. Campbell, 213–14. Separate Baptist. Simpson, I:13; Edwards, 78. Ordained 1770. Moore, 1433.
Daniel, Samuel	Caroline: Baptist, refused summons to testify at Waller trial, fined 350 lbs. tobacco, 1772. Campbell, 222.
Delaney (Dulaney), John	Culpeper: jailed for permitting another to preach, but not Baptist. Little, 421, 516. Separate Baptist. Rennie, 263.
Eastin, Augustine	Chesterfield: jailed for preaching, 1772; Cary on bench. Little, 516, 145, 312. Chesterfield: warrant for arrest, June 1772. Gewehr, 124 n.38. Chesterfield: arrested 1772, by now Cary had erected a wall around prison to discourage preaching. Lutz, 98; Edwards, 82. Chesterfield: jailed 1771. Rennie, 263. Separate Baptist. Simpson, II:70.
Elkins, Richard	Pittsylvania: two men started for warrant, frightened. Little, 516. Pittsylvania: apprehended in 1769. Rennie, 263.
Falkner (Faulkner), Richard	Middlesex: arrested but released as layman, 1771. Little, 516, 273.
Fristoe, Daniel	Fauquier: service interrupted by curses and antics; Stafford: warrant issued but not executed; gun presented to his breast. Little, 517. Regular Baptist. Simpson, I:16.
Fristoe, William	Stafford: pursued by sheriff with gun; taken by warrant, went to Philadelphia. Little, 517, 227, quoting Edwards, 33. Mobs caused bloodshed, but courts would not intervene. Rennie, 273, App. 4, citing Fristoe, 77–78. Regular Baptist. Simpson, II:76.
Gale, Mathew	Caroline: Baptist, in custody for failure to disperse on constable's order (at service), fined £5, 1772. Campbell, 222.
Goodloe, Henry	Caroline: arrested/jailed for permitting unauthorized revival (Waller) at house, 1772. Later declared insane. Campbell, 222, 437. Separate Baptist. Simpson, III:119.
Goodrich, James	Caroline: jailed for preaching, 1771. Little, 516, 235; Campbell, 212–13, 436.

Name	County/Description
Greenwood, James	King & Queen: jailed for preaching (sixteen days released on bond) 1772; Middlesex: jailed for preaching (forty-six days, thirty days without bounds); Richmond: threatened 1776. Little, 517, 288, 315, 460. Middlesex: jailed, 1771. Rennie, 258. Bread and water for four days in Middlesex. Thom, 24 (500). Separate Baptist. Simpson, III:120.
Hargate, Thomas	Amherst: jailed for preaching 1771. Little 517, 303–5; Edwards, 67.
Harriss, Samuel	Pittsylvania: opposed and slandered; Culpeper: "you shall not preach here," meeting broken up by mob (1765); door battered down during preaching; arrested as vagabond and schismatic (dismissed when said not likely to be back in county for year—preached anyway); Orange: pulled down and dragged by hair; Loudon: locked up in jail. Little, 517, 46, 48. Culpeper: arrested, 1765. Edwards, 58; Rennie, 258. Orange: pulled down by Benjamin Haley. Knocked down while preaching at Hawriver. In Hillsborough, went to preach to prisoners and locked up. Edwards, 59; Benedict, II:335–37. No record of Harriss abused in his own county (as he was gentry). Gewehr, 119–20. Separate Baptist. Simpson, I:19.
Herndon (Hearndon, Harndon), Edward	Caroline: jailed for preaching without a license, 1771. Little, 517, 235; Campbell, 212–13, 436. Baptist exhorter, "soon turned out" of jail. Semple, 102.
Holloway, Nathaniel	Caroline: Baptist, arrested for preaching without license, served jail sentence, 1772. Campbell, 220, 284.
Hubbard, James	Indicted for allowing Roan to preach. Foote, 142.
Ireland, James	Culpeper: seized by magistrates, jailed for preaching (five months), 1769–70, tried to suffocate with smoke, tried to blow up, tried to poison (injured for life), drunks put in cell, threatened with public whipping, horses ridden through crowd at jail, urinated in his face, charged for people to visit, threatened with locking in darkness. Little, 517–18, 156, 161 et seq., 176–77, citing Ireland, 140–42. See also Semple and Fristoe. Separate Baptist. Simpson, I:22. Later Regular Baptist. Benedict, II:33.
Kaufman, Martin	Shenandoah: beaten with stick. Little, 518, 222. Separate Baptist. Semple, 246.
Kelly, Thomas	Caroline: Baptist, in custody for failure to disperse on constable's order (at service), fined £5, 1772. Campbell, 222.

Name	County/Description
Koontz, John	Shenandoah: beaten with stick. Elsewhere beaten on road, arrested, and then released. Little, 518, 220–21. Beaten with sticks, dragged by hair. Thom, 17 (493) (citing Semple, Fristoe). Separate Baptist. Simpson, I:24, Rennie, 259.
Lane, Dutton	Lunenberg: told "not to come there again;" Pittsylvania: persecution, mother beaten by father for going to hear. Little, 518. Lane pursued by father. Edwards, 54; Benedict, II:340.
Leland, John	Orange: threatened with gun. Little, 518. Captain Robert Howard threatened to lash for baptizing his wife. Rennie, 168, citing Greene, *Writings of John Leland*, 21. Another women said her husband would beat her and kill the man to baptize her; he proceeded. Rennie, 168, citing Greene, 20. Separate Baptist. Rennie, 259.
Lewis, Iverson	Gloucester: violent opposition; Essex: arrested but not jailed, 1774. Little, 518, Rennie, 259. King & Queen: jailed, March 1774. Thom, 26 (502). Essex: jailed, 1774. Curry, 38. Separate Baptist. Simpson, I:27.
Lovall (Lovel), William	King & Queen: jailed for preaching (sixteen days, released on bond), 1772. Little, 518, 314. Separate Baptist. Rennie, 259.
Lunsford, Lewis	Northumberland: interrupted by mob (pistols/staves) and legal proscription, 1778; Richmond: summoned and required to bond, Landon Carter and Robert W. Carter on court, September 1775; stones thrown at house. Little, 450–52, 465, 518; see also James Barnett Taylor, *Lives of Virginia Baptist Ministers* (Richmond, 1838), cited in Rennie. Benedict, II:342. Was restrained from preaching for twelve months by securities in September 1775; August 9, 1778, "shocking tumult began and stopped him, some blows past, pistols presented and the stage broke down." Moore, 1391, 1395. Regular Baptist. Simpson, II:81.
McClanahan, William	Culpeper: jailed for preaching, John Slaughter on warrant, 1773 (apparently). Little, 369–73, 518; Rennie, 259. Captain Culpeper Minutemen, mostly Baptist. Little, 373–74 quoting Howe, *Historical Collections*, 238. Separate Baptist. Simpson, I:28.
Mackie, Samuel Sr.	Caroline: Presbyterian, bond or jail (jailed) for hurting a drunk Thomas Reynolds who entered his house to break up service, 1773. Campbell, 225.

Name	County/Description
Mackie, Samuel Jr.	Caroline: Presbyterian, bond or jail (jailed) for hurting a drunk Thomas Reynolds who entered house to break up service, 1773. Campbell, 225.
Major, Richard	Fairfax: warrants issued but not executed; Fauquier: mob, warrants issued, men intended to kill. Little, 518, 90. Loudon: met with "much opposition." Gewehr, 115 n.41. Regular Baptist. Rennie, 259; Edwards, 36.
Marsh [Mash], William	Spotsylvania: jailed for preaching, 1768 (forty-three days). Little, 518, 95, 106–7 (Henry supposedly argued case and got released; Little thinks unlikely). Torbet, 240.
Marshall, Daniel	Pittsylvania: "much persecution." Little, 518. Fauquier: arrested; Regular Baptist. Rennie, 260.
Marshall, William	Fauquier: arrested but not jailed. Little, 518.
Mastin, Thomas	Orange: presented to grand jury, 1769. Little, 518; Rennie, 263.
Maxwell (Maxfield), Thomas	Culpeper: jailed for preaching, 1774. Little, 518; Rennie, 263. Jailed for holding a prayer meeting. Riley, 66; Curry, 37. Semple, 146. Separate Baptist. Simpson, II:84.
Mintz, Edward	Nansemond: ducked and driven out, 1778. Little, 518, 462 quoting Benedict, II:249. Separate Baptist, later Regular. Simpson, I:31.
Moffett, Anderson	Culpeper: jailed for preaching. Little, 518. Separate Baptist. Rennie, 260.
Moore, Jeremiah	Assaulted by mob led by magistrates. Little, 391. Ducked in mockery of baptism, 1773. Rennie, 50 citing Semple, 400. Taylor, *Virginia*, I:220 says friend ducked, he escaped. Fairfax: apprehended and brought before magistrate; jailed (perhaps three times), 1773. Little, 519, 329. Taylor, *Virginia*, I:219. Bedford: arrested, magistrate accompanied by parson, 1773. Rennie, 162, citing Semple, 406. Regular Baptist. Rennie, 260.
Morris, Joshua	Indicted for allowing Roan to preach. Foote, 142.
Morris, Samuel	Indicted for allowing Roan to preach. Foote, 142.
Morton, Elijah	Orange: ousted as justice (1768) because Baptist. Little, 519, 92–93.
Murphy, Joseph	Brought before magistrate, not imprisoned. Little, 519, 37 (see also Taylor, *Virginia*, I:26). Separate Baptist. Rennie, 260.
Noel, Elder	Essex: Seized for baptizing a man's sister, the man tried (unsuccessfully) to duck him. Semple, 107.
Partlow, John	Caroline: Baptist, arrested for permitting preaching without a license at home, jailed, 1772. Campbell, 220, 437.

Name	County/Description
Picket (Pickett), John	Fauquier: opposition from mob and magistrate; jailed for preaching (three months), 1770; Culpeper: jailed for preaching. Little, 519, 192 (quoting Edwards). Culpeper: taunted and mocked by parson, Mr. Meldrum. Rennie, 161, citing Ireland, 130.
Pittman, Hipkins	Caroline: arrested and threatened with whipping, 1775. Little, 519, Campbell, 223, quoting Semple.
Pittman, James	Caroline: allowed unauthorized service at home, bond after sixteen days in jail, 1772. Campell, 437. Caroline: jailed for preaching (sixteen days), 1772. Little, 519, 321. Caroline: jailed 1771. Rennie, 264.
Pittman, Thomas	Caroline: allowed unauthorized service at his house, dismissed, 1771. Campbell, 436.
Pitts, Younger	Caroline: arrested, abused, released. Little, 519. Caroline: arrested, 1775; Separate Baptist. Rennie, 260.
Potter, Benjamin Sr.	Imprisoned and whipped. Regular. Hurt, 101.
Reed (Read), James	Dragged from stage, kicked, cuffed; Spotsylvania: jailed for preaching (forty-three days), 1768. Little, 519, 95, 106–7 (Henry supposedly argued case and obtained release; Little thinks highly unlikely). Separate Baptist. Rennie, 260.
Rice, Charles	Indicted for allowing Roan to preach. Foote, 142.
Roberts, Archibald	Chesterfield: apprehended, 1774. Rennie, 264.
Ross, Andrew	Caroline: Baptist, in custody for failure to disperse on constable's order (at service), fined £5, 1772. Campbell, 222.
Saunders, Nathaniel	Culpeper: summoned for preaching, John Slaughter on warrant; jailed for preaching, 1773. Little, 320, 369–72. Culpeper or Orange: tried and acquitted. Little, 519. Threatened prosecution if preached, 1775. Little, 376. Regular Baptist. Simpson, I:35. Separate Baptist. Rennie, 261.
Shackelford, John	Essex: jailed for preaching (eight days), 1774. Little, 519, 400. King & Queen: jailed, March 1774. James, 30 (James later says Essex, 215). Separate Baptist. Rennie, 261.
Spencer, Joseph	Orange: jailed for preaching at a Baptist meeting until bond given (almost one month), 1773; claims he is not an "Anabaptist." Orange County Order Book, No. 8 (1769–77), October 28, 1773, 287; November 26, 1773, 299.
Spiller, Philip	Stafford: jailed until court day for preaching. Little, 519, 70–71. Stafford: imprisoned, 1766. Rennie, 264. Regular Baptist. Rennie, 264.
Street, Henry	Middlesex: whipped, companions prevented more, 1771. Little, 519, 276.

Name	County/Description
Tanner, John	Chesterfield: Baptist jailed for preaching (Cary issued warrant), 1773, gave bond. Little, 219. Chesterfield: arrested on warrant issued by Cary for disturbing peace, not long in jail. "Prosecution," 416; Lutz, 99.
Taylor, John	Hampshire: "rage of mobs." Little 519, 307. Mob with weapons broke up meeting. Gewehr, 120, citing Taylor, *Lives*, I:233. Mob beat man (son-in-law of owner) who permitted meeting. Taylor, *Baptists*, 149. Separate Baptist. Rennie, 261.
Thomas, David	Stafford: violent opposition prevents worship; men armed with bludgeons; Culpeper or Orange: dragged out, attempt made to shoot (riot); Fauquier: pulled down and dragged out; Culpeper: opposition such that couldn't preach, 1763. Little, 519, 41, 178. See also Edwards, 26. Snake thrown in congregation. Gewehr, 115 n.41 citing Taylor, *Lives*, I:44 and Semple, 382–83, and Edwards. Dragged out of doors, another time shot at (someone knocked gun to save). Benedict, II:30–31. Regular Baptist. Little, 375; Rennie, 261.
Thompson, David	Attacked while preaching. Separate Baptist. Rennie, 261.
"Three Old Men"	Fauquier: arrested; parson acting as magistrate. Rennie, 264, 162 n.5, citing Fristoe, 80.
Tinsley, David	Chesterfield: jailed for preaching (four months and sixteen or seventeen days), 1774. Little, 520, 309; Lutz, 99. Burning tobacco and pepper. Taylor, *Virginia*, II:101. Separate Baptist. Rennie, 261. Semple, 286.
Tinsley, Philip	Caroline: indicted for permitting "unauthorized" services, dismissed, 1768. Campbell, 201–2.
Tribble, Andrew	Orange: presented for preaching. Little, 520. Separate Baptist. Simpson, I:38.
Waford, Thomas	Middlesex: beaten with whip (scarred back to death), seized but released as layman with warning to escape county on "pain of imprisonment," 1771. Little, 181, 273, 276, 300. Riley, 63 (Wofford). Essex: arrested, searched, released, 1774. Little, 520; Rennie, 264. Middlesex: imprisoned, 1771. Rennie, 264 (Wafer).
Walker, Jeremiah	James City: opposed by parson and others; Chesterfield: jailed for preaching, denied prison bounds (Cary on court), 1773; Lunenburg: sued for baptizing two boys, 1769. Little, 520, 148, 361. Chesterfield: jailed for preaching (Cary on warrant), 1773; denied prison bounds. "Prosecution," 416; Lutz, 99. Sued for baptizing two of Lester's sons (supposedly underaged); Lester dismissed but left costs on Walker. Edwards, 70. Separate Baptist. Simpson, I:39.

Name	County/Description
Waller, John	Hanover: dragged by hair; Caroline: jerked from stage, head beat on ground, whipped by sheriff about twenty lashes, 1771, jailed for preaching (ten days), Pendleton on bench, 1772. Little, 181, 229–30, 324–25, citing John Williams's journal (Henry may have defended). Essex: jailed for preaching (fourteen days), 1774; Spotsylvania: jailed for preaching (forty-three days), 1768 (Henry supposedly argued case and got released, Little thinks unlikely, Little, 106–7); Middlesex: jailed for preaching (forty-six days, thirty of which in close confinement). Little, 520, 93, 181, 288. Caroline: whipped by church clerk (Buckner) in presence of minister (Morton) and man identified as William Harris, sheriff, spring 1771; arrested/jailed unauthorized revival, 1772. Campbell, 220 ("Swearing Jack" Waller was high gentry), 224–25, citing Little at 229–31, William's journal; Edwards, 75 ("gore blood"); Rennie, 161–62. Middlesex: fed bread and water for four days in jail. Thom, 24 (500). Middlesex: jailed, parson accompany officials during arrest, 1771. Rennie, 161, 261. King & Queen: jailed, March 1774. Thom, 26 n.38, citing James, 30 (James later says Essex, 215). Middlesex: stone thrown at Waller while preaching. Benedict, II:48. Separate Baptist. Little, 375; Simpson, I:41.
Ware, James	Caroline: jailed for preaching (sixteen days), 1772. Little, 520, 321. Semple, 102, says jailed for permitting preaching (like Pittman). Campbell, 220–21 (refers to "John" Ware arrested for preaching without a license, presumably the same).
Ware, Robert	Essex: Baptist jailed for preaching (eight days), 1774; Middlesex: jailed for preaching (forty-six days, thirty days without bounds); men drinking and playing cards on stage where he preached. Little, 520, 288, 400–401, 404. Middlesex: jailed, 1771. Rennie, 261. Middlesex: bread and water for four days. Thom, 24 (500).
Watkins, Thomas	Indicted for allowing John Roan to preach. Foote, 142.
Weatherford, John	Chesterfield: jailed for preaching (five months) (Cary on bench), denied bounds of prison, hands slashed while extended beyond grated window while preaching, 1773. Little, 334, 344, 520; Lutz, 99. Henry defended and gained release (paid imprisonment costs). Little, 345–46. Separate Baptist. Simpson, I:43.

Name	County/Description
Webber, William	Middlesex: jailed for preaching (forty-six days, thirty days without bounds); Chesterfield: jailed (three months). Little, 520, 269, 288. Chesterfield: jailed, 1770–71; offered to take oath but court said doing so in county would not suffice. "Prosecution," 416; Lutz, 98. Middlesex: jailed, 1771. Benedict, II:400; Rennie, 263. Middlesex: bread and water for four days. Thom, 24 (500); Riley, 64 (fed by supporters). Middlesex: minister came at him with club (grabbed from behind). Riley, 63. Separate Baptist. Simpson, I:44.
Weeks, Alderson (Anderson)	Stafford: arrested, but not jailed. Little, 520, 71. Regular Baptist. Rennie, 264. Edwards, 28.
Winston, Isaac	Presbyterian, indicted for allowing John Roan to preach. Foote, 142. Fined for costs after Roan fled. Patrick Henry's maternal grandfather. Meade, 67.
Wyley (Wiley, Willey), Allen	Orange: jailed for preaching ("for some time"), 1768. Little, 520; Rennie, 264. Edwards, 32. Regular Baptist. Simpson, I:45. Separate Baptist. Rennie, 264.
Young, John	Caroline: jailed for preaching (four to six months), 1771; pepper burned when he tried to preach; signed petition against general assessment bill. Little, 520, 235–38. Caroline: preaching contrary to law, sentenced to jail or bond for good behavior, 1771; unauthorized preaching, case continued pending appeal earlier, 1772; Pendleton on court that convicted. Campbell, 212, 236, 437. Separate Baptist. Simpson, I:47.

Attending Unauthorized Service or Failing to Attend Anglican

Name	County/Description
Beazley, Edmond	Caroline: attending unauthorized service, dismissed, 1771. Campbell, 436.
Beazley, Elizabeth	Caroline: attending unauthorized service, dismissed, 1771. Campbell, 436.
Bennett, James	Middlesex: presented by grand jury for nonattendance, 1771, fined; presented 1772, 1773. Little, 266–67, 291.
Bennett, John	Middlesex: presented by grand jury for nonattendance, 1772. Little, 291.

Name	County/Description
Bennett, Thomas	Middlesex: presented by grand jury for nonattendance, 1772. Little, 291.
Blades, William	Caroline: indicted attending unauthorized, dismissed, 1768. Campbell, 201–2.
Bowie, James Jr.	Caroline: failure to attend, fined, 1768. Campbell, 201–2.
Bowie, John	Caroline: failure to attend, fined, 1768. Campbell, 201–2.
Brown, John	Caroline: failure to attend, 1768–70. Campbell, 207.
Burk, Thomas	Caroline: indicted attending unauthorized, dismissed, 1768. Campbell, 201–2.
Carden, John	Caroline: failure to attend, fined, 1768. Campbell, 201–2.
Chamber, Thomas	Orange: assembling unlawfully for preaching Baptists, ordered to bond or face jail. Orange County Order Book, No. 7 (1763–69), July 28, 1768, 514.
Chandler, Robert	Caroline: indictment attending unauthorized, dismissed, 1768. Campbell, 201–2.
Chewning, Charles	Caroline: attending unauthorized service, dismissed, 1771. Campbell, 436.
Collins, Thomas Jr.	Caroline: attending unauthorized service, dismissed, 1771. Campbell, 436.
Corbin, Gawin	Middlesex: presented by grand jury for absenting from church, 1771. Little, 266.
Corbley, John	Orange: assembling unlawfully for preaching Baptists, ordered to bond or face jail. Orange County Order Book, No. 7 (1763–69), July 28, 1768, 514.
Craig, Elijah	Orange: assembling unlawfully for preaching Baptists, ordered to bond or face jail. Orange County Order Book, No. 7 (1763–69), July 28, 1768, 514.
Craig, Joseph	Orange: Baptist presented for missing church, took oath and excused. Little, 516, 92.
Deagle, James	Middlesex: presented by grand jury for nonattendance 1773. Little, 291.
Deagle, William	Middlesex: presented by grand jury for nonattendance, 1771, 1772, 1773 (with wife). Little, 266, 291.
Drummel, Judith	Middlesex: presented by grand jury for nonattendance 1773. Little, 291.
Earlington, William	Caroline: failure to attend, fined, 1768. Campbell, 201–2.
Fleming, Francis	Caroline: failure to attend, fined, 1768; failure to attend 1768–70. Campbell, 201–2, 206.
Gatewood, James	Caroline: indictment attending unauthorized, dismissed, 1768. Campbell, 201–2.
George, Lodowick	Caroline: failure to attend, fined, 1768. Campbell, 201–2.
Gilkin, Firth (?)	Caroline: failure to attend, 1768–70. Campbell, 206.

Name	County/Description
Goodrich, John	Caroline: attending unauthorized service, dismissed, 1771. Campbell, 436.
Greenwood, James	Middlesex: presented for being absent from church. Little, 516.
Hoar, John	Middlesex: presented by grand jury for nonattendance, 1773. Little, 291.
Hoddon, Thomas	Middlesex: presented by grand jury for nonattendance, 1773. Little, 291.
Jones, Nicholas	Orange: presented for being absent from church. Little, 92.
Lee, Thomas	Middlesex: presented by grand jury for nonattendance, 1771, fined. Little, 266–67.
Lee, William	Middlesex: presented by grand jury for nonattendance, 1773. Little, 291.
McNails, George	Caroline: indictment attending unauthorized, dismissed, 1768. Campbell, 201–2.
Miller, Christopher	Middlesex: presented by grand jury for nonattendance, 1773. Little, 291.
Moody, Griffin	Caroline: failure to attend, fined, 1768; failure to attend, 1768–70. Campbell, 201–2, 207.
Noden, Martha	Caroline: indicted attending unauthorized, dismissed, 1768. Campbell, 201–2.
Oakes, Henry	Orange: presented for being absent from church. Little, 92.
Parker, William Jr.	Caroline: failure to attend, fined, 1768. Campbell, 201–2.
Powal, David (wife)	Middlesex: presented by grand jury for nonattendance, 1773. Little, 291.
Pritchet, Lucretia	Middlesex: presented by grand jury for nonattendance, 1772, 1773. Little, 291.
Pruit, Benjamin	Caroline: failure to attend, fined, 1768. Campbell, 201–2.
Pruit, John	Caroline: failure to attend, fined, 1768. Campbell, 201–2.
Pruit, Thadeus	Caroline: failure to attend, fined, 1768. Campbell, 201–2.
Redd, Joseph	Caroline: failure to attend, fined, 1768. Campbell, 201–2.
Rhodes, Benjamin	Middlesex: presented by grand jury for nonattendance, 1773. Little, 291.
Robinson, Christopher	Middlesex: presented by grand jury for nonattendance, 1771, fined. Little, 266.
Roy, Thomas	Caroline: failure to attend, fined, 1768. Campbell, 201–2.
Southworth, John	Caroline: failure to attend, fined, 1768; failure to attend, 1768–70. Campbell, 201–2, 206.
Spencer, Joseph	Orange: presented for being absent from church, took oath and excused. Orange County Order Book, No. 7 (1763–69), June 23, 1768, 502.
Stevens, Micajah	Caroline: attending unauthorized service, dismissed, 1771. Campbell, 436.

Name	County/Description
Stop, James	Orange: presented for being absent from church. Little, 92.
Stop, Joshua	Orange: presented for being absent from church. Little, 92.
Strother, William	Orange: presented for being absent from church, took oath and excused. Little, 92.
Tarrent, Henry	Caroline: failure to attend, fined, 1768. Campbell, 201–2.
Terrell, Christopher	Caroline: indictment attending unauthorized, dismissed, 1768. Campbell, 201–2.
Terrell, Henry	Caroline: indicted attending unauthorized, dismissed, 1768. Campbell, 201–2.
Terrell, Rachel	Caroline: indicted attending unauthorized, dismissed, 1768. Campbell, 201–2.
Terrell, Thomas	Caroline: indictment attending unauthorized, dismissed, 1768. Campbell, 201–2.
Thompson, John	Caroline: indictment attending unauthorized, dismissed, 1768. Campbell, 201–2.
Tinsley, William	Caroline: indicted attending unauthorized, dismissed, 1768. Campbell, 201–2.
Wake, Judith	Middlesex: presented by grand jury for not attending, 1771. Little, 266.
Walker, Catherine	Middlesex: presented by grand jury for not attending, 1771. Little, 266.
Ware, Edward	Middlesex: presented by grand jury for not attending, 1772. Little, 291.
Ware, Robert	Middlesex: presented by grand jury for not attending, 1771. Little, 520, 266.
Webmore, Edward	Middlesex: presented by grand jury for not attending, 1772. Little, 291.
Wiley, Allan	Orange: assembling unlawfully for preaching Baptists, ordered to bond or face jail. Orange County Order Book, No. 7 (1763–69), July 28, 1768, 514.
Wilson, Holding	Orange: presented for being absent, took oath and excused. Little, 92.
Woolfolk, Robert	Caroline: indicted attending unauthorized, dismissed, 1768. Campbell, 201–2.
Wyatt, John	Caroline: failure to attend, fined, 1768. Campbell, 201–2.

Appendix B: Denominational Support for Mobilization in Virginia during the American Revolution

Calculating the support given to mobilization by various denominations in Virginia during the American Revolution cannot be done directly and, even indirectly, poses a host of problems. Data for enlistment by denomination are not available. Moreover, even if such data did exist—either on a statewide basis or for several counties—at best rough estimates of the relative strength of denominations in revolutionary Virginia, generally or by county, are available. As noted in chapter 1, calculation of a dissenting denomination's strength in the eighteenth century is greatly complicated by the occasional conformity of many and by the fact that normally several times the number of people participated in dissenters' worship services than became "members" of the dissenting churches. Without information on the specific strength of each denomination in a given county, a detailed comparison of relative mobilization by denomination could not be made, even if enlistment by denomination was available.

Some effort to identify denominational support for mobilization can be made by identifying the relative strength of denominations by county. Beyond the general geographic distribution discussed in chapter 1, this can be done by locating dissenting churches by county.[1] Here, too, several problems arise. First, many of the early meeting houses for both Baptist and Presbyterian dissenters were simply homes or farm buildings that were used for preaching or prayer meetings on an occasional basis. Furthermore, many churches established by dissenting congregations had several associated meeting houses, even though each meeting house could not necessarily be considered a separate congregation or church. A similar pattern existed in most Anglican parishes, with each parish in 1770, on average, associated with 2.7 churches or chapels.[2] Nor can one easily identify Anglican strength by locating Anglican churches (data for which are more readily available) because the law required the presence of at least one Anglican church in each parish whether or not there were substantial numbers of Anglicans utilizing the facility.

To address these concerns, published lists of Baptist and Presbyterian churches in Virginia in 1776 from Lewis Peyton Little, *Imprisoned Preachers and Religious Liberty in Virginia* and Robert P. Davis, James H. Smylie, Dean K. Thompson, Ernest Trice Thompson, and William Newton Todd, *Virginia Presbyterians in American Life: Hanover Presbytery (1755–1980)* were used. Little's list was supplemented and revised using the underlying sources, Robert Semple's *History of the Baptists* and Morgan Edwards's journal, *Materials towards a History*, as Little failed to include a number of churches from Semple and included several churches twice using the different names for a single congregation from Semple and Edwards. The final, corrected list of Baptist churches follows at the end of this appendix. The list from *Virginia Presbyterians* appears to be relatively thorough. The resulting list of early Virginia dissenting churches yields eighty-nine Virginia Baptist churches and ninety-four Presbyterian churches from 1776.[3] Although a few other churches might also claim roots in the period, these may represent affiliated meeting houses. Certainly on an aggregate basis, these lists provide a reasonable means to identify the presence of dissenting congregations and relative strength of dissenting denominations by county.

For these purposes, the 1776 dissenting churches had to be classified by county. Whereas Semple and Edwards generally provide county data, for many of the Presbyterian churches listed in *Virginia Presbyterians*, the county in which a church was formed and in which it was located in 1776 had to be identified, a task complicated by the creation of new counties throughout the period. Problems also arose for several of the Baptist churches that were identified by Semple as in a county that was formed after the creation of the church and after 1776, for example, Fluvanna (formed in 1777) for the Fork Church founded in 1774.

Once the counties of origin were identified, the number of Baptist and Presbyterian churches in a county in 1776 was used to classify a county as "Baptist" (B) or "Presbyterian" (P) presence if there was one such dissenting church present, or "Strong Baptist" (BB) or "Strong Presbyterian" (PP) presence if there were two or more such churches in the county. If there were no dissenting churches in a county, it was classified as "Other"— for our purposes, dominated by Anglicans. Of course, because some counties might have both Baptist and Presbyterian churches, a county could be designated as both Baptist and Strong Presbyterian, for instance, resulting in data from that county being considered in both categories. This imperfect system allows at least some consideration of relative dissenter strength by county.

As most of the available data by county on recruiting and requisitions were from the 1780 to 1781 period, counties that were formed between 1776 and 1781 were categorized according to the classification of the county or counties from which they were formed using the 1776 church lists.[4] No effort was made to update the lists of churches to 1780 because all denominations faced very significant disruption during the war, and identifying churches that had been formed would be difficult and identifying those that were no longer meeting would be even more so. Certainly the information from 1776 provides an accurate general representation of the denominational strength in the counties throughout the war.[5]

The strength of dissenter presence in the various Virginia counties was then compared to four sets of mobilization data available by county. First, Thomas Jefferson's papers include a table showing militia "rais[e]d" in 1776 by county—presumably to fill newly formed Continental and Virginia regiments—along with militia strength by county. Second, in October 1780, the Virginia General Assembly asked each county to provide a specific number of men in response to a requisition from the Continental Congress. Third, in 1781, Richmond called for a specified number of "six-month men" from each county to help repel Cornwallis's invasion. Finally, with hyperinflation and administrative problems making taxation and procurement largely ineffective in the final years of active warfare, Richmond requisitioned specific allotments of clothing for soldiers from each county under the 1780 Provision Law. In each of the latter three cases, records were submitted to Richmond permitting a comparison of a county's actual response to the number of men or amount of supplies that were requisitioned. Thus, a percentage of mobilization response could be calculated for each county (in the latter years, averaging the response for the 1780 and 1781 troop mobilizations and the 1781 requisition) and the results tabulated by category (Baptist, Strong Baptist, Presbyterian, Strong Presbyterian, and other (Anglican) counties).[6]

With respect to the information in Jefferson's papers concerning militia "rais[e]d 1776" by county, although his table is not perfectly clear, and neither the context nor other documents seem to explain the table, it would appear that in his capacity as a member of the General Assembly's committee on the army, he was recording each county's response to the mobilization of Virginia militia into the Continental Army or the Virginia regiments in 1776.[7] From these data, the percentage of each county's militia that enlisted for Continental service could be calculated and then aggregated by county category (Baptist, Strong Baptist, etc.). The results are shown in table 4.1. In performing this analysis, several adjustments were necessary. First, this analysis uses Jefferson's 1776 figures for militia raised but the 1777 figures for total militia by county when available because Jefferson viewed these as more accurate than the 1776 data. In the limited instances when militia strength from 1777 was not available, 1776 data were utilized. Second, in several instances the reported data in the *Papers of Thomas Jefferson* listed a bracket ([ ]) where obviously a "0" was intended. Thus, "90[ ]" for the Albemarle militia was read as "900." These adjustments were made based on the copy of the document available from the Library of Congress American Memories site.[8] To make sense of the data, blanks left by Jefferson were treated as zeroes. Third, to calculate militia size in 1777 to compare to militia raised in 1776, Henry and Pittsylvania Counties were added together as were Albemarle and Fluvanna. Ohio, Monongalia, and Yohogania (formed from Augusta West) were excluded from this analysis because of the difficulty of creating a fair comparison between the available 1776 and 1777 data.

With respect to the three data sets from 1780 and 1781, several factors complicated calculations and analysis of the results. First and foremost, a very high percentage of the counties for each of the requisitions did not respond to Richmond's call for returns (noted as "no return" or "?" on the returns). Although it is likely that a "no return" often equated to the county's failure to supply any of the requisitioned troops or supplies, given the state of records and potential difficulties in communicating with Richmond in

1780 and 1781, this could not simply be assumed. As a result, when no return was available from a county, it was simply ignored for calculating the response to that requisition.[9]

Second, given the high "no return" rate in some categories, the "averages" presented in table 4.2 are not simply the average of the three individual data sets reported in that table (1780 troops, 1781 troops, and 1781 materials). Simply averaging these columns would weight data sets with particularly high "no return" rates equally with other data sets. For example, the 1781 troop requisition for Presbyterian counties, with an almost 88 percent no response rate, would be weighted equally with the 1780 troop requisition in Presbyterian counties, with a less than 7 percent no response rate. To resolve this problem, the final figures presented are the average of each of the county averages; thus, each county, if it had any data at all, was treated equally (whether it had data for one, two, or all three of the reports on mobilization). Another means to address this problem would be simply to average every data point available (each county, each requisition). It was found, however, that this did not result in a significant variation from relying on the compilation of the county averages and, because this analysis is based on county results, that method was used. Still, the high rate of no returns, particularly among Anglican counties, gave individual data points more significance than they probably deserved. Given the limitations on the data, this appears unavoidable. The data do, however, provide at least a tentative analytical framework.

Any conclusions concerning the impact of dissenters on mobilization have to be tentative for several reasons. One could argue, for example, that response to requisitions in 1780 and 1781 from counties would, of necessity, be limited from those counties that responded most vigorously in the early years of the war. Alternatively, one might suggest that a growing latent Toryism in a war-weary Virginia makes analysis from 1780 and 1781 most apt. For example, H. J. Eckenrode, archivist at the Library of Virginia, noted that "towards the close of the Revolution the State contained an increasing number of passive Tories."[10] One must also consider other factors that could influence support for mobilization, for example, the need of a county to respond to possible Indian attacks or the unwillingness of the men to enlist when their homes and families might be directly threatened by British troops. In that regard, the relative rate of support for mobilization tends to be strongest in those areas away from the frontier and British troops, that is, the northern Piedmont and Northern Neck (see figure B.1.)

Nonetheless, the data that are available support the notion that dissenting counties mobilized at least as effectively as nondissenting counties and, as the war progressed, more so. The relative response rates from county groups early in the war are much more comparable when compared to the average rate of response, with the relative differences being much smaller than in the 1780–81 period. For the 1780–81 data, the strongest support came from those counties designated Strong Baptist and Presbyterian, and the differences were substantial. Interestingly, these counties had the highest available response rate and, if no return often corresponded to an inadequate response, the differences might have been even greater than suggested by table 4.2. The lowest mobilization rate, although only marginally so, was from Other, that is, Anglican, counties.

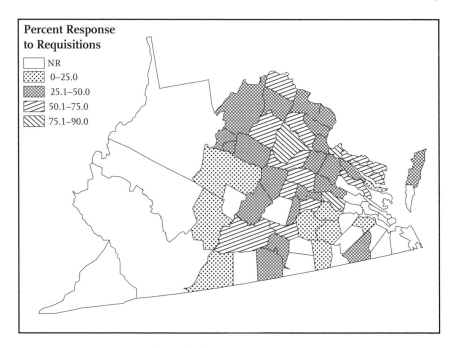

FIGURE B.1. Requisitions 1780–1781, by county. Response to Virginia's wartime requisitions were strongest in regions where dissenters had a strong presence and where British incursions had not directly disturbed the area.

On its face, this is an interesting conclusion given the prewar history of discrimination and persecution that might have justified grudging or limited support for the war by dissenters, not to mention the loyalist tendencies of many dissenters in North Carolina. In fact, one might conclude that even proportional mobilization by dissenters, given the treatment that they received at the hands of the establishment before the war, supports the notion that they negotiated for religious freedom in return for mobilization and that they delivered the promised support.

Although there are significant difficulties with this analysis, no other analysis of these data has been located, and this is a start. Previous sectarian histories lauding the bravery and loyalty of particular individuals can be fascinating but provide little comparative analysis of the relative strength of mobilization by sect.

Baptist Churches in Virginia, 1776

Ketocton	Loudon 1751
Opekon (Mill Creek)	Berkeley 1752 (1743)
Smith Linville's Creek	Rockingham 1756
Smith's Creek	Shenandoah 1758
Dan River	Pittsylvania 1760
Blackwater	Pittsylvania 1761
Stanton	Pittsylvania 1761
Broadrun	Fauquier 1762
Pungo (Oak Grove)	Pr. Anne 1762
Chappawomsick	Stafford 1766
Newvalley	Loudon 1767
Upper Spotsylvania	Spotsylvania 1767
Little-river	Loudon 1768
Mountain Run	Orange 1768
Birtchcreek	Pittsylvania 1769
Carter's Run	Culpeper 1769
Waller's	Spotsylvania 1769
Rapid-ann	Orange 1769
Nottoway	Amelia 1769
Blue Run	Orange 1769
Fall Creek	Pittsylvania 1770
Louisa	Louisa 1770
Mill Creek	Pittsylvania 1770
Culpeper	Culpeper 1771
Potomack (Hartwood)	Stafford 1771
Bedford	Bedford 1771
Amherst (Ebenezer)	Amherst 1771
Manor	Fauquier 1771
Goochland	Goochland 1771
Fiery Run	Culpeper 1771
Meherrin	Lunenburg 1771
Powhatan	Powhatan 1771
Cubb Creek*	Charlotte 1771
Buckingham	Buckingham 1772
Leatherwood	Henry 1772
Racoon Swamp	Sussex 1772
Bluestone	Mecklenburg 1772
Crooken Run	Culpeper 1772

Lower King & Queen*	King & Queen 1772
Upper Essex*	Essex 1772
Glebe Landing*	Essex 1772
Mill Creek*	Fauquier 1772
Rocks*	Pr. Edward 1772
Thumb Run*	Fauquier 1772
Buck Marsh*	Frederick 1772
Pig River	Franklin 1773
Albemarle	Albemarle 1773
Battle Run	Culpeper 1773
Burrus	Caroline 1773
Malone's (Geneto)	Mecklenburg 1773
Chesterfield	Chesterfield 1773
Harper's	Dinwiddie 1773
Catawba	Halifax 1773
Upper Banister	Pittsylvania 1773
Wynn's	Halifax 1773
Sappony	Sussex 1773
Dover*	Goochland 1773
James City*	James City 1773
Reeds*	Caroline 1773
Appomattox*	Pr. Edward 1773
Muddy Creek	Powhatan 1774
Fork	Albemarle 1774
Mill Swamp	Isle of Wight 1774
Mayo	Halifax 1774
Mountponey	Culpeper 1774
Tuckahoe*	Caroline 1774
Upper King & Queen*	King & Queen 1774
Piscataway*	Essex 1774
Guineas*	Spotsylvania 1774
N. Fork, Pamunkey*	Orange 1774
Smith's Creek*	Shenandoah 1774
Providence*	Buckingham 1774
Bethel*	Fincastle 1774
Totier	Albemarle 1775
Reedy Creek	Lunenburg 1775
Hunting Creek	Halifax 1775
Rowanty	Dinwiddie 1775

(continued)

Baptist Churches in Virginia, 1776 (*continued*)

Upper College*	King William 1775
Exol*	King & Queen 1775
Goose Creek*	Loudon 1775
Bull Run*	Fairfax 1775
Difficult*	Fairfax 1775
Simpson's Creek*	Monongalia 1775
Mathews*	?? 1775
Buffaloe	Halifax 1776
Ready Creek	Brunswick 1776
Chickahominy*	Hanover 1776
Charles City*	Charles City 1776
Licking Hole*	Goochland 1776

Note: Some churches were classified as a branch of other congregations (Edwards notes this in places) and, thus, not listed. Others on Little's list were deleted as duplicates or different names of same church (e.g., Lower Spotsylvania and Waller's).

Sources: Robert B. Semple, *A History of the Baptists in Virginia*, ed. G. W. Beale (1894, reprint, Cottonport, La.: Polyanthos, 1972), and Morgan Edwards, *Materials towards a History of the Baptists in the Provinces of Maryland, Virginia, North Carolina, South Carolina, Georgia*, vol. III (1772) (microfilm, University of Virginia Special Collections). Little's compilation of the data from Semple and Edwards (Lewis Peyton Little, *Imprisoned Preachers and Religious Liberty in Virginia* [1938, reprint, Gallatin, Tenn.: Church History Research and Archives, 1987]) leaves out approximately twenty churches from Semple (*) without explanation.

Notes

INTRODUCTION

1. Earlier suggestions that the Virginia church was fundamentally weakened by the growth of evangelical dissent, e.g., Rhys Isaac, *The Transformation of Virginia, 1740–1790* (New York: Norton, 1982), have been rightly challenged by more recent works. See generally John K. Nelson, *A Blessed Company: Parishes, Parsons and Parishioners in Anglican Virginia, 1690–1776* (Chapel Hill: University of North Carolina Press, 2001); Nancy L. Rhoden, *Revolutionary Anglicanism: The Colonial Church of England Clergy during the American Revolution* (New York: New York University Press, 1999). A number of studies also suggested that the First Great Awakening republicanized the Virginia polity prior the Revolution and left the Anglican Church subject to collapse. See Alan Heimert, *Religion in the American Mind from the Great Awakening to the Revolution* (Cambridge, Mass.: Harvard University Press, 1966); Rhys Isaac, "Religion and Authority: Problems of the Anglican Establishment in Virginia in the Era of the Great Awakening and the Parsons' Cause," *William and Mary Quarterly*, 3rd ser., 30:1 (January 1973), 4 n.5; Sydney E. Ahlstrom, *A Religious History of the American People*, 2nd ed. (New Haven, Conn.: Yale University Press, 2004), 263, 348; Wesley M. Gewehr, *The Great Awakening in Virginia, 1740–1790* (Durham, N.C.: Duke University Press, 1930).

2. William Fristoe, *A Concise History of the Ketocton Baptist Association* (1808; reprint, Harrisonburg, Va.: Sprinkle Publications, 2002), 69–70.

3. Robert B. Semple, *A History of the Baptists in Virginia*, rev. G. W. Beale (1894; reprint, Cottonport, La.: Polyanthos, 1972); Fristoe, *Concise History*; William Henry Foote, *Sketches of Virginia Historical and Biographical* (1850; reprint, Richmond, Va.: John Knox Press, 1966); Lemuel Burkitt, *A Concise History of the Kehukee Baptist Association, from its original rise down to 1803* (Halifax, N.C.: A. Hodge, 1803). See, e.g., Nelson, *Blessed Company*, 285; Brent Tarter, "Reflections on the Church of England in

Colonial Virginia," *Virginia Magazine of History and Biography*, 112:4 (2004), 354; Jon Butler, "Coercion, Miracle, Reason: Rethinking the American Religious Experience in the Revolutionary Age," in *Religion in the Revolutionary Age*, ed. Ronald Hoffman and Peter J. Albert (Charlottesville: University Press of Virginia, 1994), 23; Bishop William Meade, *Old Churches, Ministers and Families of Virginia* (1857; reprint, Baltimore, Md.: Genealogical Publishing, 1978), I:426.

4. James Madison to William Bradford, April 1, 1774, in William T. Hutchinson and William M. E. Rachal, eds., *The Papers of James Madison* (Chicago: University of Chicago Press, 1962), I:112.

5. Prince William County (June 20, 1776) (emphasis added), Early Virginia Religious Petitions, www.memory.loc.gov/ammem/collections/petitions. Most of the petitions referenced herein are available in this database and hereinafter will be cited merely by county and date. Other petitions will be cited in full. The copy of this petition from Prince William County is damaged in the Library of Congress database; language supplemented from Garnett Ryland, *The Baptists of Virginia, 1699–1926* (Richmond: Virginia Baptist Board of Missions and Education, 1955), 98.

6. Thomas Jefferson, *Autobiography*, in *Thomas Jefferson Writings*, ed. Merrill D. Peterson (New York: Library of America, 1984), 34.

7. Edmund Randolph, *History of Virginia*, ed. Arthur H. Shaffer (Charlottesville: University of Virginia Press, 1970), 263–64, 194; David John Mays, ed., *Letters and Papers of Edmund Pendleton, 1734–1803* (Charlottesville: University of Virginia Press, 1967), II:488–89. This benign characterization of Virginia's struggle for religious liberty has been accepted by some modern scholars, for example, H. J. Eckenrode, *Separation of Church and State in Virginia: A Study in the Development of the Revolution* (1910; reprint, New York: Da Capo Press, 1971), 49–51. William McLoughlin argues that "Anglican authority and power immediately ceased" with the onset of the Revolution and that "Dissenters restrained their actions against rebel legislatures, and the legislatures in turn offered more leniency." William G. McLoughlin, "The Role of Religion in the Revolution," in *Essays on the American Revolution*, ed. Stephen G. Kurtz and James H. Hutson (Chapel Hill: University of North Carolina Press, 1973), 202, 205.

8. Mecklenburg County (May 29, 1777).

9. Petitioning was a common means to seek redress of grievances in the eighteenth century. Raymond C. Bailey, *Popular Influence upon Public Policy: Petitioning in Eighteenth-Century Virginia* (Westport, Conn.: Greenwood Press, 1979). Yet Virginia's revolutionary religious petitions evidence a change in the pattern and significance of petitioning, providing further evidence of the politicization of dissenters. Whereas previous petitions focused primarily on local problems of interest to an individual or small group, the Virginia dissenters mounted a concerted campaign on a pressing issue of general import to the entire Commonwealth.

10. Other historians have properly noted the importance of the lower class and otherwise disenfranchised persons in the revolutionary movement. See Woody Holton, *Forced Founders: Indians, Debtors, Slaves, and the Making of the American Revolution in Virginia* (Chapel Hill: University of North Carolina Press, 1999), and

Michael A. McDonnell, *The Politics of War: Race, Class, and Conflict in Revolutionary Virginia* (Chapel Hill: University of North Carolina Press, 2007). Although class issues were significant in local support for the Revolution, the critically important transformation in Virginia society changed the way in which social and religious groups related. Compare Gordon S. Wood, *The Radicalism of the American Revolution* (New York: Vintage Books, 1993).

CHAPTER I

1. John K. Nelson, *A Blessed Company: Parishes, Parsons and Parishioners in Anglican Virginia, 1690–1776* (Chapel Hill: University of North Carolina Press, 2001), 4, 14, 211–25, 74–75, 344 n.17; William Waller Hening, ed., *The Statutes at Large, Being a Collection of all the Laws of Virginia from the First Session of the Legislature in the Year 1619* (Heritage Books, CD-ROM #0878, 2003), I (1642):240; IX (1776):132–33; VII (1757):93; II (1676):359; H. R. McIlwaine, ed., *Journals of the House of Burgesses of Virginia,* 1659/60–1693 (Richmond, 1906–1908), 455; William Hickman, *William Hickman 1747–1830: A Short Account of my Life and Travels. For more than fifty years; A Professed Servant of Jesus Christ* (1828; reprint, Louisville, Ken.: Kentucky Baptist Historical Commission, 1969), 8; William H. Seiler, "The Anglican Parish in Virginia," in *Seventeenth-Century America: Essays in Colonial History,* ed. James Morton Smith (Chapel Hill: University of North Carolina Press, 1959), 132. W. W. Scott, *A History of Orange County in Virginia* (Richmond, Va.: Everett Waddey, 1907), 50 (quote). Nancy Rhoden, *Revolutionary Anglicanism: The Colonial Church of England Clergy during the American Revolution* (New York: New York University Press, 1999), 10. Hening, *Statutes,* III (1705):288; VI (1753):326. Wesley M. Gewehr, *The Great Awakening in Virginia, 1749–1790* (Durham, N.C.: Duke University Press, 1930), 31. In theory, dissenters' suffrage might also have been limited, but this appears not to have occurred. Charles S. Sydnor, *American Revolutionaries in the Making: Political Practices in Washington's Virginia* (New York: Free Press, 1965), 35. Vestries had also been responsible for providing "surveyors" of the public roads and workmen to assist in repairing roads and bridges (Seiler, "Anglican Parish," 138–39), but well before the Revolution this authority was transferred to county courts. Hening, *Statutes,* VI (1749):66.

2. For example, Joseph A. Waddell, *Annals of Augusta County, Virginia, from 1726 to 1871* (1902; reprint, Bridgewater, Va.: C. J. Carter, 1958), 59; Robert E. Brown and Katherine Brown, *Virginia 1705–1786: Democracy or Aristocracy* (East Lansing: Michigan State University Press, 1964), 254. Waddell, *Annals of Augusta,* 214. Hening, *Statutes* VIII:432–33. John C. Van Horne, ed., *The Correspondence of William Nelson as Acting Governor of Virginia, 1770–1771* (Charlottesville: University Press of Virginia, 1975), 158–59 and n.2 (quote). Compare Rhys Isaac, "Religion and Authority: Problems of the Anglican Establishment in Virginia in the Era of the Great Awakening and the Parsons' Cause." *William and Mary Quarterly,* 3rd Ser., 30:1 (January 1973): 26.

3. Edmund Randolph, *History of Virginia,* ed. Arthur H. Shaffer (Charlottesville: University Press of Virginia, 1970), 158. William Fristoe, *A Concise History of the*

Ketocton Baptist Association (1808; reprint, Harrisonburg, Va.: Sprinkle Publications, 2002), 64. Robert R. Howison, *History of Virginia, from its Discovery and Settlement by Europeans to the Present Time* (Richmond, Va.: Drinker and Morris, 1848), II:175. Rhys Isaac, "'The Rage of Malice of the Old Serpent Devil': The Dissenters and the Making and Remaking of the Virginia Statute for Religious Freedom," in *The Virginia Statute for Religious Freedom: Its Evolution and Consequences in American History*, ed. Merrill D. Peterson and Robert C. Vaughan (Cambridge: Cambridge University Press, 1988), 140–41. Nelson, *Blessed Company*, 244–52. Gewehr, *Great Awakening*, 128 (Middlesex County saw fifteen presentments for nonattendance in May 1771, eight in May 1772, eleven in May 1773; "We are told there were quite as many presentments at the other quarterly terms and that 'most of those presented were fined each time five shillings and the cost—very few were excused.'"), quoting Letter of P. T. Woodward, clerk of court (April 28, 1873). Caroline County Order Book, 1768–1769, 142, 272–73, 305, 348, 457, 471 (numerous presentments and fines for failure to attend), facsimile, Heritage Center, Fredericksburg, Va. See also appendix A. Joan R. Gundersen, *The Anglican Ministry in Virginia 1723–1766: A Study of a Social Class* (New York: Garland, 1989), 183.

4. Ernest Trice Thompson, *Presbyterians in the South: Volume One: 1607–1861* (Richmond, Va.: John Knox Press, 1963), 54–56; Robert P. Davis, "The Struggle for Religious Freedom (1611–1776)," in *Virginia Presbyterians in American Life: Hanover Presbytery (1755–1980)*, ed. Robert P. Davis, James H. Smylie, Dean K. Thompson, Ernest Trice Thompson, and William Newton Todd (Richmond, Va.: Hanover Presbytery, 1982), 27; Henry R. McIlwaine, *The Struggle of Protestant Dissenters for Religious Toleration in Virginia*, Johns Hopkins University Studies, Historical and Political Science, 12th Ser., IV (Baltimore, Md.: Johns Hopkins University Press, 1894), 54. William Henry Foote, *Sketches of Virginia Historical and Biographical* (1850; reprint, Richmond, Va.: John Knox Press, 1966), 211–14. "Address to Anabaptists Imprisoned in Caroline," *Virginia Gazette* (Purdie and Dixon), February 20, 1772.

5. Frances Earle Lutz, *Chesterfield: An Old Virginia County* (Richmond, Va.: William Byrd Press, 1954), 98. Fristoe, *Concise History*, 67–68, 69–70. See also Amelia County: Baptists, Petition, *Journal of the House of Burgesses* (Feb. 24, 1772), 185–86 (only one meeting house permitted per county) (Heritage Books, CD-ROM #1547, 2000); Thompson, *Presbyterians*, 54–55.

6. Wilmer L. Hall, ed., *The Vestry Book of the Upper Parish Nansemond County, Virginia, 1743–1793* (Richmond: Virginia State Library, 1981), xxiii. See Sanford H. Cobb, *The Rise of Religious Liberty in America* (1902; reprint, New York: Burt Franklin, 1970) and Gewehr, *Great Awakening*.

7. Robert R. Hewitt III, *Where the River Flows: Finding Faith in Rockingham County, Virginia, 1726–1876* (Charlottesville: Virginia Foundation for the Humanities, 2003), 34. Gewehr, *Great Awakening*, 40–42.

8. Nelson, *Blessed Company*, 242–44, 415 n.71. Patricia Bonomi concluded that a ratio of three to four noncommunicants to members was probably too low. *Under the Cope of Heaven: Religion, Society, and Politics in Colonial America* (New York: Oxford University Press, 1986), 89. David Benedict, writing in 1813, says "we may reckon

seven adherents to one communicant." *A General History of the Baptist Denomination in America* (1813; reprint, Freeport, N.Y.: Books for Libraries Press, 1971), II:553. At that rate, Baptists would have accounted for over 10 percent of the free population in 1774, but that might be too high. William Taylor Thom, *The Struggle for Religious Freedom in Virginia: The Baptists*, Johns Hopkins University Studies, Historical and Political Science, Ser. XVIII, Nos. 10–11–12, ed. Herbert B. Adams (1900; reprint, New York: Johnson Reprint, 1973), 30–39, 39–42 n.68 (506–15, 515–18 n.68). John E. Selby, *The Revolution in Virginia 1775–1783* (Williamsburg, Va.: Colonial Williamsburg Foundation, 1988), 33 (dissenters no more than one-fifth of whites, but Baptists often attracted thousands to their meetings). Roger Finke and Rodney Stark, *The Churching of America, 1776–2005: Winners and Losers in Our Religious Economy* (New Brunswick, N.J.: Rutgers University Press, 2005), 29–30, look only to membership, but for these purposes, attendance and affiliation are more relevant. Charles Campbell, *History of the Colony and Ancient Dominion of Virginia* (Philadelphia: Lippincott, 1860), 562 (quote).

9. Thomas Jefferson, *Notes on the State of Virginia*, in *Thomas Jefferson Writings*, ed. Merrill D. Peterson (New York: Library of America, 1984), Query XVII, 283. Julian P. Boyd, Lyman H. Butterfield, and Mina R. Bryan, eds., *The Papers of Thomas Jefferson* (Princeton, N.J.: Princeton University Press, 1950), I:539. George Tucker, *The Life of Thomas Jefferson, Third President of the United States, with Parts of His Correspondence Never Before Published and Notices of His Opinions in Questions on Civil Government, National Policy and Constitutional Law* (Philadelphia: Covey, Lea and Blanchard, 1837), I:97n., 19n. "A Brief View of the State of the Church in the British Colonies," American Ecclesiastic Affairs, Lambeth Palace Library, London (Virginia Colonial Recors Project, Reel 608), 121. William C. Rives, *History of the Life and Times of James Madison* (Boston: Little, Brown, 1859), I:55n. Virginia's population at the time is estimated at 400,000 to 600,000, approximately 40–45 percent of which was slaves. Evarts B. Greene and Virginia D. Harrington, *American Population before the Federal Census of 1790* (1932; reprint, Baltimore Genealogical Publishing, 1997), 141.

10. See, e.g., Charles F. Irons, "The Spiritual Fruits of Revolution: Disestablishment and the Rise of the Virginia Baptists," *Virginia Magazine of History and Biography* 109:2 (2001), 161; Thomas E. Buckley, *Church and State in Revolutionary Virginia, 1776–1787* (Charlottesville: University Press of Virginia, 1977), 8–9; Katherine L. Brown, "The Role of Presbyterian Dissent in Colonial and Revolutionary Virginia, 1740–1785" (Ph.D. diss., Johns Hopkins University, 1969), 332–33.

11. Julius F. Prufer, "The Franchise in Virginia from Jefferson through the Convention of 1829," *William and Mary Quarterly*, 2nd Ser., 7:4 (Oct. 1927), 260–65.

12. The Presbyterian Church's early efforts in Virginia are summarized in Foote, *Sketches of Virginia*, and Davis, "Struggle for Religious Freedom." Mechal Sobel, *The World They Made Together: Black and White Values in Eighteenth-Century Virginia* (Princeton, N.J.: Princeton University Press, 1987), 183, discusses Davies's success with blacks.

13. McIlwaine, *Struggle of Protestant Dissenters*, 40 et seq.; Gewehr, *Great Awakening*, 97.

14. Isaac, "Religion and Authority," 24 ("encapsulated within this pejorative epithet ['itinerant'] was a whole view of authority and society"). Wilmer L. Hall, ed., *Executive Journals of the Council of Virginia* (Richmond: Virginia State Library, 1945), April 3, 1747, V:227–28 (quote). John Leland, *The Virginia Chronicle: With Judicious and Critical Remarks under XXIV Heads* (Norfolk: Prentis and Baxter, 1790), 13, Early American Imprints, series 1, no. 21920; Foote, *Sketches of Virginia*, 157; Gewehr, *Great Awakening*, 69. Cobb, *Rise of Religious Liberty*, 103–5.

15. Davis, "Struggle for Religious Freedom," 23–24; McIlwaine, *Struggle of Protestant Dissenters*, 50; Gewehr, *Great Awakening*, 69–70; Foote, *Sketches of Virginia*, 135–38, 164–66 (quote) (Governor Gooch supported Rodgers but could not convince council).

16. The number of ministers and churches are discussed in appendix B.

17. See Jewell L. Spangler, *Virginians Reborn: Anglican Monopoly, Evangelical Dissent, and the Rise of the Baptists in the Late Eighteenth Century* (Charlottesville: University of Virginia Press, 2008).

18. Philip N. Mulder, *A Controversial Spirit: Evangelical Awakening in the South* (Oxford: Oxford University Press, 2002), 37.

19. Cobb, *Rise of Religious Liberty*, 100. Thom, *Struggle for Religious Freedom*, 35 (511).

20. Nelson, *Blessed Company*, 246–48.

21. Quoted in Bonomi, *Under the Cope of Heaven*, 94. Fristoe, *Concise History*, 60 (quote). A. H. Newman, *A History of the Baptist Churches in the United States* (New York: Christian Literature, 1894), 303–4 (quote) (CD-ROM, Baptist History Collection, Baptist Standard Bearer, 2005). Spangler, *Virginians Reborn*, 133, 142, 186.

22. Sobel, *World They Made*, 180. Spangler, *Virginians Reborn*, 130 (4.5 percent of Baptists black in 1770, 11 percent in 1780). *Virginia Gazette* (Purdie), May 1, 1778 (emphasis in original).

23. Rhys Isaac, *The Transformation of Virginia, 1740–1790* (New York: Norton, 1982), 173; Rhys Isaac, "Preachers and Patriots: Popular Culture and the Revolution in Virginia," in *The American Revolution*, ed. Alfred F. Young (DeKalb: Northern Illinois University Press, 1976), 128. See also Thom, *Struggle for Religious Freedom*, 29–30 (505–6), 40 (516). See appendix B.

24. Rhoden, *Revolutionary*, 22. Cline Edwin Hall, "The Southern Dissenting Clergy and the American Revolution" (Ph.D. diss., University of Tennessee, 1975), 78 n.43. Finke and Stark, *Churching*, 288.

25. Isaac, "Preachers and Patriots," 128 (quote). Gewehr, *Great Awakening*, 9, 137, 151, 155 (Methodists claimed fewer than 300 members in Virginia in 1774 but almost 2,500 by 1776). Leland, *Virginia Chronicle*, 15 (Methodists "never spread much in Virginia till about 1775").

26. See McIlwaine, *Struggle of Protestant Dissenters*, 33–34.

27. Hening, *Statutes*, IX (1775):82. Michael A. McDonnell, *The Politics of War: Race, Class, and Conflict in Revolutionary Virginia* (Chapel Hill: University of North Carolina Press, 2007), 38.

28. T. E. Campbell, *Colonial Caroline: A History of Caroline County, Virginia* (Richmond, Va.: Dietz Press, 1954), 226. Foote, *Sketches of Virginia*, 133 (quote).

29. Nelson, *Blessed Company*, 285. Brent Tarter, "Reflections on the Church of England in Colonial Virginia," *Virginia Magazine of History and Biography*, 112:4 (2004), 354 ("relatively brief and insignificant"); Jon Butler, "Coercion, Miracle, Reason: Rethinking the American Religious Experience in the Revolutionary Age," in *Religion in the Revolutionary Age*, ed. Ronald Hoffman and Peter J. Albert (Charlottesville: University Press of Virginia, 1994), 23 (Enlightenment writers exaggerated); Bishop William Meade, *Old Churches, Ministers and Families of Virginia* (1857; reprint, Baltimore, Md.: Genealogical Publishing, 1978), I:426 (exaggerated for 100 years). Although it is true that parish and county records provide "little evidence of contention and disruption" (Nelson, *Blessed Company*, 285), parish records are also largely silent on the Revolution; their reporting focused on local ecclesiastic matters.

30. Robert B. Semple, *A History of the Baptists in Virginia*, rev. G. W. Beale (1894; reprint, Cottonport, La.: Polyanthos, 1972), 481–82. Morgan Edwards, *Materials towards a History of the Baptists in the Provinces of Maryland, Virginia, North Carolina, South Carolina, Georgia* (1772) (microfilm, Special Collections, University of Virginia, Charlottesville), III:75–76, 25–26; John S. Moore, ed., "John Williams' Journal, Edited with Comments," *Virginia Baptist Register*, 17 (1978), 798; G. S. Bailey, *The Trials and Victories of Religious Liberty in America* (Philadelphia: American Baptist Publication Society, 1876), 40; Benedict, *General History of the Baptist*, II:48. Fristoe, *Concise History*, 71–72. Lewis Peyton Little, *Imprisoned Preachers and Religious Liberty in Virginia* (1938; reprint, Gallatin, Tenn.: Church History Research and Archives, 1987), 227, 517–18. "Persecution of Baptists," *Religious Herald*, 6:14 (April 6, 1871).

31. Semple, *History of the Baptists*, 460, 400. James Ireland, *The Life of the Reverend James Ireland* (1819; reprint, Harrisonburg, Va.: Sprinkle Publications, 2002), 156.

32. L. F. Greene, ed., *The Writings of the late Elder John Leland, including some events in his life, written by himself, with some additional sketches* (New York: Wood, 1845), 20. Gewehr, *Great Awakening*, 119–20. Semple, *History of the Baptists*, 20, 29. Little, *Imprisoned Preachers*, 96, 404, 143–45, 66. Benedict, *General History of the Baptist*, II:21. William B. Sprague, *Annals of the American Pulpit, VI, Baptists* (New York: Robert Carter and Brothers, 1865), 81, 115. Fristoe, *Concise History*, 72. See also "Persecution of Baptists." Edwards, *Materials towards a History*, III:29–30, 54, 70, 90, 82 (quote) (emphasis added).

33. Ireland, *Life of the Reverend James Ireland*, 114–15, 141. Little, *Imprisoned Preachers*, 163. Jewell L. Spangler, "Presbyterians, Baptists, and the Making of a Slave Society in Virginia, 1740–1820" (Ph.D. diss., University of California, San Diego, 1996), 162. *Virginia Gazette* (Purdie and Dixon), February 20, 1772. *Virginia Gazette* (Purdie and Dixon), October 1, 1767; *Virginia Gazette* (Purdie), May 1, 1778, 4. Slaveowner quoted in Sobel, *World They Made*, 199.

34. Semple, *History of the Baptists*, 382. Gewehr, *Great Awakening*, 115 n.41. Jewell L. Spangler, "Becoming Baptists: Conversion in Colonial and Early National Virginia," *Journal of Southern History*, 67:2 (May 2001), 248 n.10. Spangler, "Presbyterians, Baptists," 104 ("Mobs and individuals seem to have interrupted Baptist meetings and physically attacked Baptist preachers with little regard for distinctions as 'Regular' and 'Separate'"). See appendix A. Isaac, "Religion and Authority," 32.

35. Little, *Imprisoned Preachers*, 391, 176–77, 465, 192, 520. Campbell, *Colonial Caroline*, 222. See appendix A.

36. Little, *Imprisoned Preachers*, 421, 516. Campbell, *Colonial Caroline*, 222, 225. William Jennings Terman Jr., "The American Revolution and the Baptist and Presbyterian Clergy of Virginia: A Study of Dissenter Opinion and Action" (Ph.D. diss., Michigan State University, 1974), 327–28 (quote); "Baptists in Middlesex, 1771," *William and Mary Quarterly*, 2nd Ser., 5 (July 1925), 209 (quote). Caroline County Order Book, May 1768, 142 (thirteen persons presented for attending "illegal preaching," one for preaching, and two for permitting preaching at their homes; even when charges were dismissed—as they were in this instance against all but the preacher, the process must have angered dissenters). See appendix A (almost 100 persons listed in addition to those fined for nonattendance). See also Sandra Rennie, "Virginia's Baptist Persecution, 1765–1778," *Journal of Religious History*, 12:1 (June 1982), 48–61, and Sandra Joy Rennie, "Crusaders for Virtue—The Development of the Baptist Church in Virginia from 1760 to 1790" (M.A. thesis, La Trobe University, Melbourne, 1975).

37. Isaac, "Rage of Malice," 141. Fristoe, *Concise History*, 67. Spangler, "Presbyterians, Baptists," 230. Chester Raymond Young, ed., *Westward into Kentucky: The Narrative of Daniel Trabue* (Lexington: University Press of Kentucky, 2004), 41 (quote) (notes omitted).

38. Sprague, *Annals of the American Pulpit, vol. VI, Baptists*, 81. Orange County Order Book, No. 8 (1769–77), October 28, 1773, 287.

39. Sprague, *Annals of the American Pulpit, vol. VI, Baptists*, 115. Semple, *History of the Baptists*, 34. Edwards, *Materials towards a History*, III:82. Ireland, *Life of the Reverend James Ireland*, 140–42. James B. Taylor, *Virginia Baptist Ministers, in Two Series* (New York: Sheldon, 1860), II:101. Fristoe, *Concise History*, 77. Terman, "American Revolution," 324, citing Garnett Ryland, "'James Ireland': An address delivered at the Unveiling of the Monument to James Ireland, May 20, 1931, Berryville, Clark County, VA" (Richmond: Virginia Baptist Historical Society, 1931), 12.

40. Little, *Imprisoned Preachers*, 342–44, 275. Ireland, *Life of the Reverend James Ireland*, 141. Edwards, *Material towards a History*, III:74–75. Buckley, *Church and State*, 14. Robert Doares, "The Alternative of Williams-Burg," *Colonial Williamsburg*, 28:2 (Spring 2006), 21.

41. Campbell, *Colonial Caroline*, 200, 211. Thom, *Struggle for Religious Freedom*, 27 (503) (quote). See also Catherine Greer O'Brion, "'A Mighty Fortress Is Our God': Building a Community of Faith in the Virginia Tidewater, 1772–1845" (Ph.D. diss., University of Virginia, 1997), 32; Isaac, *Transformation*, 193.

42. The one indentified instance challenging a specific claim is weak. See Campbell, *History of the Colony*, 225 (supposed inconsistency in reports of which officials were involved, "chances are that while Waller [a Baptist preacher] was abused, the extent of his abuse has been grossly exaggerated by Baptist partisans"). Moore, "John Williams' Journal," 813 n.51 (Presbyterians and Baptists sharing meeting house).

43. Thom, *Struggle for Religious Freedom*, 42, 44 (518, 520) (quote). Francis L. Hawks, *Contributions to the Ecclesiastical History of the United States of America* (New York: Harper and Brothers, 1836), 121.

44. Nelson, *Blessed Company*, 126–27, 4–5, 7, 35, 407 n.53. Rhoden, *Revolutionary Anglicanism*. David L. Holmes, "The Episcopal Church and the American Revolution," *Historical Magazine of the Protestant Episcopal Church*, 67 (1978), 264. Joan Gundersen, "The Search for Good Men: Recruiting Ministers in Colonial Virginia," *Historical Magazine of the Protestant Episcopal Church*, 48 (1979), 453, 458 (may underestimate the percentage of colonial-born by ignoring ministers for whom a birthplace is not available). See also Bonomi, *Under the Cope of Heaven*, 61.

45. Rhoden, *Revolutionary*, 91. Gundersen, "Search for Good Men," 459 (by 1775, 11 percent of clergy from families with "claims to colonial leadership"); Andrew J. Boyle, *The Church in the Fork: A History of Historic Little Fork Church* (Orange, Va.: Green Publishers, 1983), 5–7 (courtship of Governor Spotswood's widow by the Reverend John Thompson). Gundersen, *Anglican Ministry*, 81–82 (marriage to middle gentry). William Byrd III to Reverend Richard Peters, January 6, 1772, in Marion Tinling, ed., *The Correspondence of the Three William Byrds of Westover, Virginia, 1684–1776* (Charlottesville: University Press of Virginia, 1977), II:783. Clergy of New York and New Jersey to Earl of Hillsborough, October 12, 1771, in K. G. Davies, ed., *Documents of the American Revolution, 1770–1783* (Colonial Office Series) (Shannon, Ireland: Irish University Press, 1973), III: Transcripts, 1771, 209 (mortality rate and expense of ordination trip). The social rank of Anglican clergy was more subject to question in the 1750s when a much higher percentage were immigrants. Isaac, "Religion and Authority," 21.

46. Charles Frederick Irons, "'The Chief Cornerstone': The Spiritual Foundation of Virginia's Slave Society, 1776–1861" (Ph.D. diss., University of Virginia, 2003), 18. John Frederick Woolverton, *Colonial Anglicanism in North America* (Detroit, Mich.: Wayne State University Press, 1984), 16–20.

47. Sydnor, *American Revolutionaries*, 84. Meade, *Old Churches*, I:151–53. Sydnor, *American Revolutionaries*, 89–90. Campbell, *Colonial Caroline*, 95. Jefferson, *Autobiography*, 34. Cobb, *Rise of Religious Liberty*, 493. See also William Wirt Henry, *Patrick Henry: Life, Correspondence and Speeches* (New York: Scribner, 1891), I:117–19 (Pendleton and Cary). Compare William G. McLoughlin, "The Role of Religion in the Revolution," in *Essays on the American Revolution*, ed. Stephen G. Kurtz and James H. Hutson (Chapel Hill: University of North Carolina Press, 1973), 202 ("once the Revolution started, Anglican authority and power immediately ceased").

48. Campbell, *History of the Colony*, 566. Young, *Narrative of Daniel Trabue*, 128. Ireland, *Life of the Reverend James Ireland*, 136, 155.

49. Bonomi, *Under the Cope of Heaven*, 39–45, 88–90. Gundersen, "Search for Good Men," 460 n.36, 463; Gundersen, *Anglican Ministry*, 230. Nelson, *Blessed Company*, 150–55. I Cor. 11:27–29. Compare Sobel, *World They Made*, 179 (relatively small numbers taking communion) and Seiler, "Anglican Parish," 136 (unavailability of confirmation explains number of communicants). Robert Boyle C. Howell, *The Early Baptists of Virginia* (1864), 47 (CD-ROM, Baptist Standard Bearer, 2005).

50. *Virginia Gazette* (Rind), March 26, 1772. Isaac, *Transformation*, 218–22. George MacLaren Brydon, *Virginia's Mother Church and the Political Conditions under Which It Grew* (Richmond: Whittet and Shepperson, 1947), II:376–80. Madison to

William Bradford, April 1, 1774, in William T. Hutchinson and William M. E. Rachal, eds., *The Papers of James Madison* (Chicago: University of Chicago Press, 1962), 1:170, 112.

51. Compare Alan Heimert, *Religion in the American Mind from the Great Awakening to the Revolution* (Cambridge, Mass.: Harvard University Press, 1966); Isaac, *Transformation*; Isaac, "Religion and Authority," 4 n.5; Gewehr, *Great Awakening*; Sydney E. Ahlstrom, *A Religious History of the American People*, 2nd ed. (New Haven, Conn.: Yale University Press, 2004), 263, 348; McLoughlin, "Role of Religion," 198.

52. Foote, *Sketches of Virginia*, 103, 157–60, 165. Spangler, "Presbyterians, Baptists," 54. "Address to Anabaptists imprisoned in Caroline," *Virginia Gazette* (Purdie and Dixon), February 20, 1772. Otto Lohrenz, "The Virginia Clergy and the American Revolution, 1774–1799" (Ph.D. diss., University of Kansas, 1970), 11.

53. Isaac, *Transformation*, 151–52. *Virginia Gazette* (Rind), May 4, 1769. Gewehr, *Great Awakening*, 98 n.125. O'Brion, "'A Mighty Fortress Is Our God,'" 51.

54. Bonomi, *Under the Cope*, 199–209; Isaac, *Transformation*, 181–89; Carl Bridenbaugh, *Mitre and Sceptre: Transatlantic Faith, Ideas, Personalities, and Politics 1689–1775* (London: Oxford University Press, 1962), 249. *Virginia Gazette* (Purdie and Dixon), June 20, 1771, June 27, 1771, July 4, 1771, August 15, 1771, August 22, 1771, October 10, 1771, October 17, 1771, October 31, 1771, November 21, 1771; *Virginia Gazette* (Rind), July 18, 1771, August 1, 1771, August 8, 1771, September 5, 1771. This debate continued into 1772 when even the press tired of it. *Virginia Gazette* (Purdie and Dixon), March 12, 1772. But see Bridenbaugh, *Mitre*, 322 (episcopacy dispute led to religious freedom).

CHAPTER 2

1. Madison to William Bradford, January 24, 1774, in William T. Hutchinson and William M. E. Rachal, eds., *The Papers of James Madison* (Chicago: University of Chicago Press, 1962) I:105, 106 (note omitted).

2. See Michael A. McDonnell, *The Politics of War: Race, Class, and Conflict in Revolutionary Virginia* (Chapel Hill: University of North Carolina Press, 2007) and Woody Holton, *Forced Founders: Indians, Debtors, Slaves, and the Making of the American Revolution in Virginia* (Chapel Hill: University of North Carolina Press, 1999). Conflicts between slaves and white society are an entirely different matter and are addressed extensively in the literature. See Holton, *Forced Founders*; Ira Berlin and Ronald Hoffman, eds., *Slavery and Freedom in the Age of the American Revolution* (Chicago: University of Chicago Press, 1986); Robert McColley, *Slavery and Jeffersonian Virginia* (Urbana: University of Illinois Press, 1964); Paul Finkelman, *Slavery and the Founders: Race and Liberty in the Age of Jefferson* (Armonk, N.Y.: M. E. Sharpe, 1996).

3. Richard Beeman, "The Political Response to Social Conflict in the Southern Backcountry: A Comparative View of Virginia and the Carolinas during the Revolution," in *An Uncivil War: The Southern Backcountry during the American Revolution*, ed. Ronald Hoffman, Thad W. Tate, and Peter J. Albert (Charlottesville: University Press of Virginia, 1985), 235, 238–39. H. J. Eckenrode, *The Revolution in*

Virginia (1916; reprint, Hamden, Conn.: Archon Books, 1964), 171 ("public opinion was divided, but probably a majority of the people opposed the overthrow of the church they had been raised in and undoubtedly a majority of the assembly did").

4. Compare Alan Heimert, *Religion in the American Mind from the Great Awakening to the Revolution* (Cambridge, Mass.: Harvard University Press, 1966); William McLoughlin, "'Enthusiasm for Liberty': The Great Awakening as the Key to the Revolution," in *Preachers and Politicians: Two Essays on the Origins of the American Revolution* (Worcester, Mass.: American Antiquarian Society, 1977); Sydney E. Ahlstrom, *A Religious History of the American People*, 2nd ed. (New Haven, Conn.: Yale University Press, 2004); Patricia Bonomi, *Under the Cope of Heaven: Religion, Society, and Politics in Colonial America* (New York: Oxford University Press, 1986); Wesley M. Gewehr, *The Great Awakening in Virginia, 1740–1790* (Durham, N.C.: Duke University Press, 1930).

5. Rhys Isaac, "Preachers and Patriots: Popular Culture and the Revolution in Virginia," in *The American Revolution*, ed. Alfred F. Young (DeKalb: Northern Illinois University Press, 1976), 151 (quote); Rhys Isaac, *The Transformation of Virginia, 1740–1790* (New York: Norton, 1982), 280, 265. Given a citizenry "without ties of loyalty or interest to the politically dominant stratum" (Herbert Sloan and Peter Onuf, "Politics, Culture, and the Revolution in Virginia," *Virginia Magazine of History and Biography*, 91:3 [July 1983], 271–72), the negotiations were essential in achieving a united polity.

6. Miscellaneous Petition (May 26, 1784). See Thomas Cary Johnson, *Virginia Presbyterianism and Religious Liberty in Colonial and Revolutionary Times* (Richmond, Va.: Presbyterian Committee of Publication, 1907), 92 ("zeal to see the war with Britain safely ended, before pressing its desires with reference to religion on the attention of the legislature").

7. Good chronologies of the war and difficulties of mobilization in Virginia can be found in John David McBride, "The Virginia War Effort: 1775–1783: Manpower Policies and Practices" (Ph.D. diss., University of Virginia, 1977) and McDonnell, *Politics of War*.

8. Baptist Petition (May 26, 1770), Lunenburg Baptists (February 12, 1772), Mecklenburg Baptists (February 22, 1772), Amelia Baptists (February 24, 1772), Sussex Baptists (February 24, 1772), Caroline Baptists (March 14, 1772), *Journal of the House of Burgesses, 1770–1772*, 30, 160–61, 182–83, 185–86, 245. See also Loudon County (May 1774), *Journal of the House of Burgesses, 1773–76* (May 1774), 92. Presbyterians petitioned for improved toleration as early as 1751, but that request was violently opposed by Anglican clergy, including the Reverend Patrick Henry, Patrick Henry's uncle, and little came of it. Henry R. McIlwaine, *The Struggle of Protestant Dissenters for Religious Toleration in Virginia*. Johns Hopkins University Studies, Historical and Political Science, 12th Ser., IV (Baltimore, Md.: Johns Hopkins Press, April 1894), 60; William Perry, ed., *Historical Collections of the American Colonial Church* (1870; reprint, Westminster, Md.: Willow Bend Books, 2001), I:380–81.

9. George MacLaren Brydon, *Virginia's Mother Church and the Political Conditions under Which It Grew* (Richmond, Va.: Whittet and Shepperson, 1947), II:376–79. *Virginia Gazette* (Rind), March 26, 1772. Petition of Lunenburg Baptists, *Journal of the*

House of Burgesses (Feb. 12, 1772), 160–61. *Journal of the House of Burgesses, 1773–76* (May 12, 1774), 92. David Thomas, *The Virginian Baptist* (Baltimore, Md.: Enoch Story, 1774), 33, Early American Imprint Series 1, no. 13651. Bedford County (May 17, 1774). *Journal of the House of Burgesses, 1770–72* (May 26, 1770), 20 (Baptist call for toleration).

10. Madison to William Bradford, April 1, 1774, in Hutchinson and Rachal, *Papers of James Madison*, I:112.

11. *Meherrin Baptist Meeting Book* (1771–1884), 28–29 (entry after September 1774) (Virginia Baptist Historical Society, University of Richmond, Richmond). Miscellaneous Petition (June 5, 1775); Baptists and Others, *Journal of the House of Burgesses, 1773–1776* (June 13, 1775), 225.

12. See Rhys Isaac, "Evangelical Revolt: The Nature of the Baptists' Challenge to the Traditional Order in Virginia, 1765 to 1775," *William and Mary Quarterly*, 3rd ser., 31:3 (July 1974), 360–61 (Baptists admonished for fighting even in self-defense); Sandy Creek Baptist 1769 resolution regarding North Carolina Regulators: "If any of our members shall take up arms against the legal authority or aid or abet them that do so he shall be excommunicated," quoted in Cline Edwin Hall, "Southern Dissenting Clergy and the American Revolution" (Ph.D. diss., University of Tennessee, 1975), 163. Ezra Stiles, *The Literary Diary*, ed. Franklin B. Dexter (New York, 1901), I:474 (quote). L. H. Butterfield, "Elder John Leland, Jeffersonian Itinerant," *American Antiquarian Society Proceedings*, 62:2 (October 1952), 167.

13. The Library of Congress database has only a summary of this petition from the *Journal of the Virginia Convention*. Miscellaneous Petition (August 16, 1775). A full copy is available in Robert L. Scribner and Brent Tarter, eds., *Revolutionary Virginia: The Road to Independence* (Charlottesville: University Press of Virginia, 1977), III:441–42. *Virginia Gazette* (Pinkney), August 31, 1776, 3:3. See also Resolution of the Hartwood Baptist Church (September 16, 1775) ("lawful" for Christians "to take up arms in the present dispute with Great Britain and her colonies"). *Minute Book of Hartwood Baptist Church, 1775–1861*, 7 (Virginia Baptist Historical Society, University of Richmond, Richmond). William Wirt Henry, *Patrick Henry: Life, Correspondence and Speeches* (New York: Scribner, 1891), 1:317. William Waller Hening, ed., *The Statutes at Large, Being a Collection of all the Laws of Virginia from the First Session of the Legislature in the Year 1619* (CD-ROM #0878, Heritage Books, 2003), VII (1757):93 (exempting Church of England ministers); IX (1775):28, 89 (all ministers, but later limiting to ministers "licensed" by the General Court or their society). Honorable John S. Barbour, "Oration of the Life, Character, and Services of James Madison," *Daily National Intelligencer*, 7323 (Washington, D.C., August 2, 1836).

14. Henry Mayer, *A Son of Thunder: Patrick Henry and the American Republic* (New York: Frank Watts, 1986), 160. Henry, *Patrick Henry*, 118–19. William Henry Foote, *Sketches of Virginia Historical and Biographical* (1850; reprint, Richmond, Va.: John Knox Press, 1966), 161–62.

15. Sara B. Bearss, ed., *Dictionary of Virginia Biography* (Richmond: Library of Virginia, 2006), III:103.

16. *Virginia Gazette* (Purdie), April 26, 1776.

17. Hutchinson and Rachal, *Papers of James Madison*, I:171–79; Irving Brant, *James Madison: The Virginia Revolutionist, 1751–1780* (Indianapolis, Ind.: Bobbs-Merrill,

1948), 257 (Pendleton's role). Anson Phelps Stokes, *Church and State in the United States* (New York: Harper and Brothers, 1950), I:380. The language adopted in Virginia's Declaration of Rights on June 12, 1776, was not printed outside of Virginia for fifty years; many assumed that Mason's original draft calling for toleration, which was broadly published, had been adopted. See, e.g., Hugh Blair Grigsby, *The Virginia Convention of 1776: A Discourse* (Richmond, 1855), 164.

18. Henry, *Patrick Henry*, I:450; Thomas J. Curry, *The First Freedoms: Church and State in America to the Passage of the First Amendment* (New York: Oxford University Press, 1986), 135. "Petitions of the Minister and Vestrymen of the Protestant Episcopal Church in the Parish of St. Asaph to the General Assembly of Virginia" (October 1797), in David John Mays, ed., *Letters and Papers of Edmund Pendleton, 1734–1803* (Charlottesville: University Press of Virginia, 1967), II:645.

19. Prince William County (June 20, 1776) (emphasis added). The petition in the Library of Congress database is damaged; language supplemented from Garnett Ryland, *The Baptists of Virginia 1699–1926* (Richmond: Virginia Baptist Board of Missions and Education, 1955), 98.

20. The Battle of Moore's Creek Bridge, February 27, 1776, was reported, for instance, in *Virginia Gazette* (Purdie), March 15, 1776 (suppl.), March 22, 1776.

21. *Virginia Gazette* (Purdie), August 23, 1776.

22. Prince Edward County (October 11, 1776); *Journal of the House of Delegates* (*JHD*) (October 29, 1776), 41, Early American Imprints, Series I. Patrick Griffin, *American Leviathan: Empire, Nation and Revolutionary Frontier* (New York: Hill and Wang, 2007), 140.

23. Miscellaneous Petition (October 16, 1776). Evarts B. Greene and Virginia D. Harrington, *American Population before the Federal Census of 1790* (1932; reprint, Baltimore, Md.: Genealogical Publishing, 1997), 141.

24. *Virginia Gazette* (Purdie), October 18, 1776.

25. Miscellaneous Petition (October 24, 1776).

26. Albemarle, Amherst, Buckingham Counties (October 22, 1776) (emphasis added); Augusta County Committee (November 9, 1776). Also Albemarle, Amherst, Buckingham Counties (October 22, 1776) (ending establishment "would most certainly have an happy Influence upon the members of the several Churches...in warmly attaching all of every Denomination to Government"), language supplemented from Brydon, *Virginia's Mother Church*, II:563; Berkeley County (October 25, 1776); Miscellaneous Petition (October 25, 1776); Albemarle and Amherst Counties (November 1, 1776) ("struggling in the same common cause," eliminating establishment will eliminate feuds among people).

27. Miscellaneous Petition (November 8, 1776); Miscellaneous Petition (October 28, 1776). Robert Honyman, *Diary, 1776–1782*, October 27, 1776, 79–80 (Accession 28855, Personal papers collection, Library of Virginia, Richmond). *Virginia Gazette* (Purdie), November 1, 1776.

28. *Virginia Gazette* (Purdie), November 8, 1776. William H. Whitsitt, *The Life and Times of Judge Caleb Wallace* (Louisville: John P. Morton, 1888), 42–43, 53–55. Charles Campbell, *History of the Colony and Ancient Dominion of Virginia* (Philadelphia: Lippincott, 1860), 674. An Anglican advocate made exactly the opposite argument, to

no avail: "Every reasonable person will allow, that, to deprive men of what they have always enjoyed, and been taught to regard as their right, is a much juster cause of complaint, and much more likely to produce dissatisfaction and dissentions, than the withholding from them what they never had in possession, and what the distresses of their country only could have made them expect." *Virginia Gazette* (Purdie), November, 1, 1776.

29. William Fristoe, *A Concise History of the Ketocton Baptist Association* (1808; reprint, Harrisonburg, Va.: Sprinkle Publications, 2002), 82. Richard R. Beeman and Rhys Isaac, "Cultural Conflict and Social Change in the Revolutionary South: Lunenburg County, Virginia," *Journal of Southern History*, 46:4 (November 1980), 538.

30. Alfred J. Mapp Jr., *The Virginia Experiment: The Old Dominion's Role in the Making of America (1607–1781)* (Richmond, Va.: Dietz Press, 1957), 448 (quote) (notes omitted). Alonzo Thomas Dill, *Carter Braxton, Virginia Signer: A Conservative in Revolt* (Lanham, Md.: University Press of America, 1983), 165–66 ("Probably Speaker Pendleton had chosen him [Nicholas], as a conservative churchman, to cool the heated demands for immediate overthrow of the Anglican establishment").

31. *JHD* (November 5, 1776), 55; (November 6, 1776), 58; (November 9, 1776), 65; (November 19, 1776), 85; (November 23, 1776), 93; (November 29, 1776), 101; (November 30, 1776), 102–3. See Whitsitt, *Life and Times*, 53–55; *JHD* (December 4, 1776), 110. Their work on the Committee for Religion in 1776 began a fifty-year partnership between Jefferson and Madison.

32. Hening, ed., *Statutes*, IX:164–66. Thomas Jefferson, *Autobiography*, in *Thomas Jefferson Writings*, ed. Merrill D. Peterson (New York: Library of America, 1984), 35.

33. Jefferson, *Autobiography*, 34.

34. Edmund Randolph, *History of Virginia*, ed. Arthur H. Shaffer (Charlottesville: University Press of Virginia, 1970), 263–64, 194. Pendleton reportedly drafted a 1786 petition claiming "that at the period of the late glorious revolution in America they chearfully consented to an abolition of the old Church establishment." Mays, *Letters and Papers*, II:488–89.

35. See, e.g., William Cathcart, *Baptist Patriots and the American Revolution* (1876; reprint, Grand Rapids, Mich.: Guardian Press, 1976), 88–89; Hall, "Southern Dissenting Clergy," 264, discussing Robert Baylor Semple, *History of the Rise and Progress of the Baptists in Virginia* (1810), 62; W. P. Breed, *Presbyterians and the Revolution* (1876; reprint, Decatur, Miss.: Issacharian Press, 1993). Wesley Gewehr reported heroically that "the petitions to the Virginia legislature abound in expressions of loyalty to and support of the Revolutionary cause by these denominations [dissenters]," *Great Awakening*, 188 n.4. Jon Butler notes that after the war, sectarians "Christianized" it. Jon Butler, *Awash in a Sea of Faith: Christianizing the American People* (Cambridge, Mass.: Harvard University Press, 1990), 212. See, e.g., Charles F. Irons, "The Spiritual Fruits of Revolution: Disestablishment and the Rise of the Virginia Baptists," *Virginia Magazine of History and Biography* 109:2 (2001), 166 (after the war "thousands joined Baptist churches...because they had shown themselves friends of the Revolution"); Charles Frederick Irons, "'The Chief Cornerstone': The

Spiritual Foundations of Virginia's Slave Society, 1776–1861" (Ph.D. diss., University of Virginia, 2003), 31–39 (religious sects Americanize themselves by claiming a prominent role in the mythology of the Revolution).

36. Mecklenburg County (May 29, 1777), Cumberland County (May 21, 1777, and November 6, 1777) (petitions missing, summaries like Mecklenburg petition), Lunenburg County (December 11, 1777) (petition missing, summary like Mecklenburg petition), Westmoreland County (October 9, 1778). *Virginia Gazette* (Dixon and Hunter), March 28, 1777. The pamphlet *Necessity of an Established Church* has apparently been lost, but it elicited a strong dissenter rebuttal, *The Freeman's Remonstrance against an Ecclesiastical Establishment* (Williamsburg, Va.: Dixon and Hunter, 1777), Early American Imprints, Series 1, no. 43250.

37. Mecklenburg County (May 29, 1777).

38. Thomas Jefferson, *Notes on the State of Virginia*, in *Thomas Jefferson Writings*, ed. Merrill D. Peterson (New York: Library of America, 1984), Query XVII, 287. Fristoe, *Concise History*, 83.

39. Hening, *Statutes*, VII (1757):93; IX (1775):28; IX (1776):139–40; IX (1777):267. The assembly exempted dissenting ministers in late 1775, but clarified that they must be duly "licensed" by the General Court or their sect, ibid., IX (1775):89. This had apparently not been adequate for Baptist ministers in particular. The new statute referred generally to compliance with "the rules of their sect." The only other notable expansion in the exemption was for makers of firearms and workers in lead mines (after that exemption was initially removed in 1775). McDonnell, *Politics of War*, especially at 240, discusses these changes as class conflict.

40. Miscellaneous Petition (June 3, 1777). *Virginia Gazette* (Dixon and Hunter), March 28, 1777. Hening, *Statutes*, IX (1777):312, 387, 337–48.

41. Cumberland County (May 21, 1777, November 6, 1777, November 6, 1778); Amherst County (October 13, 1778); King William County (November 21, 1778).

42. Miscellaneous Petition (October 29, 1778). Hening, ed., *Statutes*, X (1779):28. Compare Hening, *Statutes*, VIII (1769):311; IX (1775):32.

43. John S. Moore, "Barrow and Mintz Sue Their Attackers," *Virginia Baptist Register*, 32 (1993): 1659–60, citing Isle of Wight Court Order Book, 1772–1780, 433, 436, 465.

44. Charles Royster, *A Revolutionary People at War: The Continental Army and American Character, 1775–1783* (New York: Norton, 1979), 267. Compare "Bill for the Better Regulation and Discipline of the Militia" passed in June. Hening, *Statutes*, X (1779):83–85.

45. *JHD* (May 28, 1779), 33. Miscellaneous Petition (Baptist Association) (October 25, 1779). *JHD* (November 29, 1779), 91.

46. Augusta County (October 20, 1779). The Amelia Baptists specified that their resolution in support of Jefferson's bill be published in the *Virginia Gazettes*. Semple, *History of the Baptists*, 89. Augusta County (October 27, 1779). Amherst County (November 1, 1779).

47. Essex County (October 22, 1779) (marked, apparently by Committee for Religion, as "rejected"). Lancaster County (October 20, 1779). See also Culpeper

County (October 21, 1779); Lunenburg County (November 3, 1779). Amherst County (November 10, 1779). The debate was also taken up in the newspapers, with opposition to Jefferson's bill receiving the most ink. Compare *Virginia Gazette* (Dixon and Nicolson), August 14, 1779, September 11, 1779, September 18, 1779, *Virginia Gazette* (Clarkson and Davis), November 6, 1779, and *Virginia Gazette* (Clarkson and Davis), October 30, 1779 (opposing assessment).

48. H. J. Eckenrode, *Separation of Church and State in Virginia: A Study in the Development of the Revolution* (1910; reprint, New York: Da Capo Press, 1971), 58–61. Charles F. James, *Documentary History of the Struggle for Religious Liberty in Virginia* (Lynchburg, Va.: J. P. Bell, 1900), 93–95. Otto Lohrenz, "The Virginia Clergy and the American Revolution, 1774–1799" (Ph.D. diss., University of Kansas, 1970), 306. Ironically, the general assessment bill was introduced by James Henry, an eastern shore Presbyterian elder. Ernest Trice Thompson, *Presbyterians in the South: Volume One: 1607–1861* (Richmond, Va.: John Knox Press, 1963), 102.

49. Hening, *Statutes*, X (1779):197–98 (eliminating clergy tax but reserving vestry power over poor tax). See *JHD* (October 16, 1779), 13; (October 25, 1779), 28; (November 4, 1779), 50; (November 5, 1779), 51; (November 8, 1779), 57; (November 15, 1779), 70–71; (November 18, 1779), 76; (November 19, 1779), 79; (November 26, 1779), 89–90; (December 10, 1779), 105; (December 11, 1779), 106; (December 13, 1779), 108.

50. Philip Slaughter, "A History of St. Mark's Parish, Culpeper County, Virginia," in *Genealogical and Historical Notes on Culpeper County, Virginia*, ed. Raleigh Travers Green (1900; reprint, Orange, Va.: Quality Printing, 1989), 84. Eckenrode, *Separation of Church and State*, 61. Robert A. Rutland, ed., *The Papers of George Mason: 1725–1792* (Kingsport, Tenn.: University of North Carolina Press, 1970), II:553–54.

51. Amelia County (May 12, 1780); Spotsylvania County (June 5, 1780); Charlotte County (November 8, 1780). See also Rockbridge County (May 20, 1780) (complaining that vestry was not acting to protect the poor). The Presbytery of Hanover also sent a petition received on April 28, 1780, apparently warning against regulation of religious societies, but the petition is missing. Foote, *Sketches of Virginia*, 332.

52. Cumberland County (November 10, 1780) (several identical petitions). Prince Edward County (November 10, 1780). Cumberland County (November 23, 1780).

53. Hening, *Statutes*, X (1780):288–90, 361–63. Jacob Harris Patton, *The Triumph of the Presbytery of Hanover; or, Separation of Church and State in Virginia* (New York: Anson D. F. Randolph, 1887), 40. Semple, *History of the Baptists*, 45. See also Eckenrode, *Separation of Church and State*, 41.

54. Quoted in Meyer Reinhold, "Opponents of Classical Learning in America during the Revolutionary Period," *American Philosophical Society, Proceedings*, 112 (1968), 230.

CHAPTER 3

1. Carl Bridenbaugh, *Mitre and Sceptre: Transatlantic Faiths, Ideas, Personalities, and Politics 1689–1775* (London: Oxford University Press, 1962), 331. John Ferling,

Almost a Miracle: The American Victory in the War of Independence (Oxford: Oxford University Press, 2007), 86. *Manifesto and Proclamation* by the Earl of Carlisle, Sir Henry Clinton, and William Eden (Carlisle Commission) (October 3, 1778), Early American Imprints, Series 1, no. 15832. Robert Honyman, *Diary, 1776–1782*, July 18, 1778, 247–48. "A Pastoral Letter from the Synod of New York and Philadelphia to the people under our charge, May 1783," *Journal of the Presbyterian Historical Society*, 5 (1909–10), 129. Britain's appeal in the Carlisle Commission *Manifesto* may have been a response to American propaganda. Both the Suffolk Resolves (no. 10) and the Continental Congress Address to the People of Great Britain (October 21, 1774) spoke to the Quebec Act, the latter stating: "Nor can we suppress our astonishment, that a British Parliament should ever consent to establish in that country a religion that has deluged your island in blood, and dispersed impiety, bigotry, persecution, murder and rebellion through every part of the world." *Journals of the Continental Congress, 1774–89*, I:88 (http://memory.loc.gov/ammem/amlaw/lwjc.html).

2. See John E. Selby, *The Revolution in Virginia 1775–1783* (Williamsburg, Va.: Colonial Williamsburg Foundation, 198), 55–127; Michael A. McDonnell, *The Politics of War: Race, Class, and Conflict in Revolutionary Virginia* (Chapel Hill: University of North Carolina Press, 2007), 49–250. Other British commanders also sought to encourage Virginia loyalists but likewise did not rely on religious affiliation. See, e.g., Virginia Colonial Record Project, Public Records Office Class C.O.5/98, Military Despatches with enclosures from General Clinton, reel 66, SR430, 23–26, 133–40, 316–21, 324–25; Public Records Office Class C.O.5/94, Military Despatches with enclosures from General Howe, reel 66, SR427, 47–50.

3. McDonnell, *Politics of War*, 66, 131–36. Selby, *Revolution in Virginia*, 56–58. Woody Holton, *Forced Founders: Indians, Debtors, Slaves, and the Making of the American Revolution in Virginia* (Chapel Hill: University of North Carolina Press, 1999), 162–63.

4. Papers of Lord Dunmore: Dunmore, John Murray, Earl of, 1732–1809, Correspondence, 1771–78, TR 13 V.2, Dunmore to Earl of Dartmouth, December 24, 1774, No. 23 (C.O. 5/1353 ff. 7–39), 448–49, Rockefeller Library, Williamsburg, Va. (quote). Ibid., 450.

5. Ibid., Dunmore to Lord George Germain, June 26, 1776, No. 3 (C.O. 5/1353 ff. 385–88), 748–49.

6. Colin Bonwick, *English Radicals and the American Revolution* (Chapel Hill: University of North Carolina Press, 1977). Joseph Priestley, *Address to Protestant Dissenters of All Denominations on the Approaching Election of Members of Parliament with Respect to the State of Public Liberty in General, and of American Affairs in Particular* (London, 1774), 5–6, Eighteenth Century Collections Online, Gale Group (http://galenet.galegroup.com). Bridenbaugh, *Mitre*, discusses cooperation between British "dissenting deputies" and colonial dissenters.

7. Loyalists were important contributors to Britain's inability to understand the conflict, and, in particular, the resilient but benighted British belief that most Americans remained loyal and if British forces would simply show the flag in a colony (New York, New Jersey, Pennsylvania, South Carolina, North Carolina, Virginia) the

king's true subjects would rally. See, e.g., Mary Beth Norton, *British Americans: Loyalist Exiles in England, 1774–1789* (Boston: Little, Brown, 1972).

8. Douglas Adair and John A. Schutz, eds., *Peter Oliver's Origin and Progress of the American Revolution: A Tory View* (Stanford, Calif.: Stanford University Press, 1967), 76. J. T. Headley, *The Chaplains and Clergy of the American Revolution* (New York: Charles Scribner, 1864), 15. Joseph Galloway, *Historical and Political Reflections on the Rise and Progress of the American Rebellion* (London: G. Wilkie, 1780), 28, 47, 49 (only Congregationalists and Presbyterians supported rebellion), Eighteenth Century Collections Online, Gale Group (http://galenet.galegroup.com). "Examination of Joseph Galloway, Esq., late Speaker of the House of Assembly of Pennsylvania, Before the House of Commons," in Edward Frank Humphrey, *Nationalism and Religion in America, 1774–1789* (New York: Russell and Russell, 1965), 67. Charles Inglis to Richard Hind, Secretary of the SPG, October 31, 1776, in John Wolfe Lydekker, *The Life and Letters of Charles Inglis* (London: Society for Promoting Christian Knowledge, 1936), 157–58.

9. Julian P. Boyd, ed., "Notes and Documents: Joseph Galloway to Charles Jenkinson on the British Constitution," *Pennsylvania Magazine of History and Biography*, 64:4 (October 1940), 535. Clergy of New York, October 28, 1780, American Papers of the Society for the Propagation of the Gospel, Lambeth Palace Library, London (microfilm), X:190–91, quoted in Patricia Bonomi, "'Hippocrates' Twins': Religion and Politicis in the American Revolution," *History Teacher*, 29:2 (February 1996), 142. Edward H. Tatum Jr., *The American Journal of Ambrose Serle, Secretary to Lord Howe, 1776–1778* (San Marino, Calif.: Huntington Library, 1940), September 29, 1776, 115–16, March 22, 1777, 201–2, March 28, 1777, 204.

10. Wesley M. Gewehr, *The Great Awakening in Virginia, 1740–1790* (Durham, N.C.: Duke University Press, 1930), 158.

11. Lord Barrington to General Gage, August 1, 1768, and General Gage to Lord Barrington, October 6, 1770, in John Shy, "Confronting Rebellion: Private Correspondence of Lord Barrington with General Gage, 1765–1775," in *Sources of American Independence: Selected Manuscripts from the Collections of the William L. Clements Library*, ed. Howard H. Peckman (Chicago: University of Chicago Press, 1978), I:44, 86. K. G. Davies, ed., *Documents of the American Revolution, 1770–1783 (Colonial Office Series)* (Shannon, Ireland: Irish University Press, 1973), VIII:227. Mr. Knox to Lord Dartmouth, "Mr. Knox on the State of Religion in America," Staffordshire County Record Office, Stafford, England, Manuscripts of the Earl of Dartmouth, quoted in James B. Bell, *A War of Religion: Dissenters, Anglicans, and the American Revolution* (Hampshire: Palgrave Macmillan, 2008), 191. Walpole quote from Egbert W. Smith, *The Creed of the Presbyterians* (Richmond, Va.: John Knox Press, 1941), 146. Judith Fingard, "Establishment of the First English Colonial Episcopate," *Dalhousie Review*, 47 (Winter 1967–68), 478, citing Guy Carleton to Lord North, August 26, 1783, Public Record Office, B.T.6/59.

12. Edmund Burke, "Speech on Moving Resolutions for Conciliation with America," in *The Works of the Right Honorable Edmund Burke*, rev. ed. (Boston: Little, Brown, 1866), II:122–23. Bonwick, *English Radicals*, 81–113. Peter M. Doll, *Revolution,*

Religion, and National Identity: Imperial Anglicanism in British North America, 1745–1795 (Madison, Wisc.: Fairleigh Dickinson University Press, 2000), 213. Bonomi, "'Hippocrates' Twins,'" 142. Tatum, *American Journal of Ambrose Serle*, September 3, 1776, 90–91.

13. William Warren Sweet, "The Role of the Anglicans in the American Revolution," *Huntington Library Quarterly*, 11:1 (1947/1948), 56. Vardill to Dartmouth, September 1, 1774, in Doll, *Revolution, Religion*, 212–13 (note omitted). Vincent T. Harlow, *The Founding of the Second British Empire: 1763–1793* (London: Longmans, Green, 1964), II:735 ("the American revolt came as a warning that the export of political institutions without their ecclesiastical counterpart could be a disastrous enterprise, depriving the monarchical system in the colonies of its principal sanction").

14. Serle to Dartmouth, November 8, 1776, in B. F. Stevens, *Facsimiles of Manuscripts in European Archives Relating to America, 1773–1783* (London: Malby and Sons, 1895), XXIV, no. 2045. Tatum, *American Journal of Ambrose Serle*, 285. Charles Inglis to Richard Hind, secretary of the SPG, October 31, 1776, in Lydekker, *Life and Letters*, 170–71. Bell, *War of Religion*, 192. West's proposal is discussed in Harlow, *Founding of the Second British Empire*, II:736. David Ramsay, *The History of the American Revolution*, ed. Lester H. Cohen (Indianapolis: Liberty Classics, 1990), II:628. William Knox, *Extra Official State Papers, Addressed to the Right Hon. Lord Rawdon, and the Other Members of the two Houses of Parliament, Associated for the Preservation of the Constitution ... By a Late Under Secretary of State* (London: 1789), I:app.V, 13–14, Eighteenth Century Collections Online, Gale Group, (http://galenet. galegroup.com). See also Serle to Dartmouth, April 25, 1777, in Stevens, *Facsimiles of Manuscripts*, XXIV, No. 2057.

15. Jeffrey Amherst to Lord Germaine, March 2, 1779, Correspondence, Commander in Chief, 1779–, C.O. 5/174, 25 et seq., National Archives, London.

16. See, e.g., Patrick J. Furlong, "Civilian–Military Conflict and the Restoration of the Royal Province of Georgia, 1778–1782," *Journal of Southern History*, 38:3 (August 1972), 415–42. Piers Mackesy, *The War for America 1775–1783* (1964; reprint, Lincoln: University of Nebraska Press, 1993), 257. John Shy, "British Strategy for Pacifying the Southern Colonies, 1778–1781," in *The Southern Experience in the American Revolution*, ed. Jeffrey J. Crow and Larry E. Tise (Chapel Hill: University of North Carolina Press, 1978), discusses Germain's efforts to Americanize military and political aspects of the war.

17. Letter from Josiah Parker, Acting Colonel, county lieutenant Isle of Wight, to Speaker of the Assembly (June 9, 1781), *Calendar of Virginia State Papers and Other Manuscripts* (1881; reprint, New York, 1968), II:152. See also Isaac Samuel Harrell, *Loyalism in Virginia* (Durham, N.C.: Seeman Printery, 1926), 65. William Watters, *A Short Account of the Christian Experience, and Ministerial Labours, of William Watters* (Alexandria, Va.: Snowden, 1806), 49–50, Early American Imprints, Series 2, no. 11808. Letter from Samuel Purviance Jr. to General Schuyler, Baltimore, May 4, 1777, "The Early Methodists and the American Revolution," *Historical Magazine, and Notes and Queries Concerning the Antiquities, History and Biography of America*, 10:12

(December 1866) (loyalism in Maryland). Jarratt quoted in Rhys Isaac, "Preachers and Patriots: Popular Culture and the Revolution in Virginia," in *The American Revolution*, ed. Alfred F. Young (DeKalb: Northern Illinois University Press, 1976), 138. See ibid., 128 (Methodists "in the early years of the war...attract[ed] a vast following").

18. Capel Lofft in *Observations on Mr. Wesley's Second Calm Address, and Incidentally on Other Writings upon the American Question* (1777), 4, quoted in Albert M. Lyles, "The Hostile Reaction to the American Views of Johnson and Wesley," *Journal of the Rutgers University Library*, 24:1 (December 1960), 2. Charles Wesley and Lord Mansfield apparently had a close relationship dating to their school days.

19. Sweet, "Role of the Anglicans," 64–65, quoting Nehemia Curnock, ed., *Journal of John Wesley* (London, 1916), VIII:325–28; Frederick V. Mills Jr., "New Light on the Methodists and the Revolutionary War," *Methodist History*, 28 (1989), 64. Lyles, "Hostile Reaction," 4–5.

20. Lynwood M. Holland, "John Wesley and the American Revolution," *Journal of Church and State*, 5 (1963), 200. Alan Raymond, "'I Fear God and Honour the King': John Wesley and the American Revolution," *Church History*, 45:3 (September 1976), 316. Lyles, "Hostile Reaction," 5.

21. Holland, "John Wesley and the American Revolution," 208–11; Raymond, "'I Fear God and Honour the King,'" 235–36. Dee E. Andrews, *The Methodists and Revolutionary America, 1760–1800: The Shaping of an Evangelical Culture* (Princeton, N.J.: Princeton University Press, 2000), 50.

22. *London Magazine*, 44 (October, 1775), 483, quoted in Lyles, "Hostile Reaction," 7. Raymond, "'I Fear God and Honour the King,'" 324. Sweet, "Role of the Anglicans," 67; Raymond, "'I Fear God and Honour the King',", 318. Rev. L. Tyerman, *The Life and Times of the Reverend John Wesley, M.A., Founder of the Methodists* (London: Hodder and Stoughton, 1876), III:194 (quote). Jon Butler, *Religion in Colonial America* (New York: Oxford University Press, 2000), 134.

23. Nehemia Curnock, ed., *The Journal of the Rev. John Wesley, A.M., Enlarged from Original MSS., with Notes from Unpublished Diaries, Annotations, Maps, and Illustrations* (reprint, Kessinger Publishing, 2006), VI:82, November 11, 1775; see also Ibid., 202, quoting Wesley from Frederick C. Gill, ed., *Selected Letters of John Wesley* (London: Epworth Press, 1956), 167–68. Raymond, "'I Fear God and Honour the King,'" 319, 327.

24. Sweet, "Role of the Anglicans," 65–66 n.30. Stephen Conway, *The British Isles and the War of American Independence* (Oxford: Oxford University Press, 2003), 243. Tyerman, *Life and Times*, III:188, 187. Kathleen Wilson, *The Sense of the People: Politics, Culture and Imperialism in England, 1715–1785* (Cambridge: Cambridge University Press, 1998), 241. Raymond, "'I Fear God and Honour the King,'" 321–22. Tyerman, *Life and Times*, III:191.

CHAPTER 4

1. Charles Irons, "'The Chief Cornerstone': The Spiritual Foundations of Virginia's Slave Society, 1776–1861" (Ph.D. diss., University of Virginia, 2003), 31–39.

Miscellaneous Petitions (May 26, 1784). Robert Boyle C. Howell, *The Early Baptists of Virginia* (1864; CD-ROM, Baptist Standard Bearer, 2005), 78. Robert R. Howison, *History of Virginia, from its Discovery and Settlement by Europeans to the Present Time* (Richmond, Va.: Drinker and Morris, 1848), II:170.

2. "Presbyterians and the Revolution," *Journal of the Presbyterian Historical Society*, 5 (1909–10), 127–28. Ernist Trice Thompson, *Presbyterians in the South: Volume One: 1607–1861* (Richmond, Va.: John Knox Press, 1963), 88, 93. Also James H. Smylie, ed., "Presbyterians and the American Revolution: A Documentary Account," *Journal of Presbyterian History*, 52:4 (Winter 1974), 299–487. Compare Ian Charles Cargill Graham, *Colonists from Scotland: Emigration to North America, 1707–1783* (Ithaca, N.Y.: Cornell University Press, 1956), 169–71. Thomas Armitage, *A History of the Baptists: Traced by Their Vital Principles and Practices* (New York: Bryan, Taylor, 1890), II:326 (CD-ROM, Baptist Standard Bearer, 2005). William Cathcart, *Baptist Patriots and the American Revolution* (1876, as *The Baptists and the American Revolution*; reprint, Grand Rapids, Mich.: Guardian Press, 1976), 68–69.

3. Cathcart, *Baptist Patriots*, 76, 73. Richard R. Beeman, "The Political Response to Social Conflict in the Southern Backcountry: A Comparative View of Virginia and the Carolinas during the Revolution," in *An Uncivil War: The Southern Backcountry during the American Revolution*, ed. Ronald Hoffman, Thad W. Tate, and Peter J. Albert (Charlottesville: University Press of Virginia, 1985), 237.

4. A. H. Newman, *A History of the Baptist Churches in the United States* *New York: Christian Literature, 1894; CD-ROM, Baptist Standard Bearer, 2005), 303–4 (no "college-bred man" among Baptist ministers). Ellis Sandoz, *Political Sermons of the American Founding Era, 1730–1805* (Indianapolis: Liberty Fund, 1998); Davis R. Williams, ed., *Revolutionary War Sermons* (Delmar, N.Y.: Scholars' Facsimiles and Reprints, 1984); John Wingate Thornton, *The Pulpit of the American Revolution or, the Political Sermons of the Period of 1776* (Boston: Gould and Lincoln, 1860). Analysis requires determining the number of clergy from each denomination. Otto Lohrenz's extensive study concludes that Virginia had 129 Anglican, 40–50 Presbyterian, and more than 100 Baptist clergy at the time of the Revolution. Otto Lohrenz, "The Virginia Clergy and the American Revolution, 1774–1799" (Ph.D. diss., University of Kansas, 1970), 19, 23 n.6, 400. This perhaps slightly overestimates Anglican clergy (as he included several from outside the state) and underestimates Presbyterian clergy. See also Nancy L. Rhoden, *Revolutionary Anglicanism: The Colonial Church of England Clergy during the American Revolution* (New York: New York University Press, 1999), 89 (130 Anglican from 1775 to 1783). William Jennings Terman Jr. lists by name ninety-three Baptist clergy in Virginia and eighty-six Presbyterian; "The American Revolution and the Baptist and Presbyterian Clergy of Virginia: A Study of Dissenter Opinion and Action" (Ph.D. diss., Michigan State University, 1974), table 1, 331 et seq., table 3, 352 et seq. Terman, though, lists sixteen Presbyterians who left Virginia before the war or began their ministries after the war. A reasonable estimate for purposes of comparison is 125 Anglican ministers (accounting for Lohrenz's out-of-state clergy and Rhoden's expanded period), 100 Baptist, and 75 Presbyterian in Virginia at the time of the American Revolution.

5. John Leland, *The Virginia Chronicle: With Judicious and Critical Remarks under XXIV Heads* (Norfolk, Va.: Prentis and Baxter, 1790), Early American Imprints, Series 1, no. 21920, 18; Lohrenz, "Virginia Clergy," 253. Alexander Miller, who had been a Presbyterian minister, was a loyalist, but he had been deposed by 1765 for misconduct. Terman, "American Revolution," 279. Baptist historian Morgan Edwards was a Tory, but, while he toured Virginia prior to the war, he was not a Virginia minister.

6. Lohrenz, "Virginia Clergy," 22–23. Rhoden, *Revolutionary Anglicanism*, 89, 180 n.3. William Parks, "Religion and the Revolution in Virginia," in *Virginia in the American Revolution: A Collection of Essays*, ed. Richard A. Rutyna and Peter C. Stewart (Norfolk, Va.: Old Dominion University, 1977), 53, found that of 105 Anglican clergymen, only 15 had been shown to be Tory; 70 signed an oath of allegiance, although 5 changed their minds. Thomas argued that of eighty-five Anglican clergy whose position can be determined, seventy-eight were patriots, but he tends to assume loyalty to Virginia in some ambiguous cases. R. S. Thomas, *The Loyalty of the Clergy of the Church of England in Virginia to the Colony in 1776 and Their Conduct* (Richmond, Va.: Wm. Ellis Jones, 1907), 5–14. George MacLaren Brydon, *Virginia's Mother Church and the Political Conditions under Which It Grew* (Richmond, Va.: Whittet and Shepperson, 1947), II:420–21.

7. Compare William Warren Sweet, "The Role of the Anglicans in the American Revolution," *Huntington Library Quarterly* 11:1 (1947/1948), 62; Francis L. Hawks, *Contributions to the Ecclesiastical History of the United States of America* (New York: Harper and Brothers, 1836), I:136–37 ("In Virginia and Maryland about two-thirds of the clergy were loyalist."). Lohrenz, "Virginia Clergy," 222–23 (Presbyterians), 253 (Baptist). Lohrenz notes that seven Presbyterian ministers "apparently were Patriots but the records credit them with no specific acts," and scores of Baptist ministers "have not been credited with any specific patriotic acts, but there is no doubt that they upheld the American side in the war to greater or lesser degrees." Ibid., 275. Assumed support for the patriot cause based on silence is eschewed by Lohrenz in the case of Anglicans.

8. Lohrenz, "Virginia Clergy," 163, 30–31, 44–45, 74. Lohrenz concludes that Lewis Gwilliam did not accept his position on the Pittsylvania committee, but the *Virginia Gazette* (Dixon and Hunter), February 11, 1775, s2:3, includes him, although by 1777, he was questioned as to loyalty. Others conclude that Gwilliam joined the committee and later fell from favor. Frances Hallam Hurt, *An Intimate History of the American Revolution in Pittsylvania County, Virginia* (Danville, Va.: Womack Press, 1976), 61–62. Thomas Hall, chairman of the Louisa committee, supported the patriots but would not do so after the Declaration of Independence. Lohrenz, "Virginia Clergy," 90. See also Parks, "Religion and the Revolution," 53; Rhoden, *Revolutionary Anglicanism*, 92.

9. Lohrenz, "Virginia Clergy," 236–37, 265; James H. Smylie, "From Revolution to Civil War (1776–1861)," in *Virginia Presbyterians in American Life: Hanover Presbytery (1755–1980)* (Richmond, Va.: Hanover Presbytery, 1982), 48; William B. Sprague, *Annals of the American Pulpit, Vol. III, Presbyterians* (New York: Robert Carter and Brothers, 1865), 287; Thompson, *Presbyterians in the South*, 93–94.

10. William Taylor Thom, *The Struggle for Religious Freedom in Virginia: The Baptists*, Johns Hopkins University Studies, Historical and Political Science, Series 18, Nos. 10–11–12, ed. Herbert B. Adams (1900; reprint, New York: Johnson Reprint, 1973), 51 (527).

11. Lohrenz, "Virginia Clergy," 218, 239–40. See Joan Gundersen, *The Anglican Ministry in Virginia 1723–1766: A Study of a Social Class* (New York: Garland Publishing, 1989), 150–51. Terman, "American Revolution," 236–41, 357. Malcolm H. Harris, *History of Louisa County, Virginia* (Richmond, Va.: Dietz Press, 1936), 184. Several chaplains listed by Terman had only been itinerants in Virginia; those who did not begin their ministry until after the war are not included here. J. T. Headley, *The Chaplains and Clergy of the American Revolution* (New York: Scribner, 1864), 58 (quote). Lohrenz, "Virginia Clergy," 163.

12. Alice M. Baldwin, "Sowers of Sedition: The Political Theories of Some of the New Light Presbyterian Clergy of Virginia and North Carolina," *William and Mary Quarterly*, 3rd Ser., 5:1 (January 1948), 72; Henry A. Muhlenberg, *The Life of Major-General Peter Muhlenberg of the Revolutionary Army* (Philadelphia, 1849); Headley, *Chaplains and Clergy*, 123–24. Klaus Wust, *The Virginia Germans* (Charlottesville: University of Virginia Press, 1969), 80. John K. Nelson, *A Blessed Company: Parishes, Parsons and Parishioners in Anglican Virginia, 1690–1776* (Chapel Hill: University of North Carolina Press, 2001), 102.

13. Bishop William Meade, *Old Churches, Ministers and Families of Virginia* (1857; reprint, Baltimore, Md.: Genealogical Publishing, 1978), I:323–25. Thomas, *Loyalty of the Clergy*, 8. Lohrenz, "Virginia Clergy," 199 et seq. Brydon, *Virginia's Mother Church*, II:418, 421, 423, 433–34 n.15.

14. Baldwin, "Sowers of Sedition," 72. Headley, *Chaplains and Clergy*, 275; Cline Edwin Hall, "Southern Dissenting Clergy and the American Revolution" (Ph.D. diss., University of Tennessee, 1975), 246–47. William Henry Foote, *Sketches of Virginia Historical and Biographical* (1850; reprint, Richmond, Va.: John Knox Press, 1966), 412; Charles Grier Sellers Jr., "John Blair Smith," *Journal of the Presbyterian Historical Society*, 34:4 (December 1956), 207. Sprague, *Annals of the American Pulpit, vol. III, Presbyterians*, 287. Thompson, *Presbyterians in the South*, 94. Lohrenz, "Virginia Clergy," 241–44. Terman, "American Revolution," 352–62.

15. B. F. Riley, *A History of the Baptists in the Southern States East of the Mississippi* (Philadelphia: American Baptist Publications Society, 1898), 91–92; Lohrenz, "Virginia Clergy," 266, 269–71. Henry Howe, *Historical Collections of Virginia* (1845; reprint, Baltimore, Md.: Regional Publishing, 1969), 238. Baldwin, "Sowers of Sedition," 72. John Taylor, *Baptists on the American Frontier: A History of Ten Baptist Churches of which the Author Has Been Alternative a Member*, ed. Chester Raymond Young (1823; reprint, Macon, Ga.: Mercer University Press, 1995), 245 nn.277–78. Robert B. Semple, *A History of the Baptists in Virginia*, rev. and extended by G. W. Beale (1894; reprint, Cottonport, La.: Polyanthos, 1972), 282. Hall, "Southern Dissenting Clergy," 243. Terman, "American Revolution," 186–90, citing Taylor, *Virginia Baptist Ministers*. John S. Moore, "John Weatherford: The Man behind the Legend," *Virginia Baptist Register*, 8 (1969), 365, citing *The Religious Herald*, March 15,

1833. William S. Simpson Jr., *Virginia Baptist Ministers, 1760–1790: A Biographical Survey* (Richmond, 1969), 10, 44, and 69. Jewell L. Spangler, *Virginians Reborn: Anglican Monopoly, Evangelical Dissent, and the Rise of the Baptists in the Late Eighteenth Century* (Charlottesville: University of Virginia Press, 2008), 221. Sandra Rennie, "Crusaders for Virtue—The Development of the Baptist Culture in Virginia from 1760 to 1790" (MA thesis, La Trobe University, Melbourne, 1975), 262, lists Burrus as a nonpreacher; Little explains that Burrus was a licensed preacher, although not yet ordained. Lewis Petyon Little, *Imprisoned Preachers and Religious Liberty in Virginia* (1938; reprint, Gallatin, Tenn.: Church History Research and Archives, 1987), 247.

16. Little, *Imprisoned Preachers*, 380–83; also L. H. Butterfield, "Elder John Leland, Jeffersonian Itinerant," *American Antiquarian Society Proceedings* 62:2 (Oct. 1952), 186. Robert A. Rutland and Charles F. Hobson, eds., *The Papers of James Madison* (Chicago: University of Chicago Press, 1977), X:542 n.5. William H. B. Thomas, *Patriots of the Upcountry, Orange County, Virginia in the Revolution* (Orange, Va.: Green Publishing, 1976), 47, 115–16.

17. Edmund Randolph, *History of Virginia*, ed. Arthur H. Shaffer (Charlottesville: University Press of Virginia, 1970), 194. Lincoln Macveagh, ed., *Journal of Nicholas Cresswell, 1774–1777* (New York: Dial Press, 1924), 165. Hawks, *Contributions to the Ecclesiastical*, 138. Honourable John S. Barbour, "Oration of the Life, Character, and Services of James Madison," Culpeper Courthouse, July 18, 1836, *Daily National Intelligencer*, 7323 (Washington, D.C., August 2, 1836).

18. *Virginia Gazette* (Purdie), February 21, 1777. Robert Honyman, *Diary, 1776–1782* (Accession 28855, Personal papers collection, Library of Virginia, Richmond), (March 4, 1777), 115–16.

19. H. R. McIlwaine, ed., *Journals of the Council of the State of Virginia* (Richmond: Virginia State Library, 1932), II:74, January 28, 1778. Harris, *History of Louisa*, 191. John S. Moore, ed., "Richard Dozier's Historical Notes, 1771–1818," *Virginia Baptist Register*, 28 (1989), 1397. Semple, *History of the Rise and Progress*, 83. John S. Moore, "Jeremiah Walker in Virginia," *Virginia Baptist Register*, 15 (1976), 719, 725. David A. Benedict, *A General History of the Baptist Denomination in America* (1813; reprint, Freeport, N.Y.: Books for Libraries Press, 1971), II:390–92 (Walker "all-powerful in Associations and other places among the Baptists"). Newman, *History of the Baptist Churches*, 258.

20. Thompson, *Presbyterians in the South*, 94. Wallace to James Caldwell, April 8, 1777, in William H. Whitsitt, *The Life and Times of Judge Caleb Wallace* (Louisville: John P. Morton, 1888), 40. Foote, *Sketches of Virginia*, 412. Lohrenz, "Virginia Clergy," 248.

21. Hall, "Southern Dissenting Clergy," 244–45. See also Lohrenz, "Virginia Clergy," 267 (Walker and Craig enlisting). Thompson, *Presbyterians in the South*, 93–94 (quote). David Campbell to editor, March 25, 1850, Sprague, *Annals of the American Pulpit, Vol. III, Presbyterians*, 287 (quote). Semple, *History of the Baptists*, 359 (quote).

22. Sprague, *Annals of the American Pulpit, Vol. III, Presbyterians*, 366–67. "A Memoir of the Late Rev. William Graham," *Evangelical and Literary Magazine and Missionary Chronicle*, 4:5 (May 1821), 257. Lohrenz, "Virginia Clergy," 226.

23. "Passive Obedience Considered in a Sermon Preached at Williamsburg, December 31st, 1775, by the Reverend David Griffith, Rector of Shelburne Parish," in Williams, *Revolutionary War Sermons*, 24. Meade, *Old Churches*, II:49. Lohrenz, "Virginia Clergy," 143. Gundersen, *Anglican Ministry*, 150. When elected bishop in 1786, Griffith could not afford a trip to England for consecration and resigned the appointment. William White quoted in Rhoden, *Revolutionary Anglicanism*, 100 (note omitted).

24. William Fristoe, *A Concise History of the Ketocton Baptist Association* (1808; reprint, Harrisonburg, Va.: Sprinkle Publications, 2002), 82–83. See also Lohrenz, "Virginia Clergy," 247–48, 278–79. Caleb Wallace to James Caldwell, April 8, 1777, in "Revolutionary Letters," *Historical Magazine and Notes and Queries Concerning the Antiquities, History and Biography of America*, 1:12 (December 1857), 355.

25. There is also some indication of support for supply requisitions among dissenting ministers. Two Presbyterian clergymen, John Brown and James Crawford, worked briefly on claims or supplies in Augusta. Terman, "American Revolution," 286. Others supplied materials. Lohrenz, "Virginia Clergy," 244 (Hugh Vance and John McKnight). Wealthy Baptist minister Samuel Harriss "wagoned military stores." Maud Carter Clement, *The History of Pittsylvania County, Virginia* (Lynchburg, Va.: Bell, 1929), 171. See Terman, "American Revolution."

26. This methodology is discussed in more detail in appendix B.

27. Marvin L. Michael Kay, "The North Carolina Regulation, 1766–1776: A Class Conflict," in *The American Revolution*, ed. Alfred F. Young (DeKalb: Northern Illinois University Press, 1976), 90. Thompson, *Presbyterians in the South*, 85. George Washington Paschal, *History of North Carolina Baptists* (Raleigh, N.C.: Edwards & Broughton, 1930), II:46. See also Harold James Dudley, ed., *Foote's Sketches of North Carolina, Historical and Bibliographical* (1846; reprint, Dunn, N.C.: Twyford Printing, 1965), 237–38. Religion was never a prominent element of Regulator protests, although they did, by 1769, seek an end to discrimination in marriage and establishment taxes. Marvin L. Michael Kay and Lorin Lee Cary, "Class, Mobility, and Conflict in North Carolina on the Eve of the Revolution," in *The Southern Experience in the American Revolution*, ed. Jeffrey J. Crow and Larry E. Tise (Chapel Hill: University of North Carolina Press, 1978), 144.

28. Kay, "North Carolina Regulation," 103. Jeffrey J. Crow, "Liberty Men and Loyalists: Disorder and Disaffection in the North Carolina Backcountry," in *An Uncivil War: The Southern Backcountry during the American Revolution*, ed. Ronald Hoffman, Thad W. Tate, and Peter J. Albert (Charlottesville: University Press of Virginia, 1985), 128. Paul D. Escott and Jeffrey J. Crow, "The Social Order and Violent Disorder: An Analysis of North Carolina in the Revolution and the Civil War," *Journal of Southern History*, 52:3 (August 1986), 379.

29. Kay, "North Carolina Regulation," 105. David Lee Russell, *The American Revolution in the Southern Colonies* (Jefferson, N.C.: McFarland, 2000), 79. Proclamation by Governour Martin, North Carolina, August 8, 1775, in Peter Force, ed., *American Archives: Fourth Series. Containing a Documentary History of the United States of America, from the King's Message to Parliament, of March 7, 1774, to the*

Declaration of Independence by the United States. Volume III (Washington, D.C.: M. St. Clair Clarke and Peter Force, 1840), 61. Governor Josiah Martin to General Gage, March 16, 1775, quoted in Crow, "Liberty Men and Loyalists," 130. Governor Josiah Martin to earl of Dartmouth, June 30, 1775, in William L. Saunders, ed., *The Colonial Records of North Carolina, Vol. X: 1775–1776* (1890; reprint, New York: AMS Press, 1968), 45–46.

30. Crow, "Liberty Men and Loyalists," 136. Kay, "North Carolina Regulation," 105.

31. John Ferling, *Almost a Miracle: The American Victory in the War of Independence* (Oxford: Oxford University Press, 2007), 386; Russell, *American Revolution in the Southern Colonies*, 105; John Buchanan, *The Road to Guilford Court House: The American Revolution in the Carolinas* (New York: Wiley, 1977), 106–10. Robert O. DeMond, *The Loyalists in North Carolina during the Revolution* (Hamden, Conn.: Archon Books, 1964), 180–81, 48 ("Only two or three Regulators of prominence were Patriots").

32. Graham, *Colonists from Scotland*, 157. Depositions of Burlin Hamrod (July 8, 1776), William Bennett, et al. (July 9, 1776), quoted in Escott and Crow, "Social Order and Violent Disorder," 389 (spelling as in original). Graham, *Colonists from Scotland*, 155. Paschal, *History of North Carolina Baptists*, I:389, 469–73.

33. William Everett Pauley Jr., "Religion and the American Revolution in the South: 1760–1781" (Ph.D. diss., Emory University, 1974), 157 (note omitted). Extracts from the Proceedings of the Continental Congress, November 28, 1775, in Saunders, *Colonial Records of North Carolina*, X:338. Joseph Hewes, N.C. Delegate to Continental Congress, to Samuel Johnston, July 8, 1775, ibid., X:86 (note omitted). *Journal of the Proceedings of the Provincial Congress of North Carolina*, September 2, 1775, ibid., X:188. Crow, "Liberty Men and Loyalists," 131. DeMond, *Loyalists*, 49. Synod Letter, July 10, 1775, in Smylie, ed., "Presbyterians and the American Revolution," 392.

34. Paschal, *History of North Carolina Baptists*, I:459, 288. See also Pauley, "Religion and the American Revolution," 182. DeMond, *Loyalists*, 75. Beeman, "Political Response," 226–27.

35. DeMond, *Loyalists*, 77. Rates of representation were calculated by comparing the adult white male population (one-fifth the white population) to the number of assemblymen. Data are from *Historical Statistics of the United States: Colonial Times to 1970* (Washington, D.C.: U.S. Government Printing Office, 1975), II:1168; McIlwaine, *Journal of the House of Burgesses of Virginia* (Richmond, Va., 1906–9), various years; Cynthia Miller Leonard, *The General Assembly of Virginia, July 30, 1619–January 11, 1978* (Richmond: Virginia State Library, 1978); John L. Cheney, ed., *North Carolina Government 1585–1979: A Narrative and Statistical History* (Raleigh: North Carolina Department of the Secretary of State, 1981), 46–47, 53–54, 205–6. Figure 4.1; Return of Militia, November 1782, Library of Virginia Special Collections, Accession No. 36912, Executive Communications, Letters and returns, 1781, November 26, Richmond. Beeman, "Political Response," 234; Nelson, *Blessed Company*, 284.

36. Jac Weller, "The Irregular War in the South," *Military Affairs*, 24:3 (Autumn 1960), 128. Pauley, "Religion and the American Revolution," 170–71, 181–82.

37. Thomas O'Brien Hanley, *The American Revolution and Religion: Maryland 1770–1800* (Washington, D.C.: Catholic University of America Press, 1971), 145. Dee E. Andrews, *The Methodists and Revolutionary America, 1760–1800: The Shaping of an Evangelical Culture* (Princeton, N.J.: Princeton University Press, 2000), 70, 54–59. Keith Mason, "Localism, Evangelicalism, and Loyalism: The Sources of Discontent in the Revolutionary Chesapeake," *Journal of Southern History*, 56:1 (February 1990), 25. Paca quoted ibid., 48. See Ronald Hoffman, *A Spirit of Dissension: Economics, Politics, and the Revolution in Maryland* (Baltimore, Md.: Johns Hopkins University Press, 1973), 227, quoting Nathaniel Potter to Governor Thomas Sim Lee, August 20, 1780; Hanley, *American Revolution and Religion*, 39. William Henry Williams, *The Garden of American Methodism: The Delmarva Penninsula, 1769–1820* (Wilmington, Del.: Scholarly Resources, 1994), 39–40.

38. Andrews, *Methodists and Revolutionary America*, 54–59. Hoffman, *Spirit of Dissension*, 229–30; Williams, *Garden of American Methodism*, 41. Robert R. Hewitt III, *Where the River Flows: Finding Faith in Rockingham County, Virginia, 1726–1876* (Charlottesville: Virginia Foundation for the Humanities, 2003), 76.

39. Mary Beth Norton, *British-Americans: Loyalist Exiles in England, 1774–1789* (Boston: Little, Brown, 1972), 37.

CHAPTER 5

1. Thomas Nelson to Virginia Delegation to the Continental Congress, October 20, 1781, in H. R. McIlwaine, ed., *Official Letters of the Governors of the State of Virginia* (Richmond: Virginia State Library, 1929), III:89.

2. William Waller Hening, ed., *The Statutes at Large, Being a Collection of all the Laws of Virginia from the First Session of the Legislature in the Year 1619* (Heritage Books, CD-ROM #0878, 2003) X (1780):363. Dissenters also complained that marriages had to be officially reported to county clerks. Ibid., XI:505, Art. VII. George MacLaren Brydon suggests that dissenters were unhappy because recording a marriage in an Anglican parish register was an "official" record. When the law was revised in 1784, all ministers were required to report marriages. *Virginia's Mother Church and the Political Conditions under Which It Grew* (Richmond, Va.: Whittet & Shepperson, 1947), II:450 n.8.

3. Hening, *Statutes*, X:288. Caroline County (November 8, 1780). The seven counties in which overseers were responsible for poor relief were Rockbridge, Botetourt, Montgomery, Washington, Greenbrier, Augusta, and Frederick. In 1782, Shenandoah, Henry, Monongalia, Ohio, and Berkeley were added. Hening, *Statutes*, XI:62.

4. Ibid., IX:165. As claims to deprive the Anglican (soon Episcopal) Church of these properties increased, some complained bitterly that the property "was all given up by the Dissenters to the said Church upon Condition they would obtain the Abolition of her Establishment." Amelia County (November 8, 1784).

5. Prince Edward County (November 22, 1781). Miscellaneous Petition (June 3, 1782).

6. Amelia County (May 1783). Essex County (May 30, 1783). Amelia County (May 31, 1783). Powhatan County (November 16, 1783). *Journal of the House of Delegates* (*JHD*) (December 19, 1783), 137.

7. King & Queen County (May 26, 1784); Miscellaneous Petition (May 26, 1784). The canard that "dissenters restrained their actions against rebel legislatures" has been used to argue that development of religious freedom was inevitable. E.g., William G. McLoughlin, "The Role of Religion in the Revolution," in *Essays on the American Revolution*, ed. Stephen G. Kurtz and James H. Hutson (Chapel Hill: University of North Carolina Press, 1973), 205.

8. Brydon, *Virginia's Mother Church*, II:442. Henry Alexander White, *Southern Presbyterian Leaders* (New York: Neale Publishing, 1911), 140. Smith had a knack for angering important patrons: enraging Madison over his support for a general assessment in 1784 and falling out with Henry in 1788 over use of a Henry speech opposing ratification of the U.S. Constitution without attribution or chance for rebuttal in a debate at Hampden-Sydney structured to support ratification. "Henry stalked from the room and refused to hear Smith's preaching ever again." Henry Mayer, *A Son of Thunder: Patrick Henry and the American Republic* (New York: Frank Watts, 1986), 391.

9. Francis L. Hawks, *Contributions to the Ecclesiastical History of the United States of America* (New York: Harper and Brothers, 1836), 156. Brydon, *Virginia's Mother Church*, II:429, 461, 470–71. Although clergy losses have been overstated, there was a serious problem in filling parishes after the war. John K. Nelson, *A Blessed Company: Parishes, Parsons and Parishioners in Anglican Virginia, 1690–1776* (Chapel Hill: University of North Carolina Press, 2001), 300–301.

10. David Griffith to John Buchanan, Fall 1783, in Bishop William Meade, *Old Churches, Ministers and Families of Virginia* (1857; reprint, Baltimore, Md.: Genealogical Publishing, 1978), II:264–65.

11. Lunenburg County (November 8, 1783). Amherst County (November 27, 1783). *JHD* (November 15, 1783), 33; (November 27, 1783), 66. *Virginia Gazette or American Advertiser*, November 15 and 22, 1783 (responding to a November 8 letter from a dissenter).

12. Warwick County (May 15, 1784). Powhatan County (June 4, 1784). See also Miscellaneous Petition from the Clergy of the Protestant Episcopal Church (June 4, 1784); Isle of Wight (November 4, 1784); Amelia County (November 8, 1784).

13. *JHD* (May 27, 1784), 30. Irving Brant, *James Madison: The Nationalist, 1780–1787* (Indianapolis: Bobbs-Merrill, 1948), 344. Marvin K. Singleton, "Colonial Virginia as First Amendment Matrix: Henry, Madison, and Assessment Establishment," *Journal of Church and State*, 8 (Autumn 1966), 350–51 ("disproportionately Episcopal House of Delegates and strong friends in the Senate").

14. *JHD* (June 8, 1784), 57–58. Robert K. Brock, *Archibald Cary of Ampthill* (Richmond: Garrett and Massie, 1937), 123. *JHD* (June 28, 1784), 111. Madison to Jefferson, July 3, 1784, Robert A. Rutland, William M. E. Rachal, Barbara D. Ripel, and Fredrika J. Teute, eds., *The Papers of James Madison* (Chicago: University of Chicago Press, 1973), VIII:93–94.

15. Madison to James Monroe, November 14, 1784, in Rutland, Rachal, Ripel, Teute, *Papers of James Madison*, VIII:136. *JHD* (November 1, 1784), 4. Although the committee was dominated by conservatives, including the chairman, William Norvell, it also had supporters of liberalization, for example, Madison, Zachariah Johnston, French Strother, and Wilson Cary Nicolas. *JHD* (November 11, 1784), 17.

16. Miscellaneous Petition (November 11, 1784). C. C. Bitting, *Notes on the History of the Strawberry Baptist Association of Virginia, for One Hundred Years,—From 1776 to 1876* (Baltimore: Strawberry Baptist Association, 1879), 18 (quote).

17. Lee to Madison, November 26, 1784, in Rutland, Rachal, Ripel, and Teute, *Papers of James Madison*, VIII:149. Ibid., VIII:390 (Harrison). Brant, *Madison: the Nationalist*, 343 (John Marshall, Philip Barbour, Joseph Jones, William Norvell, Henry Tazewell); Gaillard Hunt, "James Madison and Religious Liberty," *Annual Report of the American Historical Association for the Year 1901* (Washington, D.C., 1902), I:168 (Spencer Roane). Washington to Mason, October 3, 1785, in Robert A. Rutland, ed., *The Papers of George Mason: 1725–1792* (Kingsport, Tenn.: University of North Carolina Press, 1970), II:832 (spelling as in original). Claims that Edmund Randolph and James Currie supported the assessment (Singleton, "Colonial Virginia as a First Amendment Matrix," 351–52) do not appear justified by the sources. James Currie to Jefferson, August 5, 1785, in Julian P. Boyd, Mina R. Bryan, and Elizabeth L. Hutter, eds., *The Papers of Thomas Jefferson* (Princeton, N.J.: Princeton University Press, 1953), VIII:342–46; Moncure Daniel Conway, *Omitted Chapters of History Disclosed in the Life and Papers of Edmund Randolph* (1888), 56 (CD-ROM, Bank of Wisdom, Louisville, Ky., 1999). Similarly, while numerous sources report that Washington supported (e.g., Daniel L. Dreisbach, "George Mason's Pursuit of Religious Liberty in Revolutionary Virginia," *Virginia Magazine of History and Biography*, 108:1 [2000], 226; McLoughlin, "Role of Religion," 213; William Wirt Henry, *Patrick Henry: Life, Correspondence and Speeches* [New York: Charles Scribner and Sons, 1891], II:211; Sanford H. Cobb, *The Rise of Religious Liberty in America* [1902; reprint, New York: Burt Franklin, 1970], 495), Washington understood that an assessment would create division, something he sought to avoid. His note to Mason continued, "I wish an assessment had never been agitated—& as it has gone so far, that the Bill could die an easy death; because I think it will be productive of more quiet to the State, than by enacting it into a Law; which, in my opinion, wou'd be impolitic, admitting there is a decided majority for it, to the disgust of a respectable minority.—In the First case, the matter will soon subside;—in the latter it will rankle, & perhaps convulse the State." This is hardly a ringing endorsement. Washington also assumed, as have some modern sources (e.g., Noah Feldman, *Divided by God: America's Church State Problem—and What We Should Do about It* [New York: Farrar, Strauss and Giroux, 2005], 37), that the bill exempted non-Christians; in fact, funds not designated for a Christian denomination would go to "seminaries of learning," generally run by Christian ministers.

18. August 23, 1785, in Boyd, Bryan, and Hutter, eds., *Papers of Thomas Jefferson*, VIII:428–29. Governor Harrison wrote Jefferson, watching anxiously from Paris, that he thought it "doubtful" that the bill would pass. Benjamin Harrison to Jefferson,

November 12, 1784, in Julian P. Boyd, Mina R. Bryan, and Elizabeth L. Hutter, eds., *The Papers of Thomas Jefferson* (Princeton, N.J.: Princeton University Press, 1953), VIII:519. Harrison may have written before he was aware of the apparently supportive Presbyterian petition of November 12.

19. Miscellaneous Petition (November 12, 1784). John Holt Rice, "Memorials to the General Assembly of Virginia," *Literary and Evangelical Magazine*, 9:1 (January 1826), 38. Madison to James Monroe, April 12, 1785, in Rutland, Rachal, Ripel, and Teute, eds., *Papers of James Madison*, VIII:261. For Presbyterian petitions in opposition to a general assessment: Miscellaneous Petition (October 24, 1776); Miscellaneous Petition (June 3, 1777); Miscellaneous Petition (May 26, 1784).

20. *JHD* (November 17, 1784), 25. Perhaps not coincidentally, the statute on suffrage was also amended in this session to remove the prohibition on "recusant[s]" voting, Hening, *Statutes*, XII (1785):120–21; compare ibid., VII (1762):519, albeit dissenters had not generally been disqualified.

21. *JHD* (December 16, 1784), 68; *JHD* (December 28, 1784), 81. Edmund Pendleton to Richard Henry Lee, February 28, 1785, in David John Mays, ed., *The Letters and Papers of Edmund Pendleton, 1734–1803* (Charlottesville: University Press of Virginia, 1967), II:474. Hening, *Statutes*, XI (1784):532.

22. Hening, *Statutes*, XI:504. William W. Bennett, *Memorials of Methodism in Virginia* (Richmond, 1871), 210. *JHD* (December 24, 1784), 79.

23. Henry, *Patrick Henry*, II:206. Madison to James Madison Sr., January 6, 1785, in Rutland, Rachal, Ripel, and Teute, *Papers of James Madison*, VIII:217. Madison to Jefferson, January 9, 1785, in Boyd, Bryan, and Hutter, *The Papers of Thomas Jefferson*, VII:594.

24. For example, Brant, *Madison: The Nationalist*, 345–46. Madison to James Monroe, November 27, 1784, in Rutland, Rachal, Ripel, and Teute, *Papers of James Madison*, VIII:157–58. Robert Douthat Meade, *Patrick Henry: Practical Revolutionary* (Philadelphia: Lippincott, 1969), 281–83. H. J. Eckenrode, *The Revolution in Virginia* (1916; reprint, Hamden, Conn.: Archon Books, 1964), 297. Edmund Randolph to Jefferson, May 5, 1784, in Boyd, Bryan, and Hutter, *Papers of Thomas Jefferson*, VII:260. *JHD* (November 17, 1784), 24–25. In December, Jefferson wrote Madison that "what we have to do I think is *devoutly to pray* for *his* [Henry's] *death*." December 8, 1784, ibid., VII:558 (emphasis originally in cipher). Although this quotation has often been attributed to the assessment debate, in context it refers to Jefferson and Madison's desire to have a new Virginia constitution adopted without Henry's participation. This is one reason there was no effort at the time to have Jefferson's Statute for Establishing Religious Freedom placed in a new constitution.

25. Rockingham County, *JHD* (November 18, 1784), 26; see also *Virginia Gazette and Weekly Advertiser*, November 13, 1784 (100 inhabitants of Botetourt County urge their delegates to oppose assessment). See Lunenburg, Mecklenburg, and Amelia Counties ("stability of our government,…depend in a great measure on the influence of religion") and Halifax County, *JHD* (November 20, 1784), 29; Dinwiddie, Amelia. and Surry, *JHD* (December 3, 1784), 51; *Virginia Gazette and Weekly Advertiser*, November 20, 1784 (Prince Edward inhabitants supporting assessment).

26. Rutland, Rachal, Ripel, and Teute, *Papers of James Madison*, VIII:197–99. *JHD* (December 24, 1784), 78–79. Compare *JHD* (November 11, 1784), 17 and (December 24, 1784), 78–79. Isaac reports that support, "by the third reading," had dropped to forty-four in favor to forty-two opposed. Rhys Isaac, *The Transformation of Virginia, 1740–1790* (New York: Norton, 1982), 284. As the bill never received a third reading, Isaac is apparently referring to the motion in the Committee of the Whole to engross the bill and return it to the House for final consideration. Madison to James Monroe, December 24, 1784, in Rutland, Rachal, Ripel, and Teute, *Papers of James Madison*, VIII:200.

27. *Virginia Journal and Alexandria Advertiser*, March 31, 1785; April 7, 1785; April 14, 1785; November 17, 1785. *Virginia Gazette or American Advertiser*, August 6, 1785; August 13, 1785.

28. Hanover Presbytery Minutes: 1755–1823, May 19, 1785, microfilm reel P278a (Union Theological Seminary, Richmond). See also William Henry Foote, *Sketches of Virginia Historical and Biographical* (1850; reprint, Richmond: John Knox Press, 1966), 341. Ernest Trice Thompson, *Presbyterians in the South: Volume One: 1607–1861* (Richmond, Va.: John Knox Press, 1963), 106. See, e.g., Miscellaneous Petitions (November 12, 1785) (multiple sources, all referring to the Bethel meeting), Frederick and Berkeley Counties (November 12, 1785), Prince Edward County (November 12, 1785), Berkeley County (November 18, 1785). Miscellaneous Petitions (November 2, 1785).

29. John Blair Smith to Madison, June 21, 1784, in Rutland, Rachal, Ripel, and Teute, eds., *Papers of James Madison*, VIII:81.

30. *JHD* (November 17, 1784), 25; (December 11, 1784), 62. The specific language on "clergy" may not have been the focus of the House as the language used in the journal seemed to simply switch back and forth. Compare *JHD* (December 11, 1784), 62; (December 13, 1784), 65; (December 17, 1784), 71; (December 18, 1784), 72; (December 20, 1784), 73; (December 22, 1784), 75 ("Protestant Episcopal Church"), and *JHD* (November 17, 1784), 25; (December 21, 1784), 74 ("Clergy of the Protestant Episcopal Church").

31. Letter from Madison to Jefferson, August 20, 1785, in Boyd, Bryan, and Hutter, eds., *Papers of Thomas Jefferson*, VIII:413–16, 415 (emphasis originally in cipher).

32. Lemuel Burkitt, *A Concise History of the Kehukee Baptist Association, from its Original Rise down to 1803* (Halifax, N.C.: A. Hodge, 1803), 79. Charles F. James, *Documentary History of the Struggle for Religious Liberty in Virginia* (Lynchburg, Va.: J.P. Bell, 1900), 136–38. John Leland, *The Virginia Chronicle: With Judicious and Critical Remarks under XXIV Heads* (Norfolk: Prentis and Baxter, 1790. Early American Imprints, Series 1, no. 21920), 32n. Miscellaneous Petition (November 14, 1785) (Quakers). Madison to Jefferson, January 22, 1786, in Rutland, Rachal, Ripel, and Teute, eds., *Papers of James Madison*, VIII:473. See also J. L. M. Curry, *Struggles and Triumphs of Virginia Baptists, a Memorial Discourse* (Philadelphia: Bible and Publication Society, 1873), 52; B. F. Riley, *A History of the Baptists in the Southern States East of the Mississippi* (Philadelphia: American Baptist Publications Society, 1898), 101.

33. *JHD* (October 29, 1785), 2–3. Howard McKnight Wilson, *The Tinkling Spring, Headwater of Freedom* (Fisherville, Va.: Tinkling Spring and Heritage Presbyterian Churches, 1954), 226–27. Foote, *Sketches of Virginia,* 431.

34. Henry, *Patrick Henry,* II:208. Madison to James Monroe, June 21, 1785, in Rutland, Rachal, Ripel, and Teute, eds., *Papers of James Madison,* VIII:306. Edmund Randolph to Arthur Lee, September 24, 1785, in Conway, *Omitted Chapters,* 163. For Baptist histories that denigrate the Presbyterian effort, see Garnett Ryland, *The Baptists of Virginia, 1699–1926* (Richmond: Virginia Baptist Board of Missions and Education, 1955), 125–26 (Baptists "only organized group that opposed"); Riley, *History of the Baptists in the Southern States,* 100 ("never stood more alone"); Robert B. Semple, *A History of the Baptists in Virginia,* rev, and extended by G. W. Beale (1894; reprint, Cottonport, La.: Polyanthos, 1972), 97–98 ("only sect who plainly remonstrated.").

35. Madison to James Monroe, May 29, 1785, in Rutland, Rachal, Ripel, and Teute, eds., *Papers of James Madison,* VIII:286. See also Madison to James Monroe, April 28, 1785, in ibid., VIII:272 (James Pendleton, colonel in the Revolution, former sheriff of Culpeper, lost for support of assessment). Mays, *Papers of Edmund Pendleton,* II:478. Archibald Stuart to Jefferson, October 17, 1785, in Boyd, Bryan, and Hutter, eds., *Papers of Thomas Jefferson,* VIII:645–46.

36. George Nicholas urged Madison to draft as had, apparently, his brother Wilson Cary Nicolas. George Nicholas to Madison, April 22, 1785, in Rutland, Rachal, Ripel, and Teute, eds., *Papers of James Madison,* VIII:264; editorial note, VIII:295. *Everson v. Board of Education,* 330 U.S. 1, 11–12 (1947). Anson Phelps Stokes, *Church and State in the United States* (New York: Harper & Brothers, 1950), I:391 (quote). See Boyd, Bryan, and Hutter, *Papers of Thomas Jefferson,* VIII:416n. ("staggering blow struck in defense of religious liberty, which at a single stroke destroyed the attempt 'to establish a general assessment'"); Brant, *Madison, The Nationalist,* 350, 352 ("political effect…was staggering," "the most powerful defense of religious liberty ever written in America"). Both Baptists and Presbyterians claim to be progenitors of the *Memorial and Remonstrance.* Compare James Smylie, "From Revolution to Civil War (1776–1861)," in *Virginia Presbyterians in American Life: Hanover Presbytery (1755–1980)* (Richmond: Hanover Presbytery, 1982), 52; Robert Boyle C. Howell, *The Early Baptists of Virginia* (1864; CD-ROM, Baptist Standard Bearer, 2005), 113, 124; William Taylor Thom, *The Struggle for Religious Freedom in Virginia: The Baptists,* Johns Hopkins University Studies, Historical and Political Science, Series 18, Nos. 10–11–12, ed. Herbert B. Adams (1900; reprint, New York: Johnson Reprint, 1973), 77 (553); James, *Documentary History,* 62ff.; Thomas Cary Johnson, *Virginia Presbyterianism and Religious Liberty in Colonial and Revolutionary Times* (Richmond: Presbyterian Committee of Publication, 1907), 76ff. The editors of Madison's papers note more reasonably that "assertions of intellectual dependence are often based on slender textual coincidences." Rutland, Rachal, Ripel, and Teute, *Papers of James Madison,* VIII:297.

37. Rutland, Rachal, Ripel, and Teute, *Papers of James Madison,* VIII:298–304.

38. Thomas E. Buckley, *Church and State in Revolutionary Virginia, 1776–1787* (Charlottesville: University Press of Virginia, 1977), 148. Rutland, Rachal, Ripel, and Teute, *Papers of James Madison,* VIII:297.

39. Washington to Mason, October 3, 1785, in Rutland, *Papers of George Mason*, II:831–32. Stokes, *Church and State*, I:390. George Nicholas to Madison, April 22, 1785, in Rutland, Rachal, Ripel, and Teute, *Papers of James Madison*, VIII:264.

40. Counting these petitions is art as much as mathematics. Often, multiple copies of a petition from the same county were received on a single day (in which case this study treats them as one petition unless clearly different, e.g., Goochland County [November 2, 1785] [*Memorial and Remonstrance*] and Goochland County [November 2, 1785] ["Spirit of the Gospel"]). In some cases, the county of origin is not clear, such as the eleven "miscellaneous petitions" received on November 12, all endorsing the Presbyterian decision at Bethel. These were treated as one petition. Some appear in the *Journal of the House of Delegates* without being survived by a hard copy. Compare Buckley, *Church and State*, 145 (ninety opposed, eleven in favor). Rutland, Rachal, Ripel, and Teute, *Papers of James Madison*, VIII:298 (eighty opposed, eleven in favor); Curry, *First Freedoms*, 143 (ninety opposed, eleven in support).

41. Foote, *Sketches of Virginia*, 431. Thomas Buckley notes that support came "principally" from the Tidewater region of the Northern Neck and the Southside, *Church and State*, 145 and map, 146, but the pattern is less clear when all the petitions are considered.

42. Compare Raymond C. Bailey, *Popular Influence upon Public Policy: Petitioning in Eighteenth-Century Virginia* (Westport, Conn.: Greenwood Press, 1979), 158; Buckley, *Church and State*, 153. Editorial note, Rutland, Rachal, Ripel, and Teute, *Papers of James Madison*, VIII:36. Henry, *Patrick Henry*, II:215. Lewis Cecil Gray, *History of Agriculture in the Southern United States to 1860* (1932; reprint, Gloucester, Mass., 1958), II:604–5. Henry Howe, *Historical Collections of Virginia* (1845; reprint, Baltimore, Md.: Regional Publishing, 1969), 381 (poem). The poem was reprinted from the *Virginia Gazette* (Dixon and Hunter), October 18, 1776. Hugh Blair Grigsby, *History of the Virginia Federal Convention of 1788*, Virginia Historical Society, *Collections*, New Series, X (Richmond, 1891), II:122–30, relied on in Buckley, *Church and State*, 155.

43. Madison to James Monroe, December 17, 1785, in Rutland, Rachal, Ripel, and Teute, *Papers of James Madison*, VIII:446. Julian P. Boyd, Lyman H. Butterfield, and Mina R. Bryan, eds., *The Papers of Thomas Jefferson* (Princeton, N.J.: Princeton University Press, 1950), II:545–47.

44. *JHD* (December 16, 1785) (December 17, 1785), 93–94. *Journal of the Senate of the Commonwealth of Virginia; begun and held in the City of Richmond, On Monday, the 17th day of October, in the year of our Lord Christ, 1785* (Richmond: Thomas W. White, 1827), December 23, 1785, 61. Madison to Jefferson, January 22, 1786, in Rutland, Rachal, Ribel, and Teute, *Papers of James Madison*, VIII:474.

45. Hening, ed., *Statutes*, XII:86.

46. Ibid., XII:27–30; *JHD* (December 30, 1785), 117. *JHD* (January 16, 1786), 141. Journals of the Conventions of the Protestant Episcopal Church in Virginia, 13, in Hawks, *Ecclesiastical History. JHD* (January 6, 1787), 142; Hening, ed., *Statutes*, XII:266.

47. Buckley, *Church and State*, 167. Episcopal petition (December 5, 1786), Miscellaneous Petitions (November 2, 1785) (Presbyterian); Miscellaneous Petitions

(November 17, 1785) (Baptist). Thom, *Struggle for Religious Freedom*, 82 (558). *JHD* (December 4, 1787), 63. For example, Wesley M. Gewehr, *The Great Awakening in Virginia, 1740–1790* (Durham, N.C.: Duke University Press, 1930), 215. *Terrett v. Taylor*, 13 U.S. 43 (1815). Buckley, *Church and State*, 172 n.79. See Brydon, *Virginia's Mother Church*, II:474–535 (actions to seize silver and other property).

48. Implications of the Great Awakening have previously been discussed. Sidney Mead attributes religious freedom to postwar negotiations between dissenters and establishment intellectuals. Sidney E. Mead, *The Lively Experiment: The Shaping of Christianity in America* (New York: Harper and Row, 1963).

CHAPTER 6

1. L. F. Greene, ed., *The Writings of the Late Elder John Leland, including some events in his life, written by himself, with some additional sketches* (New York: Wood, 1845), 107. Accomac County (November 28, 1785). Noah Feldman, in criticizing Justice Hugo Black's conclusion in the *Everson* case that the First Amendment is intended to protect minorities who might suffer from establishment, argues that early American establishments were so mild that Black must have been responding to then-contemporary Nazi persecution of Jews. Noah Feldman, *Divided by God: America's Church State Problem—And What We Should Do about It* (New York: Farrar, Strauss and Giroux, 2005), 174–75. Thomas J. Curry, *The First Freedoms: Church and State in America to the Passage of the First Amendment* (New York: Oxford University Press, 1986), 211 (Virginia's establishment "relatively mild").

2. Mason to Henry, May 6, 1783, in Robert A. Rutland, ed., *The Papers of George Mason: 1725–1792* (Kingsport, Tenn.: University of North Carolina Press, 1970), II:770. Washington quoted in Michael W. McConnell, "The Origins and Historical Understanding of Free Exercise of Religion," *Harvard Law Review*, 103:7 (May 1990), 1441. Kent Greenawalt, "Common Sense about Original and Subsequent Understanding of the Religion Clauses," *University of Pennsylvania Journal of Constitutional Law*, 8 (May 2006), 501.

3. Madison to Monroe, May 29, 1785, in Robert A. Rutland, William M. E. Rachal, Barbara D. Ripel, and Frederika J. Teute, eds., *The Papers of James Madison* (Chicago: University of Chicago Press, 1973), VIII:286. McConnell, "Origins and Historical Understanding," 1442 (notes omitted). See *Board of Education of the City of Cincinnati v. Minor*, 23 Ohio St. 211, 243–44 (1872). "Religion and the Founding of the American Republic," available online at http://www.loc.gov/exhibits/religion/rel06.html. The role of "civic virtue" in America was generally addressed by checks and balances among branches of government and a federal system so that, even if not wholly virtuous, civil leaders were restrained. See Gordon S. Wood, *The Creation of the American Republic, 1776–1787* (New York: Norton, 1969), 65–70, 117–18, 427–29.

4. Philip Hamburger, *Separation of Church and State* (Cambridge, Mass.: Harvard University Press, 2002), 66–67. Vincent Philip Muñoz, "Religion and the Common Good: George Washington on Church and State," in *The Founders on God and Government*, ed. Daniel L. Dreisbach, Mark D. Hall, and Jeffery H. Morrison (Lanham, Md.: Rowman & Littlefield Publishers, 2004), 2–6 (same).

5. Miscellaneous Petition (November 2, 1785).

6. John Leland, *The Virginia Chronicle: With Judicious and Critical Remarks under XXIV Heads* (Norfolk: Prentis and Baxter, 1790. Early American Imprints, Series 1, no. 21920), 22n+.

7. *The Freeman's Remonstrance against an Ecclesiastical Establishment* (Williamsburg, Dixon and Hunter, 1777. Early American Imprints, Series 1, no. 43250, filmed), 7. Baptist petition from Convention (December 25, 1776), *Virginia Gazette* (Dixon and Hunter), March 28, 1777.

8. William Fristoe, *A Concise History of the Ketocton Baptist Association* (1808; reprint, Harrisonburg, Va.: Sprinkle Publications, 2002), 85–86. Powhatan County (November 3, 1785). Orange County (Baptists) (November 17, 1785). *Freeman's Remonstrance*, 7.

9. H. J. Eckenrode, *Separation of Church and State in Virginia: A Study in the Development of the Revolution* (1910; reprint, New York: Da Capo Press, 1971), 119, quoting Baptist Petition written in August 1786. Botetourt County (November 29, 1785). Baptist Petition, *Journal of the House of Delegates* (*JHD*), November 1, 1786, 15.

10. Miscellaneous Petition (October 24, 1776) (emphasis in original). Miscellaneous Petition (June 3, 1777) (emphasis in original). Amherst County (November 1, 1779). 1784 Resolution of the Baptist General Committee, in B. F. Riley, *A History of the Baptists in the Southern States East of the Mississippi* (Philadelphia: American Baptist Publications Society, 1898), 99–100. G. S. Bailey, *The Trials and Victories of Religious Liberty in America* (Philadelphia: American Baptist Publication Society, 1876), 13.

11. Miscellaneous Petition (October 24, 1776). Rockingham County, November 18, 1784. Orange County (Baptists) (November 17, 1785). Miscellaneous Petition (June 3, 1777). Petition, from a meeting of "Ministers and Delegates" at Dover in Goochland County, *Virginia Gazette* (Dixon and Hunter) March 28, 1777. Miscellaneous Petition (June 3, 1777). Madison to Monroe, May 29, 1785, in Rutland, Rachal, Ripel and Teute, *Papers of James Madison*, VIII:286.

12. *Virginia Gazette* (Dixon and Nicholson), September 11, 18, 1779. Essex County (October 22, 1779). Lunenburg County (November 8, 1783). See Amherst County (November 11, 1779) (no "Roman catholic, Jew, Turk or Infidel" be allowed in office) and (November 27, 1783). Mecklenburg County (November 2, 1785); Pittsylvania County (November 7, 1785); Lunenburg County (November 9, 1785); Mecklenburg County (October 26, 1785). Miscellaneous Petition (May 26, 1784).

13. Leland, *Virginia Chronicle*, 38, 24.

14. Petition, from a meeting of "Ministers and Delegates" at Dover in Goochland County, December 25, 1776, *Virginia Gazette* (Dixon and Hunter) March 28, 1777). Miscellaneous Petition (Presbyterian ministers in convention) (November 2, 1785).

15. Chesterfield County (November 14, 1785) (spelling as in original); Montgomery County (November 15, 1785) ("Why then are Pagans & Mahomitans compelled to contribute to the Support of the *Christian* Religion?"). Fristoe, *Concise History*, 85–86.

16. Curry, *First Freedoms*, 147. See also Ellis West, "The Case against a Right to Religion-Based Exemptions," *Notre Dame Journal of Law, Ethics and Public Policy*,

4 (1989–90), 628; Chester James Antieau, Arthur T. Downey, and Edward C. Roberts, *Freedom from Federal Establishment: Formation and Early History of the First Amendment Religion Clauses* (Milwaukee: Bruce Publishing, 1964), 21 (distinguishing "encouragement and support" from "establishment...exclusion and preference").

17. Surry County (October 26, 1785), Cumberland County (October 26, 1785). Thomas Jefferson, *Autobiography*, in *Thomas Jefferson Writings*, ed. Merrill D. Peterson (New York: Library of America, 1984), 40. James Madison, "Detached Memoranda," in Robert S. Alley, ed., *James Madison on Religious Liberty* (Buffalo: Prometheus Books, 1985), 90. Madison to Jefferson, January 22, 1786, in Rutland, Rachal, Ripel, and Teute, *Papers of James Madison*, VIII:474. Compare Thomas E. Buckley, *Church and State in Revolutionary Virginia, 1776–1787* (Charlottesville: University Press of Virginia, 1977), 158 n.45 ("Jesus Christ" in preamble would have been unimportant). Elizabeth Fleet, ed., "Madison's 'Detached Memoranda,'" *William and Mary Quarterly*, 3rd Ser., 3:4 (October 1946), 556. The General Assembly's bills and resolutions file for December 1785 includes an "agreed" resolution of the Committee for Religion that the "Christian [obscured] Religion be the Established Religion of this Commonwealth." Virginia General Assembly, House of Delegates, Rough Bills, Resolutions, Etc., Rough Bills, 11/1784–12/1785, Resolutions 11/1784–1/1786, Box 9 (12/1785 file), Library of Virginia, Richmond. The significance of this document is not clear; it may be misfiled, or it may refer to the controversy over insertion of "Jesus Christ."

18. Derek H. Davis, *Religion and the Continental Congress 1774–1789: Contributions to Original Intent* (Oxford: Oxford University Press, 2000), 16. Miscellaneous Petition (October 16, 1776). Compare *Board of Education v. Louis Grumet*, 512 U.S. 687, 732 (1994) (Scalia, Rehnquist, and Thomas dissenting) (only intended to prevent one sect from punishing dissenters); James M. O'Neill, *Catholics in Controversy* (New York: McMullen Books, 1954), 18. With the breadth of modern religions, nondiscriminatory aid to all religions may simply be impractical in any case. Michael J. Malbin, *Religion and Politics: The Intentions of the Authors of the First Amendment* (Washington, D.C.: American Enterprise Institute, 1978), preface. Claims of discrimination by followers of the Jedi religion in Britain come to mind.

19. Leland, *Virginia Chronicle*, 22. Thomas Jefferson, *Notes on the State of Virginia*, in *Thomas Jefferson Writings*, ed. Merrill D. Peterson (New York: Library of America, 1984), Query XVII, 285 ("it does me no injury for my neighbor to say there are twenty gods, or no God"). Miscellaneous Petition (November 2, 1785).

20. Hanover Presbytery Minutes: 1755–1823, May 19, 1785, microfilm reel P278a (Union Theological Seminary, Richmond). Richard Henry Lee to Madison (November 26, 1784), in Robert A. Rutland and William M. E. Rachal, eds., *The Papers of James Madison* (Chicago: University of Chicago Press, 1975), IX:149–50. Madison to Jefferson (January 9, 1785), in Julian P. Boyd, Mina R. Bryan, and Elizabeth L. Hutter, eds., *The Papers of Thomas Jefferson* (Princeton, N.J.: Princeton University Press, 1953), VII:595 (emphasis originally in cipher).

21. James Hutson, "Thomas Jefferson's Letter to the Danbury Baptists: A Controversy Rejoined," *William and Mary Quarterly*, 3rd Ser., 56:4 (October 1999). Daniel L. Dreisbach, "Thomas Jefferson, a Mammoth Cheese, and the 'Wall of

Separation Between Church and State,'" in *Religion and the New Republic: Faith in the Founding of America*, ed. James H. Hutson (Lanham, Md.: Rowman and Littlefield, 2000), 72–73, 75 (Jefferson saw letter as political, not a "universal principle"); Feldman, *Divided by God*, 40. Jefferson to Levi Lincoln, January 1, 1802, in Andrew A. Lipscomb and Albert Ellery Bergh, *The Writings of Thomas Jefferson: Containing His Autobiography, Notes on Virginia, Parliamentary Manual, Official Papers, Messages and Addresses, and Other Writings, Official and Private* (Washington, D.C.: Thomas Jefferson Memorial Foundation, 1903), X:305. Edwin Scott Gaustad, "Thomas Jefferson, the Danbury Baptists, and 'Eternal Hostility,'" *William and Mary Quarterly*, 3rd Ser., 56:4 (October 1999).

22. Buckley, *Church and State*, 180.

23. Powhatan County (Baptists) (November 6, 1783). Leland, *Virginia Chronicle*, 37. Botetourt County (November 29, 1785). *Virginia Gazette or American Advertiser* (November 8, 1783). *Freeman's Remonstrance*, 8. *Virginia Gazette and Weekly Advertiser* (Richmond, Nicolson), August 6 and 13, 1785. Hamburger cites this *Virginia Gazette* article favoring the assessment as evidence that some connection between church and state was anticipated, *Separation of Church and State*, 70, but this position was overwhelmed.

24. C.C. Bitting, *Notes on the History of Strawberry Baptist Association of Virginia, for One Hundred Years,—From 1776 to 1876* (Baltimore, Md.: Strawberry Baptist Association, 1879; microfilm), 22.

25. Southampton County (October 13, 1778), Caroline and King & Queen Counties (May 25, 1779), Hanover County (October 23, 1778). See Sandy Creek Baptists (October 16, 1780), Botetourt County (November 4, 1778), Charles F. James, *Documentary History of the Struggle for Religious Liberty in Virginia* (Lynchburg, Va.: J. P. Bell, 1900), 219–21.

26. Baptist petition (December 25, 1776), reprinted in *Virginia Gazette* (Dixon and Hunter), March 28, 1777. Compare William G. McLoughlin, "Role of Religion in the Revolution," in *Essays on the American Revolution*, ed. Stephen G. Kurtz and James H. Hutson (Chapel Hill: University of North Carolina Press, 1973), 222; Buckley, *Church and State*, 176–77 (Presbyterians did not advocate separation of church and state until 1785), 182, 173 (assessment "reflected the real consensus of Virginians").

27. Robert B. Semple, *A History of the Baptists in Virginia*, rev. and extended by G. W. Beale (1894; reprint, Cottonport, La.: Polyanthos, 1972), 89 (resolution of Baptist meeting at Nottoway). Leland, *Virginia Chronicle*, 37. See *Board of Education v. Mergens*, 496 U.S. 226, 250 (1990) ("crucial difference between government speech endorsing religion, which the Establishment Clause forbids, and private speech endorsing religion, which the Free Speech and Free Exercise Clauses protect"). See Jefferson to Peter Wendover, March 13, 1815, discussed in Hamburger, *Separation of Church and State*, 151–54. Feldman, *Divided by God*, 6. Much of the early nineteenth-century effort to discourage ministers' political involvement arose from some Baptist and Methodist ministers' opposition to slavery. Randolph Ferguson Scully, *Religion and the Making of Nat Turner's Virginia: Baptist Community and Conflict, 1740–1840* (Charlottesville: University of Virginia Press, 2008), 120.

28. Hamburger, *Separation of Church and State*, 19, 54–55 (quote). Ibid., 100 n.23, quoting Rhys Isaac, *The Transformation of Virginia, 1740–1790* (New York: Norton, 1982), 291. Botetourt (November 29, 1785).

29. 540 U.S. 712 (2004). See Justices Scalia and Thomas's persuasive dissent. Buckley, *Church and State*, 180 (dissenters wanted church "separated from the state precisely so that it might freely influence society and permeate it with the Gospel message"). This doctrine is discussed in Richard W. Garnett, "Religion, Division, and the First Amendment," *Georgetown Law Journal*, 94 (2006), 1667–724.

30. Prince William County (June 20, 1776). Prince Edward County (October 11, 1776); William Henry Foote, *Sketches of Virginia Historical and Biographical* (1850; reprint, Richmond, Va.: John Knox Press, 1966), 332 (April 1780 Presbyterian petition).

31. For example, Rockingham County (November 18, 1784). Eckenrode, *Separation of Church and State*, 119, quoting Baptist Petition written in August 1786; Baptist Petition, *JHD*, November 1, 1786, 15. William Wirt Henry notes that dissenters took separation of church and state so strictly that a seminary could not be incorporated or a religious charity "enforced" in Virginia for 100 years. William Wirt Henry, *Patrick Henry: Life, Correspondence and Speeches* (New York: Charles Scribner and Sons, 1891), II:210–11.

32. Greene, *Writings of the Late Elder John Leland*, 181. Miscellaneous Petition (November 12, 1784). L. H. Butterfield, "Elder John Leland, Jeffersonian Itinerant," *American Antiquarian Society Proceedings* 62:2 (Oct. 1952), 163. William Taylor Thom, *The Struggle for Religious Freedom in Virginia: The Baptists*, Johns Hopkins University Studies, Historical and Political Science, Series XVIII, Nos. 10–11–12, ed. Herbert B. Adams (1900; reprint, New York: Johnson Reprint, 1973), 19 (495).

33. In a 1776 draft of a Declaration of Rights, Jefferson noted in parentheses (presumably because he was continuing to contemplate the matter) that free exercise would not include "any seditious preaching or conversation against the authority of the civil government." Julian P. Boyd, Lyman H. Butterfield, and Mina R. Bryan, eds., *The Papers of Thomas Jefferson*, (Princeton, N.J.: Princeton University Press, 1950), I:353. This limitation was omitted from Jefferson's subsequent draft and an earlier draft referenced only "seditious behavior." Ibid., I:363, 344. Compare Malbin, *Religion and Politics*, 35 (Jefferson's "own two drafts" did not protect "seditious preaching"). Jefferson's history with seditious speech is not spotless, but it is generally agreed that the statute—only overt acts, not mere opinions, are actionable—represents his considered view.

34. See *City of Boerne v. P.F. Flores*, 521 U.S. 507 (1997). For example, *Welsh v. United States*, 398 U.S. 333, 340 (1970), (Harlan concurring) at 345, 356–58, 360 (conscientious objectors exempted from draft even if not part of traditional religious belief). Compare *Thomas v. Review Board*, 450 U.S. 707, 713 (1981) ("Only beliefs rooted in religion are protected by the Free Exercise Clause"). *Virginia Gazette* (Purdie), November 8, 1776. See Daillin H. Oaks, *Religious Freedom and the Supreme Court* (Washington, D.C.: Ethics and Public Policy Center, 1981), 118–19. Gary Glenn argues that Congress's decision to remove rights of "conscience" from Madison's draft

of the free exercise clause and restrict it to "religion" was done to exclude nontheistic beliefs. Gary B. Glenn, "Forgotten Purposes of the First Amendment Religion Clauses," *Review of Politics*, 49:3 (Summer 1987), 347–50, 359.

35. Compare McConnell, "Origins and Historical Understanding"; West, "The Case against a Right to Religion-Based Exemptions,"; Malbin, *Religion and Politics* (focusing only on Jefferson and Madison); Kurt T. Lash, "Power and the Subject of Religion," *Ohio State Law Journal* 59 (1998), 1069–154; Philip Hamburger, "A Constitutional Right of Religious Exemption: An Historical Perspective," *George Washington Law Review*, 60 (April 1992), 915–48. Greenawalt, "Common Sense."

36. West, "The Case against a Right to Religion-Based Exemptions," 624; Malbin, *Religion and Politics*, 29 et seq. McConnell, "Origins and Historical Understanding," 1453, 1452.

37. William T. Hutchinson and William M. E. Rachal, eds., *The Papers of James Madison* (Chicago: University of Chicago Press, 1962), I:173–75 (emphasis added). Isaac, *Transformation*, 280 (note omitted). Isaac cites Jefferson's ruminations about restricting seditious preaching which Jefferson, on reflection, rejected. McConnell, "Origins and Historical Understanding," 1463. *Virginia Gazette* (Dixon and Nicolson) August 14, 1779.

38. Jefferson's statute notes that religious opinions shall "in no wise diminish, enlarge, or affect [men's] civil capacities." One could argue that an exemption based on religious beliefs enlarges a person's civil capacities. Compare Michael S. Paulsen, "Religion, Equality, and the Constitution: An Equal Protection Approach to Establishment Cause Adjudication," *Notre Dame Law Review*, 61 (1987), 341–45.

39. Leland, *Virginia Chronicle*, 37. Greene, *Writings of the Late Elder John Leland*, 239 (from "A Blow at the Root" sermon given April 9, 1801). William Warren Sweet, *Religion in Colonial America* (New York: Charles Scribner's Sons, 1951), 122. Carl Bridenbaugh, *Mitre and Sceptre: Transatlantic Faiths, Ideas, Personalities, and Politics 1689–1775* (London: Oxford University Press, 1962), 51.

40. Compare Hamburger, "Constitutional Right," 942 n.111, citing Greene, *Writings of the Late Elder John Leland*, 188, 228. Other Leland examples cited by Hamburger (dunking a wife or murder based on religious beliefs) involve physical acts of violence that compromise "peace and good order." Other statements referenced by Hamburger are, at best, equally ambiguous. For example, Hamburger, "Constitutional Right," 945 n.113 (Presbyterian petition [April 25, 1777] calls upon civil government to "restrain the vicious...by wholesome laws equally extended to every individual"). Greene, *Writings of the Late Elder John Leland*, 228.

41. *City of Boerne v. P.F. Flores*, 521 U.S. at 540 (Justices Scalia and Stevens concurring), citing Hamburger, "Constitutional Right," 918–19. Stewart Rapalje and Robert L. Lawrence, *A Dictionary of American and English Law* (Jersey City: Linn, 1888), I:149–50, II:757.

42. Hamburger, "Constitutional Right," 923. *Freeman's Remonstrance*, 4-5.

43. See, e.g., New York Constitution, Art. 38 (1777) (free exercise does not excuse "acts of licentiousness, or justify practices inconsistent with the peace or safety of this State"); New Hampshire Constitution, Art. V (1784) ("provided he doth not disturb the

public peace, or disturb others"); Georgia Constitution, Art. LVI (1777) ("not repugnant to the peace and safety of the State"). Nine of the new states restricted free exercise by such limitations. McConnell, "Origins of Free Exercise," 1461.

44. Leland, *Virginia Chronicle*, 22. Semple, *History of the Baptists*, 29.

45. Miscellaneous Petition (June 3, 1777).

46. After seeming to require a compelling state interest to justify imposition on free exercise, the Supreme Court receded, essentially refusing to recognize any religious exception to an otherwise valid law of general application. *City of Boerne v. P.F. Flores*, 521 U.S. at 513–14; *Employment Division v. Smith*, 494 U.S. 872 (1990).

47. *Virginia Gazette* (Rind), March 26, 1772. Miscellaneous Petition (June 5, 1775). See David Thomas, *The Virginian Baptist* (Baltimore: Enoch Story, 1774. Early American Imprints, Series 1, no. 13651, filmed), 40. Although a restriction on baptism might be direct regulation prohibited by the free exercise clause, one could easily craft a neutral regulation to the same effect, for example, prohibiting inducting slaves into any society or organization.

EPILOGUE

1. See Connecticut Fundamental Orders (1639) (Christian); Delaware Constitution, Art. 22 (1776) (oath for office includes trinity, Old and New Testaments); Georgia Constitution, Art. VI (1777) (Protestant office holders); Maryland Declaration of Rights, Art. 33 (1776) (Christians protected); Massachusetts Constitution, Art. 3 (1780) (Protestant religion established); New Hampshire Constitution, Art. 6 (1784) (Christians protected); New Jersey Constitution, Art. 19 (1776) (Protestants protected); New York Constitution, Art. 42 (1777) (anti-Catholic); North Carolina Constitution, Art. 32 (1776) (Protestant office holders); Pennsylvania Constitution, Sec. 10 (1776) (office requires belief in God, Old and New Testaments); South Carolina Constitution, Arts. 3, 12 (1778) (Protestant office holders). See generally Francis Newton Thorpe, ed., *The Federal and State Constitutions, Colonial Charters, and Other Organic Laws of the States, Territories, and Colonies* (Washington, D.C.: Government Printing Office, 1909).

2. *Cantwell v. Connecticut*, 310 U.S. 296 (1940). *Everson*, 330 U.S. 1, 11, 13, 33 (1947). *McGowan v. Maryland*, 366 U.S. 420, 437 (1961). See also *Reynolds v. United States*, 98 U.S. 145, 162–63 (1879) (Virginia's experience and Madison's efforts).

3. See generally Merrill D. Peterson and Robert C. Vaughan, eds., *The Virginia Statute for Religious Freedom: Its Evolution and Consequence in American History* (Cambridge: Cambridge University Press, 1988). Leo Pfeffer, "Madison's 'Detached Memoranda': Then and Now," in Peterson and Vaughan, *Virginia Statute for Religious Freedom*, 285. Anson Phelps Stokes, *Church and State in the United States* (New York: Harper & Brothers, 1950), I:366. Martin E. Marty, "The Virginia Statute Two Hundred Years Later," in *Virginia Statute for Religious Freedom*, 1. Jon Butler, *Awash in a Sea of Faith: Christianizing the American People* (Cambridge, Mass.: Harvard University Press, 1990), 265.

4. *Everson v. Board of Education*, 330 U.S. 1, 11–12 (1947) ("Thomas Jefferson and James Madison led the fight against this tax"); ibid., 38 (Rutledge, Frankfurter,

Jackson, Burton dissenting) (quotes) (note omitted); *Illinois ex rel. McCollum v. Board of Education*, 333 U.S. 203, 214, 247–48 (1948) (Frankfurter, Jackson, Rutledge, Burton) (Reed dissenting); *Reynolds*, 98 U.S. at 163–64 (letter to Danbury Baptists). See *City of Boerne v. P.F. Flores*, 521 U.S. 507, 560–61 (1997) (O'Connor and Breyer dissenting) (Madison's "now-famous" *Memorial* "led thousands of Virginians to oppose the bill"). Michael J. Malbin, *Religion and Politics: The Intentions of the Authors of the First Amendment* (Washington, D.C.: American Enterprise Institute, 1978), 25 (Madison's *Memorial* and Jefferson's statute were "the most important of the views expressed during the ten years of Virginia debate"). This focus on Jefferson and Madison is sometimes used to attack a broad reading of religious freedom; McLoughlin, urging a narrow reading, argues "in many respects it was Jefferson and Madison's position that was eccentric at the time." William G. McLoughlin, "The Role of Religion in the Revolution," in *Essays on the American Revolution*, ed. Stephen G. Kurtz and James H. Hutson (Chapel Hill: University of North Carolina Press, 1973), 222. Recent criticism of the emphasis on the Virginia experience is addressed in John A. Ragosta, "Jefferson's Statute for Establishing Religious Freedom: How We Got It, What We Did with It, and Implications for the First Amendment Debate," at www.adamsjefferson.com.

 5. *Terrett v. Taylor*, 13 U.S. 43 (1815). George MacLaren Brydon, *Virginia's Mother Church and the Political Conditions under Which It Grew* (Richmond, Va.: Whittet and Shepperson, 1947); Wesley M. Gewehr, *The Great Awakening in Virginia, 1740–1790* (Durham, N.C.: Duke University Press, 1930), 215. Christine Leigh Heyrman's *Southern Cross: The Beginnings of the Bible Belt* (New York: Knopf, 1998) and Randolph Scully's *Religion and the Making of Nat Turner's Virginia: Baptist Community and Conflict, 1740–1840* (Charlottesville: University of Virginia Press, 2008) focus on the shifting roles of evangelicals in the south in the public square.

 6. Compare Robert Boyle C. Howell, *The Early Baptists of Virginia* (1864; CD-ROM, Baptist Standard Bearer, 2005), 122 (Baptist Convention proposed statute; Jefferson and Madison drafted at Reuben Ford's request) and Jacob Harris Patton, *The Triumph of the Presbytery of Hanover; or, Separation of Church and State in Virginia* (New York: Anson D.F. Randolph, 1887), 51–52 (nothing in bill not in 1776 Presbyterian petition). James H. Smylie, "From Revolution to Civil War (1776–1861)," in *Virginia Presbyterians in American Life: Hanover Presbytery (1755–1980)* (Richmond, Va.: Hanover Presbytery, 1982), 52 (ideas for *Memorial* from Presbyterian petitions). Howell refers to Madison's *Memorial* as "their" (Baptists') memorial, explaining that "it is well known that when the General Committee of the Baptists of Virginia,…had issued its Declaration of Principles,…this Declaration was placed in the hands of Mr. Madison with a request that he would embody it in their behalf, in a memorial to the Legislature." *Early Baptists*, 113, 124. Also William Taylor Thom, *The Struggle for Religious Freedom in Virginia: The Baptists*, Johns Hopkins University Studies, Historical and Political Science, Series XVIII, Nos. 10–11–12, ed. Herbert B. Adams (1900; reprint, New York: Johnson Reprint, 1973), 77 (553). Charles F. James, *Documentary History of the Struggle for Religious Liberty in Virginia* (Lynchburg, Va.: J. P. Bell, 1900), 62ff. (Baptist influence on Declaration of Rights Article 16); Thomas Cary

Johnson, *Virginia Presbyterianism and Religious Liberty in Colonial and Revolutionary Times* (Richmond, Va.: Presbyterian Committee of Publication, 1907), 76ff., and Brydon, *Virginia's Mother Church*, II:383–84 (Presbyterian influence). For the general proposition that nineteenth-century sects sought legitimacy, in part, by claiming the mantle of the Revolution, Charles Frederick Irons, "'The Chief Cornerstone': The Spiritual Foundations of Virginia's Slave Society, 1776–1861" (Ph.D. diss., University of Virginia, 2003); Peter Onuf, "Thomas Jefferson's Christian Nation," in *Religion, State and Society: Jefferson's Wall of Separation in Comparative Perspective*, ed. Robert Fatton Jr. and R. K. Ramazani (New York: Palgrave Macmillan, 2009), 25.

7. William N. Eskridge Jr., Philip P. Frickey, and Elizabeth Garrett, *Legislation and Statutory Interpretation* (New York: Foundation Press, 2000), 296. Madison to Thomas Ritchie (September 15, 1821), quoted in Philip B. Kurland and Ralph Lerner, eds., *The Founders' Constitution* (Chicago: University of Chicago Press, 1987), I:74.

8. Semple, *History of the Baptists*, 102. James Madison Sr. to James Madison Jr. (January 30, 1788), Rutland and Hobson, eds., *Papers of James Madison*, 10:446.

9. Robert B. Semple, *A History of the Baptists in Virginia*, rev. and extended by G. W. Beale (1894; reprint, Cottonport, La.: Polyanthos, 1972), 206–7 (quote). Ryland, *Baptists of Virginia*, 134. James Gordon Jr. to Madison, February 17, 1788, in Robert A. Rutland and Charles F. Hobson, eds., *The Papers of James Madison* (Chicago: University of Chicago Press, 1977), X:516; Joseph Spencer to Madison, February 28, 1788, ibid., Z:541 (spelling as in original). Elder John Leland to G. N. Briggs, governor of Massachusetts, Briggs to William B. Sprague, in William B. Sprague, *Annals of the American Pulpit, Volume VI, Baptists*, 180 (New York: Robert Carter and Brothers, 1865); Gewehr, *Great Awakening*, 189. B. F. Riley, *A History of the Baptists in the Southern States East of the Mississippi* (Philadelphia: American Baptist Publications Society, 1898), 105–6 (quoting Barbour).

10. James, *Documentary History*, 161. James provides an extended discussion of Madison's dependence on the Baptists for his election to the Virginia Convention and Congress. Ibid., 157–68. Robert A. Rutland and Charles F. Hobson, eds., *Papers of James Madison* (Charlottesville: University Press of Virginia, 1977), XI:303–4, 404–5.

11. For example, James, *Documentary History*, 152 et seq.; Thomas J. Curry, *The First Freedoms: Church and State in America to the Passage of the First Amendment* (New York: Oxford University Press, 1986), 199–200.

12. Philip Hamburger, *Separation of Church and State* (Cambridge, Mass.: Harvard University Press, 2002), 106. *Wallace v. Jaffree*, 472 U.S. 38, 97–98 (1985) (Rehnquist dissenting). Compare Pfeffer, "Madison's 'Detached Memorandum.'" Madison to George Washington, November 20, 1789, in Charles F. Hobson and Robert A. Rutland, eds., *The Papers of James Madison* (Charlottesville: University Press of Virginia, 1979), XII:453. The *Everson* dissent saw these electoral developments as an additional reason to focus on Madison's commitment to religious liberty. 330 U.S. at 39 n.26 (Rutledge, Frankfurter, Jackson, and Burton dissenting).

13. Nathan O. Hatch, "The Whirlwind of Religious Liberty in Early North America," in *Freedom and Religion in the Nineteenth Century*, ed. Richard Helmstadter (Stanford, Calif.: Sanford University Press, 1997), 30, citing Sidney E. Mead, "From Coercion to Persuasion: Another Look at the Rise of Religious Liberty and the

Emergence of Denominationalism," *Church History*, 25 (1953), 317–37, and Perry G. E. Miller, "The Contribution of the Protestant Churches to Religious Liberty in Colonial America," *Church History*, 4 (1935), 57–66.

14. Sidney E. Mead, *The Lively Experiment: The Shaping of Christianity in America* (New York: Harper and Row, 1963), 60. McLoughlin, "Role of Religion," 198 (quote).

15. Mead, *Lively Experiment*, 60. See McLoughlin, "Role of Religion," 198, 228 ("the rulers of Connecticut and Massachusetts may have been somewhat more fearful of social disruption than those in Virginia, where the upper class felt sufficiently secure to accept the dissolution of an ecclesiastical system that had never been very effective anyway"). Irons, "Chief Cornerstone," 18 ("in colonial Virginia, civil officers assumed many of the responsibilities traditionally reserved for bishops and therefore bound together church and state more closely than in the mother country").

APPENDIX B

1. Counties in present-day Kentucky, although part of Virginia until 1792, were ignored for these purposes as involving relatively few people and inadequate records. Counties in present-day West Virginia are included.

2. John K. Nelson, *A Blessed Company: Parishes, Parsons and Parishioners in Anglican Virginia, 1690–1776* (Chapel Hill: University of North Carolina Press, 2001), 29.

3. Three Baptist churches listed by Little—Isle of Wight, Surry, and Prince George—were ignored because these churches dated to 1714 and an early Baptist formation in the colony that generally died out by mid-century. See Lewis Peyton Little, *Imprisoned Preachers and Religious Liberty in Virginia* (1938; reprint, Gallatin, Tenn.: Church History Research and Archives, 1987). These aggregate figures seem reasonable. Terman says "estimates of numbers of Baptist churches in Virginia in 1776 run from seventy-four to ninety-three." William Jennings Terman Jr., "The American Revolution and the Baptist and Presbyterian Clergy of Virginia: A Study of Dissenter Opinion and Action" (Ph.D. diss., Michigan State University, 1974), 10, citing David Benedict, *A General History of the Baptist Denomination in America* (1813; reprint, Freeport, N.Y.: Books for Libraries Press, 1971), 651, and Harry P. Kerr, "The Character of Political Sermons Preached at the Time of the American Revolution" (Ph.D. diss., Cornell University, 1962), 202. Helen Hill, *George Mason: Constitutionalist* (Cambridge, Mass.: Harvard University Press, 1938), 44 (ninety Baptist churches). See also Otto Lohrenz, "The Virginia Clergy and the American Revolution, 1774–1799" (Ph.D. diss., University of Kansas, 1970), 15 (seventy-two Baptist churches in 1774). Terman estimated sixty-six Presbyterian congregations by 1778. "American Revolution," 35, citing Kerr, "Character of Political Sermons," 202. The list from Robert P. Davis, James H. Smylie, Dean K. Thompson, Ernest Trice Thompson, and William Newton Todd, *Virginia Presbyterians in American Life: Hanover Presbytery (1755–1980)* (Richmond, Va.: Hanover Presbytery, 1982) appears more complete.

4. Greenbrier was formed in 1777 from parts of Botetourt (PP) and Montgomery (B/PP). It is included in this analysis as B/PP. Other newly formed counties were listed by the designation of their predecessor county(ies) without complications.

5. See, for example, H. J. Eckenrode, *The Revolution in Virginia* (1916; reprint, Hamden, Conn.: Archon Books, 1964), 295. See also William B. Sprague, *Annals of the American Pulpit, Vol. III, Presbyterians* (New York: Robert Carter and Brothers, 1865), 398; Robert B. Semple, *A History of the Baptists in Virginia*, rev. and extended by G. W. Beale (1894; reprint, Cottonport, La.: Polyanthos, 1972), 63.

6. Julian P. Boyd, Lyman H. Butterfield, and Mina R. Bryan, eds., *The Papers of Thomas Jefferson* (Princeton, N.J.: Princeton University Press, 1950), II:130–32 (List of Militia by Counties, 1777). Returns for each of the later requisitions can be found in Virginia General Assembly, House of Delegates, Speaker, Executive Communications, Letters and returns, 1781 November 26, Accession no. 36912, state government records collection, Library of Virginia, Richmond. The 1781 requisition of materials under the 1780 Provision Law assigned to each county a quota of shirts, overalls, stockings, hats, and shoes; the response for these categories was averaged to provide a single percentage response to material requisition by county.

7. Boyd, Butterfield, and Bryan, *Papers of Thomas Jefferson*, II:130–32.

8. See http://memory.loc.gov/ammem/collections/jefferson_papers, image 754–55.

9. The supposition that a "no return" would often correspond to a "zero" or weak response is supported by data that are available. As table 4.2 shows, the highest rate of mobilization occurred in those counties (Strong Baptist and Presbyterian) that had the lowest rate of no return. The alternative conclusion—that counties with high no return rates would have shown higher rates of mobilization had more responses been made—makes little sense as a county had every incentive to provide information of a high response, especially because the state continued to seek an accounting of supplies well into 1782. For example, Virginia General Assembly, House of Delegates, Speaker, Executive Communications (May 29, 1782), Library of Virginia, Richmond, call no. 36912. Failure to apply a negative inference for no returns may be particularly telling as the no return rate for Other counties, a surrogate for Anglican, was 80 percent, by far the highest no return rate among the various groups.

10. Eckenrode, *Revolution in Virginia*, 242.

Bibliography

Adair, Douglas, and John A. Schutz, eds. *Peter Oliver's Origin and Progress of the American Rebellion: A Tory View.* Stanford, Calif.: Stanford University Press, 1967.

Ahlstrom, Sydney E. *A Religious History of the American People,* 2nd ed. New Haven, Conn.: Yale University Press, 2004.

Alderson, L. A. "Persecution of Baptists." *Religious Herald* 6:14 (April 6, 1871).

Alley, Robert S., ed. *James Madison on Religious Liberty.* Buffalo, N.Y.: Prometheus Books, 1985.

American Papers of the Society for the Propagation of the Gospel. Vol. X. Lambeth Palace Library, London (microfilm).

Andrews, Dee E. *The Methodists and Revolutionary America, 1760–1800: The Shaping of an Evangelical Culture.* Princeton, N.J.: Princeton University Press, 2000.

Antieau, Chester James, Arthur T. Downey, and Edward C. Roberts. *Freedom from Federal Establishment: Formation and Early History of the First Amendment Religion Clauses.* Milwaukee: Bruce Publishing, 1964.

Armitage, Thomas. *A History of the Baptists: Traced by Their Vital Principles and Practices.* Vol. 2. New York: Bryan, Taylor, 1890. CD-ROM, Baptist Standard Bearer, 2005.

Bailey, G. S. *The Trials and Victories of Religious Liberty in America.* Philadelphia: American Baptist Publication Society, 1876.

Bailey, Raymond C. *Popular Influence upon Public Policy: Petitioning in Eighteenth-Century Virginia.* Westport, Conn.: Greenwood Press, 1979.

Baldwin, Alice M. "Sowers of Sedition: The Political Theories of Some of the New Light Presbyterian Clergy of Virginia and North Carolina." *William and Mary Quarterly* 3rd Series, 5:1 (January 1948): 52–76.

"Baptists in Middlesex, 1771." *William and Mary Quarterly,* 2nd Series, 4 (July 1925): 208–13.

Barbour, Honourable John S. "Oration of the Life, Character, and Services of James Madison." Culpeper Courthouse, July 18, 1836. *Daily National Intelligencer*, 7323 (Washington, D.C., August 2, 1836).

Bearss, Sara B., ed. *Dictionary of Virginia Biography*. Vol. 3. Richmond: Library of Virginia, 2006.

Beeman, Richard R. "The Political Response to Social Conflict in the Southern Backcountry: A Comparative View of Virginia and the Carolinas during the Revolution." In *An Uncivil War: The Southern Backcountry During the American Revolution*, ed. Ronald Hoffman, Thad W. Tate, and Peter J. Albert, 213–39. Charlottesville: University Press of Virginia, 1985.

Beeman, Richard R., and Rhys Isaac. "Cultural Conflict and Social Change in the Revolutionary South: Lunenburg County, Virginia." *Journal of Southern History*, 46:4 (November 1980): 525–50.

Bell, James B. *A War of Religion: Dissenters, Anglicans, and the American Revolution*. Hampshire: Palgrave Macmillan, 2008.

Benedict, David. *A General History of the Baptist Denomination in America*. 2 vols. 1813. Reprint, Freeport, N.Y.: Books for Libraries Press, 1971.

Bennett, William W. *Memorials of Methodism in Virginia*. Richmond, 1871.

Berlin, Ira, and Ronald Hoffman, eds. *Slavery and Freedom in the Age of the American Revolution*. Chicago: University of Illinois Press, 1986.

Bitting, C. C. *Notes on the History of the Strawberry Baptist Association of Virginia, for One Hundred Years,—From 1776 to 1876*. Baltimore, Md.: Strawberry Baptist Association, 1879 (microfilm).

Bonomi, Patricia. "'Hippocrates' Twins': Religion and Politics in the American Revolution." *History Teacher* 29:2 (February 1996): 137–44.

———. *Under the Cope of Heaven: Religion, Society, and Politics in Colonial America*. New York: Oxford University Press, 1986.

Bonwick, Colin. *English Radicals and the American Revolution*. Chapel Hill: University of North Carolina Press, 1977.

Boyd, Julian P., ed. "Notes and Documents: Joseph Galloway to Charles Jenkinson on the British Constitution." *Pennsylvania Magazine of History and Biography*, 64:4 (October 1940): 516–44.

Boyd, Julian P., Mina R. Bryan, and Elizabeth L. Hutter, eds. *The Papers of Thomas Jefferson*. Vol. 7. Princeton, N.J.: Princeton University Press, 1953.

———, eds. *The Papers of Thomas Jefferson*. Vol. 8. Princeton, N.J.: Princeton University Press, 1953.

——— Lyman H. Butterfield, and Mina R. Bryan, eds. *The Papers of Thomas Jefferson*. Vol. 1. Princeton, N.J.: Princeton University Press, 1950.

———, eds. *The Papers of Thomas Jefferson*. Vol. 2. Princeton, N.J.: Princeton University Press, 1950.

Boyle, Andrew J. *The Church in the Fork: A History of Historic Little Fork Church*. Orange, Va.: Green Publishers, 1983.

Brant, Irving. *James Madison: The Nationalist, 1780–1787*. Indianapolis: Bobbs-Merrill, 1948.

————. *James Madison: The Virginia Revolutionist, 1751–1780*. Indianapolis: Bobbs-Merrill, 1941.

Breed, W. P. *Presbyterians and the Revolution*. 1876. Reprint, Decatur, Miss.: Issacharian Press, 1993.

Bridenbaugh, Carl. *Mitre and Sceptre: Transatlantic Faiths, Ideas, Personalities, and Politics 1689–1775*. London: Oxford University Press, 1962.

Brock, Robert K. *Archibald Cary of Ampthill*. Richmond, Va.: Garrett and Massie Publishers, 1937.

Brown, Katherine L. "The Role of Presbyterian Dissent in Colonial and Revolutionary Virginia, 1740–1785." Ph.D. diss., Johns Hopkins University, 1969.

Brown, Robert E., and Katherine Brown. *Virginia 1705–1786: Democracy or Aristocracy*. East Lansing: Michigan State University Press, 1964.

Brydon, George MacLaren. *Virginia's Mother Church and the Political Conditions under Which It Grew*. 2 vols. Richmond: Whittet and Shepperson, 1947.

Buchanan, John. *The Road to Guilford Court House: The American Revolution in the Carolinas*. New York: Wiley, 1977.

Buckley, Thomas E. *Church and State in Revolutionary Virginia, 1776–1787*. Charlottesville: University Press of Virginia, 1977.

Burke, Edmund. *The Works of the Right Honorable Edmund Burke*, rev. ed. Vol. II. Boston: Little, Brown, 1866.

Burkitt, Lemuel. *A Concise History of the Kehukee Baptist Association, from its Iriginal Rise down to 1803*. Halifax, N.C.: A. Hodge, 1803.

Butler, Jon. *Awash in a Sea of Faith: Christianizing the American People*. Cambridge, Mass.: Harvard University Press, 1990.

————. "Coercion, Miracle, Reason: Rethinking the American Religious Experience in the Revolutionary Age." In *Religion in the Revolutionary Age*, ed. Ronald Hoffman and Peter J. Albert, 1–30. Charlottesville: University Press of Virginia, 1994.

————. *Religion in Colonial America*. New York: Oxford University Press, 2000.

Butterfield, L. H. "Elder John Leland, Jeffersonian Itinerant." *American Antiquarian Society Proceedings* 62:2 (October 1952): 155–242.

Calendar of Virginia State Papers and Other Manuscripts. Vol. II. 1881. Reprint, New York, 1968.

Campbell, Charles. *History of the Colony and Ancient Dominion of Virginia*. Philadelphia: Lippincott, 1860.

Campbell, T. E. *Colonial Caroline: A History of Caroline County, Virginia*. Richmond, Va.: Dietz Press, 1954.

Caroline County Order Book, 1768–1769. Facsimile. Heritage Center, Fredricksburg, Va.

Carroll, J. M. *"The Trail of Blood": Following the Christians Down through the Centuries—or, The History of Baptist Churches from the time of Christ, Their Founder, to the Present Day*. 1931. Reprint, Lexington, Va.: Ashland Avenue Baptist Church, 1973.

Cathcart, William. *Baptist Patriots and the American Revolution*. 1876, as *The Baptists and the American Revolution*. Reprint, Grand Rapids, Mich.: Guardian Press, 1976.

Cheney, John L., ed. *North Carolina Government 1585–1979: A Narrative and Statistical History*. Raleigh: N.C. Department of the Secretary of State, 1981.

Clement, Maud Carter. *The History of Pittsylvania County, Virginia*. Lynchburg, Va.: Bell, 1929.

Cobb, Sanford H. *The Rise of Religious Liberty in America*. 1902. Reprint, New York: Burt Franklin, 1970.

Conway, Moncure Daniel. *Omitted Chapters of History Disclosed in the Life and Papers of Edmund Randolph*. 1888. CD-ROM, *America: The Historic Facts*, Bank of Wisdom, Louisville, Ky., 1999.

Conway, Stephen. *The British Isles and the War of American Independence*. Oxford: Oxford University Press, 2003.

Craig, Joseph. *A Sketch of a Journal of the Reverend Joseph Craig*. 1827. Published by Aubrey Thomas, January 1927, entered online by Ann Woodlief, 2005, http://www.geocities.com/awoodlief;/craigjournal.html.

Crow, Jeffrey J. "Liberty Men and Loyalists: Disorder and Disaffection in the North Carolina Backcountry." In *An Uncivil War: The Southern Backcountry during the American Revolution*, ed. Ronald Hoffman, Thad W. Tate, and Peter J. Albert, 125–78. Charlottesville: University Press of Virginia, 1985.

Curnock, Nehemiah, ed. *The Journal of the Rev. John Wesley, A.M., Enlarged from Original MSS., with Notes from Unpublished Diaries, Annotations, Maps, and Illustrations*. Vol. VI. Reprint, Kessinger Publishing, 2006.

———, ed. *The Journal of John Wesley*. Vol. VIII. London, 1916.

Curry, J. L. M. *Struggles and Triumphs of Virginia Baptists, a Memorial Discourse*. Philadelphia: Bible and Publication Society, 1873.

Curry, Thomas J. *The First Freedoms: Church and State in America to the Passage of the First Amendment*. New York: Oxford University Press, 1986.

Davies, K. G., ed. *Documents of the American Revolution, 1770–1783 (Colonial Office Series)*. Volume III, Transcripts, 1771. Shannon, Ireland: Irish University Press, 1973.

———, ed. *Documents of the American Revolution, 1770–1783 (Colonial Office Series)*. Volume VIII, Transcripts, 1774. Shannon, Ireland: Irish University Press, 1973.

Davis, Derek H. *Religion and the Continental Congress 1774–1789: Contributions to Original Intent*. Oxford: Oxford University Press, 2000.

Davis, Robert P., James H. Smylie, Dean K. Thompson, Ernest Trice Thompson, and William Newton Todd. *Virginia Presbyterians in American Life: Hanover Presbytery (1755–1980)*. Richmond, Va.: Hanover Presbytery, 1982.

Davis, Robert P. "The Struggle for Religious Freedom (1611–1776)." In *Virginia Presbyterians in American Life: Hanover Presbytery (1755–1980)*, ed. Robert P. Davis, James H. Smylie, Dean K. Thompson, Ernest Trice Thompson, and William Newton Todd. Richmond, Va.: Hanover Presbytery, 1982.

DeMond, Robert O. *The Loyalists in North Carolina during the Revolution*. Hamden, Conn.: Archon Books, 1964.

Dill, Alonzo Thomas. *Carter Braxton, Virginia Signer: A Conservative in Revolt*. Lanham, Md.: University Press of America, 1983.

Doares, Robert. "The Alternative of Williams-Burg." *Colonial Williamsburg*, 28:2 (Spring 2006): 20–25.

Doll, Peter M. *Revolution, Religion, and National Identity: Imperial Anglicanism in British North America, 1745–1795*. Madison, Wisc.: Fairleigh Dickinson University Press, 2000.

Dreisbach, Daniel L. "George Mason's Pursuit of Religious Liberty in Revolutionary Virginia." *Virginia Magazine of History and Biography* 108:1 (2000): 5–44.

———. "Thomas Jefferson, a Mammoth Cheese, and the 'Wall of Separation Between Church and State.'" In *Religion and the New Republic: Faith in the Founding of America*, ed. James H. Hutson, 65–114. Lanham, MD: Rowman and Littlefield Publishers, Inc., 2000.

Dudley, Harold James, ed. *Foote's Sketches of North Carolina, Historical and Biographical*. 1846. Reprint, Dunn, N.C.: Twyford Printing, 1965.

"The Early Methodists and the American Revolution." *Historical Magazine, and Notes and Queries Concerning the Antiquities, History and Biography of America*, 10:12 (December 1866).

Eckenrode, H. J. *The Revolution in Virginia*. 1916. Reprint, Hamden, Conn.: Archon Books, 1964.

———. *Separation of Church and State in Virginia: A Study in the Development of the Revolution*. 1910. Reprint, New York: Da Capo Press, 1971.

Edwards, Morgan. *Materials towards a History of the Baptists in the Provinces of Maryland, Virginia, North Carolina, South Carolina, Georgia*. Vol. III. 1772. Microfilm. Special Collections, University of Virginia, Charlottesville.

Escott, Paul D., and Jeffrey J. Crow. "The Social Order and Violent Disorder: An Analysis of North Carolina in the Revolution and the Civil War." *Journal of Southern History* 52:3 (August 1986): 373–402.

Eskridge, William N. Jr., Philip P. Frickey, and Elizabeth Garrett. *Legislation and Statutory Interpretation*. New York: Foundation Press, 2000.

Feldman, Noah. *Divided by God: America's Church State Problem—and What We Should Do about It*. New York: Farrar, Strauss and Giroux, 2005.

Ferling, John. *Almost a Miracle: The American Victory in the War of Independence*. Oxford: Oxford University Press, 2007.

Fingard, Judith. "Establishment of the First English Colonial Episcopate." *Dalhousie Review*, 47 (Winter 1967–68): 475–91.

Finke, Roger, and Rodney Stark. *The Churching of America, 1776–2005: Winners and Losers in Our Religious Economy*. New Brunswick, N.J.: Rutgers University Press, 2005.

Finkelman, Paul. *Slavery and the Founders: Race and Liberty in the Age of Jefferson*. Armonk, N.Y.: M. E. Sharpe, 1996.

Fleet, Elizabeth, ed. "Madison's 'Detached Memoranda.'" *William and Mary Quarterly*, 3rd Series, 3:4 (Oct. 1946): 534–68.

Foote, William Henry. *Sketches of Virginia Historical and Biographical*. 1850. Reprint, Richmond, Va.: John Knox Press, 1966.

Force, Peter, ed. *American Archives: Fourth Series. Containing a Documentary History of the United States of America, from the King's Message to Parliament, of March 7,*

1774, to the Declaration of Independence by the United States. Volume III. Washington, D.C.: M. St. Clair Clarke and Peter Force, 1840.

The Freeman's Remonstrance against an Ecclesiastical Establishment. Williamsburg: Dixon and Hunter, 1777. Early American Imprints, Series 1, no. 43250 (filmed).

Fristoe, William. *A Concise History of the Ketocton Baptist Association.* 1808. Reprint, Harrisonburg, Va.: Sprinkle Publications, 2002.

Furlong, Patrick J. "Civilian–Military Conflict and the Restoration of the Royal Province of Georgia, 1778–1782." *Journal of Southern History,* 38:3 (August 1972): 415–42.

Galloway, Joseph. *Historical and Political Reflections on the Rise and Progress of the American Rebellion.* London: G. Wilkie, 1780. *Eighteenth Century Collections Online.* Gale Group, http://galenet.galegroup.com.

Garnett, Richard W. "Religion, Division, and the First Amendment." *Georgetown Law Journal* 94 (2006): 1667–724.

Gaustad, Edwin Scott. "Thomas Jefferson, Danbury Baptists, and 'Eternal Hostility.'" *William and Mary Quarterly,* 3rd Ser., 56:4 (October 1999): 801–4.

Gewehr, Wesley M. *The Great Awakening in Virginia, 1740–1790.* Durham, N.C.: Duke University Press, 1930.

Gill, Frederick C., ed. *Selected Letters of John Wesley.* London: Epworth Press, 1956.

Glenn, Gary B. "Forgotten Purposes of the First Amendment Religion Clauses." *Review of Politics,* 49:3 (Summer 1987): 340–67.

Graham, Ian Charles Cargill. *Colonists from Scotland: Emigration to North America, 1707–1783.* Ithaca, N.Y.: Cornell University Press, 1956.

Gray, Lewis Cecil. *History of Agriculture in the Southern United States to 1860.* Vol. 2. 1932. Reprint, Gloucester, Mass., 1958.

Greenawalt, Kent. "Common Sense about Original and Subsequent Understandings of the Religion Clauses." *University of Pennsylvania Journal of Constitutional Law,* 8 (May 2006): 479–512.

Greene, Evarts B., and Virginia D. Harrington. *American Population before the Federal Census of 1790.* 1932. Reprint, Baltimore, Md.: Genealogical Publishing, 1997.

Greene, L. F., ed. *The Writings of the late Elder John Leland, Including Some Events in His Life, Written by Himself, with Some Additional Sketches.* New York: G. W. Wood, 1845.

Griffin, Patrick. *American Leviathan: Empire, Nation, and Revolutionary Frontier.* New York: Hill and Wang, 2007.

Grigsby, Hugh Blair. *History of the Virginia Federal Convention of 1788.* Vol. II. Virginia Historical Society, *Collections,* New Series, X, Richmond, 1891.

———. *The Virginia Convention of 1776: A Discourse.* Richmond, 1855.

Gundersen, Joan R. *The Anglican Ministry in Virginia 1723–1766: A Study of a Social Class.* New York: Garland Publishing, 1989.

Gundersen, Joan. "The Search for Good Men: Recruiting Ministers in Colonial Virginia." *Historical Magazine of the Protestant Episcopal Church,* 48 (1979): 453–64.

Hall, Cline Edwin. "The Southern Dissenting Clergy and the American Revolution." Ph.D. diss., University of Tennessee, 1975.

Hall, Wilmer L., ed. *Executive Journals of the Council of Colonial Virginia*. Vol. V (Nov. 1, 1739–May 7, 1754). Richmond: Virginia State Library, 1945.

————, ed. *The Vestry Book of the Upper Parish Nansemond County, Virginia, 1743–1793*. Richmond: Virginia State Library, 1981.

Hamburger, Philip. *Separation of Church and State*. Cambridge, Mass.: Harvard University Press, 2002.

Hamburger, Philip A. "A Constitutional Right of Religious Exemption: An Historical Perspective." *George Washington Law Review*, 60 (April 1992): 915–48.

Hanley, Thomas O'Brien. *The American Revolution and Religion: Maryland 1770–1800*. Washington, D.C.: Catholic University of America Press, 1971.

Harlow, Vincent T. *The Founding of the Second British Empire, 1763–1793*. Vol. 2. London: Longmans, Green, 1964.

Harrell, Isaac Samuel. *Loyalism in Virginia*. Durham, N.C.: Seeman Printery, 1926.

Harris, Malcolm H. *History of Louisa County, Virginia*. Richmond, Va.: Dietz Press, 1936.

Hatch, Nathan O. "The Whirlwind of Religious Liberty in Early North America." In *Freedom and Religion in the Nineteenth Century*, ed. Richard Helmstadter, 29–53. Stanford, Calif.: Stanford University Press, 1997.

Hawks, Francis L. *Contributions to the Ecclesiastical History of the United States of America*. New York: Harper and Brothers, 1836.

Headley, J. T. *The Chaplains and Clergy of the American Revolution*. New York: Scribner, 1864 (microfilm).

Heimert, Alan. *Religion in the American Mind from the Great Awakening to the Revolution*. Cambridge, Mass.: Harvard University Press, 1966.

Hening, William Waller, ed. *The Statutes at Large, Being a Collection of All the Laws of Virginia from the First Session of the Legislature in the Year 1619*. Vols. III, VII, VIII, IX, X, XI, XII. Heritage Books, CD-ROM #0878, 2003.

Henry, William Wirt. *Patrick Henry: Life, Correspondence and Speeches*. Vols. I and II. New York: Scribner, 1891.

Hewitt, Robert R. III. *Where the River Flows: Finding Faith in Rockingham County, Virginia, 1726–1876*. Charlottesville: Virginia Foundation for the Humanities, 2003.

Heyrman, Christine Leigh. *Southern Cross: The Beginnings of the Bible Belt*. New York: Knopf, 1998.

Hickman, William. *William Hickman 1747–1830 A Short Account of My Life and Travels. For More than Fifty Years; A Professed Servant of Jesus Christ*. 1828. Reprint, Louisville: Kentucky Baptist Historical Commission, 1969.

Hill, Helen. *George Mason: Constitutionalist*. Cambridge, Mass.: Harvard University Press, 1938.

Historical Statistics of the United States: Colonial Times to 1970. Part 2. Washington, D.C.: U.S. Government Printing Office, 1975.

Hobson, Charles F., and Robert A. Rutland, eds. *The Papers of James Madison*. Vol. 12. Charlottesville: University Press of Virginia, 1979.

Hoffman, Ronald. *A Spirit of Dissension: Economics, Politics, and the Revolution in Maryland*. Baltimore, Md.: Johns Hopkins University Press, 1973.

Holland, Lynwood M. "John Wesley and the American Revolution." *Journal of Church and State*, 5 (1963): 199–213.

Holmes, David L. "The Episcopal Church and the American Revolution." *Historical Magazine of the Protestant Episcopal Church*, 47 (1978): 261–91.

Holton, Woody. *Forced Founders: Indians, Debtors, Slaves, and the Making of the American Revolution in Virginia*. Chapel Hill: University of North Carolina Press, 1999.

Honyman, Robert. *Diary, 1776–1782*. Accession 28855, Personal papers collection, Library of Virginia, Richmond.

Howe, Henry. *Historical Collections of Virginia*. 1845. Reprint, Baltimore, Md.: Regional Publishing, 1969.

Howell, Robert Boyle C. *The Early Baptists of Virginia*. 1864. CD-ROM, Baptist Standard Bearer, 2005.

Howison, Robert R. *History of Virginia, from its Discovery and Settlement by Europeans to the Present Time*. Vol. II. Richmond, Va.: Drinker and Morris, 1848.

Humphrey, Edward Frank. *Nationalism and Religion in America, 1774–1789*. New York: Russell and Russell, 1965.

Hunt, Gaillard. "James Madison and Religious Liberty." *Annual Report of the American Historical Association for the Year 1901*, I (Washington, D.C., 1902): 165–71.

Hurt, Frances Hallam. *An Intimate History of the American Revolution in Pittsylvania County, Virginia*. Danville, Va.: Womack Press, 1976.

Hutchinson, William T., and William M. E. Rachal, eds. *The Papers of James Madison*. Vol. 1. Chicago: University of Chicago Press, 1962.

Hutson, James. "Thomas Jefferson's Letter to the Danbury Baptists: A Controversy Rejoined." *William and Mary Quarterly*, 3rd Ser., 56:4 (October 1999): 775–90.

Ireland, James. *The Life of the Reverend James Ireland*. 1819. Reprint, Harrisonburg, Va.: Sprinkle Publications, 2002.

Irons, Charles Frederick. "'The Chief Cornerstone': The Spiritual Foundations of Virginia's Slave Society, 1776–1861." Ph.D. diss., University of Virginia, 2003.

Irons, Charles F. "The Spiritual Fruits of Revolution: Disestablishment and the Rise of the Virginia Baptists." *Virginia Magazine of History and Biography*, 109:2 (2001): 159–86.

Isaac, Rhys. "Evangelical Revolt: The Nature of the Baptists' Challenge to the Traditional Order in Virginia, 1765 to 1775." *William and Mary Quarterly*, 3rd Ser., 31:3 (July 1974): 345–68.

———. "Preachers and Patriots: Popular Culture and the Revolution in Virginia." In *The American Revolution*, ed. Alfred F. Young, 125–56. DeKalb: Northern Illinois University Press, 1976.

———. "'The Rage of Malice of the Old Serpent Devil': The Dissenters and the Making and Remaking of the Virginia Statute for Religious Freedom." In *The Virginia Statute for Religious Freedom: Its Evolution and Consequences in American History*, ed. Merrill D. Peterson and Robert C. Vaughan, 139–69. Cambridge: Cambridge University Press, 1988.

———. "Religion and Authority: Problems of the Anglican Establishment in Virginia in the Era of the Great Awakening and the Parsons' Cause." *William and Mary Quarterly*, 3rd Ser., 30:1 (January 1973): 3–36.

———. *The Transformation of Virginia, 1740–1790*. New York: Norton, 1982.

James, Charles F. *Documentary History of the Struggle for Religious Liberty in Virginia*. Lynchburg, Va.: J. P. Bell, 1900.

Jefferson, Thomas. *Autobiography*. In *Thomas Jefferson Writings*, ed. Merrill D. Peterson. New York: Library of America, 1984.

———. *Notes on the State of Virginia*. In *Thomas Jefferson Writings*, ed. Merrill D. Peterson. New York: Library of America, 1984.

Johnson, Thomas Cary. *Virginia Presbyterianism and Religious Liberty in Colonial and Revolutionary Times*. Richmond, Va.: Presbyterian Committee of Publication, 1907.

Kay, Marvin L. Michael. "The North Carolina Regulation, 1766–1776: A Class Conflict." In *The American Revolution*, ed. Alfred F. Young, 71–123. DeKalb: Northern Illinois University Press, 1976.

Kay, Marvin L. Michael, and Lorin Lee Cary. "Class, Mobility, and Conflict in North Carolina on the Eve of the Revolution." In *The Southern Experience in the American Revolution*, ed. Jeffrey J. Crow and Larry E. Tise, 109–51. Chapel Hill: University of North Carolina Press, 1978.

Kerr, Harry P. "The Character of Political Sermons Preached at the Time of the American Revolution." Ph.D. diss., Cornell University, 1962.

Knox, William. *Extra Official State Papers. Addressed to the Right Hon. Lord Rawdon, and the other members of the two Houses of Parliament, associated for the preservation of the constitution . . . By a late under secretary of state*. Vol. 1. London, 1789. *Eighteenth Century Collections Online*. Gale Group, http://galenet.galegroup.com.

Kurland, Philip B., and Ralph Lerner, eds. *The Founders' Constitution*. Vol. I. Chicago: University of Chicago Press, 1987.

Lash, Kurt T. "Power and the Subject of Religion." *Ohio State Law Journal* 59 (1998): 1069–154.

Leland, John. *The Virginia Chronicle: With Judicious and Critical Remarks under XXIV Heads*. Norfolk: Prentis and Baxter, 1790. Early American Imprints, Series 1, no. 21920.

Leonard, Cynthia Miller. *The General Assembly of Virginia, July 30, 1619–January 11, 1978*. Richmond: Virginia State Library, 1978.

Lipscomb, Andrew A., and Albert Ellery Bergh. *The Writings of Thomas Jefferson: Containing His Autobiography, Notes on Virginia, Parliamentary Manual, Official Papers, Messages and Addresses, And Other Writings, Official and Private*. Washington, D.C.: Thomas Jefferson Memorial Foundation, 1903.

Little, Lewis Peyton. *Imprisoned Preachers and Religious Liberty in Virginia*. 1938. Reprint, Gallatin, Tenn.: Church History Research and Archives, 1987.

Lohrenz, Otto. "The Virginia Clergy and the American Revolution, 1774–1799." Ph.D. diss., University of Kansas, 1970.

Lutz, Francis Earle. *Chesterfield: An Old Virginia County.* Richmond, Va.: William Byrd Press, 1954.

Lydekker, John Wolfe. *The Life and Letters of Charles Inglis.* London: Society for Promoting Christian Knowledge, 1936.

Lyles, Albert M. "The Hostile Reaction to the American Views of Johnson and Wesley." *Journal of the Rutgers University Library,* 24:1 (December 1960): 1–13.

Mackesy, Piers. *The War for America 1775–1783.* 1964. Reprint, Lincoln: University of Nebraska Press, 1993.

Macveagh, Lincoln, ed., *Journal of Nicholas Cresswell, 1774–1777.* New York: Dial Press, 1924.

Malbin, Michael J. *Religion and Politics: The Intentions of the Authors of the First Amendment.* Washington, D.C.: American Enterprise Institute, 1978.

Manifesto and Proclamation, by the Earl of Carlisle, Sir Henry Clinton and William Eden (the Carlisle Commission) (October 3, 1778). Early American Imprints, Series 1, no. 15832 (filmed).

Mapp, Alfred J. Jr. *The Virginia Experiment: The Old Dominion's Role in the Making of America (1607–1781).* Richmond, Va.: Dietz Press, 1957.

Marty, Martin E. "The Virginia Statute Two Hundred Years Later." In *The Virginia Statute for Religious Freedom: Its Evolution and Consequences in American History,* ed. Merrill D. Peterson and Robert C. Vaughan, 1–21. Cambridge: Cambridge University Press, 1988.

Mason, Keith. "Localism, Evangelicalism, and Loyalism: The Sources of Discontent in the Revolutionary Chesapeake." *Journal of Southern History,* 56:1 (February 1990): 23–54.

Mayer, Henry. *A Son of Thunder: Patrick Henry and the American Republic.* New York: Frank Watts, 1986.

Mays, David John, ed. *The Letters and Papers of Edmund Pendleton, 1734–1803.* Vol. 2. Charlottesville: University Press of Virginia, 1967.

McBride, John David. "The Virginia War Effort; 1775–1783: Manpower Policies and Practices." Ph.D. diss., University of Virginia, 1977.

McColley, Robert. *Slavery and Jeffersonian Virginia.* Urbana: University of Illinois Press, 1964.

McConnell, Michael W. "The Origins and Historical Understanding of Free Exercise of Religion." *Harvard Law Review,* 103:7 (May 1990): 1409–517.

McDonnell, Michael A. *The Politics of War: Race, Class, and Conflict in Revolutionary Virginia.* Chapel Hill: University of North Carolina Press, 2007.

McIlwaine, H. R., ed. *Journal of the House of Burgesses of Virginia.* Various years. Richmond: 1906–8.

———, ed. *Journals of the Council of the State of Virginia.* Vol. II (Oct. 6, 1777–Nov. 30, 1781). Richmond: Virginia State Library, 1932.

———, ed. *Official Letters of the Governors of the State of Virginia.* Vol. III: The Letters of Thomas Nelson and Benjamin Harrison. Richmond: Virginia State Library, 1929.

McIlwaine, Henry R. *The Struggle of Protestant Dissenters for Religious Toleration in Virginia*. Johns Hopkins University Studies, Historical and Political Science, 12th Ser., IV. Baltimore, Md.: Johns Hopkins University Press, April 1894.

McLoughlin, William G. "'Enthusiasm for Liberty': The Great Awakening as the Key to the Revolution." In *Preachers and Politicians: Two Essays on the Origins of the American Revolution*. Worcester, Mass.: American Antiquarian Society, 1977.

———. "The Role of Religion in the Revolution." In *Essays on the American Revolution*, ed. Stephen G. Kurtz and James H. Hutson, 197–255. Chapel Hill: University of North Carolina Press, 1973.

Mead, Sidney E. *The Lively Experiment: The Shaping of Christianity in America*. New York: Harper and Row, 1963.

———. "From Coercion to Persuasion: Another Look at the Rise of Religious Liberty and the Emergence of Denominationalism." *Church History*, 25 (1953): 317–37.

Meade, Bishop William. *Old Churches, Ministers and Families of Virginia*. 2 vols. 1857. Reprint, Baltimore, Md.: Genealogical Publishing, 1978.

Meade, Robert Douthat. *Patrick Henry: Practical Revolutionary*. Philadelphia: Lippincott, 1969.

Meherrin Baptist Meeting Book (1771–1884). Virginia Baptist Historical Society. University of Richmond, Richmond, Va.

"A Memoir of the Late Rev. William Graham." *Evangelical and Literary Magazine and Missionary Chronicle*, 4:5 (May 1821): 253–63.

Miller, Perry G. E. "The Contribution of the Protestant Churches to Religious Liberty in Colonial America." *Church History*, 4 (1935): 57–66.

Mills, Frederick V. Jr. "New Light on the Methodists and the Revolutionary War." *Methodist History* 28 (1989): 57–65.

Minute Book of Hartwood Baptist Church, 1775–1861. Virginia Baptist Historical Society. University of Richmond, Richmond, Va.

Moore, John S. "Barrow and Mintz Sue Their Attackers," *Virginia Baptist Register*, 32 (1993): 1659–60.

———, ed. "Richard Dozier's Historical Notes, 1771–1818." *Virginia Baptist Register*, 28 (1989): 1387–442.

———, ed. "John Williams' Journal, Edited with Comments." *Virginia Baptist Register*, 17 (1978): 795–813.

———. "Jeremiah Walker in Virginia." *Virginia Baptist Register* 15 (1976): 719–44.

———. "John Weatherford: The Man behind the Legends." *Virginia Baptist Register*, 8 (1969): 356–74.

Muhlenberg, Henry A. *The Life of Major-General Peter Muhlenberg of the Revolutionary Army*. Philadelphia, 1849.

Mulder, Philip N. *A Controversial Spirit: Evangelical Awakenings in the South*. Oxford: Oxford University Press, 2002.

Muñoz, Vincent Philip. "Religion and the Common Good: George Washington on Church and State." In *The Founders on God and Government*, ed. Daniel L.

Dreisbach, Mark D. Hall, and Jeffry H. Morrison, 1–22. Lanham, Md.: Rowman and Littlefield Publishers, 2004.

Nelson, John K. *A Blessed Company: Parishes, Parsons and Parishioners in Anglican Virginia, 1690–1776.* Chapel Hill: University of North Carolina Press, 2001.

Newman, A.H. *A History of the Baptist Churches in the United States.* New York: Christian Literature, 1894. CD-ROM, Baptist Standard Bearer, 2005.

Norton, Mary Beth. *British Americans: Loyalist Exiles in England, 1774–1789.* Boston: Little, Brown, 1972.

Oaks, Daillin H. *Religious Freedom and the Supreme Court.* Washington, D.C.: Ethics and Public Policy Center, 1981.

O'Brion, Catherine Greer. "'A Mighty Fortress Is Our God': Building a Community of Faith in the Virginia Tidewater, 1772–1845." Ph.D. diss., University of Virginia, 1997.

Observations on Mr. Wesley's Second Calm Address, and Incidentally on Other Writings upon the American Question. London, 1777.

O'Neill, James M. *Catholics in Controversy.* New York: McMullen Books, 1954.

Onuf, Peter. "Thomas Jefferson's Christian Nation." In *Religion, State and Society: Jefferson's Wall of Separation in Comparative Perspective,* ed. Robert Fatton Jr. and R. K. Ramazani, 17–36. New York: Palgrave Macmillan, 2009.

Papers of Lord Dunmore: Dunmore, John Murray, Earl of, 1732–1809, Correspondence, 1771–1778. TR 13, Vols. 1 and 2. Rockefeller Library, Williamsburg, Va.

Parks, William. "Religion and the Revolution in Virginia." In *Virginia in the American Revolution: A Collection of Essays,* ed. Richard A. Rutyna and Peter C. Stewart, 38–56. Norfolk, Va.: Old Dominion University, 1977.

Paschal, George Washington. *History of North Carolina Baptists.* Vols. I and II. Raleigh, N.C.: Edwards and Broughton, 1930.

"A Pastoral Letter from the Synod of New York and Philadelphia to the people under our charge, May 1783." *Journal of the Presbyterian Historical Society,* 5 (1909–10): 127–31.

Patton, Jacob Harris. *The Triumph of the Presbytery of Hanover; or, Separation of Church and State in Virginia.* New York: Anson D. F. Randolph, 1887.

Pauley, William Everett Jr. "Religion and the American Revolution in the South: 1760–1781." Ph.D. diss., Emory University, 1974.

Paulsen, Michael S. "Religion, Equality, and the Constitution: An Equal Protection Approach to Establishment Clause Adjudication." *Notre Dame Law Review,* 61 (1986): 311–71.

Perry, William, ed. *Historical Collections of the American Colonial Church.* Vol. 1: Virginia. 1870. Reprint, Westminster, Md.: Willow Bend Books, 2001.

Peterson, Merrill D., and Robert C. Vaughan, eds. *The Virginia Statute for Religious Freedom: Its Evolution and Consequences in American History.* Cambridge: Cambridge University Press, 1988.

Pfeffer, Leo. "Madison's 'Detached Memoranda': Then and Now." In *The Virginia Statute for Religious Freedom: Its Evolution and Consequences in American History,* ed. Merrill D. Peterson and Robert C. Vaughan, 283–312. Cambridge: Cambridge University Press, 1988.

"Presbyterians and the Revolution," *Journal of the Presbyterian Historical Society*, 5 (1909–10): 127–31.

Priestley, Joseph. *An Address to Protestant Dissenters of All Denominations on the Approaching Election of Members of Parliament with respect to the State of Public Liberty in General, and of American Affairs in Particular.* London, 1774. *Eighteenth Century Collections Online.* Gale Group, http://galenet.galegroup.com.

"Prosecution of Baptist Ministers: Chesterfield County, Va., 1771–'73." *Virginia Magazine of History and Biography*, 11 (1903–4): 415–17.

Prufer, Julius F. "The Franchise in Virginia from Jefferson through the Convention of 1829." *William and Mary Quarterly.* 2nd Ser., 7:4 (Oct. 1927): 255–70.

Ragosta, John A. "Jefferson's Statute for Establishing Religious Freedom: How We Got It, What We Did with It, and Implications for the First Amendment Debate." At www.adamsjefferson.com.

Ramsay, David. *The History of the American Revolution*, ed. Lester H. Cohen. Vol. II. Indianapolis: Liberty Classics, 1990.

Randolph, Edmund. *History of Virginia*, ed. by Arthur H. Shaffer. Charlottesville: University Press of Virginia, 1970.

Raymond, Allan. "'I Fear God and Honour the King': John Wesley and the American Revolution." *Church History.* 45:3 (September 1976): 316–28.

Rapalje, Stewart, and Robert L. Lawrence. *A Dictionary of American and English Law.* 2 vols. Jersey City: Frederick D. Linn, 1888.

Reinhold, Meyer. "Opponents of Classical Learning in America during the Revolutionary Period." *American Philosophical Society, Proceedings*, 112 (1968): 221–34.

Rennie, Sandra. "Virginia's Baptist Persecution, 1765–1778." *Journal of Religious History*, 12:1 (June 1982): 48–61.

Rennie, Sandra Joy. "Crusaders for Virtue—The Development of the Baptist Culture in Virginia from 1760 to 1790." M.A. yhesis, La Trobe University, Melbourne, 1975.

"Revolutionary Letters." *Historical Magazine and Notes and Queries Concerning the Antiquities, History and Biography of America*, 1:12 (December 1857): 355.

Rhoden, Nancy L. *Revolutionary Anglicanism: The Colonial Church of England Clergy during the American Revolution.* New York: New York University Press, 1999.

Rice, John Holt. "Memorials to the General Assembly of Virginia." *Literary and Evangelical Magazine*, 9:1 (January 1826): 30–47.

Riley, B. F. *A History of the Baptists in the Southern States East of the Mississippi.* Philadelphia: American Baptist Publications Society, 1898.

Rives, William C. *History of the Life and Times of James Madison.* Vol. 1. Boston: Little, Brown, 1859.

Royster, Charles. *A Revolutionary People at War: The Continental Army and American Character, 1775–1783.* New York: Norton, 1979.

Russell, David Lee. *The American Revolution in the Southern Colonies.* Jefferson, N.C.: McFarland, 2000.

Rutland, Robert A., ed. *The Papers of George Mason: 1725–1792*. Vol. II. Kingsport,
    Tenn.: University of North Carolina Press, 1970.
Rutland, Robert A., and Charles F. Hobson, eds. *The Papers of James Madison*. Vol. 10.
    Chicago: University of Chicago Press, 1977.
———, eds. *The Papers of James Madison*. Vol. 11. Charlottesville: University Press of
    Virginia, 1977.
Rutland, Robert A., and William M. E. Rachal, eds. *The Papers of James Madison*.
    Vol. 9. Chicago: University of Chicago Press, 1975.
Rutland, Robert A., William M. E. Rachal, Barbara D. Ripel, and Fredrika J. Teute, eds.
    The Papers of James Madison. Vol. 8. Chicago: University of Chicago Press, 1973.
Rutland, Robert A., William M. E. Rachal, Jean Schneider, and Robert L. Scribner, eds.
    The Papers of James Madison. Vol. 7. Chicago: University of Chicago Press, 1971.
Ryland, Garnett. *The Baptists of Virginia, 1699–1926*. Richmond: Virginia Baptist Board
    of Missions and Education, 1955.
———. "'James Ireland': An address delivered at the Unveiling of the Monument to
    James Ireland, May 20, 1931, Berryville, Clarke County, VA." Richmond: Virginia
    Baptist Historical Society, 1931.
Sandoz, Ellis. *Political Sermons of the American Founding Era, 1730–1805*. 2 vols.
    Indianapolis: Liberty Fund, 1998.
Saunders, William L., ed. *The Colonial Records of North Carolina, Vol. X—1775–1776*.
    1890. Reprint, New York: AMS Press, 1968.
Scott, W. W. *A History of Orange County Virginia*. Richmond, Va.: Everett Waddey,
    1907.
Scribner, Robert L., and Brent Tarter, eds. *Revolutionary Virginia: The Road to
    Independence*. Vol. III. Charlottesville: University Press of Virginia, 1977.
Scully, Randolph Ferguson. *Religion and the Making of Nat Turner's Virginia: Baptist
    Community and Conflict, 1740–1840*. Charlottesville: University of Virginia Press,
    2008.
Seiler, William H. "The Anglican Parish in Virginia." In *Seventeenth-Century America:
    Essays in Colonial History*, ed. James Morton Smith, 119–42. Chapel Hill:
    University of North Carolina Press, 1959.
Selby, John E. *The Revolution in Virginia 1775–1783*. Williamsburg, Va.: Colonial
    Williamsburg Foundation, 1988.
Sellers, Charles Grier Jr. "John Blair Smith." *Journal of the Presbyterian Historical
    Society*, 34:4 (December 1956): 201–25.
Semple, Robert B. *A History of the Baptists in Virginia*. Rev. and extended by G. W.
    Beale. 1894. Reprint, Cottonport, La.: Polyanthos, 1972.
Shy, John. "British Strategy for Pacifying the Southern Colonies, 1778–1781." In *The
    Southern Experience in the American Revolution*, ed. Jeffrey J. Crow and Larry E.
    Tise, 155–73. Chapel Hill: University of North Carolina Press, 1978.
———. "Confronting Rebellion: Private Correspondence of Lord Barrington with
    General Gage, 1765–1775." In *Sources of American Independence: Selected
    Manuscripts from the Collections of the William L. Clements Library*, ed. Howard H.
    Peckman, Vol. I, 1–139. Chicago: University of Chicago Press, 1978.

Simpson, William S. Jr. *Virginia Baptist Ministers, 1760–1790: A Biographical Survey.* Vols. I and II. Richmond, 1990.

Singleton, Marvin K. "Colonial Virginia as First Amendment Matrix: Henry, Madison, and Assessment Establishment." *Journal of Church and State*, 8 (Autumn 1966): 345–64.

Slaughter, Philip. "A History of St. Mark's Parish, Culpeper County, Virginia." In *Genealogical and Historical Notes on Culpeper County, Virginia*, ed. Raleigh Travers Green, 1–113. 1900. Reprint, Orange, Va.: Quality Printing, 1989.

Sloan, Herbert, and Peter Onuf. "Politics, Culture, and the Revolution in Virginia," *Virginia Magazine of History and Biography*, 91:3 (July 1983): 259–84.

Smith, Egbert W. *The Creed of the Presbyterians.* Richmond, Va.: John Knox Press, 1941.

Smylie, James H. "From Revolution to Civil War (1776–1861)." In *Virginia Presbyterians in American Life: Hanover Presbytery (1755–1980)*, 45–102. Richmond, Va.: Hanover Presbytery, 1982.

———, ed. "Presbyterians and the American Revolution: A Documentary Account." *Journal of Presbyterian History*, 52:4 (Winter 1974): 299–487.

Sobel, Mechal. *The World They Made Together: Black and White Values in Eighteenth-Century Virginia.* Princeton, N.J.: Princeton University Press, 1987.

Spangler, Jewell L. "Becoming Baptists: Conversion in Colonial and Early National Virginia." *Journal of Southern History*, 67:2 (May 2001): 243–86.

———. "Presbyterians, Baptists, and the Making of a Slave Society in Virginia, 1740–1820." Ph.D. diss., University of California, San Diego, 1996.

———. *Virginians Reborn: Anglican Monopoly, Evangelical Dissent, and the Rise of the Baptists in the Late Eighteenth Century.* Charlottesville: University of Virginia Press, 2008.

Sprague, William B. *Annals of the American Pulpit, Vol. III, Presbyterians.* New York: Robert Carter and Brothers, 1865.

———. *Annals of the American Pulpit, Vol. VI, Baptists.* New York: Robert Carter and Brothers, 1865.

Stevens, B. F. *Facsimiles of Manuscripts in European Archives Relating to America, 1773–1783.* Vol. XXIV, No. 2024–2107. London: Malby and Sons, 1895.

Stiles, Ezra. *The Literary Diary.* Ed. Franklin B. Dexter. New York: Scribner, 1901.

Stokes, Anson Phelps. *Church and State in the United States.* Vol. I. New York: Harper and Brothers, 1950.

Sweet, William Warren. *Religion in Colonial America.* New York: Scribner, 1951.

———. "The Role of the Anglicans in the American Revolution." *Huntington Library Quarterly*, 11:1 (1947/1948): 51–70.

Sydnor, Charles S. *American Revolutionaries in the Making: Political Practices in Washington's Virginia.* New York: Free Press, 1965.

Tarter, Brent. "Reflections on the Church of England in Colonial Virginia." *Virginia Magazine of History and Biography*, 112:4 (2004): 339–71.

Tatum, Edward H. Jr. *The American Journal of Ambrose Serle, Secretary to Lord Howe, 1776–1778.* San Marino, Calif.: Huntington Library, 1940.

Taylor, James B. *Virginia Baptist Ministers, in Two Series.* New York: Sheldon, 1860.

Taylor, John. *Baptists on the American Frontier: A History of Ten Baptist Churches of which the Author Has Been Alternately a Member*, ed. Chester Raymond Young. 1823. Reprint, Macon, Ga.: Mercer University Press, 1995.

Terman, William Jennings Jr. "The American Revolution and the Baptist and Presbyterian Clergy of Virginia: A Study of Dissenter Opinion and Action." Ph.D. diss., Michigan State University, 1974.

Thom, William Taylor. *The Struggle for Religious Freedom in Virginia: The Baptists.* Johns Hopkins University Studies, Historical and Political Science, Series XVIII, Nos. 10–11–12. Ed. Herbert B. Adams. 1900. Reprint, New York: Johnson Reprint, 1973.

Thomas, David. *The Virginian Baptist.* Baltimore: Enoch Story, 1774. Early American Imprints, Series 1, no. 13651 (filmed).

Thomas, R. S. *The Loyalty of the Clergy of the Church of England in Virginia to the Colony in 1776 and Their Conduct.* Richmond, Va.: Wm. Ellis Jones, 1907.

Thomas, William H. B. *Patriots of the Upcountry, Orange County, Virginia in the Revolution.* Orange, Va.: Green Publishing, 1976.

Thompson, Ernest Trice. *Presbyterians in the South: Volume One: 1607–1861.* Richmond, Va.: John Knox Press, 1963.

Thornton, John Wingate. *The Pulpit of the American Revolution or, the Political Sermons of the Period of 1776.* Boston: Gould and Lincoln, 1860.

Thorpe, Francis Newton, ed. *The Federal and State Constitutions, Colonial Charters, and Other Organic Laws of the States, Territories, and Colonies.* Washington, D.C.: Government Printing Office, 1909.

Tinling, Marion, ed. *The Correspondence of the Three William Byrds of Westover, Virginia, 1684–1776.* Vol. 2. Charlottesville: University Press of Virginia, 1977.

Torbet, Robert G. *A History of the Baptists*, 2nd ed. Valley Forge, Pa.: Judson Press, 1963.

Tucker, George. *The Life of Thomas Jefferson, Third President of the United States, with Parts of His Correspondence Never Before Published and Notices of His Opinions in Questions on Civil Government, National Policy, and Constitutional Law.* Vol. I. Philadelphia: Covey, Lea and Blanchard, 1837.

Tyerman, Rev. L. *The Life and Times of the Reverend John Wesley, M.A., Founder of the Methodists.* Vol. 3. London: Hodder and Stoughton, 1876.

Van Horne, John C., ed. *The Correspondence of William Nelson as Acting Governor of Virginia, 1770–1771.* Charlottesville: University Press of Virginia, 1975.

Waddell, Joseph A. *Annals of Augusta County, Virginia, from 1726 to 1871.* 1902. Reprint, Bridgewater, Va.: C. J. Carter, 1958.

Watters, William. *A Short Account of the Christian Experience, and Ministerial Labours, of William Watters.* Alexandria: Snowden, 1806. Early American Imprints, Series 2, no. 11808 (filmed).

Weller, Jac. "The Irregular War in the South." *Military Affairs*, 24:3 (Autumn 1960): 124–36.

West, Ellis. "The Case against a Right to Religion-Based Exemptions." *Notre Dame Journal of Law, Ethics and Public Policy*, 4 (1989–90): 591–638.

White, Henry Alexander. *Southern Presbyterian Leaders*. New York: Neale Publishing, 1911.

Whitsitt, William H. *The Life and Times of Judge Caleb Wallace*. Louisville: John P. Morton, 1888.

Williams, David R. ed. *Revolutionary War Sermons*. Delmar, N.Y.: Scholars' Facsimiles and Reprints, 1984.

Williams, William Henry. *The Garden of American Methodism: The Delmarva Peninsula, 1769–1820*. Wilmington, Del.: Scholarly Resources, 1994).

Wilson, Howard McKnight. *The Tinkling Spring, Headwater of Freedom*. Fisherville, Va.: Tinkling Spring and Heritage Presbyterian Churches, 1954.

Wilson, Kathleen. *The Sense of the People: Politics, Culture and Imperialism in England, 1715–1785*. Cambridge: Cambridge University Press, 1998.

Wood, Gordon S. *The Creation of the American Republic, 1776–1787*. New York: Norton, 1969.

———. *The Radicalism of the American Revolution*. New York: Vintage Books, 1993.

Woolverton, John Frederick. *Colonial Anglicanism in North America*. Detroit: Wayne State University Press, 1984.

Wust, Klaus. *The Virginia Germans*. Charlottesville: University of Virginia Press, 1969.

Young, Chester Raymond, ed. *Westward into Kentucky: The Narrative of Daniel Trabue*. Lexington: University Press of Kentucky, 2004.

Index